GENDER, RACE, AND NATION:
A GLOBAL PERSPECTIVE

The terms 'woman' and 'women' have been the organizing concepts for feminist politics and scholarship on women in Western countries for several centuries. 'Women,' it was assumed, shared characteristics based on biology and experiences of subordination; other aspects of their lives, such as language, national or ethnic identity, 'race,' or sexual orientation were considered secondary to the identity of womanness. In this work, Vanaja Dhruvarajan and Jill Vickers call into question feminism's presumed universality of gender analysis, and bring to the foreground the voices of marginalized women in Western society, and of women outside of the Western world.

Gender, Race, and Nation discusses opening scholarship to the experiences of women in all of their diversity. Making links between the differences in local contexts and global contexts, and relating to other women with the understanding of each woman's relative position in terms of power and privilege, will facilitate coalition building and the development of strategies to address issues of common concern to usher in a just and caring world for all. This change in perspective presented by Dhruvarajan and Vickers represents a paradigm shift in the study of women and women's issues, and forges a new approach to women's studies/scholarship on women, women's movements, and global social transformation.

VANAJA DHRUVARAJAN is Professor and Senior Scholar in the Department of Sociology at the University of Winnipeg.

JILL VICKERS is Professor in the Department of Political Science at Carleton University.

Gender, Race, and Nation:
A GLOBAL PERSPECTIVE

Vanaja Dhruvarajan and Jill Vickers

UNIVERSITY OF TORONTO PRESS
Toronto Buffalo London

© University of Toronto Press Incorporated 2002
Toronto Buffalo London
Printed in Canada

ISBN 0-8020-3636-8 (cloth)
ISBN 0-8020-8473-7 (paper)

Printed on acid-free paper

National Library of Canada Cataloguing in Publication Data

Dhruvarajan, Vanaja

Gender, race, and nation : a global perspective

Includes bibliographical references and index.
ISBN 0-8020-3636-8 (bound). – ISBN 0-8020-8473-7 (pbk.)

1. Women's studies. 2. Feminism. 3. Feminist theory.
4. Minority women. I. Vickers, Jill, 1942– . II. Title.

HQ1190.D47 2002   305.4'07   C2001-904091-1

This book has been published with the help of a grant from the Humanities and Social Sciences Federation of Canada, using funds provided by the Social Sciences and Humanities Research Council of Canada.

The University of Toronto Press acknowledges the financial assistance to its publishing program of the Canada Council for the Arts and the Ontario Arts Council.

University of Toronto Press acknowledges the financial support for its publishing activities of the Government of Canada through the Book Publishing Industry Development Program (BPIDP).

We wish to dedicate this book to all those around the world engaged in collaborative efforts across differences to usher in a world that is just and caring for all.

CONTENTS

PREFACE

Women are not homogeneous. They differ because of race, nation, ethnicity, class, sexual orientation, and ability, to mention only a few categories. (We understand race, like ethnicity, to be socially constructed, not an essential or natural phenomenon.) In this book we argue that we must take these differences into account if we wish to understand and explain the life experiences of all women (indeed, of all people). The various dimensions of social status that women experience are not discrete but relational. They intersect and interlock with one another. We explain how these differences are transformed into hierarchies and get built into institutional structures, how belief systems legitimize such inequalities, and how unequal relationships among women (people) are routinely reproduced within day-to-day life. In other words, unequal relationships among different groups of women (people) become a part of commonsense knowledge.

Women may understand and interpret their issues of concern differently because they are differently located in social space. Our objective in this text is to think through these differences to understand and explain women's concerns worldwide. Women have many issues of concern, and we have selected only some of them to illustrate this argument. We have mostly used voices of women from marginalized positions and Third World locations. These voices may be more authentic, since they are spoken from the experience of marginalization. Certainly they are rarely heard. However, we have also included voices from the position of relative privilege to illustrate the argument that women can be oppressed and be oppressors at the same time. Following Walby (1997), we describe the position adopted by many main-

stream, Western women as 'stand-alone' feminism. This position focuses exclusively on gender justice as the goal of feminism and assumes that feminist movements should 'stand alone' — that is, not be
associated with other movements.

We present some but not all issues of concern to women within a
global context. In this era of globalization it is important that we understand how the way we live affects women who are differently
located and marginalized in different parts of the world. We also show
how inequalities between First World and Third World people were
created historically through colonization and imperialism and are being perpetuated through various means at the present time. This shows
historical continuity in the reproduction of dominance and subordination and the interdependence of various social systems.

We also focus on the particular experiences of indigenous peoples
who were both dispossessed and oppressed by Europeans, whose descendants still dominate their lands and are privileged, along with
more recent immigrants, as a result.

We have been able to include only some of the many diverse voices
of women globally. Our hope is that the analytical framework introduced here can be applied to other voices of the reader's own choosing. We also had to be selective in our choice of issues of concern to
women. Our method of analysis can be applied to other issues as well.

The feminist analysis we have used in this book provides insights
that we believe can be used to bring about social transformation. Our
ultimate goal is to usher in a life on this planet that is just, secure, and
caring for all people. We argue that coalition building on different
levels, especially between those who are marginalized worldwide and
those of privilege who also seek justice and peace, is necessary to
implement this project of social transformation. By exploring women's
ideas and struggles within a one-world framework informed by the
history of colonialism and prior waves of globalization, we hope feminist scholarship can develop a new paradigm that is open to women's
experiences everywhere. Whether you are working within women's
studies, in feminist courses in the disciplines, or in activist roles in
women's movements, we hope our introduction to a new one-world
paradigm will help you understand the many differences women experience globally.

ACKNOWLEDGMENTS

We wish to thank the three contributing authors for their patience as we went through the long process of revising to publish this book. We wish to acknowledge the work of Kevin Derksen of Virtual Editing for copy editing an earlier draft of this volume and Barbarah Lo, who became Jill Vickers's 'hands' during the final revisions. We also wish to thank Virgil Duff for his confidence in the project and copy editor Matthew Kudelka of the University of Toronto Press for his assistance in bringing the project to publication.

Vanaja wishes to thank Sandra Shapiro, Kathleen Shellrude, and Judi Hanson for helping with the word processing and preparation of the manuscript at various stages. She also wishes to thank the University of Winnipeg for its financial support for the copy editing of an earlier draft of the volume. Finally, she wishes to thank her husband, Raj, for his continued support of her work.

Jill Vickers wishes to acknowledge the generous financial support from the SSHRCC (Committee 15) for the research on which her chapters are based. She wishes to acknowledge with many thanks the contributions of Ikram Jama and Kiera Ladner, who worked as research assistants and who taught her important things about how women both differ and share common experiences. She wishes to thank her friend and colleague Micheline De Sève for her almost daily support and advice. Finally much love and many thanks are due to James Keith Johnson – husband and best friend.

GENDER, RACE, AND NATION

Introduction

Consider the following conflicts that have occurred in recent years. A young Somali woman is sitting in one of our classes. Although she is dressed in jeans and sneakers, she still stands out because she is Black and wears a head scarf symbolizing her commitment to her faith. Her classmates, who are mostly white and bareheaded, tell her: 'You just *cannot* be a feminist, if you let yourself be manipulated by some man into wearing that thing!' The Women's Press, established in 1972, splits up despite long, well-meant debates and affirmative action policies. The cause? According to author Marlene Norbese Philip: 'Racism ... detonated the explosion at the Women's Press' (cited in Carty, 1993: 45). Several shelters for women fleeing violence close when differences relating to racism and sexual orientation leave workers unable to resolve conflicts. A woman of South Asian descent, who immigrated to Canada to escape anti-Asian policies in Africa, is elected president of the NAC (the National Action Committee on the Status of Women), over protests by an MP in the House of Commons. Journalists whose interviews with her white predecessor had won prizes decide that the NAC is no longer newsworthy except when in crisis. Some women in the NAC's affiliates mutter that it no longer represents them and that it focuses too much on 'non-feminist' issues such as poverty and racism. This echoes the off-the-record views of many women working within government. The more the NAC, later led by a second non-white President, speaks up for marginalized women, the more it is marginalized.

What This Book Is About

'Woman' and 'women' have been the organizing concepts for much of feminist politics in 'Western' countries for several centuries. 'Women,' it has been assumed, share characteristics based on biology and experiences of subordination. In 'Western'[1] thought, 'women' has been treated as a universally valid category of being. In philosophy-speak, it has become an ontological category. The idea that a 'woman' is an essential category of existence – one that all women share and that defines all women – began with traditional male thinkers,[2] many of whom were antifeminist. So categorizing people as 'women' meant describing the most important things about them, which basically defined them. Other aspects of women's lives, such as their language, their national or ethnic identity, their 'race,' their sexual orientation, were considered secondary to this identity of woman-ness. As it emerged in Western countries in the 1970s, women's studies and feminist scholarship generally were organized around the concept of 'women.' However, recent debates in women's movements have begun to open those movements up to women's experiences in all their diversity. Furthermore, globalization is breaking down barriers among countries, with both good and bad results. As a consequence of all this, a new framework or paradigm is emerging for women's studies and feminist scholarship. We invite you to participate in this transformation by reading and thinking through this book.

Who Are 'We'?

We should introduce the principal authors. Vanaja Dhruvarajan, a Hindu woman, was born in India and educated in the United States and at present is a professor of sociology in Winnipeg. Jill Vickers, born the daughter of a war bride in England of Welsh and Scottish ancestry, is a professor of political science in Ottawa. Our close friendship of many years has enabled us to develop a deeper understanding of both our differences and our commonalities. We came together through the Canadian Research Institute for the Advancement of Women and through the Canadian Women's Studies Association, which have nurtured many friendships across differences. We believe that collaborative work of this kind is vital to the project of thinking through difference. Our experiences of understanding and misunderstanding of shared responses and conflicting perceptions constitute the basis of our approach to women's studies. The three contributing authors also have varied backgrounds. Amanda Goldrick-Jones was born in Vancouver and was educated there and in New York state and has lived in Toronto. She is now an associate professor of academic writing and women's studies in Winnipeg, where she focuses on rhetoric and computer-mediated communications. In this text she shares with us her research on men's movements. Parvin Ghorayshi is a professor of sociology at the University of Winnipeg. Her research on women's work in developing countries such as Iran gives her study of women's work in Canada a rich sense of women's commonalities and differences. Carla Rice will be one of the first women to obtain a PhD from York University's interdisciplinary women's studies program. Her BA thesis in history at Harvard University focused on feminism's contest with fashion in the dress reform movement from 1850 to 1914. Her current research on body image, eating disorders, and the politics of beauty is conducted in Toronto at Women's College Hospital's Women's Health Centre. Carla works with girls and young women grappling with body image disorders. The insights she has drawn from that work apply to many women's lives.

Women's Movements and Women's Studies

On their inception, women's movements in Western countries mobilized around issues of gender fairness and around gaining rights within liberal-democratic political regimes. They also campaigned relentlessly for the right of women to welfare-state entitlements – entitlements made possible by the wealth of 'Western' capitalism. Clearly, these early movements focused strongly on struggles within 'Western states.' Initially, women's studies and feminist scholarship in the disciplines were heavily influenced by these movements; as a consequence they largely adopted the 'fairness' model. Some feminists focused on class divisions between rich and poor women, but there was little systematic exploration of other differences among women, even within 'Western' states. The emphasis was on 'sisterhood,' and the result in general was stand-alone feminism, in which issues of gender fairness predominated.

This approach to women's activism and women's studies assumed that 'women' have common interests and needs and so 'women' was the most meaningful political and analytic category. Those whose interests, experiences, and needs were different because, for example, they experienced racism, or were lesbians, or were disabled, were still assumed to be essentially 'women' and so devoted mainly to fighting male dominance and the presumed oppression of all women. However, women oppressed or marginalized[3] by other systems of power argued the following: (1) that class, racism, language, homophobia, and the organization of society for the able-bodied ('ablism') affected their lives at least as much as being 'women'; and (2) that their experiences as 'women' were profoundly shaped by these other forces. Because these women are marginalized in or excluded from dominant women's movements and scholarship on women, privileged, mainstream women have been slow to hear and respond to their views. Moreover, feminist analysis casts all 'women' as oppressed. This ideological construction of all women as 'victims' has made it difficult for mainstream women to recognize they are privileged in relation to women marginalized by other systems of privilege and inequality such as class, racism, ablism, and homophobia. Jill, for example, saw herself as oppressed both as a 'woman' and as a consequence of being born into poverty. Through her interactions with Vanaja, she learned that she was also privileged because of her white, Celtic origin; from that perspective she was privileged relative to Vanaja. In turn Vanaja learned that although she had suffered harms because of her gender, race, and ethnicity, she was privileged because of her caste and class, and because she remains able-bodied, as Jill does not. Both learned that as immigrants, they had benefited from the fact that this continent's indigenous people had had their lands stolen from them. Both learned that their heterosexuality privileged them relative to their lesbian friends. Everywhere this expansion of vision is occurring, but the process is slow and rarely easy. White Western feminists are slowly coming to understand that embracing the commonality of the universal concept 'women' has resulted in painful fragmentation and conflict. The project some of them have advanced of a universal 'sisterhood' – that is, a unified global women's movement (which they would lead) – has foundered. But the vision of feminism as a project of social transformation continues to inspire efforts to transcend these conflicts. Indeed, all women often do have much in common – enough that the potential exists to form coalitions for change once the privileges and harms constructed on difference have been understood and addressed. At that point different women will be able to come together through their groups as equals to join in the process of transformation. This process is central to our efforts in this text.

This book was written before the tragic and shocking events in New York and Washington on 11 September 2001. It is too late for us to incorporate reflections on how they may affect the process of seeking a globally based feminism that respects differences. It is too early for us to even begin to reach conclusions about their consequences. Nonetheless, our focus on how more broadly based understandings of how women differ, and what we have to share, seems increasingly important as the forces of globalization affect us all. Women can and must find ways to promote understanding and peace.

Weaknesses of Earlier Approaches

Until recently, many feminist theories and practices did not deal well with forces such as racism, nationalism, class conflict, homophobia, and ablism. Nor did many mainstream feminists understand why some women worldwide are sceptical of feminism and as likely to be mobilized by movements dedicated to nationalism, socialism, antiracism, or gay rights, or even by antifeminist movements, and the fundamentalist movements now associated with many religions. This has done much to weaken women's movements and to limit the success of scholarship on women's studies. Moreover, women's movements and early women's studies have also largely ignored the experiences of women in countries outside 'the West.' This is mainly because from 1945 to the early 1990s most Westerners, women included, lived intellectually within a framework that divided the world into three parts: Western countries (democratic and capitalist), Communist countries, and 'the Third World,' which included all other countries, which were perceived as 'underdeveloped' or 'developing.' This period, the so-called Cold War, was marked by conflict and competition between Western countries led by the United States and Communist countries led by the Soviet Union. Because of all this, explorations of women's assumed common characteristics and interests occurred in the absence of unbiased knowledge of women's lives and movements in the other two-thirds of the world. However, these explorations did incorporate some negative stereotypes about women outside the West – for example, the notion that 'Third World women' are more oppressed by their cultures and also less advanced than 'Western' women.

Toward a New Paradigm

Despite these weaknesses, the underlying goal of women's movements and of much scholarship on women remains social transformation.

When women interact as equals to explore their experiences, they often discover they have many things in common along with their differences. In recent years in Western countries, marginalized women of different races, faiths, languages, nationalities, and sexualities have been creating their own organizations; as a result, coalitions based on equality and respect for difference have begun to emerge. The shared goal is to create fairer societies. This has required different ways of thinking and acting. These changes together are often described as a paradigm shift. In this book we present the outlines of this emerging new paradigm, with the caveat that those outlines are often provisional and based on our perceptions of the changes currently under way.

How and why is the paradigm of scholarship on women changing? There are three interrelated aspects of the new, emerging paradigm. We explore each briefly here. Each forms the basis of more extended discussions in Part I and is illustrated by the application chapters in Part II.

Women's Studies without 'Women'?

The idea of a universal 'sisterhood' based on an *assumption* of common experiences and interests – an idea that was once so central to much 'Western' feminism – is now recognized as untenable and is largely being abandoned. This is mainly because minority and marginalized women are asserting their own ideas and theories, which mainstream women's studies are beginning – albeit slowly – to take into serious consideration. These movements are challenging mainstream women's old assumption that they can represent all 'women' – that is, that what they experience can be set up as if it were the universal experience of 'women.' We explore the implications of this change especially in chapter 1, but it is a thread that runs throughout the book.

The second aspect of the new paradigm is that scholarship on women is expanding. It no longer concentrates on mainstream women in Western countries, and on their perspective; it has embraced a one-world framework. The collapse of the Soviet Union in the early 1990s removed many of the barriers preventing 'Western' culture, technology, and economic activity from expanding into the two-thirds world. As we explore in chapter 2, this process – usually referred to as 'globalization' – has had many negative consequences for women, and especially for poorer women and for women in poorer countries. But it has also increased contact among feminists from different parts of the world. Women's groups and networks are now both competing and co-operating – for example, in the United Nations system; feminists outside 'the West' are now claiming the right to speak for 'women.' All of this has led some in women's studies and doing feminist scholarship in the disciplines to adopt a one-world framework for their work.

The one-world framework has made it clear to those who hadn't noticed that women's movements exist in many countries worldwide and are often highly effective. On many issues they often have different 'takes' than mainstream movements in the West. In the same vein, women's studies also operates on different premises in different countries. The emergence of diverse women's movements and approaches to scholarship on women onto the world stage is challenging the idea of a global sisterhood led by Western women who assume their solutions can be applied everywhere. This idea has been rejected by women who don't share 'Western' cultural values. Analysing women's movements and scholarship on women within a one-world framework requires that we question old assumptions, the key ones being that women share the same experiences and needs in a generally presumed 'global sisterhood,' based on stand-alone feminism organized only around gender justice.

Given the increased evidence of such diversity worldwide, some feminists have come to believe that no systematic study of women's lives is possible. They have concluded that efforts to generalize about women's lives beyond the stories of specific local situations result only in the imposition of the views of more powerful women. This position is associated with feminists who have adopted the Western orientation of postmodernism. We discuss these ideas in more detail in chapters 1 and 2, in which we discuss our theory and methodology. Here we note only that though we are informed by postmodernism, we do not believe it is part of the emerging paradigm for a renewed women's studies with a one-world perspective. This is because, though the old category 'women' is no longer sustainable (i.e., we can no longer assume that all women share common experiences), nevertheless the practice of women's movements shows that feminism can still be a movement for social transformation when it is based on recognition of both commonalities and diverse experiences. Women have built coalitions of women's movements, and networks of women from around the world have been built successfully on some issues (e.g., reproductive rights, antiviolence efforts). Indeed, many observers of international politics assume that the emergence of coalitions of women's movements and feminist networks is now a significant development in postwar history.[4] So although we do not *assume* commonalities among women in this book, we observe and compare both similarities and differences that form the basis for independent organizations and divergent opinions, on the one hand, and coalitions and shared campaigns, on the other.

A third aspect of the paradigm shift under way in Western women's studies, and in scholarship on women more generally, which is also a consequence of globalization, is the increased presence in Western countries of women from many parts of the world who come as immigrants and refugees. These women are often informed by their experiences in women's movements elsewhere, but their views are also shaped by their lives in diaspora and by exile communities in Western countries. Women who have grown up in Western countries but have derived some of their culture, language, and values from their parents' or grandparents' country of origin develop feminist ideas inspired by their experiences within these overlapping worlds. Their insight that the 'West' and the 'Third World,' or 'North' and 'South' (as the new divisions in the world are often categorized), are not airtight compartments, but rather exist in dynamic interaction with one another, forms the third part of the paradigm shift now under way. Women who share insights from multiple contexts become the translators of difference and thereby promote this shift. Feminists living in diaspora and exile communities often use the term 'postcolonial' to describe their orientation. Our approach relies heavily on many of their insights, although there are elements of the postcolonial orientation we consider inappropriate. For example, from the perspective of many indigenous people, colonialism is still a force in settler societies such as Canada and so is not 'post.'

The stage is set for a major transformation in the nature of women's studies in 'Western' countries – a transformation we hope this text will foster. The main agents of change, however, will be the next generation of women's studies students, feminist scholars, and women's movement activists. Also included, however, will be activists and scholars in the Third and Fourth (indigenous) Worlds who may not use the term 'feminist.' For the new paradigm to emerge and take hold, however, women worldwide will need to take both their differences and commonalities seriously.

The Value and Roots of the New Approach

Demands that mainstream women acknowledge diversity can throw feminist politics into crisis. But the value of opening up feminism, scholarship on women, and women's studies to a greater understanding of the diversity of women's lives is also increasingly apparent as Western societies become increasingly multicultural. With its vision of social transformation, a one-world feminism can play an important role in the next millennium, if mainstream women come to better understand the various systems of power within which women experience subordination because of attributes other than their womanness. This is a disturbing point for many mainstream women, partly because it isn't clear what women's studies and scholarship on women generally will be about if it isn't held together by an assumption that 'women' are basically the same. Some ask whether there is a future for women's studies without the assumptions of the category 'women.' The history of women's movements shows that the feminists were among the first to challenge the notion that oppressed people can be 'thought about' in the same way as those who are oppressing them. Feminists challenged the right of male thinkers and activists to assume that men's experiences should form the basis for theory and practice applied to women. They argued that since 'women's' experiences were different from 'men's,' women had to represent their own experiences. This opened the way for others also to challenge false claims about them that were embedded in ideologies – ideologies such as racism, which like sexism has held sway for centuries. In sum, 'Western' feminist theory and practice were at one time too narrow because they failed to consult the ideas of minority, marginalized, indigenous, and non-Western women; in recent years, we have collectively begun to take 'difference' into account in a serious way. We draw on these efforts in this text. We share the task of revealing a new paradigm; we also acknowledge the efforts of the many whose ideas informed our own.

In trying to build movements based on false claims of 'universal sisterhood,' we weakened our capacity to achieve meaningful change, by provoking fragmentation. The conflicts noted earlier are but a few consequences of assuming that women are (or should be) alike. If some women are privileged, while others are disadvantaged and marginalized and their views are ignored, then coalitions for change are weak at best. This is because the insights of so many women are excluded; indeed, feminism's claim to be a project of social transformation is harmed if it replicates the privileges and harms of the dominant society in general. Because women's studies emerged in 'Western' countries in the 1970s in the heyday of ideas of sisterhood and stand-alone feminism, its key texts focused on commonalities, de-emphasized difference, and ignored the voices of marginalized women. Australian Jan Jindy Pettman (1992) has described this practice as 'normalized absence, problematized presence.' That is, women whose experiences were 'different' were invisible unless they were identified as 'a problem,' either because their 'difference' itself was constructed as a problem or because it was judged to create a problem such as violence. This was often manifested in the practice of lumping all 'different' and disadvantaged women together in a single chapter in women's studies' textbooks and courses and treating their issues as problems without exploring how these women were also similar to 'ordinary' women or how they responded to oppression. This containment of difference meant that the basic framework continued to be grounded in the experiences and ideas of mainstream women, who were mostly white, anglophone, and heterosexual. As already noted, the frameworks of women's studies and of scholarship on women generally are now more open to ideas from minority and marginalized 'Western' women and 'non-Western' women. This is the point of the paradigm shift now under way, and it is changing the underlying frameworks of scholarship on women rather than containing discussions of difference and limiting their impact.

Five 'Big Questions' Around Which This Text Is Organized

Our re-visioning of the paradigm used by women's studies and feminist scholarship is based on some of the big questions feminist theorists and activists in women's movements are tackling. Five of these big questions organize our analyses in this text. These are:

1 Why and how have human societies used differences in people's characteristics to construct and justify systems of power in which some privileged people dominate others, who are then subordinated, marginalized, exploited, and oppressed?
2 How do women in different contexts experience being 'women,' and how do they organize to contest negative aspects of their lives?

3 How do the systems of power in which men dominate women operate, and how are they related to other systems of power based on 'race,' class, sexual orientation, language, ethnicity, nation, or dis/ability, which also affect women's lives?

4 How do movements organized by women to contest male dominance relate to other movements that mobilize women – especially those that contest racism, homophobia, capitalism, colonialism, or environmental degradation, or that advance nationalism, language, faith, or ethnicity?

5 How do global systems, including colonialism, capitalism, neocolonialism, and globalization, shape movements in which women act? Do women's movements in turn affect these global movements?

These big questions are woven through the chapters, which provide insights into their complexities but do not always provide definitive answers.

Objectives of the Text

Our goal is to provide tools of thinking that will help you think through difference to some aspects of these big questions. Our approach assumes that differences are normal in the world and are central to women's experiences of their 'woman-ness.' Our theme thinking through difference has several meanings. First, it means using an understanding of women's different experiences – usually gained through comparative methods – to think about these 'big questions' in ways that move beyond the artificial commonalities embedded in the category 'women.' Second, it means thinking to understand what difference is and why it has been the basis for systems of power in which some are privileged and dominant, whereas others are subordinated, marginalized, oppressed, and exploited. Part of this thinking through will involve defining these concepts and exploring the theories from which they are drawn. Note that our emphasis on difference is a corrective; that is, we have adopted it because much scholarship on women, and many mainstream women's movements, have had difficulty with it. We will also learn, but not assume, what women have in common. In this text, then, we aim to do the following:

• Introduce multiple perspectives on issues to think through different positions, and try to explain why women may have different 'takes.'

- Explore the extent to which women worldwide share similar visions of social transformation, although they may not always call themselves feminists and may have different ideas about how to achieve their visions. To this end, we focus on whether women's movements worldwide have similar agendas, and we explore the kinds of issues around which successful coalitions and networks have emerged.
- Discuss how women in different contexts often have different ideas as to what is needed to transform their lives. This will help us locate ourselves in relation to the existing, multiple systems of power and explore how each of our relationships affects those of other women.
- Show how privileges and inequalities get built into social systems and are reproduced – often unconsciously and unintentionally – in our daily practices. That is, we show how we often participate in reproducing privileges and inequalities in our daily lives – usually without intending to do so.
- Provide insights into how each of us can identify important issues in our given circumstances.

Why Start with Diversity?

In this text, we employ as our methodological rule an initial focus on diversity, rather than an assumption of commonality. That is, we start from the premise that although 'women' may share goals and values, their experiences are often different and their interests may conflict. That being said, the majority of 'Western' women have characteristics not shared by other women – especially by women around the world. By Western women, we usually mean those who are white, often anglophone, more educated, and more affluent than most women in the world, but who still perceive themselves as victims of oppression by men. This has led them to downplay other oppressions that have harmed millions of women around the world – oppressions that mainstream, 'Western' women don't experience, such as being or having been colonized, absolute poverty, national liberation struggles, and the harms of racism, homophobia, and ablism. This does not mean that only women who are white, anglophone, affluent, and so on are the only oppressors or that they cannot themselves be oppressed. But it does reflect the positions of privilege they often experience – positions that are too often ignored.

Our purpose is to understand both the commonalities and differences among women. We have chosen issues that we think represent the concerns of women from different racial, ethnic, and class backgrounds. We have included religion and nationalism, which are important issues for many women worldwide but are often not included in Western scholarship on women. We have also included issues that are of interest to women in general, such as body image, reproduction, working with men, violence, work, race, and ethnicity. Because of space constraints, we have not been able to include topics such as pornography and feminist culture, even though they are important issues of feminist concern. Nevertheless the analyses we provide for the issues we *have* included offer a useful model that will help the reader analyse issues of her or his choice. Our focus is on developing an approach in which all of us learn to situate ourselves in relation to others who are differently situated. This method will enlighten us by making us aware of our privileges and disadvantages. In other words, it will help us understand the relational nature of our positions. Currently, we are in a time of transition. Women's studies and feminist scholarship generally are dominated by white, mainstream women. To facilitate our re-visioning, we need dialogues and partnerships between mainstream and marginalized women. Too often, the concerns of mainstream women have been central because of power differentials among women. The transformation we seek for scholarship on women requires that we explore the relational nature of women's lives in this world. The one-world perspective we adopt in this text has the goal of emphasizing how all women's destinies are tied together. This effort is strengthened by the fact that globalization and its accompanying population movements are promoting greater contact among women worldwide. Also, the analyses of postcolonial thinkers, which reflect the knowledge and experiences of those whose nations suffered colonization, are providing new visions. We can make sense of our lives only when we understand the interconnections among women, be they mainstream or marginalized.

Diversity and Globalization

To develop the capacity to 'think through' difference, we must learn to think in a one-world context. In the new millennium, globalization will make the lives of women in different parts of the world even more interconnected, although most women will continue to live their lives in a local environment. Part of the process involves learning what is meant by 'global' and 'local.' For many of us, the term 'globalization' suggests threatening economic, political, and technological changes that can be neither resisted nor controlled.[5] As we illustrate in chapter 2, the discourse and processes involved in globalization present many socially disruptive and polarizing consequences for women. We propose a one-world approach for women's studies because we believe women's movements around the world must make common cause on many of these issues, but can do so only if they are able to contest these negative consequences. In almost every country there are women's movements seeking social transformations to improve women's lives. The emergence of a vigorous international movement advocating feminist goals on the international stage – for example, in UN arenas – is an exciting harbinger of this re-visioning.

A one-world approach is different from the 'sisterhood is global' idea advanced by some 'Western' feminists in the 1980s. Studies of the women-in-development (WID) literature has shown this bias in, for example, the remarks of Western development 'experts,' who claim to know better than women of less-developed countries just what their real needs were (Goetz, 1988). To think through transnational differences within a one-world framework, we must abandon the idea that mainstream, 'Western' feminism is the best kind for all women. A true one-world approach requires that we think about differences both in local contexts and in a global context, and then make links between the two. Moreover, as women's fates worldwide become more linked, Western scholarship on women must affirmatively increase our knowledge of women's different experiences worldwide. The old compartments that separated 'us' from 'them,' multiplied many times the world over, must be broken down if feminism is to enhance its ability to promote justice for all women.

Principles of This Text

In this text we assume that mainstream Western feminist ideas are neither universal nor the norm. They will be put in debate (1) with the ideas of women who are marginalized within Western countries because of their differences and/or colonial status, and (2) with the ideas of women in the 'two-thirds world.' As much as possible, we will let women speak directly, in their own voices, in materials drawn from research often ignored. Our goal is to understand how differently located women experience both their woman-ness and their feminism, if they work within a feminist framework. Where women activists reject feminism – as do many indigenous women – we will try to understand why. The goal is not to judge whose feminism is purer, nor is it to point fingers at groups that choose to pursue justice for women outside a feminist framework.

One principle that will guide us in this exploration of the ideas of women whose lives are often quite different from our own is the idea that categories of difference are relational, not natural. For example, poor women cannot exist without rich women, whose affluence rests on an unequal distribution of the world's resources. Similarly, women with disabilities are limited in their options because the world is organized for the convenience of people who are able-bodied. These are not characteristics that are intrinsic to the people we use them to describe. For example, Jill has an impairment of function because of her arthritis, but she is further disabled by how workplaces and transportation systems are organized. To most women the privileges of being able-bodied are invisible, because they seem to be 'normal' – just the way the world is. So in Canada, Vanaja is seen to have a 'race,' whereas Jill's 'race' is invisible. Yet Jill's 'whiteness' gives her privileges, and Vanaja's brown colour brings her harms. Nor is it just a matter of which skin colour is the majority colour, since Jill enjoys privileges even where white-skinned people are in the minority because of the continuing effects of colonialism, neocolonialism, and racism.

If you are privileged in terms of the relationships described by concepts such as race, class, heterosexuality, and disability, it is important to explore how you replicate the systems of power involved in creating privileges and disadvantages. For example, if you are characterized by 'whiteness,' what consequences does your race entail in terms of how you are treated and how you experience your relationships with others? (We discuss these issues more in chapter 1.) It is also important to understand that these consequences occur whether you choose them or not. A white woman who is an antiracist still benefits from her whiteness in a racist society. And a woman who chooses heterosexual relationships is protected from the harms of homophobia, even if she is active in fighting against it. The goal is not to make mainstream women feel guilty about their privilege, nor is it to blame them; rather, it is to develop ways of understanding both sides of the power relationships constructed around these differences. It is also important to realize that conditions such as being privileged or oppressed are not all-or-nothing in character. Jill is privileged because of her whiteness, her education, and her heterosexual life choices; but she is also disadvantaged because of her origins in poverty and her disability. Likewise, Vanaja is privileged by her class, caste, education, and heterosexuality but disadvantaged by her race, her immigrant origins, and her being a Hindu.

A core problem is that we will only be exploring the ideas of many 'other' women to the extent that they are written down and published in English. This is a limitation in our effort to develop a one-world framework. In Canada, for example, Franco-Quebec and Acadian feminisms are little understood by English-Canadian women because of the language difference, which has resulted in stereotyping and misunderstanding. Nor can most of us easily access the ideas of women whose mother tongue is an indigenous language (of which forty are spoken in Canada). We must be careful, therefore, not to think that our brief encounters with the experiences of feminists from around the world give us an in-depth understanding of their situations. Even so, we must make the effort to learn about women whose lives are different from ours, and we must challenge stereotypes that exist about 'other' women. As Australian Chilla Bulbeck observes, 'within women's studies, "other" women still often appear ... as footnotes of difference on the general themes of white women's lives and experiences' (1998: 4). Studying unfamiliar feminisms widens our vision and challenges resistance to change.

Organizing Difference

The goal is to move beyond forms of scholarship on women that treat 'other' women as 'footnotes on the general themes of white women's lives,' and to engage with difference to subvert assumptions that those 'general themes' can be applied to all women with minor modifications. But descriptions of difference[6] cannot by themselves organize women's studies and stretch mainstream Western feminism to a wider vision. Like Bulbeck, we believe 'women's studies ... cannot ... dissolve into endless differences.' Like her, we think 'patterns must be sought, lines of distinction drawn, or nothing much can be said' (1998: 4). But where are these lines of distinction to come from? And on what basis can distinctions be drawn? Throughout the book we draw on theoretical insights about how some differences are actually converted systems of power based on the one hand on privilege and domination, and on the other on marginalization, oppression, and exploitation. These are linked to the big questions we introduced earlier. Of course, not all diversity results in social relations of dominance and subordination. But many forms of difference do.[7] The concept of difference, explored in detail in chapter 1, points us toward aspects of human relationships that are important as signposts. We need theoretical insights, however, to go beyond signposts to explain why one 'side' of a relationship of difference is conferred with power and privilege, while the other 'side' is not. We also need theoretical insights to explain how privileges and inequalities are replicated, often unintentionally through our daily practices. The insights on which we draw in the text come from a number of sources, including class theory, critical race theory, queer theory, and theories of patriarchy. Our main inspiration, however, is drawn from 'Third World' feminists who address the impact of the legacies of colonialism and neocolonialism on women and on indigenous women who still struggle with them.

Organization of the Text

The text is divided into two parts. In the two chapters of Part I, we explore feminist theories and contextualize both theory and practice in a one-world framework. In the second chapter of Part I we explore key issues of methodology, mainly the question of how we think through difference at the global and local levels in order to gain an understanding of the main issues that mobilize mainstream Western women, 'other' women marginalized in the West, and women in the 'two-thirds' world.

The two chapters in Part I introduce key concepts, which are tools for thinking. They also explore theoretical insights that interpret some of the patterns identified by women's studies scholars.

In Part II (nine chapters) we explore issues in women's studies from different perspectives, and apply the concepts, theoretical insights, and methods developed in Part I. Informed by 'third wave' feminist frameworks, the authors are inclusive in terms of using the perspectives of dominant and marginalized groups. Differences among women (people) are conceptualized in relational terms. The intent is to show how relations of power give differences among women (people) a certain structure. We hope these analyses will help raise consciousness among people regarding their privileges and disadvantages. Coalition building among women to transform society is possible under such conditions of awareness.

In each chapter we deal with a given issue and introduce at least two different 'takes' by different segments of the population to drive home the point that there are differences among women with regard to how they assess a given issue. Even though the method of analysis is not exactly the same in all chapters, each author is sensitive to power differences among different segments of the population and differences in experiences and, therefore, differences with regard to various concerns and preoccupations. The dimensions of differences we have consistently identified across chapters are gender, race and ethnicity, and class. Several chapters also deal with dimensions of sexuality and ability.

Notes

1 We use quotation marks to indicate when terms are controversial or imprecise. The 'West' refers to most countries populated by whites of European origin, including the United Kingdom, the United States, Canada, Australia & New Zealand. Terms such as 'the West' and 'the Third World' flatten differences within those constructed zones. In 'the West,' for example, some European countries had no colonies (Switzerland) and other countries (Canada) were colonies.

2 The Greek philosopher Aristotle, for example, believed women were immersed in necessity because of reproduction, which justified excluding all women from public roles and their subordination to men.

3 These concepts are explained in Iris Marion Young's text *Justice and the Politics of Difference* (1990). We explore them in detail in Part I.

4 Masao Miyoshi (1996: 99) identifies six interrelated developments in postwar history: (1) the Cold War and its end, (2) decolonization, (3) the development of transnational corporations, (4) the hightech revolutions (e.g., information technology), (5) the emergence of feminist movements worldwide, and (6) the environmental crisis. We explore how each shapes the new paradigm in women's studies. We would now add another major variable: the emergence of large-scale terrorism and the reduced sense of security in the West.

5 Karl Polanyi noted in 1957 that each wave of globalisation involves two parts, the economic, political and technological forces and reactions to them, including resistances of different kinds.

6 The terms 'diversity' and 'difference' are not synonyms. 'Diversity' means variety and usually has a positive value. 'Difference' is the state of being unalike but can also mean a disagreement or a quarrel.

7 Left-handedness, for example, has been the basis for discrimination in many cultures, as is seen in the term *sinister* and in the harsh treatment until recently of left-handed children.

PART I

CHAPTER 1

Gender, Race, and Nation

Jill Vickers and Vanaja Dhruvarajan

Women's studies emerged in Western countries in the 1970s in the heyday of undifferentiated 'sisterhood.' Its key texts focused on similarities among 'women's' lives and constructed 'difference' mainly as a distinction between men and women. Poor women and women of dissimilar race, faith, language, or ethnicity were marginalized. Nor were the voices of lesbians and women with disabilities often heard. Women who were 'different' were dealt with through 'normalized absence, problematized presence' (Pettman 1992). Women who were 'different' were invisible unless their 'difference' was seen as a problem or was judged to create a problem such as violence. In the past decade issues of 'difference' have seriously affected Western women's movements, causing fragmentation and demobilization. In this chapter we introduce you to some of the debates and issues about how to 'think through difference.' We also explore the limits of approaches that focus only on difference and that fail to draw on theories which explain how difference is constructed into systems of power, dominance, and oppression.

Susan Strickland asserts that *how* different experiences are to be evaluated or explained is part of the challenge of difference. Moreover: 'Women critical of, or excluded by, white/Western/middle-class/ heterosexual or whatever perspective are not just claiming a space to speak for themselves; they have been speaking out but have not really been listened to. What they are offering is not just their 'difference' to acknowledge, but a challenge at least partly in critique of my understanding of the world' (1994: 268). So, the central question we address in this chapter is this: How should we respond in full measure to the challenge of difference?

The Challenge of Difference

Globalization

The emergence of a strong international women's movement reflects the growing importance of transnational arenas where women's ideas interact. Even in our own countries, our fates are increasingly tied to those of women elsewhere. Our horizons need to be broadened so that we can better understand women's lives beyond the borders of our own country or locality. There are already important issues of difference within Western countries. With the impact of globalization, and the growing importance of transnational networks, movements, and institutions, the challenges and the stakes are even greater. Feminist scholarship, whether it is practised in women's studies or as part of activism, therefore, must come to grips with this complex phenomenon, which increasingly frames our debates about difference.

Globalization, a set of economic, technological, and social processes, is affecting women and women's movements around the world. Some of the processes became possible after the barriers dividing the Cold War world broke down. Others were working long before that. For example, colonization – the process whereby Britain and other Western European countries attempted to conquer, rule, and Christianize most non-European countries and peoples – was an earlier global process that had profound consequences for women worldwide. The civilizations associated with religions such as Hinduism, Buddhism, and Islam were an even earlier form of globalization.

Some impacts of the current wave of globalization:

- Human migration is increasing, especially from the 'two-thirds' world to Western countries.
- Information technology (IT) has speeded up communications (for those who can afford access) and freed up corporations to develop global factories, with different countries assigned different aspects of production – for example, labour-intensive work to countries with cheap (usually female) labour and weak labour and environmental protections.
- Local cultures are being swamped by Western, mainly American culture. This process began under colonialism but has been intensified by IT.

- International market forces and financial transactions are increasingly disrupting nation-state economies.
- The power of transnational agencies, such as the World Bank (WB) and the International Monetary Fund (IMF), is increasing.

Some accounts assume that the changes summed up in the term 'globalization' are inevitable. This is not our view. There is intense ideological conflict over the scope, meaning, and likely consequences of 'globalization.' For some, it involves the triumph of capitalist democracies around the world and the emergence of a 'global village' (McLuhan, 1989). These people are fascinated with the idea that globalization is open-ended – with the 'promise' of new horizons coming into view. Others are concerned about its potential to cause economic devastation, weaken the power of nation-states, and destroy cultures and identities (Chossudovsky, 1997; Hahnel, 1999; Kumar, 1996). This has led many to call for the rejection of globalization forces to create space for the flowering of individual cultures, economies, and identities. For example, Spivak (1990), an Indian feminist, has called for the rejection of all histories written by or from the perspective of the colonizers. She argues that we should write histories and other discourses that value difference in totally new spaces. Doing so would establish an independent consciousness created from the experiences and knowledge of ordinary people. Others have selectively adopted some of the changes brought about by globalization and are negotiating to redefine their identities and cultures so that some aspects change but others remain untouched (Geschiere and Meyer, 1998; Barndt, 1999). Identities and cultures were formed differently by the unique histories, politics, and cultures of specific localities (Appadurai, 1996). In some circumstances the accelerated pace of globalization can lead to intense ethnic or religious strife as people and their leaders strive for economic and political advantage. Appadurai (1998) argues that this can happen when groups must establish the 'purity' of their ethnic identities to ensure their eligibility for political and economic entitlements.

Clearly, the processes of globalization are complex. They create new boundaries and rupture old ones. But who is creating these new boundaries, and in whose interest? How do these changes affect different segments of a population? How do different people respond to these changes? These are empirical questions since these processes vary from place to place (Kaplan, 1998). One of our goals, therefore, is to demonstrate that part of 'thinking through difference' involves grappling with the impact of globalization. It is not good enough to simply reject it as entirely negative; nor is it good enough to jump on the bandwagon uncritically.

Feminism has an important role to play in this era of globalization. Without constructive/critical feminist intervention there is a danger of masculinist theories becoming dominant again (Kaplan and Grewal, 1999). The need for a dialectical relationship between theory and practice has been accepted to a greater extent in recent years; so has the need to develop interdisciplinary ways of analysing gender (Bridgman et al., 1999). Those who are developing transnational cultural studies recognize that postcolonial scholarship and international feminist theory and cultural products are important new influences (Kaplan and Grewal, 1999). It is not enough to document the existence of pluralism across the world if elites are simply going to use this knowledge to 'manage' diversity. Internationally, feminists are seeking an integrated analysis of women's economic, cultural, and political concerns. Instead of assuming that all women share a common standpoint, they contend that we should look for historically specific ways in which societies are gendered.

We argue that it is important to explore linkages among people who are differently located in their social spaces. Such an approach involves analysing economic and political relations in different countries. Linkage does not imply reciprocity or sameness. We will explore differences in women's access to power and in their ability to participate in making culture. We will examine forces such as religious fundamentalism, patriarchy, and nationalism in different parts of the globe, and consider how those forces are linked. We will emphasize the value of transnational co-operation for achieving the feminist goal of empowering women globally.

In many Western countries, women's movements are becalmed at least in part because minority and marginalized women are unwilling to accept leadership from women of the dominant culture who fail to respect differences or acknowledge their own privilege. So the ability of women's movements to build coalitions strong enough to achieve social transformation in Western countries is also at stake. Globalization is penetrating Western nation-states to the extent that powerful economic, social, and political forces are threatening women's well-being. Without the counter-power (Cohen 1989) of alliances and networks of women's movements organized transnationally, the most negative scenarios projected about globalization will be fulfilled. Thus, developing this counter-power globally as well as within Western nation-states is an important motive for addressing issues of difference. After the horrific events of 11 September 2001, it has become increasingly difficult to believe that women's counter-power could contend with the dark forces released within the context of globalization. It is all the more important, however, that we keep before us the transformative visions that women in many parts of the world have found in feminisms.

Women's Experiences and Interests

Learning to think through difference, means taking into account the fact that although 'women' may have some interests in common, they also have conflicting interests. This is especially the case when we view women's movements in a one-world framework. Colonialism and experiments with communism and neocolonialism have contoured the world so that women's views on many issues vary widely. This means we must move beyond the familiar ideological slogans about all women sharing a common oppression because we are 'women.' As Audre Lorde argues, the oppression of women transcends ethnic and racial (and national) boundaries, but it is not identical across all categories: 'To imply ... all woman suffer the same oppression simply because we are women is to lose sight of the many varied tools of patriarchy [and] to ignore how these tools are used by women without awareness against each other' (Lorde 1983: 67).

As we learn how to think through difference in a one-world framework, and as we learn from the knowledge of women living beyond the circle of Western 'sisterhood,' familiar issues take on new dimensions. Western feminists at first assumed that their experiences were universal. They adopted a method of consciousness raising (CR) that involved women exploring their experiences in small groups. In these groups they realized their experiences were shared by other women, and theorized that their supposedly private, individual issues were in fact rooted in the structures of society – perhaps even in their species. They captured this insight in slogans such as: 'the personal is political.' The shared experiences of the women involved in these groups developed into the movement's political agenda and the background

knowledge of early women's studies. This method produced a dynamic political movement, but it also blocked understanding of the
experiences of women who were not part of the CR groups, for example, because of racism, disability, or poverty, or because they were
involved in other movements such as the Red Power movement of
indigenous peoples. Knowledge created this way was intense and immediate. Feminist ideas resonated with these women because instead
of 'men' writing about 'women's' lives, 'women' were speaking and
writing about their own lives. But the CR method excluded the knowledge that 'other' women had when the category 'women' was explored more broadly.

Our method in this text is to compare different perspectives on
common themes based in the knowledge of differently situated women.
It is not our goal to recreate the ontological category of 'women' or to
reinvoke 'sisterhood' out of this process. Instead, our method recognizes that women's knowledge cannot be given a unified form, because not all 'differences' can be assimilated and not all women everywhere see their destinies as determined only (or even primarily) by
their sex or gender. For example, Winona Stevenson, an aboriginal
single mother of Cree, Assiniboine, Saulteaux, Irish, and English descent explains why she rejects the label 'feminist':

> I do not call myself a feminist. I believe in the power of Indigenous
> women and the power of all women. I believe that while feminists and
> Indigenous women have a lot in common, they are in separate move-
> ments. Feminism defines sexual oppression as the Big Ugly. The Indig-
> enous women's movement sees colonization and racial oppression as the
> Big Uglies. Issues of sexual oppression are seldom articulated separately
> because they are part of the Bigger Uglies. (Johnson, Stevenson, and
> Greschener, 1993: 159)

Difference Is Not Assimilable

When we read the different accounts – each of which is authentic in
the sense of being knowledge the authors have derived from their
experiences – it is important to think through the different 'takes' on
issues that each involves. Understanding these accounts is helpful to
the extent that we are capable of comprehending them, but the differences will not disappear once we understand them. Nor will we find it

easy to understand them fully or in great depth. But taking difference seriously usually requires us to change how we think and act:

> Difference is not something we just recognize (agreeing to differ, live and let live ...). It may require some change from us; not necessarily adopting the other's point of view, which is usually not possible, but certainly changing in order to acknowledge its legitimacy. (Lennon and Whitford, 1994: 12)

Genuine engagement with difference, then, means examining our own situation and how we are related to others from whom we are 'different.' It requires us to make honest and searching assessments of our relations with 'others,' and compels us to consider how we stand in relations of privilege or power to them. It also requires that we tap into the creative potential of our encounters with 'difference.' 'Advocating the mere tolerance of difference between women is the grossest reformism. It is a total denial of the creative function of difference in our lives' (Lorde, 1993: 111). It is our encounters with difference, in fact, that allow us to think creatively beyond the framework of 'me and people like me.' Comparison – which is a process of exploring both similarities and differences – helps us discover new approaches and strategies by providing us with new insights from women whose 'take' is different from ours.

Outline of the Chapter

This chapter has four parts:

- First, we outline the major approaches to 'thinking through difference' and the manner in which Western feminists have dealt with difference. In this discussion, we present some arguments to support the claim that women's studies ought to take 'difference' into account.
- Second, we link the difficulties Western feminists have with 'difference' conceptually and politically to basic characteristics of Western thought and political practice, which are rooted mainly in Euro-American colonialism and neocolonialism. We argue that colonial and neocolonial political practices have established knowledge monopolies associated with modernity, and that these mo-

nopolies have suppressed other – especially non-Western – ways of understanding reality. These monopolistic ways of knowing have structured 'differences' hierarchically – for example, male *over* female – and have marked each difference as a sign of inferiority or superiority. As a consequence, non-hierarchical approaches have been repressed or remain underdeveloped.

- Third, we explore some issues of overlapping and conflicting loyalties in order to highlight the weaknesses of approaches that do not go beyond difference. We note the problems that result from focusing solely on experience as a basis for understanding in a worldwide context. In particular, we discuss the limits of postmodern approaches to difference in this regard, and suggest alternatives.

- Finally, we provide a concrete example of how to engage with difference, through a discussion of gendered racism. We argue that feminist scholarship works best when it compares knowledge of differences, and when it theorizes about how systems of power based on difference develop, and how those systems work.

I. Major Approaches to Difference

In this section, although we begin with a white, majority-culture account of difference, we give priority to accounts by women who experience oppression and/or marginalization because of their 'difference.' Our goal is to help you develop the conceptual skills to understand 'the politics of difference' that is central to 'third-wave' women's movements and to the new women's studies. We begin by outlining an account of difference by a white American feminist, Nancy Fraser.

Difference – A Majority Account

Nancy Fraser in *Justice Interruptus* (1997) gives an account of the stages she believes Western feminism has gone through in its treatment of 'difference.' Fraser, a professor of political philosophy, constructs this history from within the Euro-American tradition. She identifies three attempts to 'deal with difference' and concludes that none of them was satisfactory. Each point of view was limited because it was developed within the framework of identity politics, the goal of which is recognition of identity; hence each failed to make links to the politics of redistribution, poverty, and class. In the first stage, difference was constructed mainly in terms of differences between men and women. In the second, stimulated by pressures from lesbians and race-minority women in Western countries, differences among women became the focus, and yet the majority – namely white women – remained in control.

In the current stage, Fraser sees difference being converted into the multiple, intersecting differences that are central to postmodern and multicultural challenges to theory and politics organized around 'women.' Postmodern feminists reject any generalizations about 'women'; they deny that 'women' have any common identity because of shared biological, social, or psychological experiences, and they denaturalize the body by conceptualizing sex exclusively as gender, and gender as 'performed' (Butler, 1990). Multiculturalists in this same period, she concludes, celebrate diverse cultural identities and traditions but without inquiring if they are or are not 'good for women.'

Fraser focuses on the third period – that is, the period since the collapse of the Soviet Union and the discrediting of communism marked by 'the "Postsocialist" Condition.' She asserts that 'the "struggle for recognition" is fast becoming the paradigmatic form of political conflict in the late twentieth century' (11). She associates this 'struggle for recognition' with people who are marginalized on account of race, ethnicity, and sexual orientation. Fraser believes that current demands for 'the recognition of difference' too often fail to acknowledge that material inequality is on the rise globally and that redistribution of wealth and resources is as important to the struggle for justice as cultural recognition of difference. She concludes that if claims for recognition of difference lead us to ignore material inequalities, identity politics will disrupt our progress toward justice. In sum, she believes this stage has resulted in a politics organized exclusively around the recognition of difference – a politics that ignores class and poverty, especially outside 'the West.'

Not All Differences Work the Same Way

Fraser argues that not all differences work in the same way. Those associated with race and gender, she believes, are 'bivalent.' That is, in order to achieve the social transformations feminists and antiracists seek, changes are required in both recognition and redistribution, because those suffering from race and sex oppression are usually also poor. So redressing gender injustice and eliminating the effects of racism require changes in both the political economy and in culture – that is, in both the redistribution of wealth and the reconstruction of culture. Her analysis is a useful corrective to assumptions that antiracism and gender justice movements are rooted solely in identity politics. Other differences, however, are also 'bivalent.' For example, justice for those with disabilities requires both recognition of identity (deaf culture, for example) and redistribution of resources (services for deaf people, for example). To Fraser, approaches to 'difference' that focus only on identity ignore issues of power underlying the system of wealth distribution. If identity politics always 'trump' claims for redistribution, the movements that result will not be progressive. Therefore, she advocates a politics of difference based on multiple systems of domination involving both identity and the material differences of poverty and wealth.

Limits to Fraser's Analysis

The challenge of opening Western feminism to 'difference' may be more complex than Fraser's account suggests. Although useful as a starting point, her account is largely about 'the politics of difference' in Western countries (mainly the United States) in the post–Cold War period. But when we contextualize feminism's struggles with 'difference' in a worldwide frame, challenges emerge to Western knowledge claims – challenges that are not captured by Fraser's framework. For example, Audre Lorde argues, we must take seriously the belief that many 'Third World' and aboriginal women that they are oppressed by racism, colonialism, and neo-colonialism, not only by their cultures, faiths, or nations. For these women, sex/gender oppression is not a separate, overarching system of power, domination, and oppression. Second, Fraser's account fails to integrate the insights of women in Russia and Eastern Europe, whose experience of the 'postsocialist condition' poses profound questions about socialist visions of redistribution. We must take into account that millions of women in Russia and Eastern Europe, based on their experiences, have rejected both feminism and socialism. Third, Fraser's account fails to note how Westerners are now constructing the Muslim world as the new 'Evil Empire.' Feminists who are open to a global vision of social transformation must take issue with this new monolithic identity. Finally, in order to understand them fully, we must explore categories like 'race' from the perspective of those oppressed because of them, and not just from the perspective of those they privilege. This means not constructing categories of 'difference' such as 'race' as ontological categories that are supposedly experienced in an identical fashion by all people everywhere. In deconstructing 'women,' we must avoid creating new false universals.

The Concept of 'Difference': Maynard's Account

Mary Maynard (1994) also provides a brief history of 'difference,' its definitions and uses. She acknowledges that the term has been useful for identifying diversity, but also fears that a focus on 'difference' runs the risk of maintaining and replicating oppressions based on some 'differences,' especially race. She argues that identity politics often implies that all differences operate equally in systems of power. (We are all 'different' now.) However, as she notes, oppression is not the consequence of all forms of difference, since only some kinds of difference have been constructed into hierarchical systems of dominance and oppression. Moreover, the term 'difference' assumes there is 'a norm' from which those who are labelled 'different' diverge, with the added implication that they should be assimilated into it, or aspire to be assimilated. So 'difference' is most often used to identify those marginalized from the group understood as the mainstream. Those who are 'different' are not the norm.

Maynard insists that if our goal is to achieve justice in the real world, we must recognize differences that have been developed into oppressive power structures – dominators and subordinates, oppressors and oppressed, exploiters and exploited. She also insists there is no single definition of 'difference.' She notes that the basic objective of those women (mainly women of colour) who constructed the discourse around 'difference' was to develop a strategy for challenging white majority feminists' idea of 'woman' as a universal category. She observes that there are now two approaches to challenging this idea. One is the postmodern approach, which constructs the world in terms of 'multiple intersecting differences.' This approach assumes 'there is no objective social world outside of our preexisting knowledge of discourse' (Maynard, 1994: 15). This assumes that 'differences' are what we make of them; how others use them to locate us in systems of power is not the issue. This approach posits that we have 'multiple selves'; it denies the possibility of any 'authoritative accounts' of how we experience the world, and seems to claim that patterns in women's different experiences are illicit. Susan Strickland (1994: 269) also warns us that there can be a consumerist approach to difference that fails to acknowledge the systems of power and their consequences.

The second approach, according to Maynard, focuses on experiential differences, exploring how women's positions in terms of their class, race, sexual orientation, and so on affect their interactions and relationships. This establishes previously marginalized women as the best knowers about their experiences. That is, Black women, not white women, are established as the best knowers concerning experiences of gendered racism. This requires that we affirmatively seek out their accounts about their experiences. In the sections that follow, this is the approach on which we will build. There are certain similarities between these two approaches: both distrust generalizations and emphasize diversity over sameness, and both resist universalizing labels like 'women' or 'Black.'

Some scholars argue that we should study the relational nature of differences among groups, instead of focusing on discrete accounts of the experiences of different groups. They use the metaphor of a prism to capture this idea. As Zinn et al. (2000: 7) argue, it is time to analyse group experiences 'within a framework that emphasizes differences and inequalities not as discrete areas of separation but as interrelated bands of colour that together make up a spectrum.'

Antiracist Feminisms

Significant contributions toward antiracist feminist thought have been evident in North America since the 1980s (for example, in the U.S., hooks, 1984; Collins, 1986; and in Canada, Bannerji, 1987; Ng, 1986; Gupta, 1987; Carty and Brand, 1989). As we entered the 1990s these efforts were intensified, and today they are much better recognized. There is a strong conviction among antiracist feminists that race is a primary organizing principle of life in North American society and around the globe. Race as a system of power interacts with other systems of inequality such as class, sexuality, and ability, which shape the experiences of different groups of women and men. Raising this awareness is considered especially important at a time when racism has become part of common sense – that is, part of the taken-for-granted reality of everyday life. In addition, 'this emphasis on race takes on increasing political importance in an era where discourse about race is governed by colour-evasive language and a preference for individual rather than group remedies for social inequalities' (Zinn et al., 1997: 25). These feminists consider gender, race, and class, among others as simultaneous intersecting and interlocking systems of action and meaning. All of them are interested in exploring how each system is constituted in and through the others, but they also differ sharply with regard to how they analyse these systems. Here we discuss two types of analysis: the reformulated political economy approach, and postcolonial thought. The former deals with structural racism, the latter with the experiences of marginalized people and their accrued knowledge. In our analyses of difference in this text, we draw on both types of antiracist feminism.

Feminists who adopt the antiracist political economy approach are interested in studying the political and economic impact of various policies and practices on groups of women of various racial and class backgrounds and sexual orientations. They call for a reformulation of the political economy approach to address the intersecting and interlocking nature of gender, race, class, and sexuality. They define racism in broader terms to be inclusive of language and ethnicity as well as skin colour (Stasiulis, 1990). They resist privileging skin colour, since they believe that doing so could promote race essentialism (Jhappan, 1996). As Creese and Stasiulis write (1996: 5): 'Understanding the multiple and contradictory intersections of race, class, gender and sexuality in local and international contexts is central to developing a more adequate political economy.' However, they do not explain how and why policies and practices in the economy and in politics – historically as well as in contemporary society – are implicated in promoting inequalities among women (people) of different racial and class backgrounds. Nonetheless, they explore the political/economic implications of these differences for women.

Feminists who adopt postcolonial thought privilege skin colour when defining race. This has sometimes led to the criticism that they are promoting race essentialism (Jhappan, 1996). However, a careful reading shows that postcolonial analyses conceptualize race as a social construction – albeit one that has serious social consequences. These feminists show how policies and practices on the economic and political levels are informed by a concern for maintaining the hegemony of white people and their culture. For example, starting from her own personal experiences as an immigrant woman of colour in Canada, Bannerji carefully analyses the intersections of history and biography in Canadian society. She documents how her own experience as an outsider in Canada was not unique; rather, it was part of a pattern of experiences of colonized people (1995). During the era of colonization and imperialism, Third World people were constructed as beset by all kinds of deficiencies, including deficient biology and culture (Said, 1979; Fanon, 1963). Furthermore, the colonizers embraced a civilizing mission, and in doing so legitimized their superiority to the colonized. These notions of superiority became embedded in institutional structures and social practices. As these practices were naturalized over the years, the resulting inequalities took on an immutable character (Hall, 1990). Making use of Gramsci's ideas, Bannerji shows how the hegemonic status of colonizers was established and how racial inequalities have become part of commonsense knowledge (1995). She argues that deconstructing commonsense knowledge requires altering the very foundations of Western societies. At the present time in Canada, there is an all-pervasive conviction that Canada is an open society in which all citizens have equal access to opportunity structures. This conviction persists even though there are inequalities among groups of people of different races and classes. In fact, Canadians suffer from historical amnesia, and collectively deny that there is racism in Canadian society (Henry et al., 1995).

To raise people's awareness of the predicament of women of colour, Bannerji gives primacy to the experiences of the marginalized. Women of colour must represent themselves and articulate their own perspectives on all issues of concern. In this sense, Bannerji's position is similar to that of standpoint theorists. But she also differs from them in significant ways. For example, she states that being on the margin does not automatically mean that one is aware of one's subordinate position; furthermore, one may not be able to articulate one's concerns. It is only when marginalized people have access to knowledge that they are able to raise their critical consciousness to articulate their concerns. Knowledge is power. Without it, marginalized people are a muted group and are subjected to interpretations of their experiences by those who have power. She shows how historically women of colour in Canada have been a muted group. This has enabled mainstream feminists to generalize their own particular experiences and declare their validity for all women.

Nourbese Philip (1992) shows how difference and hierarchy between whiteness and non-whiteness are reinforced by maintaining and reproducing cultural hegemony. Writers who are women of colour are treated as outsiders within. For example, the standards of literary criticism are developed within the mainstream, and the work of people of colour is not treated as contributing to Canadian life. Their work was turned down by prominent Canadian publishers because it is deemed 'ethnic,' not 'Canadian' (Dickenson, 1988: 118). In addition, stereotypes of Third World people – persistent and enduring residues of the colonial era – are presented in different media as normal and natural. The need for women of colour to validate their own work as authentic and to claim a place for themselves is as urgent as ever in the new century. Marginalized people should be able to name and define their experiences. These experiences have to be brought from the margins to the centre.

The process of bringing things from the margins to the centre of our analyses, as bell hooks (1984) argues, is an approach that helps open new ways of knowing. Since the conditions of one's life determine one's consciousness these analyses provide new knowledge from the perspectives of those who are oppressed. It helps us question the prevalent assumptions about the marginalized as well as the privileged. It offers those at the centre access to the experiences of the marginalized and also provides them with a new vantage point from which to view their privileges. This new way of knowing also leads to different definitions of knowledge itself. For example, as Collins (1990) argues, conventional methods of deciding who is to be regarded as an intellectual do not work in contexts where Black women learn alternative methods for expressing their creativity on account of their marginal position. In the same way, a wise elder has invaluable knowledge regarding an indigenous way of life that may not be expressed in conventional ways.

Contextualizing 'Women'

In this text we present many contextual accounts of difference. We do not essentialize experiences associated with socially constructed categories such as 'race,' 'disability,' 'ethnicity,' or 'class,' because race, ethnicity, or class, lesbianism, and disability do not involve the same experiences for women in different contexts. We identify four dimensions of women's situations within which we will analyse difference:

• Geographic location and location in the global political economy.
• Class and/or caste.
• Communal affiliation, including race, faith, language, ethnicity, and/or nationality.

• Personal status, including age, marital or reproductive status, sexual orientation, reproductive status, and dis/ability.

Place Matters

Universalist assumptions are especially resistant to claims that women's experiences vary as a function of where they live (i.e., rural/urban, Africa/North America; Western Canada/Quebec). For example, Fraser's analysis ignores differences related to where women live. Debates about globalization often replicate the homogenization many fear, as for example when they assume there is a single 'Third World' that will be affected uniformly by global forces. As we will show in chapter 2, people are affected by globalization virtually everywhere. But they experience the effects within their local context, so their responses will vary accordingly.

We assume that place matters when it comes to understanding differences among women – that 'a place on the map is also a place in history' (Rich, in Mohanty, 1992: 77). Where women live profoundly affects how they experience being 'women.' It also affects how they experience other aspects of their identities. This dimension of our contextual approach goes against the grain of much modern Western thought, which stresses the importance of time and linear history in people's lives while neglecting the effects of place and contextualized histories. For example, it is often assumed that people experience 'modernity' the same way in different places. Feminist geographer Doreen Massey disagrees: 'Most people still live their lives locally [and] their consciousness is formed in a distinct geographic place' (in Agnew 1987: 36). Moreover, place may matter more to many women who are generally tied to locales because of childrearing responsibilities; their menfolk often are more mobile. For example, globalization and migration involve gendered processes: far more men move from rural to urban areas and across national borders; in contrast, in general women experience barriers to spatial mobility. This may make place especially important for understanding many women's lives, especially as economic restructuring threatens local infrastructures on which women and their children especially depend.

Class and Caste Matter

Class and caste also raise significant contextual issues for understanding differences among women. Interlocking systems of domination and oppression are both symbiotic and hierarchical. Within each country, for example, 'domestic workers and professional women are produced so that neither exists without the other' (Razack, 1998: 13). But we also need to understand how colonialism and neocolonialism produced a global economy in which the impoverishment and indebtedness of non-Western countries created the affluence that funded welfare state programs in the 'West.' Poverty both within and outside Western countries creates a supply of women who need jobs and so end up looking after the children and cleaning the bathrooms of professional women who participate in the paid workforce. Accounts of difference that fail to highlight how systems of dominance and oppression intersect are seriously deficient. Women professionals who need other women to perform their domestic and motherwork form part of a system with poor women, who seek employment as domestics either at home or, increasingly, in Western countries to support their own families.

Despite the importance of class in understanding women's different experiences, theories of class are often difficult to apply to women. Class originally referred to a categorical division in society between those who owned 'the means of production' (such as land) and those who didn't. It was hard to fit women into this analysis, because understood this way, they both are and are not part of a class. For example, because of their relationships to fathers, brothers, or husbands, they can be part of a dominant class, while owning nothing in their own right and experiencing oppression – often in the form of violence. They can be part of the working class without ever going near a factory where 'work,' as defined by the theory, is performed and without being paid for the work they do at home. Moreover, the significance of class for the political mobilization of women varies significantly from place to place and across time.

Caste is a system of hereditary social divisions based on occupation. It is most often associated with Hindu societies, but elements of caste organization exist elsewhere. For example, the concept of 'untouchability' associated with those who do the most menial tasks in society also survives in Japan. Caste barriers are not as permeable as class barriers, and both may affect people's lives. Elements of caste are involved in systems of segregation based on race, although the origins are different. The Hindu caste system affects what work people do, where they live, whom they marry, and even what they eat. In some parts of India there are long-standing connections between the anticaste *dalit* movement and feminism:

The *dalits*, classified as untouchable under the Hindu caste system for their association with such polluting tasks as curing leather or clearing excreta, had a long history of anti-caste protest in Maharashtra. In the late nineteenth century, *dalits* had also espoused women's rights to education, against purdah, and for widow remarriage. (Radah Kumar, 1995: 63)

Despite the problems noted, class and caste are too significant as aspects of women's experience to discard as concepts. In this text we conceptualize class and its consequences for differently located women. First, we assume that women's experiences and life choices are affected by their access to economic resources, whether or not class or caste conflict are salient in their society at a particular time. We also note that the class/caste of women's natal families may differ from that of their conjugal families. Second, we assume that women's ability to identify with other women, with their community, and with a personal status group is related to how central the struggle for survival is in their lives. For women whose political actions revolve mainly around the survival and/or the security of their families, class or caste location may overwhelm other aspects of their identity. However, class oppression often works in tandem with other forms of domination, so for many women the experience of class and race or ethnicity may be inseparable. Moreover, where state power is organized to benefit a dominant, owning class, and where the coercive power of the state is used to repress challenges to it, other possible political identities may be muted because class struggle takes precedence.

Communal Affiliation Matters

The third important area of difference is women's communal affiliation based on shared experiences of race, faith, ethnicity, language, and/or nationality. In these contexts women are part of communities that reproduce themselves physically and culturally. This is the dimension of difference that stand-alone feminists have the most difficulty understanding and respecting. From their perspective as members of dominant communities in their society, stand-alone feminists seem not to 'have' race or ethnicity because their identity is the norm within a territory and is transmitted and replicated through state and market institutions, including the media and the education system. But for women who are part of communal minorities that do 'have' race, or ethnicity, the reproduction of their community's identity and culture depends heavily on these things, which shape their experiences profoundly if their community suffers oppression or marginalization. Through acts as diverse as bearing children, handing down their folk wisdom, and organizing festivals that celebrate collective identity, women of minority communities reproduce their identities and their communities. This frames their responses to sexism within their communities, and to racism and other forms of oppression imposed from outside.

Minority women's participation in community projects has often made them seem 'less feminist' to majority feminists, who can afford the luxury of an uncomplicated, stand-alone feminism. Women who are part of minority communities can rarely depend on the state to reproduce their identities, as majority feminists can. Moreover, states often privilege members of the majority race, nation, faith or ethnicity, while marginalizing, disadvantaging, or oppressing members of minority communities. It follows that in this context, few women can easily separate experiences that result from their sex or gender from those that result from their communal affiliation.

Personal Status Matters

The final dimension of a woman's situation that is of significance here is her personal status, including her age, sexual orientation, marital and reproductive status, dis/ability, and/or size. Characteristics like these often result in discrimination or oppression of individual women, who then commonly join together in groups, which are often hard to distinguish from reproducing communities. Groups in this category are often bivalent, seeking both recognition of their identity and a redistribution of resources to alleviate the negative material consequences of their 'difference.' That being said, groups like these often pursue different solutions. For example, lesbians and gay men are currently divided on how to overcome the disadvantages their 'difference' brings: Should compulsory heterosexuality be abolished so that 'sexual orientation' no longer has any importance in society? Or should gay and lesbian relationships be 'normalized,' through pursuit of legal rights and recognition of same-sex 'marriages,' so that partners are entitled to state benefits on the same basis as heterosexual partners?

'Women' in different situations may or may not share the same take on issues, and may or may not feel they have interests in common. So it is a basic point of our methodology not to assume that differently located women share political values, goals, and interests simply because they are 'women,' and not to impute differences to women who share a communal affiliation or individual characteristic. Contextualizing women's experiences of differences helps us learn through empirical evidence what ideas, interests, and values many women have in common that could be the basis of coalition building.

II. Knowledge Monopolies

In this section we discuss some aspects of Euro-American culture and explore the question of who controls meaning and whose knowledge gets accepted as valid or as 'reality.' Most knowledge available to us is Euro-American centred, androcentric, and generated by people in heterosexual relationships who experience the world without disabilities. Other ways of knowing are simply unknown and also often devalued, ignored, ridiculed, denied, trivialized, or rejected. If you doubt this, try offering a feminist account of women's poverty in a mainstream economics class, or writing a letter defending employment equity and affirmative action to your local newspaper. The institutions that construct what our society regards as 'knowledge' include science, the universities, religions, cultural institutions, and the media.

It is not just knowledge that is monopolized. For example, aesthetic standards governing norms of beauty are also determined by the mainstream. Marginalized groups come up short whenever they are judged against these models (Bannerji, 1993). Most aspects of meaning are monopolized because Euro-Americans are dominant and act as gatekeepers in the process of determining what will be legitimized as knowledge. Moreover, those within the knowledge production centres and communications media limit our ability to form or gain access to alternative interpretations and visions. Because these monopolies exist, the ideas and values of the dominant majorities in the core Euro-American states shape the sense of reality of many millions of people, who do not share the experiences of those majorities except through the media. In the mainly American-made movies and television programs that blanket most of the world, the young, white, pretty, skinny, sexualized women of California and Florida project an image of womanhood, against which older, darker, plumper women are measured. The privileging of white, majority culture by dominant institutions that produce and disseminate knowledge and transmit images cannot be transcended simply by 'tolerance' within women's movements and women's studies classes. As long as these knowledge monopolies remain, majority feminists will stay more or less ignorant of the ideas and images held by people on the 'margins' and outside the Western world, unless they undertake affirmative steps to broaden their horizons. Our method in this text is based on such affirmative actions.

Western Theories of Knowledge and the Enlightenment

Pilomena Essed (1991) argues that Euro-American culture has a problem with 'difference' because it has not unlearned the thought patterns of colonialism and is in denial about the existence of racism. She observes that Euro-American culture contains an awkward balance between racist and non-racist tendencies (vii). These cultures are democratic and value liberty, equality, and individual rights. But '[another] general feature of these societies is ... that the superiority of Euro-American culture is taken for granted' (vii). Many scholars note this combination of democracy and racism (Henry et al., 1995). The concept of democratic racism, used in the study of race regimes, identifies this capacity of people in Western democracies to hold both egalitarian and racist ideas at the same time. Essed's study of everyday racism, as experienced by Black women in Holland and the United States, illustrates how democratic racism works and what it reveals about our problems with 'difference.' She locates the problem with 'difference' as developed by majority, white feminists in 'the notion, inherent in Euro-American culture, that human progress demands increasing control over "nature," that "reason" is ... superior to "emotion," and that so-called non-Western peoples must be subjected to Western dominance to "free" themselves from the constraints of "nature"' (189). These values, she notes, are also used to privilege men over women within culture and to justify male dominance in Western societies.

Audre Lorde also believes that Western culture has difficulty with 'difference.' She contends that much of Western history has conditioned people to see themselves 'in simplistic opposition to each other, dominant/subordinate, good/bad, up/down, superior/inferior' (1984: 114). She believes this binary, oppositional treatment of 'difference' is functional because 'in a society where good is defined in terms of profit rather than in terms of human need, there must always be some group of people who, through systematized oppression, can be made to feel surplus, to occupy the place of the dehumanized inferior' (114).

She concludes that denial of difference is the central problem: 'Somewhere, on the edge of consciousness, there is ... a *mythical norm*. In America, this norm is usually defined as white, thin, male, young, heterosexual, Christian, and financially secure' (116). This denial, she argues, reflects how threatening the acknowledgment of 'difference' is in Euro-American culture.

Lorde suggests that we are paralyzed by difference, within women's movements and in women's studies and feminist scholarship generally, because we don't know what to do with it or about it. She believes Euro-American culture is based on paradigms that use difference to divide and conquer. As a result, the choices we can imagine for 'dealing with difference' are limited to suppression, emulation, or tolerance. For Lorde, in contrast, 'the interdependence of mutual (nondominant) differences' provides 'the security which enables us to descend into the chaos of knowledge and return with true visions of our future' (111). Lorde sees the task of 'thinking through' difference together as 'learning to take our differences and make them our strengths' (112). But for this to happen, the barriers that divide women from one another must be transcended and white, majority women must affirmatively search out the insights, ideas, and participation of women who have been 'othered.' But the causes of the threat that difference poses within our intellectual frameworks are deep and cannot be deconstructed easily.

Until recently, feminist theories of knowledge shared assumptions of universalism with Western knowledge systems in general, with one crucial exception. Feminist epistemologies challenged universalist thinking by arguing that 'women's ways' of knowing differed from 'men's.' As we've seen, in the 1960s and 1970s Western feminism placed heavy emphasis on 'women's experience' as the basis of feminist knowledge. Consciousness raising generated knowledge that 'women' 'knew' intuitively to be true because it accorded with their lived experience. This was often described as *the* standpoint of women. Through consciousness raising, majority women challenged the claim that male-centric knowledge, which had been represented as 'Western civilization,' was universal and eternally valid. But as they did this, they also replicated knowledge monopolies within women's movements, feminist scholarship, and women's studies on a smaller scale by excluding the knowledge of minority, marginalized, and 'Third World' women. Eventually this 'woman's standpoint' was challenged as being the standpoint of only some women. This created a dead-end, since a feminist understanding of women's studies implies that we must grapple with 'difference' beyond the simple binary opposition of 'women' and 'men.' But to do this we need much greater knowledge of diversity – for example, knowledge gathered from those who experience racism.

Similar insights are offered by the distinguished Indian physicist Vandana Shiva, who in *Biopiracy* (1997) argues that there is a link between the West's long thought-war against cultural diversity and its legal and economic 'war' against biodiversity – a war that currently threatens the global environment. She illustrates how knowledge monopolies work by enclosing, controlling, and privatizing both biodiversity (diverse species) and cultural diversity (marginalized and 'Third World' knowledges). Her account of the links between Western knowledge systems and the worldwide environmental crisis makes it clear that neo-imperialism is a world system that privileges Western countries and transnational corporations and the institutions they control, such as the World Bank.

Patricia Hill Collins argues that knowledge monopolies work through 'institutions, paradigms and other elements of the knowledge validation procedure controlled by elite white men [which] constitute the Eurocentric masculinist knowledge validation process' (1990: 205). She links universalist knowledge claims with positivism – a social science methodology that 'aim[s] to create scientific descriptions of reality by producing objective generalizations' (205). This approach to producing social knowledge seeks to apply 'the scientific method' to understanding social phenomena. The scientific method, which characterizes the main knowledge-production system of the modern Western world, works by producing and testing generalizations that aim at universal explanations. Collins notes that within positivism, 'genuine science is thought to be unattainable unless all human characteristics except rationality are eliminated from the research process' (205). This results in context stripping, or decontextualizing researchers and their 'subjects.' Collins demonstrates that this kind of Western, epistemological thought presents insurmountable problems for understanding her Afrocentric, feminist epistemology, which is rooted in the everyday experiences of African-American women (207). She concludes that Black feminist epistemology is not assimilable to Western knowledge norms – even feminist ones. Instead, its value lies in its ability to create alternative knowledge that can foster the resistance that Black women need.

'Difference' Challenges Western Knowledge Monopolies

Much current Western thought has underlying it 'the Enlightenment idea of a ... point where a universal knower can stand and see the world without perspective' (Lennon and Whitford, 1994: 3). That is, Western science and the positivist social sciences patterned on it claim for themselves an objectivity in a paradigm they assume can have universal validity. Objectivity is achieved by the researchers literally being nowhere, having insulated themselves from context ('assume a perfect vacuum'), history, and values. Feminist claims that all knowers are situated or located by being either 'women' or 'men' initiated a process that is challenging these knowledge monopolies. What is developing in the present day, according to Lorde, Essed, and Collins, is a newer idea that the subjective knowledges or standpoints of those who are oppressed or marginalized should be privileged, and universalizing paradigms abandoned.

The struggle to dislodge dominant knowledge monopolies is far from over, and Western feminism has epistemological battles to fight on two fronts. As Lennon and Whitford argue, 'feminism as a political project required that the feminist claims of distorting and subordinating trends within masculine knowledge be regarded as legitimate, and ... not only for feminists. This makes it difficult to simply abandon objectivity' (1994: 4). Western feminists find it difficult to make their case with governments and dominant knowledge producers that 'women' are oppressed, without adopting the standards of the Western scientific and social scientific discourses. Yet at the same time, postcolonial women in the 'Third' and 'Fourth' worlds, and those who represent their views in the West, are challenging Western knowledge monopolies (including feminism), perceiving them as the basis of colonial and postcolonial oppression and exploitation. To legitimate their knowledge and their claims for justice, majority culture feminists working within knowledge-production centres must present their claims in forms that are comprehensible to those who monopolize meaning. This sets them at odds with those who reject such engagement. How can those who are building women's studies respond to these conflicting pressures?

Deconstructing Monopolies without 'Lapsing into Boundless Difference'

Some advocate the practice embodied in the slogan 'let many flowers bloom.' That is, they contend that women's studies and feminist scholarship generally should foster a postmodern array of many different accounts of women's experiences. Others fear this could lead to a pluralist 'tolerance' that doesn't engage with 'difference' in any deep way. Since white, Western, heterosexual culture is dominant now, they conclude that such 'tolerance' of difference would not disrupt the power systems on which this dominance rests. For many mainstream feminists, a deeper engagement with difference poses a danger of 'a postmodern pluralist free-for-all' (Lennon and Whitford, 1994: 4). Or they fear, as Donna Haraway puts it, that 'consciousness of our failures' will lead to us 'lapsing into boundless difference' (1991: 202). Resistance to a deep engagement with difference, therefore, is rooted in the knowledge form that mainstream women believe is needed to make their case and disrupt the domination of male-centred knowledge. But it also reflects a reluctance to acknowledge the legitimacy of other standpoints and to transfer leadership to 'other women' when appropriate. Moreover, when the issue is considered in a global context, mainstream, Western feminists' task of achieving a deep engagement with diversity seems even more difficult, although the task is ever more pressing.

Creative Uses of 'Difference' in Constructing New Knowledge

Trinh Minh-ha (1997) has distinguished between the creative use of the concept of difference and its use as a tool of segregation: 'Many of us still hold on to the concept of difference not as a tool of creativity to question multiple forms of repression and dominance, but as a tool of segregation, to exert power on the basis of racial and sexual essences, the apartheid type of difference.'

How can we use 'difference' creatively – that is, without engaging in apartheid? First, it is important to recognize that differences and commonalities are both important parts of the picture. Put another way, segregation – as in *'they'* are different from *'us'* – can only happen when we focus exclusively on the differences between women. The same focus can lead to fears that *'we'* cannot possibly understand *'them'* well enough to do research (or write an essay) about other women's lives. To use the concept of 'difference' creatively, therefore, we must combine it with the concept of commonalities, so that we are always asking what we share as women, as well as how we are different. Good comparison is always about identifying both differences and similarities. Nonetheless, some mainstream feminist philosophers persist in attempting to develop new understandings of difference and of what is needed for genuine inclusion. Iris Marion Young (1990b), for example, in *Inclusion and Democracy*, conceptualizes social difference as a political resource central to the deepening of democracy on a global basis. In particular, she shows that struggles by excluded or oppressed groups and societies for justice must not be dismissed as being only about identity. She concludes that communication across differences is possible and essential.

The second problem to be overcome is the fear held by many mainstream feminists that becoming concerned with issues of difference will distract us from our common goals. But this often expressed fear that engaging seriously with 'difference' will disrupt mainstream feminism as a project of social transformation is misguided. For example, Haleh Afshar in *Women and Politics in the Third World* (1996) shows the value of focusing on difference as a theoretical basis for investigating different forms of women's activism. She shows how privileging 'difference' helped her explain the importance of motherhood, marriage, and domesticity as choices made by many 'Third World' women – choices that Western feminists often conceptualize as a source of weakness for women. By focusing on 'difference,' Afshar and her collaborators were able to show that many 'Third World' women use motherhood, marriage, and domesticity as strategies to seek resources to avoid poverty and to achieve freedom from oppression for their children. She concludes that if one takes an approach that begins with difference, 'these strategies ... can be [understood as] highly effective even within such discourses as Islamic fundamentalism' (i). This approach also helps us better understand the choices made by many marginalized women in Western countries, who identify racism, continuing colonialism, heterosexism, and ablism as 'the Big Uglies' rather than sex oppression on its own. This allows us to link feminist explanations of oppression to other theories that offer explanations based on class theory, race theory, queer theory, and theories about disablement.

One consequence of this shift, Afshar maintains, is that it 'becomes impossible to say, in any uncomplicated way, that all women are oppressed by all men' (9). Men are repositioned so that they may be oppressors or potential allies. She argues that 'the need to forge commonality across difference, through alliances and coalitions becomes a key issue within feminism' (9). When we recentre women's studies on difference and on the systems of power that construct dominance and oppression based on difference, we stop perceiving minority, marginalized, or 'Third World' women as misguided or as 'passive victims of barbaric and primitive practices' (9). 'Other' women can be seen as agents with different strategies and hence as potential allies in concrete campaigns. Those who reject feminism as ideology or politics may still be potential allies. Thus, a creative use of 'difference' leads us directly to a discussion of commonalities and of establishing solidarity based on recognition of both difference and commonality.

This combination of (1) a comparative focus on difference, (2) identification of commonalities, and (3) use of both feminist and other theories about systems of power forms the basis of our approach in this text.

Whose 'Difference'?

A crucial point of controversy within women's studies, feminist scholarship, and feminist politics more broadly centres around these questions: Whose story gets told? And who gets to tell it? In the international arena – for example, in the UN conferences on women – Western feminists often resist giving space to women engaged in 'ordinary' political conflicts. Palestinian-Canadian feminist Nahla Abdo observes: 'In almost every international women's gathering Palestinian women have had to wage double if not triple struggles to affirm their identity as Arabs, Palestinians and women' (1993: 92). Like women engaged in anticolonial struggles elsewhere, Palestinian women meet resistance from Western feminists when they try to tell their stories in international political arenas that are focused on 'women' and gender justice. Western feminists perceive such struggles as unrelated to 'women's' concerns, and don't make the links between women's pursuit of security and well-being for themselves and their families and the struggles of the collectivities of which they are a part. Under the influence of such views, Senator Nancy Kassebaum (Republican–Kansas) introduced a bill, later passed by the U.S. Congress, authorizing the president to 'use every available means to ensure that the final Nairobi meeting [ending the UN Women's Decade] wouldn't be dominated by unrelated political issues' (in Abdo, 1993: 93). Her bill reflected the views of many Western feminists, who resented what they considered the 'highjacking' of conferences that they believed should focus solely on gender struggles.

All of this has silenced Palestinian women, who do not enjoy the luxury of separating their fate as women from their fate as Palestinians. Abdo also argues that state-constructed hierarchies of oppressions 'have tended to be reproduced rather than rejected by Western feminists, both academics and activists' (74–5). In Canada the hierarchy of oppressions 'places the Natives as the "most" affected by racism; the second place is reserved for Blacks and the third for an unspecified category called "people of colour"' (74). Abdo concludes that by reproducing this hierarchy of oppressions uncritically, many Canadian feminists are silencing Arab and Palestinian women. In part because many Arabs in Canada are light-skinned, they – ironically, like Jewish women victims of anti-Semitism – find their stories excluded. She contends that systems of oppression are historically specific; and that women's studies and feminist scholarship, as collective projects of social transformation, must stop fueling arguments over who is most oppressed, and begin exploring the many different historical experiences of oppression and resistance within which women struggle.

Abdo argues that there are positive feminist practices on which we can build. For example, she points out that the banner behind which more than 3,000 women marched on International Women's Day in Toronto in 1991 read: 'Make the Links: From Oka to the Gulf, Self-Determination for Native People, Self-Determination for the Palestinian People and Fight Racism' (95). Achieving consensus on this wording required a political practice centred on solidarity through respect for difference. A second practice is represented by the Women in Black movement, which started in the Middle East and has since spread to the former Yugoslavia, in which women who are part of different 'sides' in a conflict join together to demonstrate their rejection of the oppression it represents and their solidarity with women 'othered' by the conflict. Palestinian and Israeli Women in Black stand together in silent demonstration of solidarity across difference-in-conflict. Using *solidarity-in-difference* to overcome *difference-in-conflict* is an important practice of women's movements that we need to keep in mind in women's studies.

III. Overlapping and Conflicting Loyalties

In this section we explore in a preliminary way how women experience their identities as women in relation to their other identities. We argue that Western feminism is focused mainly on gender struggle, and demands women's full loyalties – an approach many women elsewhere in the world cannot or do not wish to share. Women from postcolonial states and 'Fourth World' women, in particular, suspect that this kind of mainstream, Western feminism is a form of cultural imperialism. Moreover, this stand-alone feminism consists of 'the (implicit) self-representation of Western women as educated, as modern, as having control over their bodies and sexualities and the freedom to make their own decisions' (Mohanty, 1991: 36). That is, it presents mainstream, Western women as the ideal. But this 'ideal' is also individualist, preoccupied with autonomy, eager to compete with men in the public realm, and inclined to undervalue women's roles in relation to family and community. These are not values that women who are not part of modern, Euro-American culture necessarily value or regard as ideal. In mainstream, Western feminism, women's identity and experiences as sexed and gendered beings are seen as determining their role and status. For many women whose experiences are also deeply shaped by their class (or caste), race, faith, or ethnicity, or by the nation to which they belong, stand-alone feminism ignores how their lives are shaped in common with their menfolk by racism, imperialism, and poverty, and by a shared faith, ethnicity, language and nationality. Mainstream Western feminists have tended to dismiss 'other' women's other identities as a flaw in their feminism, believing that 'true' feminists should be exclusively committed to issues of gender justice.

Amrita Basu argues that 'women's identities within and across nations are shaped by a complex amalgam of national, racial, religious, ethnic, class and sexual identities' (1995: 4) When we explore what women's movements worldwide have achieved or not achieved, we find that the stand-alone identity of 'woman' may be the anomaly rather than the rule. As Basu notes, many movements mobilize women that might be described not as 'women's movements' but rather as movements of women linked to national liberation, democratization, class conflict, or language and ethnic conflicts. Furthermore, many movements that champion women's rights and empowerment reject or are sceptical about feminism, which they view as individualistic, bourgeois, and Western. So we must begin by examining how women who are not white, mainstream, Western feminists experience their identities.

Contextual Analysis and Identity Politics

In this section we explore how the politics of identity affect women in several different contexts. Relationships between women's sex/gender identities and their other identities are the result of their context; this prevents us attributing such relationships to essential, unchanging characteristics. For example, Black feminist Rosemary Brown (1989) observed that growing up 'Brown' is experienced differently in a country where the majority population is white than where it is Black. Though the history of slavery and widespread race prejudice creates common elements in the two contexts, how women experience and combine being 'women' with being 'Black' differs. A contextual approach, therefore, helps us understand how women balance their identities and loyalties and how they choose which aspects of their identities to mobilize around. A contextual approach also exposes the privileges enjoyed by some women as a function of their class or caste and membership in a dominant majority culture – privileges that free them to focus exclusively on sex/gender issues. It may also remind us that women who enjoy the luxury of stand-alone feminism may do so at the expense of others.

In this section we first explore two main contexts within which women form and balance their identities:

- When women are part of secure majorities that dominate their state.
- When women are part of insecure minorities or disadvantaged classes that do not control the institutions in the society in which they live.

Note that there are two parts to each of these contexts: first, whether a community is a majority or minority; and second, whether it is dominant and controls the main institutions of the society or is subordinate. Context also includes issues of legitimacy. For example, aboriginal peoples, now reduced to tiny minorities by disease and state racism in settler societies like Canada, nonetheless believe they are the legitimate occupants of their lands. So they seek self-government as 'First

Nations,' and identify themselves as citizens of autonomous nations rather than as minorities within Canada. Context also involves forces such as colonialism and neocolonialism, which transcend the nation-state. In countries fighting against these forces or their aftermaths, the contexts for women differ from those of women living in imperialist or neo-imperialist countries. Women are not often the state decision-makers in neo-imperialist countries; but they still benefit from the resulting affluence and cultural dominance. Since stand-alone feminism developed in countries associated with colonialism and neo-imperialism, this is an important consideration. The recent demise of the Soviet Union and the Communist Bloc presents another context affecting women's capacity to assert their sex/gender interests, as the old states organized around communism collapse and communities struggle for dominance and security in the aftermath. Moreover, these contexts change over time. For example, the impact of mass terrorism in the West has reduced the sense of security felt by majority-culture women and changed the context in which they work.

As Mohanty notes, a view commonly held by mainstream, Western feminists is that women who are loyal to their communities and/or to other movements such as nationalism are not 'real feminists' and are 'dupes' of male political leaders who want to control them. Women not 'in sync' with stand-alone feminism are often portrayed as 'politically immature' – as victimized or suffering from 'false consciousness' (57). But since many women around the world share important struggles – such as the struggle for national liberation – with men in their groups, we might ask whether the exclusion of women from influence within such struggles would not be more problematic than their efforts to be included. Also, women who are oppressed because of their race, faith, or ethnicity cannot simply 'choose' to devote themselves exclusively to the feminist cause. Identities, which form the basis for power relationships of oppression and privilege such as 'Black,' 'disabled,' and 'lesbian,' are not freely chosen from among a number of possibilities – they are imposed by others. Moreover, racism and other prejudices often exclude these women from mainstream movements even if they wish to be involved.

Examples of the Difference Conundrum

Consider how feminists in different contexts understand issues concerning reproduction. Vickers argues that 'women and men of secure, dominant cultures who have access to state institutions ... understand reproduction and its links to political power differently from members of threatened minority communities' (1994: 190). Most white Western feminists know that their national, cultural, and ethnic identities will survive without their personal involvement in reproduction because it is reproduced through state and societal institutions. Consequently, many view reproduction negatively as a barrier to women's participation in the public realm and not (as do many other women) as a source of power and continuity of identity. Freedom *from* reproduction ('choice') is their bottom-line demand. Also, many mainstream Western feminists construct 'the family' as a site of women's oppression – a view reinforced by the contraction and devaluation of domestic activities in urban life in the West and by frequent violence in family relationships. In contrast, many marginalized and 'Third' and 'Fourth World' women – equally eager for justice for women – value their families and wish to reproduce their identities. Many also value the family as a retreat from racism and as a site for nurturing cultural values that are different from those of mainstream society, although they also often experience violence in these retreats.

One example involves the rejection of the label 'feminist' by many aboriginal women, for whom the term strongly suggests an antinatal and antifamily stance that is offensive to them as they rebuild their nations. They had formed the majority population until disease and other consequences of colonial invasion reduced them to a tiny group within the new settler societies, and then they experienced a system of state racism in which 'Indian' children were forced into residential schools, with the result that aboriginal languages, spiritual practices, and cultural traditions were banned. Although not in government, white women were implicated in state racism through their organizations and as teachers, nurses, social workers, and public servants. Given this history, mainstream feminist values seem like a continuation of policies threatening aboriginal peoples by denying them the right to rear their own children. White women who promote stand-alone feminism, then, may seem not like 'sisters' but more like agents of continuing colonialism.

Second Example: Race and Sexual Orientation in Diaspora Communities

In the early 1990s, a film made by a Canadian woman of South Asian origin was the subject of protest riots by radical Hindu nationalists in

India, because it portrayed two Hindu women, trapped in unhappy marriages, finding love for one another. The demonstrators declared that lesbianism is a threat to Hindu culture. Kaushalya Bannerji, a woman of South Asian descent who grew up in Canada, explores the conflicting identities involved in her article 'No Apologies' (1993). She asserts: 'To be a lesbian is not, as I used to think, a Westernized rejection of our Indian identities' (63). She describes herself as 'living in two overlapping worlds' and expresses 'a fundamental fear of not having a real sense of community and country' (63). Her immediate family, living in the South Asian diaspora in North America, has 'come to terms' with her lesbianism; unfortunately, homophobia, racist assumptions held by white feminists about South Asian women, and the normative white, androgynous image of lesbians make it hard to integrate her cultures and her choices (61). Her physical type (not boyish) and her choices about hair length (long) and dress ('feminine') are read within a Western, lesbian frame of 'sexist eroticism' (i.e., she is 'a femme') rather than as a reflection of her South Asian origins and cultural choices.

Audre Lorde's thesis that the 'institutionalized rejection of difference' means 'we have no patterns for relating across our human differences as equals' (1993: 4) may usefully be recalled here as we consider why it is made so difficult for Bannerji to knit together the complex elements in her life. Lorde believes 'we have *all* been programmed to respond to human differences ... with fear and loathing,' so we mainly deal with 'difference' by ignoring it, by imitating it, or by trying to eliminate it. Bannerji experienced racism from white lesbians and feminists from whom she should have received solidarity, and she experienced homophobia and exclusion, although not from her immediate family, but from those who should have supported her against racism. She does not fit into the categories constructed within majority feminism to deal with 'difference.' In this framework, 'women of colour' are categorized according to their 'race,' while 'lesbians' are categorized according to their 'sexual orientation,' and this leaves little room for more complex combinations of identities. Nor does a postmodern account of choosing among a fluid variety of differences work: both racism and homophobia worked on her differences to harm her. She experienced gendered racism and racialized homophobia, in both of which women and feminists participated.

Third Example: The Identity Crisis of Fragmentation

The tendency in Western 'identity politics' to construct differences in simple, binary, oppositional categories, such as 'white' versus 'women of colour,' or 'lesbian' versus 'heterosexual,' makes complex identities difficult to analyse. Fawzia Ahmad, a Trinidadian of Indian heritage now living in Canada, makes the point this way:

> There are so many fragments to my identity that it is frustrating when I am asked the 'simple' question *'how do you identify?'* It is a question I have extreme difficulties with ... Living in Trinidad, I was clear who I was and who the other people around me were. In Canada's white feminist movement, where identity justifies your existence and experiences, I feel great resentment. I 'thank' colonialism for my dilemma. I 'thank' white supremacy for the identity crisis women of my heritage face. (1994: 29)

Ahmad believes that her 'identity crisis' is imposed by white feminists – that is, through the workings of 'white supremacy' and the continuing effects of colonialism. Around the world, the colonial powers once relocated people as slaves or workers; the descendants of those so relocated now live in tension and conflict, a prime example being the Blacks and Indians from Asia in Trinidad. In Western countries the category 'women of colour' includes women whose ancestors of many different origins, were moved from their home countries by colonialism. The removals took place generations ago, and many now living have no direct experience of the 'home' culture. How, Ahmad asks, can white feminists grasp the complex identity her life involves, if they have no understanding the history of Trinidad?

Many race minority women choose to describe themselves as 'women of colour' or 'Black,' adopting political identities of solidarity that are useful for mobilization in antiracism movements. Yet within women's movements, these women share only the characteristic of not being white – that is, 'whiteness' remains the norm. Ahmad argues that, 'women of colour' are expected to fit into slots provided by white women, 'to make their concepts of ethnicity easier' (29). These categories of difference used by white feminists lump together women of vastly different origins, cultures, and experiences, including aboriginal women, who have a much greater claim to the idea of being 'from here' than white women. Ahmad also believes that the white racism contained in these categories divides and creates resentment because 'some women of colour are treated with more respect by the white women's movement, they are given more space ... in *your* organizations' (29). The categories also let white women remain ignorant of the complex identities of other women. Thus, although they expect other women to fit into the category 'woman of colour,' white, majority feminists – like fish who swim in water without realizing it – continue to enjoy a clear and unconflicted identity. 'Others' must struggle to define themselves around majority women's whiteness.

Not Just a Matter of Choice

In Western states some people, because of their physical attributes, are clearly marked as subject to – or having in the past been subject to – a regime of state racism and/or slavery. Although 'race' is socially constructed and is not essential in people's beings, because states of European descent have administered regimes ranging from slavery and apartheid to colonial expropriation to segregation, 'race' matters profoundly. The identities of 'African', 'Oriental,' 'Indian,' and 'aboriginal' were constructed with highly negative meanings (as 'heathen,' 'primitive,' or 'savage') to legitimize laws sanctioning loss of life, liberty, labour, lands, culture, language, and family. The continuing oppression, stigmatization, and marginalization of aboriginal peoples and those subjected to state racism cannot be captured within the concepts of 'difference' or 'tolerance.' Nor can they be captured by postcolonial theories that assume the colonizers can be thrown out along with most of their ideas.

In societies like Canada, the United States, Australia, New Zealand, and South Africa, for example, white settler states were formed by dispossessing and oppressing aboriginal peoples and by importing slaves or indentured workers. Indigenous, 'Black,' and 'white' women are inheritors of official race regimes that harmed the first two while privileging the third. These facts cannot be integrated into feminist theories of patriarchy. That is, feminism cannot assimilate 'differences' based on race oppression with those based on sex/gender oppression. Nor can it assimilate oppressions based on nation, faith, culture, language, or disability with oppressions rooted in the political economies of colonialism and neocolonialism. To understand how women are oppressed within these systems of power we must use 'some larger-scale structural analyses of social and economic systems' (Strickland, 1994: 268). This does not mean that we must abandon the insights of feminism about systems of oppression based on sex/gender; these insights are feminism's most important contribution to human understanding. However, it does mean that Western feminism's claim to being a total theory that can deal with all forms of oppression must be abandoned for a more modest account. As Ien Ang (1995) argues, it also means that feminism cannot be a complete politics for most women within Western states whose difference marginalizes them from mainstream social and political life.

IV. Taking Difference Seriously

In this final section we provide a concrete example of how we can engage with difference within women's studies in a meaningful way. We do so by exploring Philomeda Essed's work on gendered racism. We argue that women's studies, and feminist scholarship generally, work best by comparing women's knowledge of their experiences, which are consequences of their differences and their commonalities, and by theorizing about how systems of power based on difference work. We begin by examining briefly how feminist scholars have used the concept of experience, which underlies much women's studies methodology.

The Problem with 'Experience'

Women's studies and feminist scholarship within the disciplines in Western countries moved quickly from the streets and social movements to sweeping critiques of *everything* that had gone before. These critiques assumed that sex/gender is central to all dimensions of human life everywhere. They assumed, for example, that white women's experience of sex/gender oppression as the foundation of all other forms of oppression was something shared by 'other' women. In fact, many other women resist such a formulation and yet are also deeply committed to the advancement of women. This has produced a stalemate: mainstream Western feminists have made 'experience' the foundation of their project, yet they are unable to deal with groups of women whose experiences differ from their own.

In exploring this stalemate, Algerian sociologist Marnia Lazreg concludes: 'The assumed collective character of women's experience may be necessary to engage in the act of negating antecedent knowledge but it is not sufficient to rectify that knowledge and transform it' (1994: 57). She traces the problem to the way that individual experiences of female subjects were elevated to ontological status because they were thought to have privileged access to truth. This set 'experience' and 'science' in opposition to each other. Lazreg agrees that positivist science can't be the basis for women's studies, but she also thinks that elevating individual experience to the same plane as science is an obstacle to understanding women's situated knowledge:

> Women's experience writ large may and should be used as a way of defining a 'problematique' requiring the application of self-critical rational thought to immediate experience as it encounters constituted knowledge. Experience may and can provide insights into the relationship between gender and social structure. However, the establishment of a subjectivist epistemology based on the body may only end where it began: in the body. (58)

Simply put, to take difference seriously, women need a knowledge system that is based on more than what their experiences as sexed and gendered people (as women) can tell them. If difference is to be taken seriously, women cannot be reduced only to their sex/gender experiences.

Anzanian Oshadi Mangena (1994) also explores problems in Western feminists' approach of making experience the ground for knowledge. But her critique focuses on the problem of separating female from male experiences and the resulting fragmentation. For Mangena, human experience is situational and so is our knowledge of it. She argues that when Western feminists (correctly) argued that 'women's' knowledge was left out, they were also acknowledging the incompleteness of having knowledge based only on the experiences of one-half of the community. But the idea that the perspective of women, like that of men, is also incomplete was lost in the construction of feminist theory. Nonetheless, women's studies and feminist scholarly practices have retained the insight and sought to restore holistic knowledge through approaches such as participatory research, which many feminist researchers have adopted. African and aboriginal women tend to avoid knowledge claims, which facilitate antagonistic struggles with men, who also 'undergo extreme exploitation and oppression internally and internationally' (280). Mangena believes that many women's experiences of oppression and exploitation are 'intertwined' with men's in this way:

> Forms of feminist thinking which explain female subjugation ... from the idea that all human societies transform biology into culture by effecting a common sex/gender system, cannot be accepted. Various human societies ... did not historically understand nature and human life in a similar manner. The fact of difference is a characteristic of human beings proper ... Consequently, *gender oppression ... is very different in different situations.* It is not the case that we all have a common experience as a consequence of our gender with differences of race, class and nationality simply added on. (281; our emphasis)

Essed's Account of Gendered Racism

Building on these insights, we move to Essed's account in *Understanding Everyday Racism: An Interdisciplinary Theory* (1991) of her research to understand gendered racism as experienced by 'Black' women in the Netherlands and California. Essed's goal was to understand the mechanics of racism in the Netherlands. She adopted a comparative method, theorizing that there is not one universal form of 'racism' – rather, there are many different forms, each with its own structure, ideology, and processes. Each form of racism is historically specific. For example, the racism experienced by African Americans is shaped by the history of slavery in the United States, whereas 'the Black Diaspora in Europe is a different story, one of colonialism rather than slavery' (14). Moreover, racism changes form over time and is experienced differently by men and women of different classes. In contrast to most research, which focuses on the perpetrators, Essed based her study on the experiences of those suffering harms because of racism. She relied on in-depth, non-directed interviews with fifty-five university-educated 'Black' women in the Netherlands and California– university educated, to control for the effects of class – all but two of whom were between twenty and forty-five. Her reconstructions of their experience from these accounts 'provide the best basis for the analysis of the simultaneous impact of racism in different sites and in different relations' (3). Essed began her reconstruction of women's accounts by exploring the similarities and differences in how racism works in the two situations. For example, in both, a common factor is white denial of racism. But Black women in California knew about the long history in the United States of movements resisting slavery and racism, whereas most of the Afro-Surinamese women were recent immigrants to the Netherlands and had little knowledge of anticolonial and antiracism movements. In Europe, Afro-Surinamese women were perceived as sexually exotic and permissive; the legacy of slavery assigned Black Californian women the Aunt Jemima stereotype.

In both the Netherlands and California, Black women's experiences of racism and gender oppression were so intertwined that Essed developed the concept of gendered racism to conceptualize it. But, she notes, 'not only Black women but also Black men are confronted with racism structured by racist constructions of gender roles, notable examples being the absent father stereotype or the myth of the Black rapist' (31). So gendered racism describes the experiences of both women and men. Essed's research reconstructs the situated knowledges that Black women have about their particular experiences. Her analysis is informed by feminism, and her research is women-centred. But the interactions between racism and sexism affect both women and men, and she acknowledges this theoretically. Moreover, the interactions that constitute gendered racism cannot be understood simply from within feminist theory, because that theory offers no systematic account of the nature of racism in different contexts or of racism's links to slavery, colonialism, and neocolonialism. In sum, Essed draws insights from theories other than feminism – that is, from comparative theories of racism. In the next chapter we examine in detail methods for 'doing' women's studies that are based on both differences and commonalities.

CHAPTER 2

Methodologies for Scholarship about Women

Jill Vickers

In this chapter we explore issues of methodology for scholarship about women. Women's studies as an interdisciplinary field draws on many different disciplines and fields, so methodology has always been controversial. Moreover, scholarship about women now exists in many different disciplines and fields, each of which uses a different methodology. We believe it is important for students to understand the basis on which feminist and women-centred knowledge claims are made. So our goal in this chapter is to outline some key methodological issues and to suggest ways of choosing among available methods.

The chapter has two parts. In Part I, we explore debates about methodology that have arisen as Western feminists put forward women-centred knowledge and have it accepted by male gatekeepers, who control what is deemed to be 'knowledge.' Many feminist activists in the early days of women's studies – in the 1970s and 1980s – were suspicious of how male-dominated disciplines did research 'on' women. In Europe and Latin America, activists did research in autonomous women's centres, not in universities. This led to the development of an approach called *action* research, which had its own principles and ethical rules. Eventually this approach worked its way into scholarship on women within universities. We explore this by discussing Dutch feminist Maria Mies's seven postulates to guide feminist scholarship on women. We then explore three methodological orientations that have developed within academia: empiricism, standpoint theories, and postmodernism. We also consider how feminist debates about method have been affected by the challenge of difference. We conclude that scholarship on women cannot have only one methodological approach. Far better to identify examples of excellent work, explore what makes them effective, and model our methodology on them.

In Part II, we make methodology practical through a case study on women's poverty. We outline methodological approaches that can integrate local causes of women's poverty with explanations of global causes, distinguishing between gender gap approaches focused on gender-specific effects worldwide and development gap approaches focused on poverty in affluent versus poor states. We conclude that scholarship on women needs a variety of methods and must equip students to learn which are needed to produce particular kinds of knowledge claims. What all of these 'best case' approaches have in common is a set of basic ethical principles to ensure that scholarship *about* women also serves women's needs.

I. Methodologies for Scholarship on Women

Sandra Burt, in a ground-breaking article on public policy research, concluded: 'For the most part feminist approaches have involved frame-shifting rather than the adoption of new methodologies' (in Burt and Code, 1995: 358). In her field the old 'frame' saw public policy as what governments decide and do. The new frame has women at the centre and as the reference point. The problem of women being excluded underlies many attempts by women to change knowledge making. The flip side of this is false inclusion, when knowledge claims incorrectly include women or any group by making sweeping assertions. There are different ways of developing women-centred knowledge to contest both the exclusion of women and their false inclusion. A common approach has been to use feminist theory, as Burt does, to 'change the frame.' A second approach is to develop women-centred methodologies such as action research. Either approach changes the process of knowledge making.

First we should distinguish between theory and methodology. This is not a simple matter, as people often disagree about what each concept means and how they are linked. At its most basic level, a theory is *a set of ideas*, usually derived by reasoning from a set of facts or premises. It is supposed to *explain* something; an example is Darwin's theory of evolution. A theory is a *tentative* explanation; thus, there are many facts that support Darwin's theory, but it isn't proven and some scientists question its validity. A methodology is *a set of methods* (ways of doing research) *and procedures* for a particular discipline, field of study, or professional practice. Burt has argued that scholarship on women in her field, by using women-centred theories, has changed the theoretical framework for public policy research, but so far hasn't changed its methodology.

There are four kinds of questions commonly involved in feminist debates about knowledge making. The first deals specifically with questions of methodology, including these:

- How can we make knowledge claims about women's experiences?
- What kinds of knowledge claims can we make?
- How can we gain legitimacy for feminist knowledge about women so that we can persuade people to change their minds?

The second set of questions involves issues of epistemology, including how we know what we know. The third set of questions asks how feminist methods are affected by 'the challenge of difference.' The fourth set of questions concerns how women's studies can best create trustworthy knowledge. The 'methodological rebellions of feminist research' (Vickers, 1983) posed a set of challenges to traditional, male-centred theories of knowledge on all fronts, so attention to these issues is also necessary.

How have scholars doing research on women dealt with methodological issues? The involvement of women's studies in so many disciplines and fields makes this a complex question. For example, feminist work raises different methodological issues in the medical sciences than in literature, sociology, or interdisciplinary women's studies. In the 1970s, feminist methodological rebellions were mainly in the social sciences. Since the 1990s, however, the humanities and cultural studies have also became sites of radical challenges. In Western countries, many researchers in the social sciences opposed the dominant rules of knowledge making usually described by the term positivism. These methodological upheavals are mainly about feminist attempts to make space for women-centred knowledge within the Western system of knowledge. Second-wave feminists largely accepted the idea that there is a common, universal knowledge about women. For them the trick was to uncover it and have it included in place of the male-centred knowledge that prevailed. Since 1990, however, the idea that knowledge developed by Western scholars can be applied around the world has been discredited. Moreover, Western women and men are now linked to their counterparts elsewhere. Hence a new set of methodological challenges has emerged. The puzzle is this: How do we develop reliable knowledge about people – about men and women in their many different locations and circumstances? What we need is a one-world approach that nonetheless respects the specificities of difference.

Maria Mies developed seven methodological 'postulates' that she believed could be used by activist scholars worldwide. We focus on Mies's postulates here because they guide scholarship on women by scholars from around the globe working through the Women and Development Program of the Institute of Social Studies in The Hague.[1] According to Mies, just to 'add women' to existing approaches 'and stir' would not have developed the kind of knowledge about women that activists need: 'Therefore we had to search for an altogether new paradigm of knowledge and science, a new epistemology and methodology, a new relationship between practice and theory, between politics and knowledge, between living and knowing, a relationship which would no longer separate, fragment and hierarchize these areas of reality' (1996: 12). Writing in 1996, she recalled the historical context in which this radical agenda for doing research about women around the globe emerged. The revolutionary ideas of Mao Zedong were influential, and so were the teachings of Paulo Freire, especially his 1970 text *Pedagogy of the Oppressed*. Many drew methods from Mao's 'speak bitterness' campaigns, in which oppressed people spoke out against their oppressors, and from Freire's *conscientization* – studies of oppressive reality by those oppressed. Feminists adopted the method of consciousness raising, which emphasized women's subjective experiences, beliefs, and feelings. But unless those gaining knowledge through consciousness raising were open to other forms of knowledge, and in touch with many different kinds of women in different places and circumstances, they risked mistaking their own experiences and feelings for universal truths. Hence, the desire to 'know' women versus men had serious pitfalls.

Mies's postulates represented a reaction against traditional ways of doing social research. They generalized from how activist feminists sought to transform knowledge making. They assumed that the concerns of ordinary women active in women's movements must form part of knowledge making in women's studies. She asserted the following:

1 The postulate of value-free research, of neutrality [which characterized male-centred scholarship] ... is replaced by conscious partiality.

2 The vertical relationship between researchers and researched is ... replaced by the view from below [in which those without power tell researchers what they experience or feel].
3 The contemplative, uninvolved attitude of the researchers ... is replaced by active participation in actions, movements and struggles for women's liberation. Feminist research must serve this goal.
4 Participation in social actions and struggles ... becomes the starting point for a scientific quest. 'If you want to know a thing you must change it.'
5 The research process must become a process of conscientization ... for all participants in the research process.
6 This ... should be accompanied by recording women's individual and social history, so that women can appropriate their history.
7 Women cannot reclaim ... their history unless they begin to share and collectivize their experience, insights and theories. (1996: 13)

These postulates form the basis of research about women practised in many countries by feminist activists and many feminist academics as well. Mies and other feminists who are both activists and researchers call the kind of research which resulted *action research*. Action research upends the basic premises of traditional social science methodology. Traditional research was detached and 'objective'; action re-search would be engaged, passionate and consciously partial. It would eliminate hierarchical distance between researchers and researched in favour of collective discovery. Knowledge of social phenomena such as oppression was only obtainable through participation in movements for change, so activism and research must proceed together. In this way, action research would fuse together activism and feminist scholarship.

All feminist debates about methodology in Western countries were informed by this transformative vision to some degree. Much attention was focused on quantification; the use and manipulation of numbers as the main medium for knowledge claims. But quantification as a research practice was suspect because it stripped the context from women's experiences and hid specificity, agency, and history. Mies's criticism of quantification also highlighted the role that quantification played in the censuses and surveys used by colonial oppressors: rendering people's experiences as 'data' made it easier to objectify and control them. Mies's view that quantitative methodologies are 'instruments of repression' (1983: 118) became common in interdisciplinary women's studies. For example, Stanley and Wise in their widely used 1983 text *Breaking Out: Feminist Consciousness and Feminist Research* rejected quantitative methods, believing that because they aggregated and generalized to construct 'facts,' they were inherently coercive and created hierarchical relationships. Many feminists now use qualitative approaches; indeed, for a time the act of rejecting quantitative methods was a symbol of feminist rebellion.

In recent years, Western feminists have developed a more complex view that partly rehabilitates quantification. For example, in Burt and Code's 1995 text *Changing Methods: Feminists Transforming Practices*, Lorraine Greaves, Alison Wylie, and colleagues report on the cautious use of quantitative methods by the Battered Women's Advocacy Centre in London, Ontario. But they argue that quantitative methods 'will be non-coercive and productive of new understanding only to the extent that their organization and content reflect a sophisticated, qualitative understanding of the experiences they are meant to capture' (322). Although (women's studies) scholars with strong activist credentials have focused their resistance on traditional practices such as quantification, those active within social science and humanities disciplines have developed the main orientations to feminist research, which we discuss in the next section. Note, however, that their concern is usually how to 'do' scholarship on women within their previously existing disciplines or fields. Less often are they determined to generate purely women-centred knowledge. And they do not generally address the problem of how to develop knowledges that reflect women's diverse locations and circumstances – that is, a one-world approach.

Orientations to Feminist Research

In this section we outline three general orientations to methodology – empiricism, standpoint positions, and postmodernism – within which scholarship on women has been developed. First we outline the nature of positivism,[2] which is the dominant paradigm for research in the social sciences, and thus the paradigm against which feminist methodological rebellions have been fought. Positivism is an orientation to human knowledge based on rules about (1) what can and cannot be known, (2) what 'knowledge' is and how it is validated, and (3) what kinds of knowledge claims can be made based on what kinds of evidence. Positivism is normative: it regulates how we use such terms as 'knowledge,' 'facts,' and 'validity.' The rules reflect 'the scientific method' adapted for social phenomena. Postitivism distinguishes between philosophical issues (about 'values') and scientific ones (about 'facts') and declares that a logical gulf exists between the two. Those who work within this framework claim that the knowledge they produce is as universally 'valid' as knowledge in the natural sciences. This establishes a 'hard' knowledge claim captured in the concept of 'facts.'

Feminists argued that these rules excluded women's experiences and falsely represented male experience as universal. Moreover, for positivists a major rule is that for knowledge to be reliable, researchers must be 'objective'; put another way, 'knowers are detached and neutral spectators, and objects of knowledge are separate from them, inert items in knowledge-gathering processes, yielding knowledge best verified by appeals to observational data' (Code, 1995: 17). The basic idea is of a point somewhere outside the world 'where a universal knower can stand and see the world without perspective' (Lennon and Whitford, 1994: 3). 'Objectivity' is acting as if you occupy such a point of detachment. But most feminists believe that all knowers are situated in time and space – in specific histories and cultures and in the class, sex/gender, and other social aspects of their lives – and most feminist methodologies begin with this premise.

Positivist rules are tests of what constitutes 'reliable' knowledge. Though feminists can use other approaches to knowledge making, the results are harder to legitimize. So feminist knowledge claims are often seen as 'biased'; that is, in positivist terms they fail the test of objectivity. Each of the three main feminist orientations to methodology is to some extent a reaction to positivism and its claims.

Many feminist scholars in the social sciences work with the same methods used by positivist social science but with altered assumptions. Like Burt, they change the frame. Canadian sociologist Margrit Eichler, for example, argues that 'the answer to the puzzle posed by the existence of sexism in the social sciences does not lie at the level of any one particular method employed, but at a meta-level' (1987: 22). For Eichler the problem is the presence of sexism in social science paradigms and theoretical frameworks. Eichler asserts that sexism is embedded in the language used, the questions posed, the interpretations of data, and the policy recommendations made – indeed, in the overall perspective. She also believes that sexism can enter social science through the use made of methods, but that in themselves methods are neither sexist nor non-sexist; to her, the key is choosing methods appropriate to the kind of knowledge women want and need.

Eichler's position is *empiricist*. That is, she assumes there is a concrete social world ('reality') about which women and men can have knowledge in common, so the key is to reform the social sciences so they are no longer sexist. This would allow feminists in various fields to develop non-sexist knowledge about women's lives that can be legitimized as valid and so accepted by others in the field and by policymakers. Sandra Harding associates feminist empiricism entirely with this project of cleansing social science of its antiwoman biases through a stricter application of the rules of scientific method enforced by a greater presence of women in the enterprise (1991). The scientific method arose during the Enlightenment. The Enlightenment philosophers, whose ideas shaped positivism, believed that the five senses were the only reliable sources of knowledge and that everyone's sense experiences were the same. The Enlightenment was a movement that developed in the eighteenth century in those Western countries that were then engaged in establishing colonies, and in exploiting the peoples thereby dominated within systems of imperialism. The Enlightenment philosophers and the social theorists and scientists who followed them believed the scientific method also could be applied to social phenomena. They went beyond the idea that, for example, gravity and evolution apply everywhere on the globe, to argue that human behaviour – both individual and collective – is also the same everywhere and so can be studied scientifically.

Clearly, in a framework that assumes human behaviour is the same everywhere, 'experience' is a questionable basis for knowledge. Marnia Lazreg (1994) notes that many feminists use the concept of experience uncritically and resist positivism by reifying 'women's experience' as the 'true source' of knowledge (1994: 52–3). But this leads to situations in which 'other' women's experiences are denied, subsumed, or deemed incomprehensible. In sum, many women's studies scholars have rejected positivism, but in doing so they have adopted many of its most questionable assumptions.

Fortunately, this is not the only way of being empiricist. There are also postpositivist research approaches that have trustworthy knowledge[3] as their goal. Naturalist inquiry is one of these. Guba outlines its characteristics:

> Most proponents of naturalistic inquiry assume ... that ... there are multiple realities rather than a single reality; that subjective inquiry is the

only kind possible to do and that as a result all studies will be value-influenced to an indeterminate degree; that the aim of inquiry is the development of shared constructions (including constructions for action) among members of a particular group, society or culture, and that if others wish to learn from the given inquiry, they do so chiefly through the 'vicarious experience' that a good case study report provides. (in Erlandson et al., 1993: xi)

There are similarities between naturalistic inquiry and what are called *feminist standpoint approaches*. But naturalistic inquiry practitioners have developed a set of rules so that knowledge claims thereby generated can be evaluated; feminist approaches have not. These rules determine whether research findings are trustworthy – that is, whether other researchers who are part of the same group, society, or culture can test them to see if they are credible. The goal is not universal 'validity,' but rather confirmability and dependability using specific techniques for establishing trustworthiness. One practice is triangulation, which enhances credibility by using multiple sources of data, multiple methods, multiple investigators, and multiple theories. Naturalistic inquiry assumes that although there are multiple realities, these realities can be shared to some degree so that collective accounts are possible, although the collectivities vary. There are other postpositivist forms of empirical inquiry, but few have systematized their rules in this way. Feminist action research as described by Mies resists the rules established by positivism but pays little attention to establishing the legitimacy of the resulting women-centred knowledge claims.[4] We believe the next stage for women's studies is to establish some rules of trustworthiness for feminist and women-centred research by observing the best practices in our current scholarship. (For this, see Part II.)

Feminist standpoint theorists take the view that 'neither orthodox nor feminist empiricists can adequately account for the varied historical and material conditions out of which people produce knowledge' (Code, 1995: 41). Code defines feminist standpoint theory as a 'hard-won product of consciousness raising and social-political engagement' that starts from the 'material realities' of women's lives and analyses their oppressions as the structural consequences of an 'unjust social order' (1995: 41). Standpoint approaches assume that the knowledge held by the oppressed should be privileged because it is more complete than the knowledge held by their oppressors. But they provide only one criterion for evaluating women-centred knowledge claims:

the extent to which their conclusions 'ring true' to those who accept them. There has been a proliferation of standpoints and standpoint theories, as we discuss in the next section. Collins (1990), for example, presents a Black women's standpoint, based on an Afrocentric, feminist epistemology that is the result of Black women having access to both Afrocentric and feminist standpoints. She argues that Black women's consciousness is formed by being both part of and not part of these groups simultaneously (207). Neither Collins nor Code provides insights into how differences among standpoints can be resolved. As globalization progresses, for example, there are also postcolonial standpoints that express the insights of Third World peoples. Indeed, the lowering of national barriers and the development of information technology are exposing us to many standpoints. How are these to be resolved?

It is now common to refer to dominant knowledge systems as standpoints, as in Eurocentric knowledge and masculine knowledge systems. The result is a pluralist world of alternative, competing standpoints of knowledges in which the power of the knower's group may ultimately be the only determinant of 'truth.' For some scholars on women, the development of formal rules of trustworthiness is the solution. Others conclude that knowledge – in the Enlightenment sense of something reliable and trustworthy that can be universally valid and shared among people – is impossible. This is the view of *postmodernists*. Postmodernism as an approach to knowledge has its origins mainly in studies of culture, but it is also a critique of modernist feminisms, and of other modernist projects to change the world based on Enlightenment values. Anna Yeatman contends that 'postmodernism is a contested zone' (1994: 187). However, there are almost as many versions of postmodernism as there are postmodernists, and this makes it difficult to offer an account of postmodernism's methodological practices. Here we distinguish between two tendencies as they affect women's studies: postmodernism as a cultural method, and postmodernism as political critique.

Some postmodern approaches, Yeatman believes, take the standpoint of 'the master subject contemplating the issues of legitimacy for his authority which arise from the refusal of those cast as other to stay silent' (1994: 187). From this perspective, postmodernism aims to collapse the idea of stable knowledge by deconstructing general statements and showing them to be deficient. The method used is deconstruction. Yeatman argues that this form of postmodernism represents an effort by dominant groups and societies to manage the threat their knowledge faces from feminists, postcolonialists, antiracists, and others who reject the Enlightenment idea that there is one universally legitimate knowledge (theirs). In Yeatman's view, dominant Euro-American men are in effect saying: 'If my knowledge isn't universally valid, there is no universally valid knowledge.'

Other postmodern approaches proceed 'from the standpoint of those who are placed as the disruptive and challenging voices of the Other' (Yeatman, 1994: 187). From the margins, they use postmodernism as a political critique of dominant knowledge systems. Postcolonialists in this tradition reveal the biases in social science statements that are supposedly universal, and show these statements to be partial, Eurocentric, and masculinist. There is no organized set of methodological rules associated with this approach. Only pluralist accounts of culturally relative knowledge are possible. Critical postmodernism, however, works largely by changing the frame of analysis. One of its valuable contributions to research on women has been the exploration of 'the global' and 'the local' as categories for understanding the diversity of women's experiences. For example, Grewal and Kaplan in *Scattered Hegemonies* (1994) suggested how the politics of location developed within a feminist standpoint can deconstruct universalizing uses of concepts such as 'local' and 'global,' so that we can employ them critically to understand both diversity and commonality. Indeed, in the late 1990s a number of feminist texts worked to develop a one-world approach to understanding such things as the impact of globalization, and its concomitant localization, on differently located women. For example, Sally Cole and colleagues (eds., 1999) in *Making Worlds: Ethnographic Insights*, Caren Kaplan (1999) in *Between Women and Nations*, and Susan Aiken and colleagues (1998) in *Making Worlds: Gender, Metaphor and Materiality* have all contributed to the creation of a new paradigm for scholarship on women in which diversity is not only taken into account, but understood in a one-world context. Yet the methodological procedures (as in Mies's account) and rules are not clearly expressed in these valuable contributions. In the next section, we begin to discuss what they could entail.

Methodology and the Challenge of Difference

To date, debates about methodology for scholarship on women have largely been disconnected from the difference debates discussed in chapter 1, but there are points of connection between them, as expressed for instance in Black feminist standpoint approaches and feminist critical postmodernism. The issues have been raised, however, by feminists trying to conduct research on women that is both cross-cultural and respectful of difference within each country. Maria Mies used the precepts of action research in the multicountry 'Women's Movements and Organisations in Historical Perspective' study. She reported on the difficulties faced by researchers in different countries and communities in comparing results and documentary evidence – problems often related to cross-cultural definitions. Nelson and Chowdhury's study *Women and Politics Worldwide* (1994), which included forty-three countries, also raised important methodological issues. Nelson and Chowdhury accepted the judgment of 'local' researchers about what constituted women's political engagement and what the most pressing issues were for women in their countries. But they were unable to penetrate below the nation-state level to tap diverse women's views within each country. A few authors, living under state socialist regimes, 'used a standpoint approach ... that privileged the perspectives on women offered by Marxist or revolutionary interpretations of the needs of women in the working, peasant or popular classes' (1994: 36). But most adopted some form of action research or a modified empiricism. Although the key weakness of the research design was that it retained a nation-state framework so that the country reports presented dominant-culture women's experiences as 'women's experiences,' with little attention to marginalized women, the authors and editors did identify the most significant issues within their local frameworks and did construct an agenda of broadly conceived issues that they argued, mobilize women worldwide. They also abstracted from the country studies a number of transnational 'forces,' which they argued affect women's political engagement in a number of countries. The project resulted in systematic cross-cultural comparisons, although the combination of local action research findings and transnational issues and forces required a cross-cultural editorial team. However, the frame remained feminist – that is, centred on gender issues – and this muted the importance of poverty and security concerns both outside the West and among minorities within Western countries.

To this point we have explored some of the problems that women's studies faces in the matter of developing trustworthy knowledge. Should scholarship on women commit its energies to developing a single, reliable methodology through which strong knowledge claims can be made? We agree with Lorraine Code: 'The most viable strategy for feminist research is to abandon any quest for one true method, or for a universalism ... At this ... juncture an experimental pluralism recommends itself' (1995: 42). We agree in general with her conclusion, but this does not mean that 'anything goes.' Rather, it is important for us to become more conscious of our methodological options. We recommend emulating work that seems most effective at putting issues of diversity front and centre.

Philomeda Essed's project was to understand Black women's experiences of racism by considering systematically how gendered racism works in two different countries. Initially, she focused on the experiential, that is, on how two groups of Black women – one in the Netherlands, the other in California – experienced 'everyday' racism. She sought to understand both the local and the transnational forces that shaped the experiences of each group. Her method was to reconstruct raw reports of Black women's experiences, using documentary, historical, and theoretical materials, to understand the impact of 'racism' on the two different sites. Her methodology assumed that 'racism' both is and is not a transnational force, in that its local manifestations will be both similar and different. Some aspects of any two local contexts will be similar (e.g., denial of racism); others will always be different (e.g., women's knowledge of antiracism movements in California but not the Netherlands). In the same vein, some aspects of the transnational forces will be similar (e.g., racism resulted from European colonialism in both cases); other aspects will be different (e.g., slavery in the United States, as opposed to colonial occupation for Dutch Blacks). Essed's approaches to data gathering (unstructured interviews), analysis, and interpretation were flexible, but her comparisons were systematic. She constructed categories so that her analysis was informed by women's reports of their experiences and by historical and theoretical factors. The systematic character of her methodological approach allowed her to make generalizations about how racism works – results that are accepted by many as trustworthy. Essed's work does not provide *the* method for women's studies, but it provides one example we can emulate. In particular, we should note that Essed's method involved a dual focus – on racism, and on women *and* men's experiences of it. Although she began with Black *women's* experiences of racism, she concluded that both women's and men's experiences involved racism and gender stereotypes that were intertwined.

So Black men as well as Black women had their sexuality distorted through stereotypes, not just the women. In the next section we will draw on some of Essed's practices in looking for an appropriate one-world approach to studying women's diverse experiences and learning from them.

II. Methodology in Practice

In this section, we put methodological issues into practice through a case study of women's poverty in which we identify and compare both local and global causes. First we explore why we think 'poverty' is a 'women's issue.' Then we explore two different approaches to understanding women's poverty: a gender gap approach that places women at the centre, and a development gap approach. We conclude that trustworthy knowledge also depends on the theoretical framework we adopt.

Poverty is a problem, but is it a 'Women's Issue'? Some mainstream women's movements focus on poverty mainly as a problem of some 'forgotten' women. So the 'feminization of poverty' is increasingly being raised as an issue in Western countries as neoliberal governments reduce welfare benefits and policymakers try to 'fix' the dependency of persistently poor people – most of whom are women – while also lowering government costs to increase competitiveness in the global economy. Texts that deal with poor groups or poor countries highlight poverty but often use an apartheid approach to difference in such a way that rigid compartmentalization constructs problems of poverty as separate from 'women's issues.' We explore this issue of segregation below, asking whether women share an agenda of issues worldwide in spite of this practice.

First, consider some basic statistics: 820 million people worldwide were unemployed in 1994. That was 30 per cent of the global labour force. In 1996 one-third of the population of 'the South' – 1.3 billion people – lived in abject poverty without health care, sanitation, or safe water. About 1 billion people go hungry every day (Bandarage, 1997: 1). More than half these people are women and their children. With such wide disparities, can there be a common women's agenda worldwide? We begin by exploring issues that are demonstrably important to women in many countries as evident from debates in the international arena, reports from UN conferences, and publications of UNIFEM, a UN status-of-women agency. We use the core issues that

Nelson and Chowdhury derived from the forty-three country studies in their project.

There is evidence that four broad goals mobilize women's struggles worldwide:

1 *Physical security for women and their families.* Security from violence is a key issue around which women mobilize in every country. It is an issue for rich and poor women, for women in rich and poor countries, and for women in both capitalist democracies and state-socialist and authoritarian regimes.

2 *Meaningful control for women over their reproduction.* Achieving this control has quite different meanings in different parts of the world. In some cases it means the ability not to have children or to limit numbers. Elsewhere, especially where coercive population control is a state goal, women's control means the freedom *to* reproduce.

3 *Economic well-being for women and their families.* The focus here is most often on access to resources, education, and employment so that women can feed, shelter, clothe, and educate themselves and their dependents.

4 *Equal benefits, rights, and responsibilities of citizenship.* Gaining the power to make decisions does not mobilize women as much as the first three issues because most women worldwide have more pressing security concerns. But women worldwide do link their lack of security and rights to the fact that 'half of the world's population routinely hold only 5–10 percent of the formal positions of political leadership' (Nelson and Chowdhury, 1994: 15). So becoming equal as citizens is a goal because it can help women achieve their other goals.

Women's Struggles in Different Contexts

Although women's movements share the goal of achieving greater gender fairness in the organization of society, there are also class conflicts among women within each country and among countries, and especially between countries in the West and the rest. The organization of both the global economy and of individual societies affects women's struggles for economic security and well-being. Almost everywhere, it is overwhelmingly women and their dependents who are poor and who lack access to the resources needed to transcend poverty. They also lack the physical mobility to move to where there are better resources. So we find the countryside in many 'Third World' countries emptied of men, who migrate to the cities and to more affluent countries to find work. Women and children are overrepresented in refugee camps because they are more likely to be displaced by violence at home and at the same time less often able to migrate to new homes, because of family responsibilities. So women are poor both because of how societies organize the sexual division of labour and because of how the global economy works. Not all women are poor, of course, and poverty has different implications for women depending on their country's location in the global economy. As a result of pressure from labour and women's movements, countries that are affluent because of their past role in colonialism and/or their present position in the global economy have developed welfare state programs that ameliorate women's poverty. In poorer countries, welfare state supports are rare. Women everywhere must struggle to gain or maintain economic security, but that struggle is different for women in various countries. It is also different within each country: some women share the best their country has, others do not.

In the 1990s, women's movements in 'Western,' capitalist countries mobilized against neoliberal governments' roll-backs of welfare state programs that had promoted gender fairness. 'Western' women's movements are perceived by neoliberal ideologies as 'special interests' and are being increasingly marginalized politically (Brodie, 1994). Nonetheless, women are participating more and more in paid work, training, and education. The mobilization against neoliberalism reflects most 'Western' feminists' belief that women are entitled as citizens to programs to achieve greater gender fairness. In contrast, since 1990 women in postcommunist countries have lost programs aimed, however ineffectually, at gender fairness. Although state socialism made it a priority to provide work for all citizens, and to provide public services such as childcare, any approach to gender fairness associated with the old regimes has little chance of acceptance from governments or from women. The backlash against state-imposed employment quotas that benefited women, and the ending of subsidized childcare, have made it harder for women to participate in the labour market, although women's need to support themselves hasn't lessened.

The situation is different again for women in the poorest countries of the 'Third World.' Here, states are either unable or unwilling to provide programs to foster greater gender fairness, and women's struggles are often against structural adjustment policies imposed by their governments under pressure from the World Bank or the IMF – policies that often eliminate food subsidies, health care, and free education. The consequences include more street children, more violence within families, and more sexual attacks on women. Furthermore, most women work on the streets providing food and services or in the informal sector. In Islamic countries, women may face governments opposed to feminism on religious grounds; that, or the secular government is under pressure from fundamentalist movements that associate feminism with Western, neocolonial values. Past failures of 'modernizing' regimes trigger the rise of fundamentalist movements; in the climate that results, Islamic fundamentalism becomes a way of resisting economic and cultural globalization (Ahmed and Donnan, 1994: 3). This can make women's struggles for economic well-being more difficult, especially where extreme gender apartheid is imposed (as in Afghanistan), thus denying women access to paid work. Even so, women in most Muslim states engage in economic activity and mobilize around struggles for economic security. And in some countries, Islamist policies provide women with opportunities to participate in gender-segregated economies, especially in health care and education.

In the re-emerging democracies of Latin America and Asia, neoliberal economic policies, first imposed by authoritarian and military regimes, are hampering women's efforts to improve their economic well-being. Women played key roles in movements against repressive regimes, but further gains are limited by internal class divisions and by the virtual exclusion of non-elite women from state decision-making in the new democracies. In countries such as Mexico and the Philippines, governments are offering transnational corporations (TNCs) export production zones (EPZs), where young mostly women workers produce everything from running shoes to computer chips for consumers in affluent countries. Global assembly lines locate production activities in rapidly industrializing countries, where there are few government regulations, low wages, and weak unions. This provides jobs for young women, but they work for low pay in poor conditions and often experience work-related health problems. They often burn out after a few years and end up in the sex trades or in abject poverty. This 'global assembly line,' by which many jobs previously located in affluent countries have been moved to poor, Third World countries, links women in many locales. Women workers in affluent countries – for example, in the textile and information technology industries – lose jobs to women in EPZs in rapidly industrializing countries. But at the same time, consumers in the affluent countries, including women, benefit from lower prices for the resulting products. Without transnational movements, women cannot control their work situations in any meaningful way in any locale.

How are we to understand the similarities and differences in these situations? The different circumstances in which 'women' around the world find themselves produce different self-contained discourses[5] about these issues. Feminism needs approaches that incorporate local *and* transnational factors. By bringing these previously isolated discourses together, we can better understand women's struggles in different situations. Nelson and Chowdhury conclude from the forty-three country reports in their project that there are 'localizing and internationalizing trends in women's political organizing' (1994: 8). Therefore, our method must include local, national, and transnational dimensions, because although women worldwide face similar international forces, they live in different local situations, their movements are locally situated, and the nation-states in which they live may be responding differently to both international forces and local reactions. Because local and global are connected, location in the global economy cannot be separated from the local situation, or from women's responses to that situation. For instance, where there are no welfare state programs to support them in old age, less affluent women perceive adult children as the best way to provide for their security. So they are reluctant to limit their reproduction, especially if high infant mortality, caused by poor health care or malnutrition, means that having only a few children is risky. In contrast, most women in industrial societies can choose to avoid motherhood, participate in paid work, and limit their childbearing; there is no risk to this as long as they have access to pensions and state services. In each case, 'women' share a common goal – achieving economic security and maintaining it through old age. Their different contexts, however, result in different perceptions of the issues, in that each woman's reproduction is differently related to her economic well-being.

Creating a Framework

Women worldwide share elements of a common agenda and mobilize around similar issues. But the forces they address vary with their country's location in the global system and with where in a given country women are living. Nelson and Chowdhury concluded that in a given historical period, 'international forces' result in a shared agenda, and in different responses to common issues according to women's individual and collective locations. So our framework must have at least two dimensions: (1) common experiences of transnational ('global') forces that produce a shared agenda, and (2) diverse responses to the issues on this agenda according to a given country's location and to women's different location within their country. Essed's methodology involved systematic comparison, because although gendered racism seems like a global or transnational force (and is to some degree), it has different causes and contexts and provokes different responses in different places. But her respondents also reported common experiences in the two different locales. With these insights, we can add two more dimensions: (3) diverse experiences of transnational ('global') forces because of historical and ideological differences in the local site resulting in different 'takes' on these forces; (4) similar responses to common experiences despite the countries' and/or women's different situations. So besides studying direct accounts of women's experiences, we must identify historic and current economic and social trends and engage in systematic comparisons.

This approach assumes that women's struggles are not just about 'women's issues,' narrowly conceived, since women have practical and theoretical knowledge about, and interest in, all of the major issues their societies face, as well as about their own lives. Women worldwide understand that their fates as women are linked to the fates of their countries, communities, nations, and classes, although mainstream Western women may experience these solidarities less often and so be less conscious of them. How can we understand the transnational forces that shape women's lives with both different and shared consequences? In chapter 1 we introduced the phenomenon of globalization, which, we argued, is affecting women's lives everywhere such that we require a one-world approach to scholarship on women that takes women's different and common experiences into account. Globalization is not a fixed, certain entity that is easily described; indeed, it involves complex trends with conflicting consequences. Consequently, people disagree on its future effects and construct sets of ideas (ideologies) to capture people's minds. 'Globalization' also involves using these ideological constructs to argue about complex sets of processes. In our framework we do not use the term to mean inevitable forces that are the same everywhere and cannot be resisted. Our approach identifies both transnational and local manifestations of the concerns that mobilized women in various countries from the 1960s to 1990, and during the decade that followed the collapse of the Soviet Union and the end of apartheid in South Africa. Nelson and Chowdhury identify four 'international' forces that they believe shaped women's agendas in this period:

- International economic forces, including 'policies promoting macro-economic stabilization and internal structural transformation introduced by the World Bank and the International Monetary Fund to respond to economic instability' (1994: 4).
- The changing nature of nationalism, with a decline in the state-focused nationalisms that promoted formal, legal equality for women, but a rise of religious and ethnic nationalisms that many believe have negative consequences for women.
- The rise of religious fundamentalisms.
- The growth of international feminism.

How do these forces affect women's poverty and their struggles for economic well-being? And how do they link to the post-1990 forms of globalization in which capitalism expanded into the post-communist world and both capitalism and democracy expanded into much of Latin America and new parts of Asia?

Gender Gap versus Development Gap

Can our contextualized approach help us understand 'women's' struggles for economic well-being for themselves and their families in these complex times? First, do we have evidence that poverty is being 'feminized' – that it is increasingly becoming a problem of women and gender justice? A 1995 UNIFEM publication reported that 564 million women were living in absolute poverty, especially in rural areas, where they comprise 60 per cent of the world's 1 billion rural poor (Heyzer, ed., 1995: 5). This basic *gender gap* represents a 50 per cent increase recently in the percentage of women living in absolute poverty, compared to a 30 per cent increase for men. Because women are often solely responsible for caring for children, the elderly, the sick, and those with severe disabilities, when women live in absolute poverty, so do their dependants. The impoverishment of women and the absolute poverty of so many of them is a fundamental issue for women worldwide. But not all women are poor, even in the poorest countries, and not all countries are poor.[6] So there is also a *development gap* that our analysis must also take into account. Chen's research identifies several gaps between 'developed' (industrialized) countries and the 'least developed' countries (1995: 24). For example, 98 per cent of women giving birth in 'developed' nations were assisted by trained health personnel, compared to only 27 per cent in the 'least developed' countries. There were comparable development gaps in literacy, schooling, access to paid work, availability of contraceptives, maternal and infant mortality, and women's life expectancy. There is a less extreme development gap between women in industrialized countries and in 'developing' (medium-poor) countries.[7] So poor women in the 'least developed' and 'developing' countries are poor because of a 'development' gap *and* because of their gender. But the forces causing each of these 'gaps' are different, and interpretations of their causes may conflict.[8]

So when we ask, 'Why are so many women poor?' there are different answers (Tinker, 1990). While many argued for the integration of women into development projects and planning, others maintain that women's integration into the global economy actually makes their poverty worse. Approaches that focus on narrowing the 'development' gap assume that if women have greater access to paid employment, poverty and exploitation will be reduced. But research on the impact of women's employment suggests variable consequences. For example, women's work in the new 'global assembly line' typically involves young women who are exploited (their wages are only 20 to 50 per cent of men's) and often sexually abused, and whose employment lasts only as long as their dexterity and docility – three to five years (Simmons, 1997: 249; Nash and Fernandez-Kelly, 1983). Yet Lim (1997: 224) concludes:

Continued imperialist and patriarchal exploitation in multinational factories in developing countries does not ... imply that the women employed in these factories are worse off than they would have been without such employment. On the contrary, the vast majority are clearly better off, at least but not only in the narrow economic sense. Wages and working conditions are generally better in multinational factories ... Although in the relative economic sense ... they may be more exploited ..., in an absolute sense their incomes tend to be higher. This is true also when compared with women's traditional economic roles as housewives and unpaid family labour. (224)

Therefore, development gap analysis of women's poverty and theories of how 'development' (here employment) alleviates poverty must carefully link 'women's' poverty to international forces through specific empirical observations. Moreover, it is important for Western scholars to find out what networks of women workers in such contexts think about their employment, instead of simply objectifying them as 'exploited.'

Gender gap explanations assume that 'women' are poor because they perform physical and social reproduction (care work) that is neither valued nor remunerated, or not enough of either. Marilyn Waring (1988) believes that the categorization of women in value systems that treat them as non-producers except when they are paid wages is central to the problem. She demonstrates that according to mainstream economic theory and the UN System of National Accounts, women's work of feeding, clothing, sheltering, educating, and nursing children, elders and sick or disabled relatives is not categorized as 'productive.' So even in the richest countries, gender gap analysts argue, the price women pay for being reproducers is greater vulnerability to poverty. Feminists explain increases in women's poverty at three levels:

- Transformations in the world economy.
- The different resource bases of countries, which partly reflect their present and past positions because of colonialism and neocolonialism.
- The causes of women's impoverishment within countries.

Next we look briefly at analyses at the global and local levels; this will allow us to compare development and gender gap approaches.

Noleen Heyzer offers a gender gap explanation of women's impoverishment, which she believes is exacerbated by 'trade deregulation, rapid technological changes, changes in industrial production, the transition to a market economy, structural adjustment programs, and the power of global financial markets' (1995: 5). She shows how 'globalization' affects women more than men in relation to these six dimensions. Each creates 'new patterns of wealth,' from which men benefit more than women because of 'the gender hierarchy imposed on women's ownership of assets, education and employment opportunities, physical and social mobility' (5). She argues that women begin with fewer resources, and because of care work are less mobile, and as a result, these transformations make them poorer. Heyzer's gender gap explanation focuses on how 'women' in countries from the richest to the poorest are affected by such transformations. Impacts at the local level include the following: displacement of women's wage labour by technology; imposition of user fees in health and education, which especially affect women and those they care for; roll-backs of social security programs and women's employment by states; the diversion of resources that women saved for investing (e.g., for tools, education) to daily use; and increased violence from unemployed men. However, a gender gap explanation does not explain why such international forces also disproportionately affect people marginalized by racism, class, caste or religious bias, disability, or rural residence, or acknowledge that marginalized men are also affected. Recall that Heyzer also found a 30 per cent increase in *men* living in abject poverty.

In contrast, a development gap explanation focuses on the severity of the impact of these transformations in the poorest countries. Some of the local impacts include the following: loss of food subsidies and basic services; loss of land used by women to feed their families to production of export crops, often resulting in starvation; the favouring of men and boys in access to food, education, and other resources as families become poorer; the flight of men to the cities seeking work, with increased workloads and greater poverty for women, who become the sole supports for their families; deteriorating nutrition and health for women and their dependents; loss of employment as men take 'women's work'; and growth in the sex trades and sex-related illnesses (such as AIDS) as men and women live apart.

Also greatly worsening women's poverty is the expansion of market values. Structural adjustment programs involve governments reshaping their economies by increasing production for export and by decreasing government spending. In general terms, they become more market-oriented. Governments 'agree' to such programs because they must if they wish their debts to be forgiven, or if they hope to receive new loans from the IMF, the World Bank, foreign banks, or aid agencies. Many 'Third World' countries experienced structural adjustment after 1982–3; often it was imposed by dictatorships. Jamaica's experience in the 1980s illustrates this.[9] Because of historical patterns, including slavery, Jamaican women head a relatively high number of households on that island, and as a result they and their dependents bore the full brunt of adjustment policies, which included wage freezes and public service layoffs, especially in health, education, and social security programs, where women were both the main employees and the principal clients. Layoffs resulted in deteriorating health services (especially in the rural areas), in deteriorated female health, and in increases in infant malnutrition (Egeawali, 1995). Yet mainstream economics, which shapes structural adjustment programs, sees women as 'unproductive and dependent wives and mothers' unless they are paid wages. In Nigeria, structural adjustment policies ended a scheme of free, compulsory education; the result was a steep decline in grammar school enrolment after 1985, especially in girls' enrolment (Obasi, 1996).

Clearly, analyses of women's poverty arrive at different results when approached from a gender gap as opposed to a development gap perspective. For example, many 'Western' feminists believe that global assembly lines result in gendered harms to women in 'Western' countries (from which corporations are removing jobs) that are comparable to the harms experienced by women in the rapidly developing 'Third World' countries to which the work is moved. Women working in EPZs do suffer gendered harms, including sexual harassment, assault on the job, and – for many – few alternatives after a period of wage earning other than selling their bodies (Grossman, 1979). But factory work also allows young women to avoid forced marriages; it is also an alternative to domestic work or earlier entry into the sex trades. Parents may sometimes force their daughters into factory work because it is a relatively lucrative thing for them to be doing. But it may also lead parents to value their daughters more highly because of their earning potential. The complex and contradictory effects of work on women's poverty, then, need exploration within particular locales. Considered through a development gap lens, Third World women avoid absolute poverty through waged employment, and their families benefit from their wages. The effects may *seem* similar for Western and 'Third World' women, but the development gap lens reveals that their interests often diverge.

Our methodology must alert us to any false assumptions that all women have interests in common. This is especially important as we choose our theoretical framework. The development gap approach reveals that wealth is concentrated in 'Western' countries; postcolonial theorists argue that this concentration contributes to the mass poverty of women worldwide. The gender gap approach identifies variables that contribute to women's poverty in rich and poor countries alike. Both explanatory systems are needed, as are two levels of analysis – local and transnational. Moreover, an issue as complex as women's poverty requires careful, systematic comparison and a mix of methods including historical analysis, economic analysis, and ideological/discourse analysis to reveal both differences and similarities in women's experiences.

Women's studies as a field is very much a work in progress; so is scholarship on women in the disciplines. Many of the most insightful early texts draw on the original 'rebellions' of feminist methodologies. As Vickers (1994b) argues, however, there is increasing divergence between the knowledge needs of women's movements and the knowledge strategies adopted by feminists within the academic disciplines. The controversies over knowledge claims posed by standpoint theorists, critical postmodernists, and postcolonialists, and especially by previously marginalized women, oblige us to pay careful attention to the bases on which we make knowledge claims about 'women.' We are suggesting in this chapter that the most effective approach is to emulate the methods adopted by scholars such as Essed, whose work encompasses both gender dimensions and careful attention to the ways in which 'difference' is converted into systems of power. A combination of insights from action research (local) and historical and theoretical analysis (global) seems especially powerful.[10]

Conclusion

When we look back to Part I of this chapter, it becomes apparent that scholarship on women can be undertaken within a variety of empiricist, standpoint, and postmodern orientations. There is no right one, although social scientists may lean more toward empiricism, women's studies scholars toward standpoint orientations, and humanities scholars toward postmodern orientations. Mies's seven postulates to guide feminist scholarship on women, on the other hand, represent ethical values for research that interact constantly with women's movements. Although the agenda they represent was common in the 1970s and 1980s – and remains common in many places around the world where scholarship on women is conducted mainly outside the universities in NGOs (non-governmental organizations) and women's centres – it is becoming less common in Western countries, where women's studies is now largely university based. The main reason for this is the success of women's studies, and of feminist scholarship in the disciplines. This has attracted new generations of scholars with little or no experience within women's movements. Furthermore, the field of women's studies has begun to professionalize and to offer its own PhDs. These new cohorts tend to look more within the academy. Nonetheless, each new generation must ask what this research is for. In this context, Mies's postulates are important, and so is the challenge of opening women's studies up to difference on a global scale.

Notes

1 Mies engages in collaborative work with Third World scholars, most recently with Vandana Shiva. Others trained in this method include Kumari Jaywardena and Saskia Wieringa.
2 Positivism, or positive philosophy, was coined by the French founder of sociology, Auguste Comte, in the nineteenth century.
3 The concept of 'trustworthiness' in making knowledge claims involves transferability, confirmability, and dependability.
4 Two examples are Maquire, 1987, *Doing Participatory Research: A Feminist Approach*, and [Vancouver] Women's Research Centre, 1987, *The Women's Research Centre and Our Assumptions About Action Research.*
5 See, for example, Diane Sainsbury (ed.), 1994, *Gendering Welfare States*, London: Sage. There is little interaction among analysts working on common themes even within the 'Western,' 'developed' world. The network led by Sainsbury is not acknowledged in the excellent analyses by the restructuring network led by feminist economist Isa Bakker.
6 Nelson and Chowdhury (1994: 29–31), use these empirical categories:
   • *Low income* (less than US$400) includes 26 African countries, 14 Asian countries, and 1 Latin American country (Haiti).
   • *Low-middle income* (US$400–999) includes 16 African countries, 6 Asian/Middle Eastern countries, 10 Latin American/Carribean countries, 5 countries in Oceania, and 2 (state-socialist countries) in Europe.
   • *High-middle income* (US$1,000–3,499) includes 8 African countries, 10 Asian/Middle-Eastern countries, 17 Latin American countries, 1 Oceanic country, and 4 European countries.
   • *High income* (US$3,5000 and up) includes 3 African countries, 11 Asian/Middle-Eastern countries, 2 North American countries, 7 Latin American/Carribean countries, 4 Oceanic countries, and 24 European countries (including 4 postcommunist).
   This analysis doesn't reveal the pockets of gross poverty within states – for example, on reserves or in communities of indigenous peoples. Nonetheless, it usefully illustrates that the poorest countries are African and Asian and the most affluent states are mainly in Europe and North

America. The categories, however, are based on data from the early 1980s. More recent data show greater impoverishment in most countries in Asia and Africa and in the postcommunist world since the 1980s, although few countries have changed categories.

7 Chen's data are pre-1991 – that is, before the collapse of Soviet Bloc economies, which has affected the ability and opportunity for women in the former communist countries to support themselves. These industrialized nations are now systematically poorer – especially Russia, because of the near collapse of its economic and political systems. Women have suffered disproportionately from unemployment and abject poverty; and older women especially face abject poverty.

8 The concept of 'development' is controversial. It often is interpreted to mean that nations are rich because they did positive things, which other countries 'failed' to do. Central to Cold War and neoliberal ideologies is the belief that the 'development' gap will ease as poorer countries 'develop' themselves.

9 Jamaica's average income is between US$1,000 and $3,499. This is also the category within which we find Portugal, Greece, and most Latin American nations (Nelson and Chowdhury, 1994: 30).

10 For a deeper exploration of the recent literature on globalization and localization, see Arjun Appadurai, 1996, *Modernity and Large Cultural Dimensions of Globalization*, Minneapolis: University of Minnesota Press; Anthony King, ed., 1991, *Culture, Globalization and the World-System*. Binghampton: State University of New York; and B. Meyer and P. Geschiere, eds., 1999, *Globalization and Identity*, Oxford: Blackwell Publishers.

PART II

Introduction

The paradigm we outline in this book is based on a one-world approach that respects both the commonalities and the differences women experience. Methodologically, this requires that we think through differences among women – indeed among people – as they are manifested in both local and global contexts. We critically analyse differences in power and privilege because we believe such understanding is vital if we are to resist oppression and exploitation and usher in a society that is just and caring for all. In this emerging new paradigm, globalization can be perceived in two somewhat conflicting ways. We challenge the corporate-sponsored globalization initiatives that are becoming dominant in many places around the globe. This kind of globalization has far-reaching and usually negative implications for women everywhere. It creates new structures of oppression and exploitation, which are then overlaid on existing structures of power, including patriarchy, internal colonialism, neocolonialism, imperialism, racism, heterosexism, ablism, and classism. This dimension of globalization involves forces such as the exponential growth in technology, which gives tremendous speed and reach for the project. Since the collapse of the Soviet Union and the end of the Cold War, global economic structures such as the World Trade Organization (WTO) have taken on more authority; they now wield enormous power to implement corporate agendas around the world. The result is that many political leaders are allowing the powers of nation-states to be weakened; this in turn has led to the erosion of democracy and to deterioration in policies and programs in the public interest.

The weakening of nation-states has resulted in a democratic deficit. Citizens are losing control over decisions, which are made in distant centres. The privileging of corporate interests negatively affects women, many of whom depend more heavily on services provided by the state, because everywhere the gender gap assigns them more responsibility for the welfare of children, elders, and the disabled and infirm. Another consequence is increasing disparity between rich and poor people within countries, and a widening development gap between countries – especially between countries of the affluent West and the rest. Another crucial feature of globalization is that it makes it much more difficult to control environmental decay as corporations focus on their profit margins at the expense of human well-being and environmental sustainability. Finally, new information and communications technologies are homogenizing cultures and institutional structures around the world. There is a fear that the Americans will impose their model of capitalist democracy on the entire world, which will become a monoculture as a result.

But globalization has other tendencies as well. The same forces that are threatening to homogenize cultures are also causing outbreaks of ethnonationalism; many peoples are showing fierce determination to protect and foster their unique cultures. Also, information technology is fostering global movements. Networks of women's movements worldwide worked successfully to get violence against women included as part of the UN's international human rights framework. Simple and fast communication technology has fostered a growing awareness among peoples everywhere that they can and should resist the negative aspects of globalization. The protests against the WTO agenda in Seattle, Washington, in 1999, and against the Free Trade Areas of the Americas (FTAA) in Quebec City, are signs that people are increasingly recognizing the urgent need to build movements to resist the negative dimensions of globalization. Movements like these are freely using the tools of globalization, such as information technology. The globalization of discourse is important for breaking down old barriers; for example, the isolation and demonization of the Islamic world can no longer hold in a world where communication has become so simple.

The chapters in Part II of this book critically analyse the structures of power pertaining to this paradox. They also show how women around the world are developing strategies to challenge domination, exploitation, and oppression, and how they can overcome their differences to develop broad-based movements to challenge the negative dimensions of globalization.

In chapter 3, 'Women of Colour in Canada,' Vanaja Dhruvarajan delineates the experiences of women of colour with sexism, racism, ethnocentrism, and classism, based on selected studies dealing with those women's experiences and their struggles to counteract the negative impacts of government policies pertaining to them. Canada's multiculturalism policies do not address their concerns. The legacies of colonialism and imperialism are built into the structures of power and have resulted in policies and practices that are doing these women harm. She also discusses the activism engaged in by women of colour, and argues that grassroots organizing in autonomous organizations led by women of colour is the best way for them to confront their challenges.

In chapter 4, 'Working Canadian Women: Continuity despite Change,' Parvin Ghorayshi discusses the importance of paid and unpaid work for women in Canada. She shows that even though the economy has changed considerably, women of different racial and class backgrounds continue to face disparities in opportunity. The structures of patriarchy, capitalism, and racism perpetuate inequalities over time; changes in the structure of the economy are overlaid on these unequal structures and determine policies and practices. Gender, race, and class equality will not be realized until these structures of inequality are dismantled. This discussion is highly relevant in the context of globalization.

For chapter 5, 'Between Body and Culture: Beauty, Ability, and Growing Up Female,' Carla Rice interviewed women of various backgrounds in terms of race, class, and sexual orientation. She discusses how the dominant culture constructs the standards of beauty for women. These standards of beauty are normalized by media practices and socialization practices, and women are made to accept these norms to the detriment of their health and well-being. Only after women are made aware of how their decisions are influenced can conditions for resistance be created. The global communications media are popularizing Western models of beauty and romantic love.

In chapter 6, 'Men and Feminism: Relationships and Differences,' Amanda Goldrick-Jones reports on the various activities of profeminist men in North America and Britain over the past thirty years. She discusses the conundrums faced by profeminist men as they try to forge solidarity with feminists while struggling to relinquish their power and privilege. It is beneficial for all women to have profeminist men as allies, provided those men work to dismantle patriarchal structures and deconstruct patriarchal ideologies. Profeminist men can also help the cause of justice and equality by forging alliances among men across differences, including class, race, sexuality, and ability, both within countries and globally, using the tools of global communications. Only through such broad-based movements can a resistance against hegemonic structures of power be successfully mounted.

In chapter 7, 'Feminism, Reproduction, and Reproductive Technologies,' Vanaja Dhruvarajan discusses the challenges faced by feminists as they confront the misuse of old and new reproductive technologies, especially in profit-oriented liberal democracies. She also elaborates on the challenges faced by women, especially those who are marginalized all over the world, as scientists develop new reproductive and genetic technologies, usually without any moral, ethical or legal guidelines. Feminists must actively participate in the decision-making processes when new agendas to transform social life are being developed. These initiatives are taken when new frontiers are conquered in science and technology. Women must participate heavily in struggles – both local and global – to curtail corporate power and influence in determining the directions of social life.

In chapter 8, 'Thinking about Violence,' Jill Vickers argues that the subordination of women is maintained worldwide through violence and threats of violence. She maintains that for their struggles to end such violence to be successful, and for them to achieve security for themselves and their families, women must be empowered and violence against people must be addressed at the structural/material and ideological levels. If we are to mount effective struggles to resist this kind of oppression, we must make careful and systematic analyses of the conditions under which some women are especially vulnerable to violence. Globalization can produce conditions that exacerbate violence against women. But it can also facilitate the development of global networks of solidarity in women's antiviolence campaigns.

In chapter 9, 'Feminists and Nationalism,' Jill Vickers demonstrates how globalization promotes tendencies toward both nationalism and a cultural homogenization. Scholarship on women cannot ignore the power of nation-states both to maintain and to undo systems of power and privilege. Relationships between nationalist and feminist movements can be positive, especially when both movements are peaceful and democratic and women's involvement can lessen the democratic deficit. But in other contexts – especially in antimodernizing nationalisms and in nationalisms resisting the breakdown of states (as in postcommunist countries) – the relationship is generally negative. This makes the question 'Is nationalism good or bad for women?' a complex one, as well as critical to our efforts to build transnational solidarity.

Vanaja Dhruvarajan, in chapter 10, 'Religion, Spirituality, and Feminism,' argues that patriarchal religious ideologies maintain and perpetuate social inequalities. However, religion is too central to the maintenance of power and privilege for feminists to ignore. Many women, including feminists, are struggling to transform religions to make them responsive to spiritual needs of all people. If this project is successful, religion may become an important source of support in feminist struggles. By foregrounding ethical and moral issues, religion may make it easier to dismantle the hegemonic status of corporate structures.

In chapter 11, 'Feminism and Social Transformation,' Vanaja Dhruvarajan shows how a feminist paradigm that is life affirming and life enhancing, and that promotes harmony with nature, cooperation, and mutual respect among people, and that has a pervasive concern for justice and care of all people, can provide a framework for forging alliances across differences. She identifies various insights that can enhance women's – and all people's – capacity to build coalitions to promote social transformation. She recognizes the need to work in collaboration with other movements, including the ecology movement, the peace movement, the antiracism movement, the labour movement, the movement for democratic socialism, and the movements against homophobia and heterosexism, all of which share common goals. Only a broad-based movement will be able to challenge successfully the entrenched structures and ideologies of power and privilege.

CHAPTER 3

Women of Colour in Canada

Vanaja Dhruvarajan

Women of colour have been victims of racism, sexism, and classism. They share the burden of racism with men in their ethnic groups, and they share the burden of sexism along with all women living in patriarchal contexts. They also suffer because of class inequalities in society. Their struggles against racism, sexism, and classism continue in the present day.

In this chapter I first discuss the experiences of women of colour in Canada. Then, I examine how multiculturalism policies address issues pertaining to racism at various levels. I also scrutinize the impact of these policies on women of colour, as well as on people of colour in general. Finally, I discuss the role that women-of-colour activism can play in addressing issues that are of concern to marginalized people, and in influencing the women's movement in Canada.

Experiences of Women of Colour in Canada

Attitudes and Social Practices toward Women of Colour

The experiences of women of colour in Canada are different from those of women of European origin. Women of colour are not a homogeneous population. The ethnic groups to which they belong vary significantly in culture and history. Also, there are class differences within ethnic groups. Even so, they have faced the same experiences of racism in Canadian society – albeit in varying degrees – because of their historical legacy as victims of colonization and imperialism. Women of colour also share the experiences of racism with men in their ethnic groups.

People of colour are not included in Canada's self-image. Canadians perceive their country as one of white settlers, and quite often look on people of colour as strangers and outsiders. Many don't realize that people of colour have been settling in Canada for centuries and have been involved for that long in nation-building activities. For example, runaway slaves and loyalists had settled in Ontario and Nova Scotia as long as two centuries ago, and Sikhs and the Chinese have lived in British Columbia for over a century. Yet these groups are still perceived as transient. Technically, the term 'immigrant' refers to recent arrivals who lack citizenship status; in daily use, the term is synonymous with 'non-white' (Ng, 1986). It is not unusual for a non-white person, even one who has lived in the country for many years, to be asked how long he or she plans to stay in Canada (Brown, 1989). Because non-whites are considered outsiders, they are often blamed for taking jobs away from 'Canadians,' especially in times of economic downturn. These attitudes persist even though people of colour have always participated actively in nation building. Chinese labourers built the railways. Professional people have taught at universities, doctored people in hospitals, and worked in private industry. Domestic workers have done the housework for white people and cared for their children.

People of colour have long experienced restrictions when immigrating to Canada; for many decades racism was built into the laws of the land. But since the 1950s, mainly as a result of changes in the global political climate after the Second World War, these laws have changed gradually to become less and less discriminatory. It is now illegal to discriminate against anyone on the basis of race. Nevertheless, individual immigration officers, most of whom are white, are provided with discretionary powers, and, according to many testimonies, often use those powers to keep people of colour out (NFB, Video: 'Who Gets In').

Canada's standard practice is to let in immigrants on the basis of the country's labour force requirements. For example, in the late 1960s and 1970s, Canadian universities and industries were expanding, and those with professional qualifications were allowed to immigrate. At present, domestic workers, computer experts, and those with money to invest are the favoured immigrants. Many researchers have shown that people of colour are allowed to immigrate only when white immigrants with required qualifications are not available (Calliste, 1989).

In the past, women of colour confronted more problems with immigration because the immigration laws were not only racist but also sexist. For example, in the early part of the last century only able-bodied men of colour were allowed into Canada. The intent was to discourage these people from settling in Canada. The expectation was that these men would return to where they came from after the jobs for which they had been hired were completed. The gender disparity that once existed as a result of these practices has been corrected in recent years: discrimination on the basis of sex is now also illegal. But there is still a disparity in terms of 'class' of entry: men enter mainly under 'independent class,' whereas women enter under 'family class.' This has far-reaching implications for women, because those who immigrate under family class are not eligible for certain government services, such as an allowance for learning one of the official languages. The reasoning behind this particular discriminatory practice is that only those who need to be integrated into the labour market should be eligible for the language-training allowance. Women who immigrate under the family class are expected to be economically subsidized by their sponsors. In reality, most immigrant women have to take paid work to make ends meet. Those who lack knowledge of one of the official languages get trapped in low-paying, dead-end jobs such as sewing machine operator. Also, those who remain economically dependent on their sponsors become isolated from the larger society and experience profound alienation. Those who immigrate with professional qualifications acquired in the home country suffer in different ways. For example, only those who acquired their qualifications in European or North American countries are recognized as professionals in Canada. Furthermore, Canadian experience is considered necessary to qualify for a job. Arbitrary rules like these keep immigrant women out of the labour market and economically dependent on men. Training allowances for the labour market are available only for those who immigrate under the 'independent class' (Agnew, 1996).

Eurocentric attitudes have led to the development of negative stereotypes about women of colour. The prevailing stereotype of South Asian women is that they are docile, subservient, and traditional (Agnew, 1990). This image persists despite the many struggles of resistance these women have mounted in the workplace against racism, wage disparity, and poor working conditions (Aggarwal, 1987). Black women are subject to a different set of negative stereotypes. Their sexuality is maligned, and their femininity is questioned. Women of colour are also not thought of as beautiful or as sexually desirable, because in Canada, conceptions of beauty are based on white standards (Bannerji, 1993). People of colour are conceptualized as the 'other,' the 'outsider' – with the inescapable implication of 'inferior' – and this significantly influences social practices.

Social distance is most extreme between mainstream Canadians and people of colour. Prejudice and discrimination in schools, housing, and the workplace are quite widespread (Dhruvarajan, 1992; Henry and Ginsberg, 1992). Official policies and practices also reveal a racial bias. For example, domestic workers and nannies from Europe have been treated far better than those from, for example, the Caribbean (Silvera, 1983). According to a 1981 study, people of colour are least preferred as friends, co-workers, neighbours, and marital partners (Driedger and Mazoff, 1981).

Canadians often look down on the cultures of people of colour. These cultures are perceived as primitive, traditional, and backward, and as a consequence are devalued. Specifically, religion, food, dress, habits, and language are fair game for criticism, and outsiders' accents are often a source of humour. A Chinese student related how one of her professors criticized her accent yet in the same class complimented another student's French accent. Other cultures' cooking odours can be annoying if one is not used to them. The smell of burning flesh is intolerable to those who are not used to it, yet more often than not it is the smell of curry that is the subject of jokes and ridicule.

Patterns of Adaptation

Women of colour who immigrated to Canada as adults tend to isolate themselves within their own ethnic groups after they experience being treated as inferior outsiders. They often become highly defensive about their cultural practices, even to the detriment of their own welfare. And women of colour, just like white women, suffer from sexism in their families and communities (Dhruvarajan, 1992; Ralston, 1988). Some of them are victims of domestic violence. In Canadian society there are facilities such as women's shelters and counselling services for women to protect themselves from violence. Some women of colour are unable to access these services because of their lack of facility in one of the official languages. Even those who are able to do so are reluctant to expose their men to the justice system, which reflects the racist prejudices of the larger society. In addition, the very thought of further stigmatizing their cultures and ethnic groups makes them cringe. The end result is that they choose to suffer silently. Faced with the challenges of confronting racism, they tend to de-emphasize the sexism they face within their own ethnic groups (Brah, 1992). They also find it very difficult to develop trusting relationships with white people, even in the caring professions. Agnew (1990) reports that South Asian women are reluctant to go to mainstream women's shelters. Only very recently, because of the struggles of many women of colour, have linguistically appropriate, culturally sensitive services become available. The providers of these services are also women of colour, which makes trusting relationships easier to develop. There is some indication that these facilities will in fact be used by some women.

The experience of growing up in an environment suffused with racism is difficult indeed. Many personal accounts of young people of colour reveal painful memories of being excluded, stigmatized, and subjected to name calling (Yee, 1993). As they try to cope with daily life, many feel profoundly confused about where they belong and what their identity is. First-generation immigrants can cope with their alienation by maintaining links with the home country and with their own ethnic groups in this country; most people of colour of the second and subsequent generations do not find this a viable option. For them, it is important to be accepted by the mainstream society. They do not have any other 'home,' and exclusive membership in an ethnic group is too confining. When people are consistently exposed to hostile and racist experiences during their formative years, they begin to internalize racism and to devalue themselves and those to whom they are similar. The psychological problem of internalized racism is evident not only among young people who grow up in a racist environment, but also among some adults. For example, it is common for men of colour to perceive white women as more beautiful and alluring than women in their own ethnic groups. Some women of colour also are susceptible to this phenomenon. For example, some of them undergo eye surgery to make their eyes resemble those of European women.

Impact of Historical Legacy

Mainstream Canadians are rarely aware of the aftereffects of European colonialism and imperialism on the victims. They are not aware of how entire peoples can be forced to look for better opportunities elsewhere after their homelands have been devastated economically and politically. Mainstream Canadians are also not aware of how various theories of white racial and ethnic superiority gained scientific legitimacy in the eighteenth and nineteenth centuries. These theories confirmed white people's sense of their own superiority and also eroded self-confidence among the colonized, even though all these peoples had developed societies with viable cultures and structures prior to the colonial devastation (Mies and Shiva, 1993a). If there were such an awareness, it would quickly become clear that white privilege and the marginalization of people of colour are not a part of the natural order of things, but rather the result of sociohistorical processes.

In 1986 1.6 million people in Canada were racial minorities – that was 6.3 per cent of the population. By 1991 the figures were 2.6 million or 9.6 per cent. The present figures are roughly 5.7 million and 17.7 per cent (Samuels, 1992). Most of these people live in metropolitan areas, where social supports from their own ethnic groups are available.

The general tendency in Canadian society is to deny that there is prejudice and discrimination against people of colour (Henry et al., 1995). The assumption at work here is that Canada is a democracy, so the individual rights of all Canadians are enshrined in the Constitution. What is forgotten is that racism was built into state policies and practices until the 1950s. This earlier racism has become part of the common sense knowledge that routinely structures social practices in daily life, even today. In other words, racism has become systemic – part of how life is lived.

In the popular media, people of colour are either invisible or portrayed in stereotypic ways. They appear in news items only when something exotic – an arranged marriage, or Hijab, or clitoridectomy – is the topic of investigation. One rarely witnesses these people living 'normal' lives.

Canada's universities routinely marginalize people of colour through their policies and practices relating to curriculum, teaching, and administration. Curriculum decisions are made by those who administer the programs and by those who teach in those programs. Most university administrators and teachers have been white men, and most still are. The curricula they have fashioned reflect their own interests and experiences. Even where there is some student interest in a more diversified course content, this is difficult to achieve because professors tend to teach and provide mentoring services only in topics in which they are well versed. More often than not, male professors of European origin take an interest in subjects that reflect their own life experiences. Even when they do show interest in the study of people of colour, their perspectives may not reflect the interests of those they are studying. Thus, the experiences of people of colour are either left out of the curriculum, or they are constructed from an Eurocentric/androcentric perspective. Even in universities that operate under liberal-democratic ideological principles, and where a climate of academic freedom to explore knowledge prevails, people of colour continue to be marginalized. This is partly because of how universities are structured, and partly because of people who are oriented toward Eurocentric/androcentric traditions are teaching and making curriculum decisions.

The practice of using the term 'woman' in the generic sense in courses and research reports – in universities in general and in women's studies in particular – and the linked practice of labelling women of colour as 'visible minority women,' together promote the differentiation between 'we' and 'they.' The assumption is that mainstream women do not belong to a race/ethnicity. In an important sense, white women are perceived as the 'norm,' and women of colour as the deviation. Educational and research practices will not be inclusive until we start assuming that all women – all people, for that matter, including the mainstream – have the attributes of class, race/ethnicity, and gender, among others. Furthermore, the term 'visible minority' is problematic. 'Visible to whom?' one may ask. Again, the reference point is the mainstream population. When one segment of the population is placed in the centre, other segments can only be at the margins.[1]

When one devalues other cultures and considers one's own culture as superior, cultural racism results. Negative stereotypes about racial minorities have developed over time as a result of colonization and imperialism. In societies in which racism is the ruling ideology, discrimination toward racial minorities comes to be built into institutional structures. An excellent example relates to Canada's earlier immigration laws. When racist attitudes and discriminatory behaviour prevail over a period of time, they become part of the taken-for-granted realities of day-to-day life and get embedded in daily routines. Making a critical evaluation of morris dance, an English dance practice, Greenhill (in press) shows how not only cultural practices but also folklore scholarship is complicit in fostering racist ideologies and practices that reinforce unequal relations between dominant and marginalized groups.

On an analytical level, it helps to consider racism's various manifestations. But that does not mean that each type of racism is independent of the others. At any given time, one can observe one or more forms of racism. Even so, distinctions between different types of racism are helpful because different strategies must be adopted to address them. For example, educating people about cultural differences can lead to better understanding. Cultural racism can be addressed by showing how values cherished by other different peoples are equally valid and deserve equal respect and acceptance. This is the objective of multiculturalism policies.

Laws that prohibit discrimination provide a framework for determining acceptable behaviour. The historical trend in Canada has been for immigration laws to become more inclusive. However, more conscious effort is needed to address systemic racism. We have to carefully assess the impact of those routine practices of daily life that exclude marginalized people. The inclusive and exclusionary practices encountered in workplaces, media representations, and university teaching are only some good illustrations of this. Where environments are suffused with persistent racism, that racism becomes internalized. The best way to prevent the internalization of racism is by ensuring that the environments in which children are raised and in which people live are free of racism. Another way, albeit more difficult, is for individuals to find and internalize strategies for guarding themselves against racist influences.

Multiculturalism and Antiracism

Canada's postwar immigration policies reflected the country's need for a labour force that would help the country develop economically. As a result of these policies, Canada was transformed into an ethnically pluralistic nation. In the 1970s, political imperatives were such that the aspirations of non-British, non-French immigrants, who now constituted close to one-third of the Canadian population, had to be addressed. Taking direction from the recommendations of the Bilingual and Bicultural Commission, the federal government embraced the policy of multiculturalism within a bilingual framework as a response to the needs of this segment of the population. In 1988 a multiculturalism act was passed that crystallized this policy within the Canadian legal framework. Multiculturalism is an ideology which holds that racial, cultural, religious, and linguistic diversity is an integral, beneficial, and necessary part of Canadian society and identity. It operates through various social institutions and levels of government, including the federal government (Henry et al., 1995: 328). This policy was a clear departure from the earlier policy of Anglo-conformity, under which British culture was considered Canada's norm and was promoted as such. The new policy sent a clear signal to all Canadians that they lived in a pluralistic society in which all citizens had the right to practise their culture as long as doing so did not interfere with the similar rights of others or with the functioning of public institutions.

Multiculturalism is considered to be the best policy in a society such as Canada. The assumption is that this policy is adequate to deal with issues of diversity and difference. Canadians are proud of being different from other countries such as the United States, and of recognizing the diversity of their fellow citizens.

This policy has had critics as well as supporters. In the next section I review the positions taken by different segments of the Canadian population and provide explanations for those positions. This review is not intended to be exhaustive, but I hope it will indicate the kinds of debates now going on in Canada with regard to multiculturalism. For more details, the references will be useful.

Multiculturalism and the 'Mainline' Ethnic Groups

Multiculturalism was received with great enthusiasm by 'mainline' ethnic groups – that is, by non-British, non-French ethnic groups of European origin who, even though they were politically and economically integrated, were historically denied the right to retain their cultural identity under the official policy of Anglo-conformity. This policy has resulted in the proliferation of heritage language programs and has rejuvenated ethnic cultural associations among these ethnic groups. Federal financial assistance has helped many of these ethnic groups revive their language, music, art, and culture in general. Some researchers contend that this policy was implemented to garner political support from this segment of the population (Buchignani, 1983).

Multiculturalism and Liberal Individualism

Some of the strongest criticisms of multiculturalism come from those who maintain a liberal individualistic stance. The main argument along these lines is that multiculturalism is divisive, because it encourages ethnic loyalties instead of promoting national loyalty. In other words, harmony would be better promoted among Canadians by encouraging assimilation – that is, by encouraging ethnic groups to adopt Canada's dominant cultural mores, be they Anglo or French (Bisoondath, 1991). These liberal individualists disapprove of using public funds to promote ethnic languages, religions, and cultures. They are also impatient with efforts to place different ethnic cultural beliefs and social practices on the same footing as those of the dominant groups. An example of these debates is the one over whether army officers who are Sikhs should be permitted to wear a turban as part of their uniform. Another relates to whether Christian prayers should be permitted in schools, and whether Christmas concerts should be required to be inclusive of all religions. In all these situations, some argue that Canadian (read *Anglo-Saxon Christian*) identity is being eroded. The implication seems to be that other cultural practices should remain private and that Anglo-Saxon Christian practices should maintain their privileged status.

The greatest weakness of this position is that it considers people as atomistic individuals without history, culture, or a sense of community. Furthermore, relinquishing one's culture, history, and identity is no guarantee that one will be accepted by the dominant groups. In other words, the proponents of this position do not take into account the dangers of marginalization inherent in this strategy of assimilation. Canada's aboriginal peoples were over centuries forced to abandon their cultures and communities, but this did nothing to integrate them with the mainstream. In fact, the sole result was marginalization, with all the pain this entailed.

Multiculturalism and Antiracism

Another set of criticisms comes from those who advocate antiracism policies, which focus on issues of justice and equality. Focusing on the topic of education, Dei discusses some of his personal experiences, to which many of us can relate, to highlight the need for antiracism policies and practices (1996: 196). He refers to how non-white people are made to feel inadequate because of their accents. He also points to the non-inclusive curricula in universities, which leave the impression that non-white people have not contributed to the development of knowledge. He also criticizes educational practices that make non-white students feel they are outsiders. 'Anti-racism explicitly names the issues of race and social difference as issues of power and equity, rather than as matters of cultural and ethnic variety' (Dei, 1996: 25). These inequalities exist because people who have power and privilege are deeply reluctant to share these with people who have been deprived of them. Even more importantly, some people possess power and privilege precisely *because* others have been deprived of them. Antiracism projects go beyond education to embrace political activism. They endeavour, for all people, to establish the legitimacy of claims to equality. Thus, they question the legitimacy of practices that privilege some groups over others. Educating people about cultural diversity is necessary, but it is not sufficient to address issues of privilege and power.

Multiculturalism policies do not directly address issues of privilege, power, and exploitation; they focus instead on establishing cultural pluralism and promoting cross-cultural understanding. Proponents of antiracism policies are firmly convinced that issues of justice and equality cannot be addressed directly under the policy rubric that has been developed to establish cultural pluralism. People can become enlightened about the cultural backgrounds of others; this does not necessarily motivate people with power and privilege to relinquish either.

Race and Class

Among those who argue for antiracism policies, some privilege class issues over cultural ones. These critics point out that for most immigrants, access to jobs, childcare, housing, and education is more important than preserving language and culture. As Wallerstein (Balibar and Wallerstein, 1988) argues, in the European capitalist quest to accumulate wealth, people of colour have always been exploited. The processes of colonialism and neocolonialism continue to exploit people of colour to the benefit of those who control the capitalist modes of production. Transnational corporations (TNCs) are now consolidating their power and building structures that will provide them with unlimited access to markets all around the globe. In the context of this venture, no attention is being paid to the impact of TNCs on the lives of local people. In the name of development financing, the World Bank and the International Monetary Fund are increasing the debt burdens of Third World economies. For most Third World countries, the hard-won independence from colonial domination has meant submission to a different kind of domination – namely, economic domination. The world's nation-states are losing control over their own economies, under the new world order that is being created by agreements such as the North American Free Trade Agreement (NAFTA), the Free Trade Areas of the Americas (FTAA), the General Agreement on Tariffs and Trade (GATT), and the like. More recently, attempts have been made to provide a level playing field for capital through the Multilateral Agreement on Investment (MAI). Just as these global economic initiatives are taking effect, the disparities between rich and poor countries are increasing, and so are the disparities between rich and poor people within countries.

People of colour are directly affected by these processes, since most of them come from Third World countries. As these countries become impoverished, people try to immigrate in search of better opportunities, only to find that 'the Third World' is being replicated in the heart of 'the First World.' It is no wonder that for these people, economic considerations far outweigh any other considerations. Many social scientists who have studied the opportunity structures available to people of colour have found that multiculturalism policies do not actually improve the situation of these people (Gupta, 1996; Calliste, 1992; Henry et al., 1995). Kallen (1989) contends that such policies promote folk festivals and ethnic performing arts but are reluctant to support minority demands for collective rights or socioeconomic enhancement. These policies are more about containing and neutralizing dissent; hardly do they address social and economic inequalities.

Race, Class, and Culture

Not all of those who argue for antiracism policies and who criticize multiculturalism policies consider culture, language, and identity less important. Some base their position on the premise that people of colour are not only exploited economically but also stigmatized culturally – indeed, they are often devalued as peoples on the basis of their biological characteristics. Dominant groups have long endeavoured to maintain their cultural hegemony as a means of legitimizing their portion of privilege and power. It follows that antiracism initiatives must question the legitimacy of the hegemonic status of dominant cultures. Social practices that construct people of colour as 'other' and therefore as not eligible for certain rights and privileges are legitimized precisely because of the hegemonic status accorded to the cultures of dominant groups. As Balibar (Balibar and Wallerstein 1988) points out, in the construction of a nation those who have hegemonic status define the mythical citizen. Even though people of colour have long contributed significantly to the building of Canada and have been in this country for generations, more often than not they are not included in this national imagery. This has had far-reaching consequences, since only those who are defined as belonging to a nation are seen as eligible to share privileges and power. Thus, issues of justice and equality are not simply economic; it is just as important to end cultural stigmatization. The racialization of peoples and the racialization of their cultures are integrally linked, so both issues must be addressed.

Gender, Race, Class, and Culture

Multicultural rights are enshrined in the Canadian Charter of Rights and Freedoms. This is welcomed by some ethnic groups, especially those of European origin; however, people of colour, and especially women of colour, are wary of the implications. Their concern is that in some circumstances multicultural rights could override other important rights, including gender equality rights. Patriarchal beliefs and practices are prevalent in many ethnic groups, and if these were given free rein, many women would be found to relinquish their gender equality rights in the name of ethnic culture. If the Charter were to uphold marriages without consent, restrictions on freedom of movement, or the imposition of certain dress codes, women could find it much harder to resist such practices. Also, there is a tendency to consider ethnic cultures as monolithic and static. But no culture is monolithic or static. Patriarchal beliefs and practices prevail in some ethnic groups, but within those same groups there is also resistance to these beliefs and practices. But because of the social distance between dominant and marginalized ethnic groups, the tendency to essentialize one version of an ethnic culture can result in cultural relativism in its most damaging form. This was evident in the debate over fetal sex determination tests. Even though there was resistance within South Asian ethnic groups against these tests, the ethnic culture was essentialized as promoting female foeticide (Dhruvarajan, 1996; Thobani, in Mukherjee, 1993b). Similar debates have arisen over the custom of Hijab and the practice of genital mutilation. In each case the issues are complex. Attempts to homogenize opinions within ethnic cultures and to trivialize the resistance strategies within ethnic groups can lead to the essentialization of ethnic cultures. Debates over gender justice can be fruitful only when there is genuine respect toward all ethnic groups.

Table 3.1: The faces of racism

	What: Core slogan	Why: Degree of intent	How: Style of expression	Where: Magnitude of scope	When: Locus of expression
Red-necked	'X get out!'	Conscious	Personal and explicit	Personal	Interpersonal
Polite	'Sorry, the job is taken.'	Moderate	Discreet and subtle	Personal	Interpersonal
Subliminal	'I'm not a racist, but ...'	Ambivalent	Oblique	Cultural	Value conflicts
Institutional	'X need not apply.'	Deliberate	Blatant	Institutional	Rewards and entitlements
Systemic	'We treat everyone the same here.'	Unintentional	Impersonal	Societal	Rules and procedure

Source: A. Fleras and J.L. Elliot, *Unequal Relations*, Scarborough: Prentice Hall Canada, 1995: 84

And this can only happen when the issue of racialization of ethnic cultures is addressed.

Institutionalization of Racism

Implementing multicultural policies without addressing racism can lead to the institutionalization of inequality between ethnic cultures. Peter Li (1994), in his study of funding policies for the arts in Canadian society under multiculturalism, shows how the art and music of European ethnic groups are judged as real art, whereas the art and music of non-European ethnic groups are judged as folk art. In addition, 'real' art is promoted on the basis of its creativity and originality, whereas 'folk' art is promoted for its display, drama, and pageantry. All of this has led to two-tier funding: 'real' art is funded by the Canada Council, whereas folk art is under direct funding of the Canadian government through multicultural programs. Until underlying biases are addressed directly, it will be difficult to show that every ethnic group, dominant or not, has both folk and 'real' art traditions that need to be promoted. Similar trends are documented on a global level: even science suffers from a differentiation between 'real science' and 'ethnic science.' For example, in the medical field only Western medical practices are accepted as 'scientific'; all others, such as acupuncture, homeopathy, and *ayurveda*, are considered forms of quackery.

So it is important to question the hegemonic status of dominant cultures in the context of antiracism policies and practices. Class issues and cultural issues are integrally related. On the global level, the unquestioned acceptance and valorization of the Western model of development has largely foreclosed the envisioning of any other models (Mies and Shiva, 1993a). The unexamined assumption that modernization means progress has helped perpetuate the process of devaluing other cultures and other ways of life. Third World countries and peoples – that is, those who were under colonial domination in earlier centuries – are pictured as underdeveloped, primitive, traditional, conservative, and so on. The implicit argument is that all of them need to be modernized, and that modernization means progress. Under a mindset like this, people don't even try to assess the impact of modernization on different segments of population in different parts of the world. If alternative models of life and living are ever to be considered equally valid, we must end the hegemonic status of the Western culture. Whether we are talking about art or the economy or science and technology, there is always a cultural context to the discussion.

Systemic Racism

Systemic racism refers to the processes whereby racial and ethnic inequalities are routinely reproduced in daily life in particular social contexts.

Because cultural assumptions mediate social relations, the implications of systemic racism are enormous. Multicultural policies that do not address systemic racism do nothing to reduce the social distance between dominant and marginalized groups, because they do not challenge the assumptions that have developed over time about marginalized groups. Many stereotypes prevail about women of colour. Black women are labelled as strident and aggressive, South Asian and Chinese women are thought of as passive and docile, and so on. It is well established that women in many of these ethnic groups have to mount resistance on different fronts as they confront racism, sexism, heterosexism, ableism, and so on. When multiculturalism policies don't take these struggles into account, they don't just fail to deconstruct stereotypes – they actually reinforce them. Only when antiracism strategies are implemented to address systemic racism will these issues be confronted and resolved.

It is well established that how daily routines are carried out in workplaces and informal networks determines to a large extent who has access to information about job openings, opportunities for promotion, job enrichment experiences, and so on. Decision makers rely on their personal acquaintances to promote people within their spheres of influence. So it should come as no surprise that familiarity with the players is central to the processes of job promotion. Who has coffee with whom? Who discusses their research with whom? These and similar questions are the important ones. Systemic racism persists because of how informal networks operate. More often than not, members of marginalized groups lack access to the informal networks that would point them toward new opportunities. It is a formidable task to infiltrate old boys' networks – or old girls' networks for that matter. It is in this context that the process of deconstructing cultural assumptions regarding people of different backgrounds assumes importance. Respecting and accepting differences is crucial. Structures provide a framework, and they also provide legitimacy, but it is the informal processes that bring about meaningful change in opportunity structures.

Equality Now, the report of the Special Committee on Visible Minorities in Canada, (1984), criticized multiculturalism policy for not addressing discrimination and for focusing exclusively on attitudinal change. This document helped draw attention to individual experiences of discrimination. Human rights commissions, however bogged down they are by bureaucratic procedures, have been helpful in getting compensation to at least some of the victims of discrimination. But these efforts address issues on an individual level and leave the systemic racism intact (Bolaria and Li, 1988). As a whole, *Equality Now* focused on means of empowering visible minorities, not on convincing the dominant majority to share its privileges, which Canada has to offer fairly to everyone. As Moodley (1984) rightly argues, empowering visible minorities will not accomplish much if the majority are not convinced of the legitimacy of their claims.

Multiculturalism Evaluated

The rejection of multiculturalism policies by people of colour does not imply that these people favour liberal individualism. In a racist society, liberal individualistic strategies of assimilation are counterproductive, since they involve marginalized individuals denying their culture, community, and personal identity. Such a strategy may facilitate individual achievement, but it does not improve the status of the individual's ethnic or cultural group. Instead, it disconnects individuals from their culture and community, and thus renders them vulnerable to marginalization. In addition, these people are co-opted into the dominant groups/cultures and tend to suffer from internalized racism. In these circumstances, the project to usher in a just and equal society for all is put on hold, and status quo in power relations is maintained.

The implication is that multiculturalism policies by themselves cannot achieve equality and justice; for this, they must be implemented within an antiracism policy framework. The language, religion, and culture of non-white people in general can be racialized in a racist societal context; this can negatively affect both dominant and marginalized groups.

The intent of multiculturalism policy is to integrate non-British and non-French ethnic groups into the Canadian cultural mosaic. The ethnic groups of European origin have understandably welcomed these initiatives, since they have already achieved economic and political integration and their main concern is now cultural survival. But for ethnic groups of non-European origin, the struggle is against economic, political, and cultural marginality, which they suffer because of racism, colonialism, and imperialism. This means that for them, antiracism strategies must take precedence over multicultural initiatives. Antiracism initiatives must be mounted on personal, interpersonal, institutional, and systemic levels. The objective is to go beyond education, and beyond raising awareness about diversity and difference among ethnic groups, to confront issues of power and privilege. It is not enough to exhort people to be civil to one another. They have to be convinced – especially particularly those in positions of control – to share power and privilege. Only when we succeed in these endeavours will Canada become a true cultural mosaic and will justice and equality prevail for all people.

Women of Colour and Feminism

The critique of patriarchy and the delineation of male privilege and female subordination were the sole topics of inquiry among second-wave feminists. The general conviction at that time was that although women are not a homogeneous group, experience with patriarchy is common to all women. So that aspect of women's lives could be analysed separately.

These efforts were empowering to many women, since they brought women's perspectives to the fore. But as women from marginalized groups examined their life experiences, they became convinced that besides patriarchy, other systems of oppression existed such as race, class, and sexuality, which were just as important for explaining their life experiences. Many women-of-colour scholars have shown how all of these dimensions of social status are fused together, and how it is impossible to explain and understand women's life experiences without analysing how these various dimensions of social status intersect with one another. For example, Bannerji, in discussing the harassment suffered by a lower-class black woman, showed how the harassment she suffered was due to her race, class, nationality, *and* gender (Bannerji, 1993). In a similar fashion, Joseph (in Hale, 1992: 418) argued that to understand the predicament of women of colour, all of us have to study history from the point of view of marginalized peoples. In one of my studies of women of colour, several respondents pointed out that one of the goals of the feminist movement – to obtain equal pay for work of equal value – is also important for women of colour. But this becomes relevant only when one is able to get a job (Dhruvarajan, 1994).

As a result of persistent efforts by women of colour, thinking about gender had entered a new stage by the mid-1980s. There was a growing awareness of the differences in experiences among women and among men. A number of early studies discussed these differences in detail, and these were catalogued to create a 'patchwork quilt.' But it was soon realized that this approach did not go far enough for us to understand how the various dimensions of social status intersect to produce the kinds of results that women of colour experience. That is when women-of-colour scholars conducted studies to show how these dimensions are fused together.

More recently, women-of-colour scholars have been showing how various systems of oppression interlock to produce hierarchical relationships among women and men. This kind of analysis is useful because people tend to take their privileges for granted and to dwell on their disadvantages. More importantly, we may not even aware that we are part of the problem, not a solution to it. As McIntosh (1995: 77) writes, 'As a white person, I realized I had been taught about racism as something which puts others at a disadvantage, but had been taught not to see one of its corollary aspects, white privilege, which puts me at an advantage.' Sherene Razack (1998: 14) elaborates on these ideas:

> An interlocking analysis reminds us of the ease with which we slip into positions of subordination (for example, the sexually vulnerable woman, the woman with sole responsibility for child care, or the woman without access to managerial positions) without seeing how this very subordinate location simultaneously reflects and upholds race and class privilege. In focusing on our subordination and not on our privilege, and in failing to see the connections between them, we perform what Mary Louise Fellows and I call 'the race to innocence,' a belief that we are uninvolved in subordinating others. More to the point, we fail to realize that we cannot undo our own marginality without simultaneously undoing all the systems of oppression.

Thus, hierarchical relationships exist not just on the basis of gender but also on the basis of race, ethnicity, class, and nation, to name a few. Patricia Hill Collins suggests that we start thinking of race, class, and gender as a socially structured matrix of domination (1990). Such analysis will help us understand how women are produced symbiotically and hierarchically.

In academia, women-of-colour scholars through their research and teaching are developing and promoting women-of-colour perspectives and are arguing for the inclusion of women-of-colour content in courses. These efforts are especially evident among those working in women's studies, and have led to some rethinking in many women's studies programs across Canada. Women's studies programs as academic arms of the women's movement have been dominated by white, middle-class women since their inception in the 1970s and reflect the concerns of those women. Some programs and departments are including women-of-colour issues and perspectives in some of their courses. But more often than not, these topics appear in the last chapter of the textbook being used, and are covered in the last week of the course and are not integrated into the course as a whole. This strategy of 'adding difference and stirring' probably will continue until women of colour are able to participate effectively in curriculum development, administration, and teaching in women's studies programs. At the present time these functions are generally in the hands of white, middle-class women. Nevertheless, all of these efforts are leading to at least some rethinking of feminist theories and to some reorganizing of women's studies programs.

The persistent calls by many women of colour for their perspectives to be included are influencing feminist policies and practices. Women-of-colour activism in Canada has done much to change the structure and functioning of organizations such as the Women's Educational Press of Toronto (commonly referred to as the Women's Press) and the National Action Committee on the Status of Women (NAC). The politics involved in these processes mirrors the politics of the Canadian women's movement as a whole.

Until the 1980s women of colour had at best token representation on the collective of the Women's Press. In the 1980s women of colour made their presence felt at the press and insisted that their voices be heard and their perspectives included in its policies and practices. They resisted the usual practice whereby white feminists were in charge and allowed others to participate on their terms. As a result of this resistance, the press has been restructured and its policies have been rewritten (Gabriel and Scott, 1997). The books now being published by the press address issues of concern to women of colour and other marginalized women. The content of the books the press publishes has changed dramatically in the past decade. Taking just one example, in 1972 the Women's Press published *Women Unite*, in 1982 *Still Ain't Satisfied*, and in 1993 *And Still We Rise*. Clearly, the politics of the press have changed. Women of colour are now closely involved in making policies for the press and in implementing them. But these changes have come at some cost. Many white feminists have left the collective, having chosen not to work in the new climate. Similar processes can be observed within the NAC.

The NAC, an umbrella group for women's organizations in Canada, was formed in 1972 with a mandate to lobby the government to implement the recommendations of the Royal Commission on the Status of Women. It maintained a multiparty stance, worked within the framework provided by the government, and functioned with government funds. But since the 1980s a radical grassroots has been grafted onto the original alliance (Vickers et al., 1993). Declines in government funding, especially in the 1990s, have driven the organization to seek private donations. There is now more grassroots participation from diverse organizations. The NAC has begun to embrace diversity and has taken strong positions in political debates on behalf of all women, including those from marginalized groups. For example, it came out strongly against the Charlottetown Accord in 1992, mainly because the Accord would have jeopardized the interests of aboriginal women and women of colour. It also took a position against the federal panel on family violence when the panel refused to include a woman of colour on the panel and to address the concerns of women of colour, aboriginal women, and women with disabilities. It is evident from all this that the NAC has moved beyond liberal, 'politically correct' feminism. It has evolved from mainly a lobby group into a viable political force, and now sees itself as part of the women's movement (Vickers et al., 1993). But these changes in structure, composition, and process have resulted in the loss of traditional allies such as some white, middle-class women and elite women. One white, middle-class woman told Gottlieb (1993: 381) why she, and by extension many other white women, had left the NAC: 'You know, I just don't know how to relate to the women's movement any more. For a long time there I felt that it was all about lesbians. And now I feel like it's all about women of colour, and I think that's probably a good thing. But you know, I just don't know what it has to do with me.'

The relationship between the NAC and government funding bodies has become distant and formal. The politics of inclusion is perceived by many as radical and anti-government, and this has led to a significant backlash from both inside and outside the government. The media have become overtly hostile to the NAC, mainly because for the most part they cannot accept the leadership and active involvement of women of colour. In becoming a truly inclusive organization, the NAC has become a truly political organization. Only time will tell how effective it will be in influencing the direction of social life. In an important sense that effectiveness will depend greatly on how many women's organizations in Canada show a willingness to support the 'new' NAC and participate in its projects.

Besides trying to influence the mainstream women's organizations, women of colour have organized themselves autonomously and are lobbying the public and the government on their own behalf (Black, 1988; Gupta, 1986). These organizations provide various services to women – for example, they hold English or French language classes, offer workshops on preparing résumés and job applications, and provide meeting places. These associations have also been instrumental in making culturally sensitive and linguistically appropriate counselling services available to women of colour. Furthermore, these organizations are doing much to help women of colour empower themselves.

A Filipino woman (in Agnew 1996: 150) explained why women of colour need their own organizations: 'We decided to take common action, educate ourselves about what the issues were and how to do things together. As a group we also wanted to create a support system in our struggle against racism and sexism in immigration, housing, health, social services, and the justice system.'

Many women of colour, especially those of the middle class, are also working to raise general awareness of their cultural values and life-styles. To this end, they are trying to influence the curricula in schools and the content of visual and print media. They are holding confer-ences and colloquia on various issues of concern for people of colour. They are lobbying different levels of governments on various issues, including immigration, education, and employment opportunities.

They are also lobbying hard for women-of-colour service providers to be employed in mainstream women's shelters. These services, where they exist, are very valuable to women of colour, many of whom are not fluent in one of the official languages, and many of whom do not feel comfortable confiding in service providers from the mainstream population because of past experiences of racism and classism. The practice of counselling victims of domestic abuse in mainstream women's shelters does not work for women of colour. In an unfriendly and often hostile society, families are often sites of refuge for women of colour, and ethnic groups their support systems. It follows that leaving one's family and going against one's cultural norms are not viable options for many women of colour. In cases of abuse, these women would rather try to work it out than leave the relationship, which is what most victims of abuse in the mainstream culture are counselled to do. This is why family counselling programs, aimed especially at abusive men, are considered the best strategy. Women of colour tend to privilege racism and classism rather than sexism, but this does not mean they are unaware of sexism within their families and communities. It only means that the strategies they adopt to ad-dress sexism are complicated by the racism and classism they encoun-ter in the broader society.

The shelter movement, like all other aspects of the women's move-ment, is dominated by white, middle-class women. It has been a long struggle for women of colour to make the case that they require ser-vices designed specifically for them. Those who operate shelters for mainstream women are beginning to understand that until they provide linguistically and culturally sensitive services, women of colour will not make use of them. As a result of persistent lobbying by women-of-colour community organizations, these services are being made available in many shelters. But we still have some distance to cover before these services are integrated into the mainstream shelters. The services currently provided are add-ons to existing services. Careful analysis of policies and practices to address the needs of all women is yet to be done (Kohli, 1993).

Conclusion

As a consequence of women-of-colour activism, feminist theory is being revised and a new canon is being developed. The struggles of many women of colour have resulted in race as an issue being brought into feminist discourse. This activism has also resulted in the recasting of feminist policies and practices, and in changes in the politics of the women's movement in Canada. For example, the NAC is now viewed as a political organization rather than just a lobby group. The Women's Press has become truly inclusive of all women. The shelter movement is becoming more receptive to the needs of marginalized women. The curricula in educational institutions, especially in women's studies programs, are gradually becoming inclusive. In almost every city in Canada there is a women-of-colour organization. In the biggest cities there are multiple ones. Human rights legislation and multiculturalism policies have made funds available to help women of colour address their issues of concern.

We have a long way to go before women of colour can feel that they are accepted as legitimate members of Canadian society, with all the rights and duties that entails. At the same time, it is important to realize that a significant start has been made to this project. Women of colour are insisting that their voices be heard and that their perspectives be integrated in the policies and practices of organizations representing the women's movement in Canada. They are asserting their right to name and define issues that concern them specifically. Whether the movement will achieve the goal of ushering in a society that is just and caring for all will depend on how unified the women's movement succeeds in becoming. As Carty writes (1993: 16): 'It is not our identities or location that create change but our vision of the future. The question we must ask is do we have a vision for the future which can bring all women together in a common politics – the politics of inclusion – fighting for a common cause, for freedom for *all* women regardless of race, colour, class or sexual orientation?'

The issues that women of colour face are complex, and the problems are formidable. So the struggle to address those issues and overcome those problems must continue.

Note

1 It is true that the terms 'women of colour' and 'people of colour' seem to assume that white is not a colour. The strategy being adopted by scholars in the area is to use the terms that are chosen by the groups themselves. The term 'visible minority' is a label created by the federal government. Other terms, such as racial minorities, people of non-European origin, Third World people, non-white people, and so on are used interchangeably with people of colour. The intent generally is to indicate commonality of experiences. When I refer to the experiences of particular groups, I use terms such as Indo-Canadian, South Asian, Black, and Chinese-Canadian. The strategy I adopt is to refer to particular ethnic groups by their name while they are being studied, such as Chinese-Canadian, Indo-Canadian, and use people of colour when referring to them together. I also use non-white, racial minorities, and people of non-European origin interchangeably with people of colour.

CHAPTER 4

Working Canadian Women: Continuity despite Change

Parvin Ghorayshi

More than ever before, problems of work are at the forefront of both public and academic debates. The twentieth century experienced a major transformation in the workplace: the nature of work evolved gradually, but the character of the labour force changed drastically. Many factors, including technology, the changing structure of the family, the diversity of workers and their experiences, and above all the growing participation of women in the paid labour force, have generated heated discussions. Over the past century there have been profound changes in how and where Canadian women work and for whom they work. These changes must be viewed in the context of the transformation of the Canadian economy.

The early 1900s was a time of rapid industrialization and capitalist development in Canada. Increasingly, labour shifted away from agriculture and domestic service toward manufacturing. For example, at the beginning of the twentieth century around 35 per cent of the Canadian labour force was engaged in farming. By 1961 this proportion had fallen to 13 per cent; by 1991, to 5 per cent. Over the same period, manufacturing itself gradually changed from predominantly skilled craft and artisan work to unskilled and semiskilled factory work. The postwar era saw a shift away from the manufacturing sector toward the service sector. By the 1960s the Canadian world of work had been largely transformed, and it is still changing. In 1971, 23 per cent of Canadian workers were employed in manufacturing; in 1991, 15 per cent. Over the same period, more and more people were employed in the service sector (www.statcan.ca). At present, the overwhelming majority of Canadians work in the service sector.

Integral to all of these societal changes has been technological transformation – specifically, computer technology. The Information Revolution is changing the character of work just as factories did two centuries ago. This is true in Canada and everywhere else. With the help of this new technology we see the increasing globalization of the capitalist economy. Both capital and labour are facing new challenges, and national governments can no longer control all of the economic activities conducted within their borders. In the new century, the world economy is becoming more interconnected.

The global economy is restructuring itself. In Canada this has especially affected the manufacturing sector and has reduced the number of so-called blue-collar jobs. In the 1980s the service sector – the site of white-collar jobs – seemed immune from restructuring. But since the 1990s the service sector, like the manufacturing sector, has been restructuring itself, with the goal of reducing labour costs and keeping Canada's competitive edge in the global market.

Opinions differ about what is changing and how much (Wood, 1989); that being said, social scientists agree that changes *are* happening. Capital is becoming increasingly internationalized, and production is increasingly oriented toward international markets (Taylor, 1991). Both private and public employers are trying to reduce labour costs and achieve greater flexibility (Standing, 1989; Nash, 1983). Some look at these trends and contend that fewer and fewer of the world's workers will have 'good' jobs (i.e., jobs that guarantee life-time employment and that offer adequate pay and pensions). Employers are gaining the flexibility they need to remain competitive by offering only part-time, contract, and temporary work. However, research shows that restructuring can lead to the creation and retention of good jobs. In some situations restructuring meant that jobs have become more complex; also, technology can lead to skill development and improve working conditions. So the prognosis for the world's workforce is neither all bad nor all good; much depends on the specific industry being discussed, on where the industry is located, and on the characteristics of the workers involved – their race/ethnicity, class, gender, and so on (Higginbotham, 1992). Thus, the answer to the question, 'What does this new world of work mean for women?' depends on where women are located on the job market ladder, and on which theoretical perspective we adopt to explain women's experience of work.

Technology, restructuring, and the labour movement are all key issues in the study of women and work, but a comprehensive analysis of these is beyond the scope of this chapter.[1] My goal in this chapter is to provide a general, introductory profile of women's work in Canada and to discuss some of the basic issues relating to Canadian women's working lives. I focus on the present-day work of women, and define work as including both paid and unpaid activities. I present three different views on how the labour market operates, and I show how some academic analyses are biased and sex-blind. I use a feminist perspective to discuss women's work in Canada. Later, I analyse Canadian women's paid and unpaid work. I consider the type of work women do, how much they earn, and their unequal position in the labour market. After this, I look at the divisions and inequalities among women themselves. In this chapter I provide strong evidence that there is a hierarchy in the Canadian labour market that is deeply influenced by sexism and racism. Within each category of work, men are at the top and aboriginal women and women of colour[2] are at the bottom. Of course, men are also a diverse category,[3] but in this paper, I concentrate on the differences among women.

In section 1, I outline three schools of thought regarding inequality – especially gender inequality – in the world of work. This will provide the reader with sufficient background to understand the real world of work in general, and women's work in particular.

Making Sense: Three Different Points of View

Considerable changes in both the world of work and the academic analysis of the nature of work have occurred, and this increasingly complex field of study has developed an impressive body of knowledge (Ghorayshi, 1990a). Social scientists have raised key questions about the structure and processes of work in our society: What is work? How is it divided up, organized, and rewarded, and why? Why there are unequal pay and skill levels, and why do some people have better jobs than others? Could it be different? This discussion will help the reader understand the common views held about inequalities in the world of work.

Human Capital

From this perspective, the allocation of jobs generally results in a close match between the demands of the work and the skills and abilities of the person in the job. The result at the societal level is a more efficient and productive economy. Those jobs requiring the most effort, training, and skill usually receive the greatest rewards. This model assumes that all employees with the necessary qualifications have equal access to job openings. When it comes to hiring decisions, employers make only rational decisions, which they base on their assessment of an individual's qualifications. Followers of this outlook emphasize the supply side of the labour market and overlook the impact of social and behavioural factors on that market. Substantial differences in pay, benefits, job security, and occupational status are attributed mainly to differences in the characteristics of the workers themselves. People are assumed to make rational choices about investing in their own development, for example, by improving their education and upgrading their skills, and by reinvesting when the demand for skills changes.

According to this perspective, women and minorities are paid less because they have invested less in their own development and because they are less productive. Women are segregated into women's jobs because they have only developed women's skills and have failed to acquire more appropriate skills. Market forces and rational choice are all-powerful. Women and men have equal information, as well as equal power to make choices for themselves (e.g., to weigh leisure against economic gain). The household is understood as a unit of consumption rather than as a place of work. This perspective ignores power differences between women and men and between potential workers and employers (Armstrong and Armstrong, 1990; Krahn and Lowe, 1998).

Segmented Labour Theory

This model, which challenges the human capital view of work, is based on the premise that there is not a single, open labour market operating in our society. Instead, better and worse jobs tend to be found in different settings and are usually obtained in different ways. There are primary labour markets with better jobs, and secondary labour markets with worse jobs. The better jobs are usually unionized and full-time and are characterized by high wages, good working conditions, and opportunities for advancement. Jobs in the secondary labour market are characterized by weak unions, poor wages, insecure employment, poor working conditions, minimal advancement, and arbitrary management practices. Immigrants and minorities tend to be concentrated in the secondary labour markets, where their chances of rising into the primary labour market are poor. Strong structural barriers block many qualified individuals from the better-paying jobs. Many well-trained, well-educated people do not have well-paying jobs. Researchers who take this perspective do not focus on women; usually, their main concern is to show that the links between education, occupation, and income are not nearly as cut and dried as the human capital model suggests (Apostle et al., 1985).

The Feminist Outlook

Feminists have challenged the sex-blind analysis of work, arguing that gender is an important factor in how both labour markets and trade unions are organized, and how their politics play out (Cavendish, 1982; Briskin and Yanz, 1983; Cohen, 1982). They have shown that traditional theories of work have at best been sex-blind (Ganage, 1986; Armstrong and Armstrong, 1990). They have also criticized the literature for presenting women's paid work as less important than that of men for the survival of households. The sexual division of labour, like assumed sex differences in skills, capacities, and attitudes, has been accepted rather than questioned. The segregation of women into a limited range of low-level paid jobs, and women's responsibility for domestic chores, have long been justified on the basis of women's physical size or shape, their 'natural' skills and capacities, their maternal instincts or emotional makeup, and their weakness or strength in bearing children.

Feminists question any explanation that attributes women's work primarily to biologically determined factors. They use the term 'gender' when discussing the socially constructed differences between women and men and when drawing attention to the non-biological origins of the position of women. They have established that for the most part, these differences are socially structured rather than biologically determined at birth. They reject biological determinism, arguing that social conditions can be altered in order to change women's work. The movement of women into virtually every occupation is making it increasingly difficult to argue that women are biologically incapable of doing particular types of paid work. Furthermore, feminists of colour stress the importance of race/ethnicity for understanding the diversity among women and the complexity of women's working lives. Though the concept of gender certainly helps us understand women's place in the labour force, we must also realize there is no common experience of gender oppression among women.

Feminist scholars have brought to our attention the importance of women's work inside the home, and the interplay between paid work and family life (Fox, 1980; Ganage, 1986). Feminists rightly point out that theories of work must consider all types of labour – paid or unpaid. This means including the unpaid labour done for family enterprises and the volunteer work performed at every level of society. It means including all unpaid domestic work – managing the household, bearing and rearing children, and providing services for family members. It also means including the work done for pay in the underground economy: babysitting, piece work, selling sex, and so on.

Working Women in the Canadian Economy

An Overview

Women of all backgrounds have been essential to the development of the Canadian economy. A quick glance into the past reveals that women have always performed a vital though unacknowledged economic role. In Huron and Ojibwa societies, women had considerable influence. Huron women of the seventeenth century enjoyed respect and autonomy that possibly today's white female Canadians haven't yet even dreamed of. But the settlement of Upper Canada in the nineteenth century had a shattering impact on all native groups: 'The majority of native women became, for generations, very private persons, attending to their traditional tasks, largely invisible to the mainstream of Canadian society' (Brant Castellano, 1991: 7).

Aboriginal women were indispensable to the fur trade, which was Canada's main industry for most of the colonial era. Male traders relied on aboriginal women to interpret for them, prepare their food, clean animal pelts for market, and teach them survival skills (Van Kirk, 1980). Women also had important and difficult tasks to perform in their everyday life. 'With all the cooking, dry meat-making, hide-tanning, clothes-sewing, looking after the children, and work with fires, women only rested when they went to sleep at night' (Blondin, 1997: 202). Women's household work was indispensable to the direct provisioning of their families' needs. Through their labour within families, women also contributed to the production of goods and services for sale to others. Few women spent their lives in leisure; most worked from dawn to dusk and cared for themselves and their families. 'Women chopped trees, ploughed the land, threshed grain with flails, butchered livestock and fowl, planted, hoed, weeded, raked, and bound field crops, during harvesting, pulled flax, hauled manure and mangles (large turnips used for animal feed), picked stones from fields, washed and sheared sheep, and drove farm machinery' (Crowley, 1995: 32).

To be an Inuk woman a couple of decades ago wasn't complicated, for gender roles were clearly defined and religiously followed to survive up North. You were a wife to your husband, a mother to your children, a housewife who cleans and cares for animal skins and furs your husband brings back home from the hunt. You have dexterous skills which are essential for making clothes, for making transportation facilities and shelters, and you were trained at an early age. (Caroline Palliser, in Issennman 1997: 179)

When an agrarian economy began to develop in Upper Canada during the nineteenth century, pioneer women played a key part in the household economy. Males worked the fields, and women looked after all domestic work associated with childrearing, tending the livestock and garden, making clothes, and preparing food. The death of a wife was a major setback for the subsistence farmer (Prentice and Trofimenkoff, 1985). As well, the non-waged winter work of women and children on the farm freed the men to seek wage labour in the forests (Radforth, 1995: 212). Life for pioneer women was hard:

'Time passes rapidly with our varied employments,' wrote Anne Bellamy in her diary of 29 January 1856. Well it might. The tasks that this Upper Canadian miller and farmer's wife listed during one year of her diary included making various kinds of clothing, cooking a wide variety of foodstuffs, nursing sick and pregnant neighbors and relatives, performing domestic labour such as daily dish washing and spring cleaning, and working in the garden. Her work kept her busy throughout the day and across the seasons; indeed 'busy' was one of the words she used most frequently in her diary. (Bradbury, 1995: 312)

Women were a vital part of the industrial transformation of Canada. For example, in Montreal, Canada's first large industrial city, women accounted for 35 per cent of the city's industrial workforce in the

1870s. In certain industries such as domestic work, sewing, and dress-making, four out of five workers were female (Bradbury, 1984). At the time, the vast majority of working women were young and single. Once married, women were expected to retreat into the home. Power-ful social values justified the employment of single women in sex-segregated jobs. By the late nineteenth century, teaching, social work, nursing, and domestic work were socially acceptable for women. At the same time, the fight by working men for protective legislation and the family wage provided men with a better position in the labour market and reinforced women's role in domestic work. In the twenti-eth century, immigration to Canada continued to create diversity and to add still more facets to women's family and work lives. Immigrant women performed crucial economic roles, both within and outside their families. They grew vegetables in their backyards, took in sew-ing and tailoring piecework, and cared for their family members.

Clearly, women have always worked. What has changed in the past few decades in Canada is that women are now flooding into the paid labour force. Women are now almost half the full-time and part-time labour force; they have entered occupational categories that were once closed to them; and like men, they are entering and staying in the paid labour force for most of their adult lives. In spite of all these changes, most working women are still found in only a few occupations – the lowest paid, and those with the fewest opportunities – and women who have entered previously male-dominated occupations still earn less money than their male colleagues. And women still bear most of the responsibility for childcare and domestic work. Family responsi-bilities prevent many women from taking on full-time employment or fast-lane jobs.

In short, as the Canadian economy became more market oriented, 'work' became defined as that which resulted in a wage; domestic labour, childcare, and clothing and food preparation became hidden, trivialized, and devalued.

Paid Work

Paid employment has been the criterion used to determine women's labour force participation in Canada. Narrowing the definition of women's work to paid work has major shortcomings and ignores many of the contributions that women make to the household, to the economy, and to society as a whole. The 'labour force participation rate' is based on official government statistics and on predetermined categories and assumptions about 'work.' It does not include people who have given up looking for work, or do volunteer work, or are retired; nor does it recognize the work women do in the home. The unemployed, defined as those who are out of work but who actively looked for work in the previous four weeks, are considered part of the labour force, but individuals who work in their homes are not. Official labour force statistics also omit Canadians who work 'underground,' that is, who engage in illegal activities such as prostitution and drug dealing, or who do legal work on a cash basis or in exchange for other services:

> Angela Lo in Toronto, together with thousands of her counterparts across Canada, make up the vast, hidden homework labour force. All of them women, most of them immigrants, homeworkers produce a remarkable share of the clothing manufactured in Canada. Homeworkers also work on uniforms, linens, toys and other articles produced in the highly labour-intensive needle trade industries. (Johnson and Johnson, 1982: 18)

Keeping all of the above in mind, let us now consider women's participation in the labour force.

In 1996, 15 million Canadians were in the labour force – that was two-thirds of all people over fifteen. As Table 4.1 shows, historically, more men than women have been in the labour force. However, significant changes have occurred in women's labour force participation. In 1901 only 16.1 per cent of women fifteen or older were in the paid labour force. Since the Second World War women's participation in the paid labour force has increased substantially. There was an especially big rise in the 1960s: between 1961 and 1971, female labour force participation jumped from 29.1 per cent to 39.9 per cent. By 1980, Canadian women were the majority of the paid labour force (Women in Canada 1995; Phillips and Phillips, 1983).

Many factors are responsible for women's increasing participation in the labour force. Changes in the Canadian economy, a tremendous expansion in white-collar service jobs, rising educational levels, and a plunging birth rate brought more women into the paid labour market. As well, with the decline of household economy, the growth of cities, shrinking family size, a rising divorce rate, and the fact that 65 per cent of married couples rely on two incomes (Women in Canada, 1995), we see more and more women who are in the paid labour force.

Table 4.1: Labour force participation by sex, 1901–1996

Year	Female	Male
1901	16.1%	87.8%
1911	18.6	90.6
1921	19.9	89.8
1931	21.8	87.2
1941	22.9	85.6
1951	24.2	84.1
1961	29.1	80.8
1971	39.9	75.4
1981	51.8	78.3
1986	55.1	76.7
1996	58.6	72.7

Source: (Krahn and Lowe, 1988: 40); www.statcan.ca.

More and more women with children are entering the workforce. In 1981, 50 per cent of women with children under sixteen living at home belonged to the labour force; by 1994 the rate was 63 per cent. Shrinking family sizes are allowing married women to pursue employment plans, and rising separation and divorce rates are forcing more and more women to find their own sources of income. Catherine Alpha (1997: 11), reflecting on her own life, writes: 'I am among several women I know who have become teachers in mid-life. Some of us were changing careers; some of us were starting a career after raising children. Married, divorced, with children or without, we all share the challenges of being beginning teachers who don't fit the usual picture.'

It is important to note that many of the women who have recently entered the labour force are part-time. Part-time work is the fastest-growing segment of the paid labour force and is a common form of work for many women, especially married women with children. Many women work part-time (i.e., fewer than thirty hours a week). Roughly one out of every four women in the Canadian labour force works part-time, and one of every three who is married with children is a part-time worker (Khosla, 1993). In 1994, 1.6 million women – 26 per cent of all those with jobs – were working part-time. In comparison, just 9 per cent of employed men held part-time jobs. In fact, the vast majority of all part-time jobs are held by women. In 1994, 69 per cent of all part-time workers in Canada were female – a figure that has changed little in the past two decades. Young women are more likely than older women to work part-time. In 1994 close to half of all women between fifteen and twenty-five were working part-time. In the same year over half a million women – 34 per cent of all female part-time workers – indicated that they wanted full-time employment but could only find part-time work.

Unpaid Family Work: What Is the Fuss?

Traditional approaches to analysing the labour market define work as that which is done for pay or profit in the market. Unpaid work done in the market or at home is excluded. This definition of work has major implications for our understanding of women's work at home.

Despite important changes in the nature of work in Canada, reproductive work – childbearing, childrearing, and feeding, clothing, and caring for the household members – stayed within the sphere of the family, and became more separate and distinct from market-oriented work. Most wage work takes place in factories and offices; reproductive work takes place in the home. Wage labour is paid, reproductive labour is not. The wage labourer works under the direction of a 'boss,' reproductive labour is done independently, if ultimately under the authority of the household head. In all racial-ethnic groups, mothers continue to bear the main responsibility for reproductive work. Housework – cleaning and cooking, and caring for children – remains the province of women. Though housework is essential for the survival of the household, it carries little prestige or reward, and is not counted as real work.

We have witnessed growing equality in the division of labour within households, but inequalities persist, and changes in this area of domestic life have not kept pace with wives' rising employment rates. Many working wives carry a double-burden (Ganage, 1986). Women still bear most of the responsibility for unpaid household work, shoulder the burden of most parenting work, and structure their labour force participation around such work (Hartmann, 1981).

A wife's household work varies with her class position and her husband's occupation. Upper-class women are able to wield their economic power to reassign some domestic work and infant care to lower-class women of their own or different racial/ethnic groups. Often, these women have been forced to leave their own infants alone or with relatives or friends. Generally speaking, working-class wives are more likely to face the combined burden of poverty and menial employment. In contrast, wives of managerial and professional men often are caught up in two-person careers: a male manager climbs the career ladder with the help of the unpaid services of his wife; the wife becomes a servant of the corporation (Krahn and Lowe, 1998).

'Family' and 'work' intersect in complex ways. Combining family work and paid work is a problem for all women. A professional woman stated it this way:

> I am a female in an administrative position and I want to have children. There seem to be so many barriers that the whole idea is overwhelming. First of all, the issue of time – need I say more. I already have 2–3 night meetings per week and I seldom arrive home before 6:30 PM each day. Then, of course, I am zonked because I have been enthusiastic, energetic, optimistic, etc. all day and come home to an infant child who desperately needs the same enthusiasm, energy, etc. My husband is quite supportive, but given his traditional home environment I still have my 'work' to do with him. The second issue, while related to time, is somewhat different – fairness. Can I do a good job of both – family and work? I think I can, but I'm scared. I am very organized and efficient and caring! To be a mother I must put my child first. It is a concern. How will my superiors view my roles? (Hajnal, 1995: 145)

The care of family and children makes a difference in terms of how women experience their work. An immigrant working-class woman in the Winnipeg garment industry sums up her double-day:

> It is hard to work when you have a kid ... When my children get sick, I don't know how I concentrate ... I am lucky, I have a sister who helps ... I am a presser ... I spend all day standing in steaming heat ... when I get home, I am exhausted ... I cook, vacuum, wash ... I do most of the chores on the weekend, but there is always something to do ... the kids get sick ... there is the family. (Ghorayshi 1990:283)

Injuries of Sexism

Occupational Segregation

To better understand women's work, it helps if we consider the occupations women join. In our society, occupation is a major determinant of income, wealth, and power. It also serves as a key source of social prestige, since we commonly evaluate one another according to the kind of work we do, respecting some jobs while looking down on others. Sociologists have measured the relative social prestige of various occupations (Blishen et al., 1987). Physicians, lawyers, and engineers are ranked at the top; low-income occupations such as janitor and cashier are ranked near the bottom. This is interesting enough, but at the heart of gender inequalities in the world of work is the division of the labour into male and female segments.

When women first began entering the paid labour force, they performed tasks that were continuations of what they had been doing at home. They became domestic workers, they performed 'feminine' tasks in factories, and they took care of children in schools. With the rise in industrialization in the twentieth century came a decline in some female jobs, such as domestic work and seamstressing, and a rise in employment opportunities in the expanding service industries. By 1981 the three leading female occupations were all in the clerical areas, and waitressing and nursing, both long-standing female economic roles, had become even more important sources of employment. Women have always been channelled into a limited range of occupations in which other females are employed. This was the case for an immigrant woman in Winnipeg: 'I have never worked before ... I started to look for job when my husband was laid off ... It took me three months ... it was 1975 ... A friend told me to go to Manpower ... I could not type ... I did not want to work in a hotel ... When the officer found that I can sew, he arranged a factory work for me ... I thought, I'll stay a short while ... but I am in this job for over ten years' (Ghorayshi 1990: 285). Another immigrant woman in Winnipeg was working as a dress maker, after looking unsuccessfully for work as a dental assistant, her field of specialization.

Table 4.2 makes it clear that job ghettos still exist. This attests to the deep roots of occupational sex segregation. Certain occupations, such as nursing, clerical work, and elementary school teaching, remain predominantly female occupations; manufacturing, construction, and upper management remain male occupations. The paid work that women perform remains a distinct category. One-quarter of working women are engaged in clerical work (secretary, typist, stenographer, etc.); almost one-fifth are in service jobs, often waitressing and other food-service work. Both of these categories of jobs are at the low end of the

Table 4.2: Women as percentage of occupation, 1982 and 1994

Occupation	1982	1994
Managerial/administrative	29.3	43.1
Professional:		
Natural Sciences/		
engineering/mathematics	14.9	19.2
Social sciences/religion	42.7	56.8
Teaching	58.9	63.4
Doctors/dentists	18.3	32.1
Nursing/therapy/other health related	84.7	86.1
Artistic/literacy/recreational	38.6	46.4
Clerical	78.8	80.2
Sales	39.7	45.7
Service	54.2	56.2
Primary	19.6	21.3
Manufacturing	18.4	18.5
Construction	1.4	2.4
Material handling/other crafts	19.3	21.0

Source: Statistics Canada, Women in Canada, Cat. 89-503E, Table 6.10.

pay scale and offer limited advancement. Men control the construction trades and hold the lion's share of positions that provide a great deal of income, prestige, and power. More than 90 per cent of engineers, 75 per cent of judges and magistrates, 70 per cent of physicians, 70 per cent of corporate managers, and 65 per cent of computer specialists are men (Statistics Canada, 1992); among the top executives of the largest corporations in Canada, there are only a handful of women.

In general, men still enjoy positions of greater authority in organizations; consequently, they usually receive better job rewards than women. Even in fields where women have made some inroads, they tend toward the lower strata in those fields. For example, in the teaching profession over half of female teachers are in elementary classrooms; males are concentrated in universities, colleges, and high schools, and in administration. In sales work, two-thirds of women are sales clerks – the bottom of the ladder in this occupation. Men are overrepresented in sales supervisory positions. Women have made significant inroads, especially in law and medicine, but even within these professions they tend to enter 'women's' specialties such as family law or family medicine (Krahn and Lowe, 1988: 133). Overall, gender stratification permeates the workplace; men tend to hold occupational positions that confer more wealth and power.

Table 4.3: Average income for selected occupations, by sex, 1990

Occupation	Male	Female	Female as % of male income
Physicians and surgeons	$111,261	$73,071	65.7
Lawyers and notaries	86,108	50,012	58.1
Managers/senior officials	74,425	40,633	54.6
University teachers	65,671	49,000	74.6
Architects	53,083	36,083	70.0
Civil engineers	50,389	38,137	75.7
Members of legislative bodies	47,539	37,360	78.6
System analysts/computer programmers	43,025	35,932	83.5
Nurses	35,964	33,317	92.6
Carpenters	29,565	19,512	66.0
Musicians and singers	27,036	20,066	74.2
Cashiers and tellers	21,913	17,243	78.7
Child-care workers	20,987	13,252	63.1
Farmers	19,649	12,871	65.5
Housekeepers/servants	19,210	14,053	73.2

Source: Statistics Canada, 1991, Cat. 93-332.

Wage Gap

A woman's position in the labour market has a significant impact on her income. At least two forms of discrimination affect female earnings. The first is wage discrimination (i.e., the employer pays a woman less than a man for performing the same job). The second stems from the segregated structure of the labour market (i.e., women are paid less because they have been channelled into lower-paying jobs).

In 1996, women working full-time earned an average of $30,717, whereas men working full-time earned $41,848. For every dollar earned by men, women earned about 73 cents. Table 4.3 shows very clearly that in all occupational categories, including those known as female occupations, on average, women make less than men. In 1993 the average annual pretax income of women over fifteen from all sources was $16,500 – just 58 per cent the average income of men, which was $28,600. Women with a university degree earn considerably more than women with lower levels of education. However, at all levels of educational attainment, women's earnings are lower than those of men. In 1993 even female university graduates employed full-time, full year, earned 75 per cent as much as their male colleagues (Women in Canada,

1995: 87). The difference in earnings is even more pronounced for those with lower levels of education. The earnings of women as a percentage of those of men is only 62 per cent among those with some secondary schooling, and 69 per cent among those with less than a grade nine education (Women in Canada, 1995).

The most important reason Canadian working women earn less is the kind of work they do: most are in clerical and service jobs. The wage gap is a result of the gendered nature of work (Lee, 1993). Men's jobs are distinct from women's jobs. Most of the former are full-time, well-paying, and secure; most of the latter are part-time, low-paid, and transitory. As well, people tend to perceive jobs with less clout as 'women's work,' and women's work and skills are devalued (Huffman et al., 1996). A female clerical worker sheds light on this point:

> I do not think a lot of people realize that a lot of work done in offices isn't done by the boss ... most of it is done by the staff and everyone doesn't look at it that way. A man [manager] was hired at one time who had no experience, and he got twice as much wages as I did. You know I had to train him. And it really got under my skin. (Gaskell, 1993: 209)

Another cause of gender-based income disparity has to do with women's family responsibilities. Taking care of the family keeps many women out of the labour force and makes it difficult for them to maintain fast-paced jobs. As well, discrimination against women contributes to income disparities between men and women (Benokraitis and Feagain, 1995).

In general terms, all women face wage discrimination to some degree. A male machine operator in Winnipeg states: 'Oh, yes. Women do get paid less than me. My job is seen as skilled work, and I have a higher pay than a simple machine operator. I get paid $6.10 per hour, but my sister-in-law does the same job in another shop for this company and only makes $4.75' (Ghorayshi 1990: 282). Similarly, there is plenty of evidence that corporate women often encounter a 'glass ceiling,' that is, a barrier to advancement that is hard to see and that is formally denied by high company officials, but that effectively prevents women from rising above middle management:

> Diane McGarry, Chairwoman, CEO, and president of Xerox Canada Inc., gets together for 'girls' lunches' every three months with other executive women to talk about the pressure they share. These women agree that

ambition has its price – at the expense of family and social life. Noting the small number of women at the top, McGarry points out the institutional and psychological obstacles women face – a plastic ceiling 'because plastic is even harder to break than glass.' (Macionis and Gerber, 1997: 309)

Injuries of Racism: Inequalities within Women

Race/Ethnic Division

The above general outline of women's work masks differences among groups of women. The work experiences of women in Canada are varied and multidimensional. The class position of women is one of the key factors affecting their life chances in Canadian society. Canadian society is highly stratified, and women are an integral part of it. There is no doubt that upper-, middle-, and working-class women have different work experiences. Statistics and research demonstrate the difficulties facing working-class women and how they struggle for daily survival (Luxton, 1986; www.statcan.ca, 1999; Little, 1998). Ethnicity and race, discussed in this section, introduce yet another dimension to our understanding of diversity among women. The ethnic division of labour is an important factor in the study of work. Immigrant women, women of colour, and aboriginal women have different experiences of work. As early as 1975, Monica Boyd showed that recent female immigrants held subordinate positions relative to women born in Canada. By 1980 she was also able to show that differences exist among immigrant women. Those who came to Canada from the United States and Great Britain have fared much better than those who came from Third World or eastern European countries (cited in Armstrong and Armstrong, 1990: 65).

Similarly, Lian and Mathews, in their analysis of stratification in Canada, arrive at this conclusion:

Whereas we began this paper with the question, 'Does the Vertical Mosaic Still Exist?,' we must end it with an even more serious question, namely, 'Is Canada a Racist Society?' Canadians have long prided themselves on their policy of ethnic pluralism in contrast to the 'melting pot' of the United States ... While we are apparently willing to accept cultural differences (particularly from a wide range of European cultures) in terms of the income received relative to level of education, we show no such tolerance for those who are racially 'visible' from the white majority in Canadian society. All our evidence suggests that, while our traditional 'vertical mosaic' of ethnic differences may be disappearing, it has been replaced by a strong 'coloured mosaic' of racial differences in terms of income rewards and income benefits ..., Our evidence leads us to conclude that there is some considerable level of racial discrimination in Canada in terms of financial rewards for educational achievement. In this respect at least, yes, we are a racist society. (1998: 476)

Immigrant Women

In 1991 there were 2.2 million female immigrants living in Canada. The proportion of immigrants in the female population has increased slightly since 1951. In 1991, 16 per cent of women of all ages were immigrants, up from 15 per cent in 1971 and 14 per cent in 1951 (Women in Canada, 1995: 117). Many immigrant women are regarded as women of colour. Visible minority women – defined as non-Caucasian or non-white women – encounter barriers in addition to the ones based on sex that other women often face. The women-of-colour subgroups that can be identified in the 1986 and 1991 censuses include Blacks, South Asians (referred to as Indo-Pakistanis in 1986), Chinese, Koreans, Japanese, Southeast Asians, Filipinos, West Asians and Arabs, Latin Americans, and Pacific Islanders. In 1991 an estimated 1.3 million women in Canada belonged to a visible minority group, up from 800,000 in 1986 (Women in Canada, 1995).

Many immigrant women, especially women of colour, face strong barriers when they come to Canada (Phi Thi Que and Rozza, in Mukherjee, 1993). Their past experience is not recognized in their new country. Also, their lack of fluency in English and their lack of familiarity with the rules of the new culture place them at a disadvantage. One immigrant woman noted that like most Italian women immigrants, she had been sponsored by her extended family, which was already settled in Toronto. Isolated by her inability to speak English, she found job hunting difficult. 'I don't know where to go, [which] streets. Nothing. I look in the newspaper. I say to my eldest son. "You come with me. I don't know whether to take a streetcar, where is that place"' (Ganage, 1986: 48).

Immigrant women face both ethnic and gender discrimination. In the case noted by Ganage (1986), a Portuguese women was not hired as a machine operator, even though she had proven her expertise. It was not her workmanship but her ethnicity and sex that determined her ability to get that specific manufacturing job: 'The foreman say, "Oh you make a nice coat. You go home. Now not so busy. We going to call you."' The result is that many immigrant women end up in low-paying jobs with long working days and hard working conditions. They get caught in vicious circles and keep hoping to find work that matches their potential, skills, and experience.

Immigrant women tend to have more education than their Canadian-born counterparts. Even so, they are assigned to lower-level occupations and earn lower wages. Immigrant women under sixty-five are slightly more likely than their Canadian-born counterparts to have a university degree. In 1991, 15 per cent of women of colour over fifteen were university graduates, in contrast to 9 per cent of other women. They are also more likely than other women to have some postsecondary training. Visible-minority women are more likely than other women to have obtained their education in science-related fields. In 1991, 20 per cent of visible minority women with university degrees had graduated from a science program, compared with 11 per cent of other female graduates. Like Canadian-born women, they are active in the labour force and tend to be concentrated in occupations held by women. In 1991, 53 per cent of employed female immigrants worked in clerical, sales, and service jobs. This figure was lower for Canadian-born women (58 per cent), but double for immigrant men (26 per cent).

Despite their university training, women of colour are much less likely than other women with degrees to be employed in professional or management positions. In 1991, 30 per cent of visible minority women with a university degree worked in professional occupations, compared to 48 per cent of their non-visible minority counterparts. University-educated women of colour tend to work in different occupations than other female graduates. In 1991, 18 per cent of employed women of colour who held university degrees were working in clerical occupations, compared to just 10 per cent of other university-educated women. Women of colour with university degrees were also more likely than other women to be employed in service, sales, or manual jobs; the comparative figures on this were 15 per cent versus 8 per cent (Women in Canada, 1995).

In 1991, immigrant women were somewhat more likely than Canadian-born women to be unemployed (10.7 versus 10 per cent). The unemployment rate is especially high for recent immigrants. In 1991, it was 18.4 per cent for those who had arrived between 1986 and 1991, but 13.5 per cent for those who had arrived between 1981 and 1985. Women of colour experience higher levels of unemployment than other women. In 1991, 13.4 per cent of women-of-colour labour force participants were unemployed, compared to 9.8 per cent of other women who were active in the labour force.

Women of colour who are employed on a full-time, full-year basis earn less than other women. In 1990 the average employment income for women of colour was $24,700 – about $1,400 less than for other women, who earned an average of $26,000. Roughly one in five immigrant women living in Canada has an income that falls below Statistics Canada's low income cut-offs.[4] In 1991, 21 per cent of all immigrant women over fifteen lived on low incomes, compared to 16 per cent of other Canadian women and 18 per cent of immigrant men. Women of colour have relatively low incomes. In 1990, women of colour over fifteen had an average annual income of $13,800. This was $1,800 less than the figure for other women ($15,600), and almost $9,000 less than that for men of colour ($22,600).

Aboriginal Women

European settlement drastically altered the economy and way of life of Canada's aboriginal peoples. Ellen Smallboy, a Cree woman, illustrates the situation:

> Now I am not supposed to be able to buy a goose. No non-registered person can participate in the spring goose-hunt. For the fall hunt they [non-registered people] may get a licence but the bag is limited. Nobody bothers to make *namestek* [dried goose meat] anymore, they just threw in the freezer the geese, without gutting or plucking them and they remain there perhaps all winter, get all dried out and do not taste good. (Flannery, 1995)

Aboriginal women, like other women, have come to depend more and more on paid labour for their daily survival. Thus, aboriginal women now form another group of disadvantaged women.

In 1991 there were 522,000 aboriginal women living in Canada – representing 4 per cent of all women. This percentage is even higher in the western provinces. Aboriginal women tend to have less formal education than other women in Canada. In 1991 only 6 per cent of aboriginal women over fifteen had a university degree, compared to 13 per cent of non-aboriginal women. As well, aboriginal women are more likely than other women to have less than a high school diploma. In 1991, 31 per cent of aboriginal women, compared to 24 per cent of other women, had attended but not completed high school, and 18 per cent of aboriginal women, versus 14 per cent of their non-aboriginal counterparts, had less than a grade nine education (Women in Canada, 1995).

In 1991, 47 per cent of aboriginal women aged over fifteen were employed, compared to 54 per cent of non-aboriginal women. Also, aboriginal women were less likely than their male counterparts to be employed that year (47 per cent versus 57 per cent). As with other women, a large proportion of aboriginal women only work part-time. In 1991, 30 per cent of employed aboriginal women worked part-time – about the same figure as for non-aboriginal women. About half of all aboriginal women work in jobs traditionally held by women. In 1991, 52 per cent of employed aboriginal women worked in clerical, service, and sales jobs – about the same figure as for other women (51 per cent).

Aboriginal women are less likely than other women to be employed in professional and managerial positions. In 1991, 12 per cent of employed aboriginal women worked in professional positions, compared to 15 per cent of their non-aboriginal counterparts. Another 7 per cent of aboriginal women, versus 8 per cent of other women, were managers. Aboriginal women are more likely than other Canadian women to be unemployed. In 1991, 17.7 per cent of female aboriginal participants in the labour force were unemployed, compared to 9.9 per cent in the equivalent non-aboriginal group. Aboriginal women are more likely than other women not to participate in the labour force, that is they are neither employed nor looking for work. In 1991, 40 per cent of aboriginal women between fifteen and sixty-four were not participating in the labour force, compared to 30 per cent of non-aboriginal women.

The average employment earnings of aboriginal women are lower than those of other women in Canada. In 1991, aboriginal women working full-time, full-year, earned an average of $23,800. This was over $2,000 less than the average earnings for non-aboriginal women. A relatively large proportion of aboriginal women have incomes that fall below Statistics Canada's low-income cut-offs. In 1990, 33 per cent of aboriginal women of all ages, compared to 17 per cent of non-aboriginal women and 28 per cent of aboriginal men, lived on low incomes.

Conclusion

Women's work has always been crucial for the survival of households and for the development of the Canadian economy. As a result of fundamental changes in the Canadian economy, more and more women have been entering the paid labour force. In this chapter I have demonstrated that gender and ethnic/racial stratification has permeated Canadian workplaces. Men are more likely than women to hold occupations that confer wealth and power. The work women do remains distinct. Women's work is devalued and underpaid and tends to be in areas that are secondary according to the segmented labour theory. Women in general face structural barriers that prevent them from getting full-time, better-paying jobs.

Even though women are flooding into the labour force, they are still responsible for the unpaid family work. Clearly, women to various degrees are still responsible for reproductive work – childbearing, childrearing, and feeding, clothing, and caring for household members. Many women are burdened with multiple tasks – both paid and unpaid. The unpaid work that women do is essential for the survival of both individual households and the economy as a whole, yet it carries little prestige or reward.

The data and life stories presented in this chapter make it clear that gender stratification in the labour market is intertwined with race/ethnicity and class factors. There are significant differences among working women. Class is an important factor in discussing women's working lives. As well, immigrant women, women of colour, and aboriginal women have different work experiences. Immigrant women and aboriginal women face major barriers in their struggles to earn a living. Those who came to Canada from the United States and Great Britain have fared much better than those who came from the Third World. Women of colour face both sexism and racism. As Lian and Mathews clearly state:

> Aboriginal peoples still remain mired at the bottom of Canadian society. Almost all Asian groups and most of those of Latin American and Middle Eastern ethnicity were also similarly disadvantaged. In sum, the evidence indicates that similar educational qualifications carried different

economic values in the Canadian labour market for individuals of different 'racial' origins. All visible minority groups had below-average earnings in each of the categories, while most of those of European ethnicity had above-average earnings. (1998: 475)

An understanding of the divisions among working Canadian women is essential if feminists are to make gains toward equality. Diversity can be a source of strength and direction. As bell hooks states, we need an appropriate direction for feminist organizing, but 'we do not need to share common oppression to fight equally to end oppression ... We can be sisters united by shared interests and beliefs, united in our appreciation for diversity, united in our struggle to end sexist oppression' (1984).

Women's greater presence in the labour force has strengthened the women's movement in many ways. Women, whether they are married or not, are spending a larger proportion of their lives in the labour market. Their increased participation in the labour force has spurred their struggles to improve wages and working conditions and strengthened their various attacks on discrimination. Greater labour force participation has also created new opportunities for women of colour, who have been able to progress up the job hierarchy a step behind middle-class and upper-class women. The net effect of women's shift into work for pay has been an increase in their financial independence.

As men and women of different racial/ethnic groups have been incorporated into paid work, the struggle for economic survival has become more and more a struggle for advancement in the labour market. Unfortunately, the capitalist economy is a pyramid: only a small percentage of workers can be highly paid managers and professionals; most workers are consigned to lower-level white and blue collar occupations. Individual efforts to scale the labour market pyramid will not eliminate economic injustice as long as hierarchies persist. Collective struggles must begin to challenge the labour market hierarchy itself, as well as the other social institutions that reproduce inequality. This will require structural changes across the economy and the polity and also within families. The historical record suggests that struggles against labour market hierarchy will be most effective in the context of a national commitment to full employment and an adequate minimum wage, so that all who want to work can find a living-wage job. Changes in the economics of the family, and in the relationship between family and work life, are necessary. Given the power that accompanies money in a capitalist economy, a sexual division of labour that assigns the greater share of unpaid work in the home to women reproduces inequality. Not only does it disempower married women, especially mothers, but it also impoverishes single mothers, assigning them both responsibility for children and jobs that cannot support those children.

In Canada there have been attempts to rectify some of the most glaring inequalities that working women confront. There are grounds for optimism; however, as I have shown in this chapter, progress toward full gender and ethnic equality in the workplace has been slow.

Notes

1 For a more detailed discussion of technology and its impact, see Boyce, 1999; Menzies, 1996; Tan, 1998.
2 I use 'women of colour' instead of 'visible minority.' This is the term used in the Statistics Canada publications.
3 In fact, there is a broad literature in the subdiscipline of sociology of work that discusses the divisions among male workers.
4 The poverty line is also referred to as low-income cut-off. People who spend at least 55 per cent of their pretax income on food, clothing, and shelter are considered below the poverty line. In 1995 the income cut-offs for families of four were $21,944 in rural areas and $31,753 in cities such as Vancouver.

CHAPTER 5

Between Body and Culture:
Beauty, Ability, and Growing Up Female

Carla Rice

Of all the concerns young women face growing up in the Western world, their changing relationships with their bodies is one of the most challenging. Young women today receive a confusing range of messages about their bodies in Western culture, from the affirming to the derogatory. These messages can strongly affect a young woman's developing sense of her body as well as her evolving sense of self. However, though body image is an important topic for many women exposed to or immersed in Western culture when they are growing up, all women do not develop the same body image problems. More-over, not all women experience body issues with the same intensity, nor do they all find similar solutions to the body image problems with which they struggle.

What accounts for such differences among women? Recently, femi-nists have begun to explore variations in experiences of body among women, asking a number of compelling questions regarding why di-verse populations of women relate to their bodies differently. Explor-ing the significance of differences in race, class, age, size, sexual orien-tation, and dis/ability to women's experiences of their bodies, they are asking how standards of beauty differ across populations of women, and how beauty practices vary from group to group. Do body image issues differ among diverse groups of women? If they do, what are the roots of these variations? How do women vary in their ability to ap-proximate ideals of beauty and how does this affect their life aspira-tions and choices? And finally, in what different ways do women respond to dominant images of beauty, and why do some embrace these ideals while others reject them?

In this chapter I explore the challenges that diverse populations of women face concerning their developing bodies and selves as they grow up female. First, I discuss the various body image struggles that women experience. Then, I relate these problems to the pressures girls and young women confront concerning their developing bodies and identities as they mature. After this, I illustrate differences among women, explaining how women become trapped in various body struggles as a function of their physical abilities, race, skin colour, ethnic identity, body size, and gender identity. Finally, I talk about how young and adult women respond to Western ideals of the body, and how and why their responses vary so widely.

Body Image: The Intersection of Body and Culture

Body image is a woman's experience of her body, which includes the mental picture she has of her body as well as her associated feelings, judgments, and sensations. Body image is not static; rather, it is a fluid picture developed through a woman's interactions with other people and the social world. It changes throughout her life in response to changing feedback about her body from the environment. The development of body image is a social and psychological process: a woman internalizes a range of social views to create a mental image, understanding, and assessment of her body. In other words, body image is the product of the messages she receives from other people (family, friends, strangers), from her networks (peer groups), systems (the school or medical system), communities (her geographic community, or her subculture), and also from her culture. In sum, body image is not fixed; rather, it develops through social relationships. It is formed and re-formed through continuous interaction between the woman and her cultural world(s) (adapted from Rice, 1995; Rice and Russell, unpublished manuscript).

What are some of the messages girls receive as they make their way from childhood into adulthood? Most young women growing to maturity in our Western culture internalize destructive messages regarding their developing bodies: between 80 and 90 per cent of North American women come to dislike their bodies or some aspect of their bodies (Hutchinson, 1985); over 80 per cent of adolescent girls worry 'a lot' about their appearance (Canadian Teachers Federation, 1990); 65 per cent of adolescent girls feel 'too fat,' and close to half have tried dieting (Day, 1990); almost 40 per cent of adult Canadian women engage in yo-yo dieting (Canadian Gallop Poll, 1994); and from 15 to 20 per cent develop health-threatening eating problems (National Eating Disorder Information Centre, 1989). The current widespread preoccupation with thinness is rooted in a struggle between biology and ideals of beauty, a conflict experienced by a significant number of young women as evidence of their personal failure.

It is interesting that weight and eating problems are presented in the popular media as psychological disorders primarily affecting young, affluent white women. Think about the popular books and movies that focus on eating problems. What are the gender, race, and class of the character with the eating disorder? How are the roots of the problem explained? How is it understood, treated, and resolved? In popular culture one of the predominant myths about eating problems is that they are mental illnesses having little to do with culture. Another is that those who are struggling with serious body image problems are invariably spoiled young women who are looking for attention or are motivated by vanity. Stereotypes like these are damaging to any girl, whatever her class or race, who is dealing with food and weight problems, not only because they trivialize her suffering, but also because they ignore the complicated roots of these problems (Rice and Russell, 1995a/b).

Researchers are finding that the 'rich white girl' stereotype is false. British girls of South Asian origin engage in just as much dieting and unhealthy eating as white girls (Hill and Bhatti, 1995; Ahmad et al., 1994). A study conducted through *Essence* magazine found that 65 per cent of African-American women were dieting, and that 21 per cent were engaging in bulimia as a means of weight control (Pumariega et al., 1994). A survey of young Native women found that almost half were dieting, 27 per cent reported that they induced vomiting to lose weight, and 11 per cent have used diet pills (Story et al., 1994). Weight and eating problems also cross class and income lines. Most studies have found that bulimia is more common among poor than affluent women (Gard and Freeman, 1996). Feminist researchers exploring eating problems among lesbians and women of colour are finding that a woman's relationship with food and her body is also affected by sexism, racism, class bias, and homophobia (Hall, 1995; Thompson, 1994).

The 'rich white girl' stereotype does not fit with the realities of many women who are dealing with eating and weight concerns. Moreover, weight issues are not the only body issues that girls can experience, nor are they necessarily the most salient ones. Girls are faced with the reality of having a female body, which can be experienced as pleasurable or problematic depending on the messages received from others. Weight is only one of the criteria by which girls are assessed. A girl's hair texture and style, her breast and hip size, her eye and skin colour, and her body shape and facial features can become focuses of concern, especially when these are evaluated against white ideals of beauty (Camper, 1994; Featherston, 1994; Rooks, 1996). Furthermore, physical differences such as a scar or burn, or visible physical disabilities, become concerns for women when their looks and bodies are compared with the able-bodied beauty ideal (Driedger and D'aubin, 1992; Hahn, 1992; Ridington, 1989).

The culture assesses a young woman's beauty and abilities, and this is how she is assigned a value in the world; her physical attributes influence whether she is accepted, or rejected, or harassed, or even physically attacked. The social meanings attached to a girl's physical traits – meanings that are learned through interactions with others – can greatly affect her developing feelings about her body and self. In discussing how social interactions shape body image, I draw from the 'body histories' of diverse groups of women. These histories have emerged from interviews I have been conducting with women between eighteen and forty-five, from all social classes, with diverse ethnic, racial, and sexual identities and with a range of disabilities. Almost 40 per cent of the interviews have been with women with disabilities and chronic illnesses. Over half the women I have interviewed are women of colour, including African-Canadian, Indo-Canadian, Asian-Canadian, and Aboriginal women. The rest are Eastern, Northern, and Southern European in background. Though most of the participants spent their formative years in Canada, I have also interviewed some recent immigrants to foregound the impact of context on body and self-image.

In these interviews I have focused on the histories of women's bodies. The emphasis has been on family background, school and peer group histories, health history, sexual history, and behaviours toward the body. The goal is to capture experiences that participants feel have shaped or altered their body images across their life span. In the next section I use excerpts of participants' stories to illustrate the early lessons that women learn about the importance of their looks. After this, I examine the lessons that women learn about their race and ethnicity and how these experiences shape their developing sense of body and self. In the final sections I discuss the pressures that women with disabilities face as they relate to body appearance and functioning, and outline the strategies the women I have interviewed use to resist the body beautiful.

Growing Up Female: Lessons in Beauty and Being a Woman

Body Confidence and Mastery

In Western culture, bodies are a primary source of identity. For example, bodies are given a gender, a race, and sometimes a disability from birth, and these labels often shape the options and life possibilities of the person in that body (Fanon, 1967; L. Davis, 1995; Butler, 1990). Though many life-shaping identities are assigned to babies from birth, most women who talk about the histories of their bodies do not recall feeling burdened by these labels in early childhood. Instead, they remember feeling a lack of body consciousness, and a lack of concern about their appearance and physical traits. Most say that as young children they acquired a sense of confidence in their bodies, whatever their body type or abilities. Tara, a young Scottish-Italian woman, remembers: 'I was really active when I was young. I sort of dwindled when I got older, I never thought there wasn't anything I could do when I was younger. I think most kids probably think that way, though. You're indestructible. You could just do anything.'

This is true for girls who are disabled as well as for those who are not. Jan, an Irish-French Canadian woman with a mobility disability, recalls: 'I used to have this "crazy car" and I would get out of my wheelchair, and I would be in this "crazy car" and I would be just like the rest of them. I was pretty fast and I was pretty proud that I was able to do this ... Yeah, that comes to mind as to how much freedom there was with that.' Regina, a Jamaican-Canadian woman, also remembers this time as idyllic: 'I remember running, playing, and trying to climb a tree. My dad built me a treehouse in the backyard. Climbing up there, I could look over the whole neighbourhood and see everything. I am happy with the childhood I had, I felt really fortunate.'

The First Socializing Messages

Many women learn about societal values regarding having a beautiful and able body as they begin to receive negative messages from other people. Mainly, it is peers and adults who send girls messages that their female bodies are not acceptable. Charlene, a Jamaican-Canadian woman, was made to feel abnormal because of her muscular body: 'I was a tomboy, a muscular child. I remember I was doing track and field and somebody made a comment that my legs were big. That really disturbed me because I thought to myself, "Gee, that means I'm different." I thought I was normal. It was the boys, I think they were threatened and that's why they tormented the hell out of me.' Messages like this reinforce society's gender norms, and make girls who do not conform vulnerable to harassment. These girls then internalize the message that they are not normal.

The education and medical systems often send girls harmful messages about their bodies. One compelling message that most children learn in these systems is that fat is stigmatized (Feldman et al., 1988). As young as five, they develop extremely negative associations with the idea of obesity – for example, they learn to perceive fat people as lazy, sloppy, ugly, mean, and stupid (Staffieri, 1967). Gina, an Estonian-Canadian woman who attended a school for kids with disabilities, recalls how overweight students were treated:

> They stuck any kids that they perceived to be too big or too fat on the diet table in the cafeteria, right? So for years, myself and a number of my friends that I'm still friendly with, were on this diet table ... In a way that was very damaging because it was at public school and everybody was young and there's peer pressure. So we were segregated like that at a very young age. It's incredible.

Though children of both sexes internalize a prejudice against fatness, the preoccupation with appearance is socialized in girls more than in boys. For example, more girls than boys are put on diets by their parents or caretakers (Pierce and Wardle, 1993). Also, parents stress the importance of girls being beautiful and boys being strong; this teaches children of both sexes that girls' bodies are to be worked on and made more beautiful (Freedman, 1984). The interviewees suggest that the importance of appearance is communicated to them through evaluative comments about their bodies and looks. Jenny, a young Chinese-Canadian woman, explains: 'We got just the sort of straight everyday kind of comments that would follow us throughout, like "Oh she's so cute." "What a pretty girl!" "Look at her cheeks." "Look, she's so little."'

These stories demonstrate that early messages can have a significant impact on girls' developing body and self-images. The interviewees suggest that messages about the importance of gender norms, body size, and looks tend to be sent more frequently in late childhood, when adults begin engaging in overt interventions to control girls' bodies.

Media Influences

The popular media reinforce socializing messages and practices concerning weight and beauty. Children watch an average of four hours of television every day. By the time they reach high school, they have watched approximately 15,000 hours of TV and have seen 350,000 advertisements, over half of which stress the importance of being thin and beautiful (Moe, 1991). Television images affect a child's developing sense of self: only fifteen minutes of exposure to beauty advertisements is enough to persuade girls that beauty is even more important to their popularity with boys (Freedman, 1984). Shavonne, an adult woman of West Indian–Black and Carib Indian heritage, relates how popular images affected her – specifically, how the gender stereotypes prevalent in children's cartoons affected her feelings about her developing body:

> Growing up I was always bigger than the other kids. My mom used to refer to my sister and I as BamBam and Pebbles. Well, I wasn't Pebbles, okay [laughs]. So at a very early age I was really conscious of the fact that it's not good to be BamBam. And do whatever you can to look like Pebbles ... I remember that my mother when she had her friends over, there'd be a laugh, it would be a joke, there's BamBam, there's Pebbles. I remember that did bother me very much. I didn't feel good. I felt yucky, I felt like, well, I'm not as good as my sister.

Most of the women I interviewed said that the messages they received in childhood about their bodies did damage their developing images of body and self. However, they also reported that they did not fully integrate these. Overall, this suggests that in preadolescence, a girl's positive experiences of her body offset any negative messages she receives whatever her race or physical abilities. Between the ages of eleven and fourteen, however, many girls face increasing challenges to their body and self-esteem. The interviewees relate these challenges to their changing bodies and developing sexualities, which are sources of power and pleasure for them but which also become targets of increased scrutiny and external control. It is during this time that girls begin to experience body ideals more intensely.

The Body as an Instrument of Femininity

Many women experience a period of foment in relation to their bodies, spanning from early adolescence into young adulthood. Though the development of a girl's gender identity begins at birth, it is through adolescence that becoming feminine is 'taught and enforced by complex social forces including adults, peers, and society at large through books, magazines, the media and even the responses of strangers in public' (Kaschak, 1992, 90). As French-Canadian Marie-Claire suggests, the process of learning to be a woman can be both exciting and frightful: 'So, I started shaving my legs, so that was something new. And I had to start wearing deodorant, right? Not you had to, but you did, because that's just the way that it worked, right? You had to start wearing a bra ... Yeah, it was kind of a mixture of excitement and sort of, ah ... fear?' A girl learns the rules for proper behaviour and appearance from peers and adults, who often direct the regulation of a girl's body. Some of the tasks she learns include using makeup, removing body hair, concealing odors, experimenting with clothing, styling her hair, managing her period, controlling her sexuality, watching her weight, and concealing figure 'flaws' (Bartky, 1990).

Growing up with a disability, Jan recalls experimenting with her appearance as a means of helping her fit in with her non-disabled peers: 'My mom didn't want me to wear makeup until I was fifteen and then I just went hog wild on the makeup. Liner, mascara. You name it, I had to have it done every single day. Had to curl my hair. I thought, "I got to look like everyone else. I got to aspire to do that."' In the process of beautifying their bodies, young women try to create acceptable selves. They often talk about losing weight, getting a new hairstyle or receiving a make-over as means of self-liberation; by improving her body, a girl expects to enhance her self (K. Davis, 1995; Székely, 1988). As adults, the interviewees reflect on how learning to be a woman was an interactional process. A girl develops a feminine body by observing others, experimenting with her own body, getting feedback, correcting herself, and gradually internalizing how she is supposed to look and act, learning what is acceptable and what is taboo (Young, 1990a; Tseëlon, 1995).

The Body as a Subject of Public Scrutiny

During the transition from childhood to adulthood, which Western culture identifies as the time of self-experimentation and definition, young women face the greatest external challenges to their body images. For example, many find that while their bodies are changing, they are subjected to unwanted assessment and attention (Lee and Sasser-Coen, 1996). For Dana, a young Romanian immigrant, as for most young women, this began to happen when she first got her period:

> Well, actually my period started when I was twelve ... I expected it since I was eleven, I was waiting and waiting for it to happen. And it did, and my body started to change, and I really didn't like it because it wasn't changing the way I wanted it to. I wanted it to stay the way it was, sort of like nothing on it, just like bones and skin. It was my hips and then chest and everything, sort of more rounded. I just couldn't do anything about it because I started getting this attention that I didn't need at the time and then also getting a lot of attention from older people. From older men, not from guys my age. That's why I didn't really like it, it was almost sort of scary.

Dana points out that during this time, girls become increasingly vulnerable to the predatory sexual gazes of older men. Venita, an young Indo-Canadian woman, notes that a girl's awareness of her appearance is heightened by the evaluative gazes she absorbs: 'If you were a tomboy in elementary school, it just meant that you played with the boys more than you played with the girls. But in high school it meant that you weren't pretty enough to get a guy to like you. You didn't dress cool enough for a popular group to want to be with you.' In puberty, girls become increasingly focused on regulating, managing, and controlling their bodies to meet an internalized ideal (Bordo, 1993). Becoming a woman involved internalizing cultural strictures relating to appropriate appearance and behaviour, and learning to adjust one's body in an effort to reproduce an acceptable or desirable form.

The 'body work' required to create an acceptable female form can become tedious, as Marie-Clair suggests:

I was about eleven when I started shaving my legs, right ... So you start to, you do stuff to your body because certain pressures you are under, right? Not that there's necessarily anything wrong with the pressures. But you start doing it and then, later down the line, you're stuck with it, right? ... And it was that everybody else was doing it, so I had to do it. Especially when you have dark hair, right? So everyone can see, everyone can see in gym class, right?

Studies of female and male high school students have shown that young women are much more dissatisfied with their bodies than their male counterparts (Paxton et al., 1991). Weight and appearance become salient issues for young women, who diet more, feel more body consciousness through adolescence, and report that their appearance interferes more with social activities than it does for young men (Rodriquez-Tomé et al., 1993).

Tara offers one of the reasons why she became so body conscious in adolescence: 'It [her high school clique] created standards you felt you had to live up to ... Even though you're sort of in that sort of circle, you have to maintain ... It's like a sick little clique. Everyone has to maintain their image. Look the same.' Venita concurs and talks about the effects of not fitting in on her changing body image: 'That's a lot of the conflict associated with high school, trying to find that group where you can actually fit in. You might morph your image every three months so that you can try to find or fit in with the group that has that image. So we had the stoner group, so you could try to fit in with the stoner group by not washing your hair for a year, which is what I did.' It should come as no surprise that adolescent girls are more conscious of their appearance than adolescent boys. Unlike boys' bodies, girls' bodies become topics for discussion and objects of scrutiny at the beginning of adolescence. This undermines the body- and self-confidence instilled in early childhood.

The Body as an Object of Social Control

Why do some young women develop more serious body dissatisfactions and weight struggles than others? Girls' satisfaction with their bodies is related to their feelings of belonging and of being accepted by others (Paxton, 1996). The messages they receive about their developing bodies from their family, peers, communities, and the larger culture during this crucial period strongly affect how good they feel about their bodies (Striegel-Moore and Kearney-Cooke, 1994). The greater the acceptance and affirmation of a young woman's physicality and sexuality as she moves through adolescence, the more likely she is to develop a positive sense of body. Conversely, the more actively a girl's body is monitored and regulated by adults and peers, the greater the chance she will develop serious body image problems. Shavonne relates how messages from her mother and doctor caused her to feel guilty about eating, and later to develop compulsive eating problems:

> Even my doctor said, 'You should try and lose some weight. Don't you want to go to your high school prom?' Oh yeah. He said to me that boys don't go out with fat girls ... My mother, she just sat there quietly when he said this, 'cause she had brought me to him to try and help me to lose weight. Yup. They put me on pills, they just made me sleep. I was just tired all the time. See, I just didn't lose weight. I liked food, too. I love food. So don't tell a kid, okay, yeah, she's a little big, but Jesus Christ, she wants to eat. And that was when I started to hide the food ... I would go to the store 'cause also I worked at an early age. I always had part-time money, sort of like pocket money. So I'd buy stuff, put it in my bag, and go to my room.

Shavonne suggests that girls' body perceptions and practices shift when their bodies become targets of social control. If there are few trusted people countering hurtful messages and punitive rules, a young woman's chances of developing serious body struggles are greatly increased.

The Body as Currency

In adolescence, a girl's body becomes her currency, its value measured according to heterosexual standards of desirability. This means young women develop a negative or positive sense of body as a result of others' assessments of their sexual attractiveness. Gina learned the early lesson that losing weight not only changed how people treated her but also whether they even saw her: 'I tell people I was thin for ten minutes once when I was fourteen! I lost quite a bit of weight in three weeks and it was incredible the difference it made in the way that people reacted. All of a sudden those same boys that used to put me down, were clamouring for my attention ... It was like they had never seen me before I lost the weight.'

Physical traits such as body size and skin colour have a significant impact on the future socioeconomic status, subsequent educational attainment, and life chances of young women (Gortmaker et al., 1993; Russell et al., 1992). A range of stresses placed on young women – including changes in their bodies, public reaction to these changes, messages from family, peers, and culture about the importance of appearance, and assessments of girls' attractiveness – can increase or decrease the probability that they will develop serious body image problems (Levine et al., 1994).

The Body as a Target of Harassment

Harassment is a common source of stress in young women's lives, and often undermines their sense of body esteem. Shavonne relates the following experience, which was one in a series of pressures that caused her to develop eating problems:

> I was bigger than the other kids at school. So I was called names. I was teased a lot. Being fat and being a pig and porky and black cow and all those ugly things. And I never got any sort of reinforcement say from teachers or, you know, saying, 'Stop that, don't tease her.' Nothing. So that was really difficult. And I internalized that, so I never brought it home. I never told anybody. I don't know why I never told anybody. Maybe cause I internalized it and I believed it. I didn't want to spring it on anybody.

Many young women experience 'body-based' harassment during adolescence. Researchers are only now exploring how this kind of abuse may relate to the development of body image and eating problems (Larkin, Rice, and Russell, 1996). The 'body-based' harassment that Shavonne faced in her early adolescence not only targeted her size but also her skin colour, which compounded her hurt.

The Impact of Violence

Sexual violence also is implicated in the development of serious body image and eating problems. Most studies exploring the possible links between violence and eating problems have documented a significant relationship between sexual and physical assaults and the later development of serious eating issues (Rice and Langdon, 1991). This does not mean that all women with eating problems have experienced childhood sexual abuse, sexual assault, or partner abuse – only that such violence makes it more likely that women will develop eating concerns (Rice, 1996). A boyfriend's abusive attitude and behaviour pushed Tara into a destructive cycle of bingeing and purging:

> He was very controlling ... Very tough on me about what I ate, how much I ate, how I looked, to the point where he would try to pick my clothes, tell me what I could wear. It actually turned out to be a very abusive relationship, emotionally without question, and it eventually turned physical ... I was bulimic for years and it started when I met him, 'cause he would just go crazy 'cause I would eat normally. I ate and he hated it; he had this perfect image of the way a girl should be, should eat, very feminine, very petite. I got to be very conscious of that ... I got to the point where I started sneaking food. Then it got out of control, I was literally never eating around him and then I would go on binges – he'd walk out the door and I would go nuts.

Messages from friends, lovers, peers, and adults about appearance, ability, and desirability can shape young women's perceptions of their bodies and selves. Relationships are an extremely important influence on body image development; young women report that connections with families, peer groups, and other support systems can prevent them from, or propel them into, taking drastic action to communicate the stresses to which they are subjected. This discussion demonstrates how young women are united in the lessons they learn in growing up female, and how they typically internalize a desire to be seen as attractive and normal. That being said, bodily standards are experienced differently by women according to their race, ethnicity, and physical abilities and this causes them to experience their bodies and the ideals in very different ways.

Lessons in Colour, Race and Ethnicity

Much of Western feminist work on body image has focused on gender – on the ways in which growing up female places young women at risk for developing body image problems. Yet every woman born in the Western world is also given a racial identity, and the reality of growing up with such an identity shapes her body image in complicated ways. Race is believed by many people to be a biological trait, like sex. However, not all people of a racial group share the same biological traits, nor do they have chromosomes that identify them as genetic members of that group (Zack, 1997). This suggests that a person's race is not in their genes – in other words, that race does not have a biological basis beyond superficial physical traits. Many social theorists now agree that race is nothing more than a changing range of attributes that have been labelled as racial – that race, in short, is socially created (Westley, 1997). Though race shapes many aspects of an individual's experiences, many researchers believe it is a cultural invention that changes over time and with historical circumstances (Thompson, 1996).

Historians have traced the origins of our modern concept of race to the seventeenth and eighteenth centuries, when Europeans were seeking ways to justify enslaving and exploiting African and Asian people (Schiebinger, 1993). Scientists of that era developed bogus theories about a hierarchy of races, theories that European governments used to defend their exploitation of the world's peoples. By creating biological differences between groups of people, Europeans were able to justify colonizing and enslaving non-Europeans while still seeing themselves as 'civilized.' In the nineteenth century, Charles Darwin continued in this tradition by falsely claiming that there was an evolutionary hierarchy of races and that Europeans were the most intelligent racial group (Darwin, 1871/1981). He also argued that light skin was more beautiful than dark skin; in doing so he was creating a purported scientific basis for Western ideals of beauty.

Modern-day cross-cultural studies have proven Darwin wrong: there is a wide variability in what people around the globe consider beautiful, and standards of beauty have everything to do with culture and power and little to do with genetics. Despite this evidence, science continues to seek genetic justifications for Western beauty ideals, to promote the illusion that beauty can be measured objectively, and to render invisible the role that social and political factors play in shaping our ideals (Cohen et al., 1996). The myth of universal beauty standards raises problems in that it reduces the rich variation in what people consider beautiful and advances one ideal throughout the world. Increasingly, the global image of beauty has become a Western one: fair skin, long hair, and European facial features are the universal standards.

Colour Consciousness: Fair Skin versus Unfair Skin

How do Western ideals of beauty affect the body and self-images of women of colour growing up in this culture? Western conceptions of beauty are creating a hierarchy in which women are ranked strictly according to their closeness to the ideal. This hierarchy ranks and divides women within and across racial groups, separating those who merit visibility and personhood from those who are condemned to invisibility and dehumanization (Derricotte, 1997). Sonia, a South-Asian Canadian woman of Pakistani and West Indian heritage, recalls how she became both invisible as a person and visible as a target of racism when a white kid living next door became aware of her colour:

> When I was five some people moved in next door. I was in the front yard and the new kid was indoors so he was looking at me through the mesh of the window. He said 'Hi, sweet lips.' But the thing that was really strange was that because he was looking at me through the mesh he didn't realize what colour I was ... When he did realize what colour I was, he was terrible to me. He was racist and there was one point when he would throw rocks at me and my brother. I became aware of my colour because of that.

Girls who grow up learning that their skin colour and physical features are unfavourably compared to those of Western beauty ideals often feel ashamed and humiliated (hooks, 1992b, 1993). Shavonne was aware of the significance of skin colour and hair texture from the time she was a young child. Her classmates, who noticed a variation in skin colour between her and her sister, first instilled this consciousness in her:

> But it wasn't so much size, it was also about racial colouring, colour lines, 'cause in my family, I'm lighter skinned than the other kids. And it wasn't till I left home to go to school that the other kids would tease me: 'Oh, how come you don't look like your sister?' And so then I realized about the world that people are looked on differently or are judged and people make assumptions about appearance ... How you look, your hairstyle, has always been something that has impacted my life.

Shavonne and Sonia developed colour consciousness early, recognizing that differences in their hair and skin tone were considered significant by peers and made them vulnerable to racist teasing and stereotyping. Colour consciousness, or colourism, has been defined as the prejudicial or preferential treatment of people based on their colour. As shown by Shavonne's and Sonia's experiences, colour conscious-ness often develops through a child's first encounters with other, often white, children in her neighbourhood or school. Children of all races pick up colourist ideas embedded in Western languages and culture, learning from books, movies, and stories which physical features are deemed beautiful and which are considered ugly (duCille, 1996). Think about the associations people have with the words black and white. And consider the books children read, the stories they are told, and the movies they see. What do the heroines and villains look like? What are the physical features of the 'good' characters, and what are the traits of those who are 'bad'?

From their early social interactions, children internalize colourist values and learn to rank one another based on Western notions of beauty and colour (Russell et al., 1992). As a young child, Patrice, a Trinidadian women of Black and Chinese heritage, learned her first lessons in the importance of colour when she was singled out and teased because of her light skin.

> I was adopted, and the family I was adopted into was much darker-skinned than I was. And nobody had the kind of hair that I had when I was little ... Some of the other kids in the family thought I was getting preferential treatment because I was lighter skinned. My adopted mother, I grew up calling her Auntie. They would say that I was her angel child ... I always got the indication that it had something to do with my skin colour as well.

The sting of being different from the rest of her family made Patrice want to be dark like them. Yet she and her siblings were also aware that light skin was to be envied and desired. They believed she re-ceived preferential treatment because of it, and their calling her 'angel child' suggests they both mocked and admired her light skin.

Cassandra, a young Guyanese woman of South American and Black heritage, is blind. Yet even she learned at an early age what others thought about her skin tone: 'I know that there were people around me that thought I was really cute. And we lived in a part of New York where it was full of blacks and I was very fair. So people thought that I was beautiful.' As with Patrice and Cassandra, colour consciousness is often reinforced in girls' families and communities. The above accounts suggest that caretakers perceive light skin to be a feminine attribute. Adjectives such as 'angel,' 'cute,' and 'beautiful' are clearly associated with femininity. Associations between light skin and femininity are widespread in our culture; so are associations between dark-skin and masculinity (Russell et al., 1992).

Hair Tales

The hierarchy of beauty, perpetuated today through Western popular culture, is based not only on skin colour but also on hair texture and facial features. The dominant culture defines fair skin, flowing hair, and European facial features as beautiful; it follows that the same culture must define something else as ugly. That 'something else' is darkness: brown skin, kinky hair, and classical African features have become synonymous with ugliness (Collins, 1990). Cassandra received glowing compliments from adults because of the lightness of her skin; but this positive view was undermined by her kinky hair, which she felt was unmanageable.

> I hated my hair as a kid. I remember thinking, why did God send me this horrible hair. It was long and unruly and hard to manage. So that was part of my blackness and I hated that part of it. I didn't have the right hair. My mom could manage [my hair] but no one else could. I was at boarding school, so they couldn't manage my hair. My hair was a problem.

It is significant that Cassandra's hair became a problem at boarding school, a school for the blind with few other black students in attendance or black teachers who could help her groom her hair. Experiences like this one demonstrate that beauty is political and that culturally defined ideals give women with the desired biological traits privilege over those who do not possess such features. They also indicate that ideals of beauty are tools of racial oppression. Like Cassandra, young women of colour can grow up feeling flawed as a result of unfavourable comparisons to white ideals of beauty.

Colourism on the Global Stage

Though rarely officially sanctioned, colourist beauty standards are deeply entrenched in the economic and cultural fabric of many nations. In countries such as Mexico, Brazil, and India, and regions such as the Caribbean, light-skinned people tend to form the political, social, and economic elite; those who are dark-skinned are often marginalized (Chapkis, 1986). As Cassandra explains: 'I learned I was lighter than a lot of people from Guyana ... I learned that they had a class system ... If you were black you married someone dark, if you were dark you married someone light, if you were light, you married someone white. That's how you move up. I learned that by just talking to my mom.'

Cassandra learned lessons about colour and class by discussing these issues with her mother and father. Though ambivalent about the preferential treatment she received as a light-skinned child, Patrice felt the shock of losing such privilege when she left Trinidad and immigrated to Canada.

> But I realize that in Trinidad, the feeling of internalized superiority ... was what I felt in Trinidad. Because in Trinidad, because I'm lighter-skinned and I'm multiracial and I was from an upper-income bracket, I did have the privileges that someone, a white male or a white female there would have. So I've gone from one extreme to the next. Pretty much everything that I had in my initial socialization has gone the complete opposite. It's almost like I'm being resocialized ... I've gone from feelings of internalized superiority and privilege to feeling powerless in society, feeling out of place, feeling I have no, I don't belong.

The value placed on light skin is especially marked in Europe and America and in countries on every continent colonized by European nations. This includes the Caribbean, where Patrice spent her early years. Because of their light skin and hair, northern Europeans have been considered more beautiful than those from the southern parts of Europe. In the same vein, North Africans are perceived as more attractive than central and southern Africans, and Indians from the northern parts of India are perceived as more attractive than those from the southern parts of the country (Russell et al., 1992; Tyagi, 1996). It is significant that what has made each of these groups 'good-looking' is their tendency to have lighter skin.

Racial Stereotyping and Isolation

Feelings of being unattractive can be especially strong in adolescence, a time when the messages about beauty received by young women may be strengthened by experiences of racial stereotyping and isolation. Patrice suggests that this sort of stereotyping both limited her choices and robbed her of her sense of control:

> I remember feeling very angry at not seeming to have any control over how other people saw me ... I hate stereotypes of any kind and sometimes in the quest for control, I've actually even denied my own self just to go against whatever stereotypes they've put me in, just to say well, that's not me. So control has always been a big issue ... Feeling like I don't fit in, feeling unattractive, feeling ugly, the whole bit. And feeling no control.

Stereotyping diminished Patrice's sense of body and self-esteem. Her lack of control over people's stereotypical reactions to her caused her to starve and cut herself, and to engage in binge-and-purge behaviour. She believes that the harm she inflicted on her body was a means of controlling and punishing herself for the harm that was being inflicted upon her.

As a young African-Canadian girl of Caribbean heritage growing up in a predominantly white society and community, Kathryn also internalized mainstream values regarding beauty: 'In my high school, out of say 1,800, there might've been ten blacks. So, yeah, sure, I used to look at the mirror and kind of think, "What's going on here? Why am I that, why am I so dark?" I wished to be white, actually. I used to close my eyes like this and when I opened my eyes I'll be white.'

Kathryn's desire to have light skin and features was strongly reinforced by the fact that she grew up in a city that had no discernible black community and attended a school with no significant black student population. The reality of racial isolation meant she wasn't exposed to alternative images and more positive views of Black women. Her mother organized other Black parents to hold periodic classes for their children, but this strategy had little impact on Kathryn's developing body and self-image, because it was not, in her words, 'an everyday thing.'

The feeling of being unattractive and unfeminine can be heightened if a young woman's peers do not see her as 'dating material.' In Kathryn's predominantly white high school, white males simply did not date black girls. 'There weren't any black guys to date and back then it was just pretty well unheard of for a white guy to date a black girl ... So then nobody else was going to ask me out. I remember there was one white guy who went out with a Chinese girl and boy, that was like, man, risky. Oh boy – what are you guys *doing*?'

Racial Harassment

Whether a woman of colour becomes a target of racial harassment is often related to her looks and to how easily others can categorize her as a member of a racial group that has been made to feel inferior. Darker-skinned people are more likely to report being victimized by racial discrimination than lighter-skinned people (Russell, et al., 1992). Patrice understands how this fact has played out in her own life: when her hair is short she becomes a target of overt racial harassment; when it is long people are unable to categorize her so easily, and this enables her to dodge their racism, at least temporarily.

> I had someone running down the street calling me nigger the other day. When my hair was longer a lot of times people's comments were more curiosity because they weren't sure, they weren't able to put me into a bracket. They weren't sure if I was black. Some people thought I was South American, some people thought I was multiracial, but they weren't sure exactly what the racial mix was. So I think the visual that they got didn't allow them to stereotype me right away. Whenever I cut my hair, the visual allowed them to put me in a bracket right away and thereby allow them to feel comfortable saying whatever they needed to me, whereas with long hair, they went through a process of well, we're not sure what she is. [laughs]

The internalization of colourist values from childhood and experiences with racial stereotyping, isolation, and harassment, drive many women to lighten their skin colour using cosmetics, to straighten their hair with chemicals and hot irons, and sometimes even to change their facial features through cosmetic surgery. Although light skin, straight hair, and European facial features have privileged some women of colour relative to their peers, continued racism in our culture ensures that a woman's race usually supersedes her skin colour or hair texture when it comes to determining how she is treated in white society.

The Economic Imperative

Women want to be beautiful, and they strive to avoid harassment and stereotyping. Economics is another important reason why women change their hair texture, hairstyle, skin colour, facial features, or eye colour. More and more studies are showing that men and women of any race who approximate Western ideals earn significantly higher wages than those who do not (Cohen et al., 1996). In white-dominated institutions or companies, conformity to the acceptable 'look' may be necessary to get and keep a job (Buchanan, 1993). Shavonne noticed a marked difference in white employers' reactions to her when she started braiding her hair:

> I, when I put in a bid to ———, it was all paper, right? They went through the bids. They took the three best bids. And then they interviewed us ... So it wasn't until the interview that they met me. And of course, there was a conversation over the telephone, da, da, da. So you go into a room of ten people and they're all white. Right? Then in walks in little blackie in her braids. And you can see the shock on their faces. Like, you *see* it. And it's, like, holy fuck. Like this person, oh wow, she can read, she can write, and she can articulate. And it's almost like it's a shock.

The idea that economic advantages accrue to those who conform to Western ideals may be especially true for women in developing countries. For these women to move up socially and economically, they have to 'marry up,' and their chances of doing that are profoundly influenced by their physical appearance. Patrice reflects on the economic and social privileges associated with light skin:

> Now I realize that even though things like education and so on make a difference now, me being of a lower income bracket and living in poverty in Toronto, probably one of the primary things that makes it appealing to men who are from upper-income brackets or come from an upper-income background, is [that] I'm lighter skinned. I'm still different enough to be 'exotic', quote unquote, but I'm not too different where it's not comfortable for them.

Integrationist versus Oppositional Ideals

Beauty rituals that enable women to conform to mainstream ideals have been labelled 'integrationist' beauty practices (Mama, 1995). Trying to conform to dominant ideals does not mean that a woman wants to be white (Buchanan, 1993). The emphasis on fair skin, straightened hair, or a small nose is less about Black or South Asian women wanting to be white than about them wanting to be attractive. This is especially the case 'in a patriarchal world that assumes beauty to be blond and blue-eyed, and makes it imperative for women to be attractive enough to succeed with men' (Mama, 1995: 151).

Some women of colour feel caught between two different ideals: the dominant, white ideal, and the ideals of their culture of origin. They are being asked to look and behave in two different ways; they have been told from very early on that they have to conform to two standards of beauty. Maria, a young Ecuadorian woman, explains:

> Especially in Latin American society, the image of the perfect woman is a curvaceous woman, and I never fit that image. And that was another struggle I used to have with my self-image. I never had the curves. I never had the voluptuous body. How am I going to get a guy interested in me? ... And there is also difference as to what Latin men are looking for ... Latin American men have to, in order to feel more assimilated, more integrated with Canadian society, they have to go out with blondes.

Maria feels pressured to conform to traditional Latin American ideals, which tend to be more curvaceous than Western ideals. Yet at the same time she feels pressured to conform to Western ideals, which tend to be fair, thin and blond. She recognizes that Latin American men themselves are split in terms of what they view as attractive. This leaves her wondering exactly what look she should aspire to in order to find a mate.

Some women cope with the pressures they face concerning their looks and bodies by rejecting mainstream definitions of beauty, and with them, mainstream ideas about what is sexually attractive and feminine. Thus, some women of colour have tried to conform to dominant Western ideals or to the traditional ideals of their culture of origin, and others have tried to create new 'oppositional standards.' Oppositional ideals are 'anti-ideals' of beauty that directly oppose dominant standards and that value the very physical traits that mainstream culture devalues. Oppositional ideals challenge the assumption that women need to conform to mainstream images; in doing so, they offer women of colour alternative notions of beauty. Maria explains how she has used her pride in her indigenous features and heritage to create her own oppositional ideal:

I'm a Latin American woman. I have Latin American features. I have an indigenous background, ancestry. I have some indigenous features. It makes me who I am ... If you look at indigenous women, they're very strong women ... And I look at my own family and my own grandmother and my own mother, despite all the adversities that they've had to face throughout their childhood, throughout their lifespan, I look at their strengths and that's when [I see] the strengths that I learned and I take my strengths and try to blossom them ... I would say yes it is important, my appearance to my identity.

As Maria suggests, oppositional ideals are a source of strength and inspiration for many women. But attempts to conform to oppositional ideals can generate their own problems, especially if the opposing ideal replaces one standard of beauty with another one which is equally narrow (Mama, 1995). Patrice explains:

I find it amazing that when I talk to other women identified as Black in the Black community, there [are] such expensive rituals to try to look Caucasian, and I'm amazed that people don't acknowledge it ... And there's sort of like another movement of people trying to be completely the opposite, where they're being entirely ethnocentric and trying to be visually African, identified as of African descendant. I think that both extremes show that they're not, we're not comfortable with who we are. Being somewhere in the middle or it has to be one extreme or the next. No one's able to just be themselves. For me, and I think for other people too, it's just a matter of whether they're aware of it or not. It's really painful.

Patrice has thought a lot about diverging beauty practices among Black women; she describes both integrationist beauty rituals and oppositional ones. She suggests that both extremes reveal a discomfort among black women about what it means to be black and female. This insecurity can develop as a result of the yearning to be beautiful according to mainstream standards versus the conflicting desire to embrace oppositional ideals of black beauty. Her insights are supported by the research of Amina Mama (1995), who has found that tension about beauty among black women places them in a position of having to choose between integrationist beauty practices and oppositional ones. Many women of colour are left having to confront what they really look like, which often does not match traditional standards of their own community, *or* the new oppositional ideals, *or* the white ideals of the dominant culture (Camper, 1994; Moraga and Anzaldua, 1983; Root, 1996).

Lessons in Ethnic Looks

Women of colour receive lessons about colour and race growing up in a white society; white women who have a strong ethnic or religious heritage also grow up aware that they don't conform to dominant beauty ideals. In fact, women report that any physical trait perceived as different from the Canadian mainstream is a liability, and one that they tried to conceal when they were growing up. As the only 'Jewish looking' girl in her class, Mira tried to alter features that she felt made her look different from her classmates:

> I was sort of short and squat and dark, curly haired and Jewish looking. And they were all tall and blonde and skinny. And I felt bad ... I spent all my time wanting to have my hair straight. I spent untold hours and money and everything trying to straighten my hair. I used to go to bed with Scotch tape around my hair, rolls and rolls of Scotch tape around my hair and clips down here. It was a whole procedure every night before I went to bed and I'd wake up and kind of rip the Scotch tape off and there'd be these little wrinkles in my hair where the Scotch tape was. I just wanted to look like them and there was no way I ever could ... So it was definitely a feeling of looking different and really striving to be like everybody else.

Lessons about colour and race are prominent in the early experiences of women of colour; these same lessons are present in the childhood and adolescent experiences of only a minority of white women – specifically, those women who look different because of their ethnicity. In the stories of most white women, lessons about colour, race, and ethnicity are not prominent because at least in terms of colour, the white woman is the ideal. Whiteness privileges white women in a colourist beauty system in which fair skin, blue eyes, and long, flowing hair are synonymous with beauty.

Very early on, women of colour develop a colour consciousness, which is often reinforced in their adolescence and adult years by experiences of racial discrimination, racial harassment, and economic marginalization. Some women of colour aspire to mainstream standards of beauty, some to oppositional standards, some to the traditional standards of their culture, and some to a look somewhere between mainstream, traditional, and oppositional ideals; this suggests that they differ in response to beauty ideals. The ideal that a woman aspires to is connected to her personal history and to the particular realities of her body. Next I explore another facet of the ideal that affects diverse groups of women in different ways – the pressure to have a 'normal' body.

Lessons in the Importance of Body Norms

In recent years, researchers have begun to note that we live in a world of norms. Weight, height, intelligence, and accuracy of vision are calculated from below to above average, and individuals measure both themselves and others against predetermined norms (L. Davis, 1995). Individuals learn they must aspire to body norms. Body norms are standards in weight, height, vision, hearing, size, shape, mobility, and other physical traits. By focusing on the pressure that exists for people to achieve body norms, we expose how these norms create the problem of abnormality for those who deviate from them.

Historians have traced the processes through which the 'average' or 'norm' became a kind of ideal in Western culture. In the past hundred years the modern concept of the norm has spread along with the implication that individuals should aspire to achieve it (L. Davis, 1995). Before the nineteenth century, human variations were seen as having many different causes and were given different interpretations (Garland, 1995); gradually, these variations came to be seen as examples of disease and disintegration. According to some historians, the primary goal of modern science is the victory of the normal body over the abnormal one through the eradication of disabilities (L. Davis, 1995).

The development of body norms has resulted in people with significant physical differences being seen as abnormal, deviant, and 'disabled.' *Disability* refers to human variation, including mental, physical, and emotional impairments, which a society defines as significantly different (Higgins, 1992). Researchers have considered how the dividing line between 'disabled' and 'non-disabled' is drawn. They contend that because disability is mainly an acquired state, it cannot be defined using simple genetic criteria. Furthermore, many suggest that the definition of disability is arbitrary – that disabilities exist on a continuum of variation in ability and that most people experience some degree of disability throughout their lives (Collins et al., 1995; Hevey, 1992; Linton et al., 1995).

Early Lessons in the Importance of Being Normal

It is from this history that themes relating to being abnormal emerge for women with disabilities. Women with disabilities are confronted from a very young age with the pressure to be normal, and grow up aware of their failure to conform to the ideal of the normal body. These pressures are encountered in virtually every sphere of life – in their interactions with family and friends, and especially in their contacts with educational and health care systems (Harris and Wideman, 1988). Gina, who has cerebral palsy, remembers that the focus of her early schooling was not on her intellectual or emotional development, but rather on her body being as normal as possible:

> I remember going to these therapy classes and swimming in this really hot therapy pool with this steel chaise lounge in it. And having them focus more on our physical bodies rather than what we were inside. And you have to strive to be normal and be mobile, and the ultimate was to get up and walk. If you didn't walk, then it was sort of like a hierarchy of disability. If you didn't walk, they kind of made you feel like you were less than was the ultimate goal.

Women with disabilities report that much of the pressure to be normal comes from the medical system. Fatima, who was born with cerebral palsy after her family immigrated from Portugal, remembers her doctors telling her parents she was faking not being able to walk:

> They said I didn't want to go to school so I was faking it. [Was that true?] No, it wasn't. I don't think they thought I was lying, they didn't know what the hell was going on. But no, I couldn't walk, from one day to the next. I stopped walking. There wasn't any reason for it. I don't need a reason for it. But they didn't believe me. And I really knew that when they told my parents I was lying, 'cause I wasn't. That was very hard. They believed the doctors.

Because the doctors could find no medical explanation for the change in Fatima's mobility, they could not believe that she was suddenly unable to walk. So they blamed her. This suggests that disabled women are taught to strive to be 'normal.' For them, being normal at first meant having normal body functioning; but as they got older the struggle to be normal evolved not into a desire for increased mobility, but rather into the desire to be seen as 'normal' women.

Becoming a Damaged Woman

Like able-bodied girls, girls with disabilities grow up yearning to be loved and desired. Yet at the same time, they are told by both family and friends that they are not normal women – that they should not aspire to normal women's desires because their bodies are not 'viable' (Rousso, 1988). In the contemporary Western world, one of the identities that disabled women are socialized to assume – namely, that of being a woman – is highly sexualized; while another identity – that of being a person with a disability – is almost completely de-sexed. Many women with disabilities report considering suicide when in their late teens and early twenties, after they realize the consequences of being denied a sexual identity and sexual intimacy. Fatima explains:

> It was the worst time of my life. I had a really hard time, wanted to die ... My whole family was aware of something going on, they couldn't relate to it. And I don't understand that, but they couldn't. Maybe they didn't want to, maybe they couldn't cope. But my brother, I was twenty-three, he was twenty-one, single guy, no commitments. I don't know, we developed a relationship where we didn't have to talk about my problem but we were very in tune to it. And yeah, there were nights where I thought, 'if I don't get him over here, I am going to kill myself.'

Gina also found herself on the brink of suicide in her early adulthood. This demonstrates how devastating it can be for a woman with a disability to realize that she will be seen by others as defective. Some women with disabilities respond to the knowledge that they are not seen as normal women by developing a more masculine gender identity. Gina illustrates this idea: 'I remember when I was younger I would always enjoyed watching sports and that kind of thing, so I would become like one of the guys ... That was great. But no one else thought of me as anything other than one of the guys. So it was kind of hard to shake that.'

Gina recognizes that she made herself into 'one of the guys,' but she also realizes that one of the reasons she did this was to initiate intimate relationships with young men, in the hope that romance would develop. In other words, she hid her gender and sexual identity in the hope that someone would get past her disability and eventually see that she was a woman who had 'normal' desires and aspirations. Jan took a more radical step: she attempted to create a gender identity that was neither masculine nor feminine:

> I saw myself as a person with a disability – my gender was not ever something that I considered in terms of my experience and was not ever something that was highlighted in terms of my growing up. I was just Jan and yes, I had a disability, but my sort of identity as a female – young, adolescent girl – even now, is pretty much non-existent, or at least does not exist very much.

Women with disabilities who create a masculine or neutral gender identity are not necessarily rejecting beauty ideals. On the contrary, they talk about wearing make-up, fixing their hair, controlling their weight, and generally working on their appearance. What is happening here is that to cope with being seen as damaged, they learn to downplay their sexuality and relate to others as desexed women. In sum, though they are gendered female in childhood, women with disabilities are often sexually 'neutered' in adolescence – that is, they are socialized to develop an identity that they are never fully allowed to become. Fatima sums up the effects of this suppression succinctly: 'For us, we're looked at as asexual, we're looked at as not being perfect, and our bodies being damaged and not worthy of love. And that puts us at a very high risk for abuse. But even without the abuse factor, that does a lot of damage to ourselves internally.'

The Abnormal Body as a Target of Social Control

Though felt on an intensely personal level, the 'abnormalities' of disabled women are publicly noted. These women are repeatedly sent the message that sexual expression is taboo. Jan recalls how this affected her ability to be sexual:

> I maybe found myself in a situation where there was heavy petting or whatever, but it just didn't do it for me. Because I think I believed that was not what was right for me. I am not supposed to be sexual. I would stop it. I mean I just didn't, something was stopping it for me. Something was blocking me from being able to express that, probably because I thought it was wrong ... Because I'm not supposed to be sexual.

As a result of the culture's view that their bodies are defective, disabled women often find that the right to reproductive choice is denied to them. Many disabled women report that their ability to reproduce is hidden from them at an early age. For example, when Fatima was thirteen she was placed on a powerful birth control drug, Depo Provera: 'I remember being thirteen and the doctor examining me, she told my mother I would never have kids. Now at thirteen, you don't ask questions. So for a very long time, I really thought that physically, I couldn't have kids, that inside, physically, that I couldn't have kids.'

Fatima was told at first that Depo controlled her epileptic seizures; she later found that out her fertility was also being controlled by the drug. Studies show that women with disabilities are regularly sterilized, lied to about the effects of various medications, and given birth control methods without their informed consent (Asch and Fine, 1988). Throughout the twentieth century, control of the reproductive capacities of women with disabilities has been fuelled by theories about the survival of the fittest and by the modern scientific push to eradicate disabilities. Though the bodies of all people in our society are supposed to be legally protected from medical procedures to which informed consent has not been given, the bodies of women with disabilities are regularly stripped of such protection (Bordo, 1993).

Concealing Flaws and Abnormalities

Most women know that failure to achieve a minimum standard of sexual attractiveness in our society renders a woman untouchable. In other words, any woman who is perceived by others as in some way abnormal is also seen as repulsive. The pressure to be normal can also affect non-disabled women, and analysing some of the ways that able-bodied women react to women with disabilities brings this to the foreground. Fatima candidly talks about the hostility that able-bodied women have directed toward her when she is with a man:

And I know for me, there have been times when I am with [my husband] and even when I am alone with my brother, out, and we are joking around and I get very dirty looks, from other women ... Women can be pretty hard. And see, guys don't see that, they don't get it, they don't see it, it's all in my head. I know it's not all in my head, I know it's not my insecurities. I know this because, for one thing, if it was, it wouldn't be happening when I'm with my brother.

Why this reaction from able-bodied women? The fear and hostility directed toward women with disabilities may reflect the normal woman's need to reject women who are damaged. Being disabled, disfigured, and female is a frightening thought for many able-bodied women. At the same time, most able-bodied women secretly understand being abnormal because most 'normal' women are 'deformed' by their inability to achieve the ideal body. As Fatima's story suggests, women who are able-bodied must reject disabled women in order to hide their secret fear of their failures to achieve the ideal. By erasing the damaged woman, the 'normal' woman erases the ways in which she too is damaged – in which she too is imperfect.

This suggests that able-bodied women also contend with body norms. In the Western world, all women inherit clear ideas about what a normal woman's body looks like, and this does not include cellulite, body hair, well-developed muscles, and so on. Able-bodied women regularly work to maintain the façade of being normal, to acquire the privileges that having a normal body may bring. In fact, the pressure to be normal is a primary motivation for women seeking cosmetic surgery or struggling to lose weight (K. Davis, 1995; Spitzack, 1990). Marie-Claire's experience provides insight into the work required to maintain the façade 'normal': 'I have a lot of hair on my face which I tend to bleach my lip, and sometimes there's hair on my face. And that's something I'm trying to deal with because I don't like this sort of having to do this everyday ... I wish there was a way that I could, that it wouldn't be an issue, right?'

Marie-Claire's story suggests that pressure to achieve a normal body is felt by both able-bodied and disabled women. But there is a crucial difference. Able-bodied women confront their failings and abnormalities alone, whereas for disabled women, this confrontation is hardly secret. Because women with disabilities cannot hide their imperfections, their bodies disrupt the illusion of normality.

Though our society looks at failure to live up to body norms as a tragedy, it is possible to imagine that such disadvantage could be a resource. Feminists have argued recently that people with disabilities have knowledge of how to live with suffering and how cultures reject certain aspects of bodily life, but that this knowledge has not been acknowledged or respected (Charmaz, 1995). Some women with disabilities know how to live with a body in pain; others have mastered the art of living with physical difficulties. These experiences could be seen not as liabilities but rather as resources for teaching people how to live fully despite their limitations or suffering. Such knowledge could enrich all our lives (Wendell, 1996).

Resistance and Resolution

Many young and adult women find body and self-confidence through a wide range of strategies for resisting dominant beauty ideals. The term *resistance* is an ambiguous one, 'meaning diverse things, translating into different practices and strategies that must be assessed and developed each in its sociohistorical situation' (de Lauretis, 1986: 3). Resistance can be lived privately or practised publicly; it can be open and confrontational or quietly subversive; it can be humourous and playful or serious and painful; it can be individually motivated or socially organized in group action. The following are some of the resistance strategies that women have used to counter cultural ideals of the body.

Making Connections

For many women, overcoming struggles with body image involves making connections with people who give them positive messages about themselves and severing relationships with people who are destructive to them. Tara saw a therapist who specialized in abusive relationships, who helped her break up with her abusive boyfriend and overcome her eating problem. She talks about why their relationship worked:

> He didn't judge me. I mean, he knew every deep, dark, little bit of my soul. And I think it made a difference because I accepted what he said to me. Nobody else could say anything to me about anything ... especially where my boyfriend was concerned. I just trusted him implicitly. There was like a connection I felt to him that he could reach a level with me that no one else could. I had such barriers with everyone else for so long. I didn't have with him ... And it's almost like I was hurting him when I was at a low weight ... He's the one person I just couldn't hurt.

Many young women suggest that protecting body esteem and self esteem involves making friends, especially the kind of friends who are not into dieting or other body-harming practices. According to Dana:

If people have a problem talking with others, if you don't have many friends or something, they usually have those kinds of problems because they are so inside of themselves and they have no one to talk to and no one to sort of tell their problems to. Yeah, having a friend would help a lot. A good friend, not a dieting friend. Not the kind of friend who sort of goes, 'Yeah!! You lost another ten pounds.' No, but a friend who would sort of help you.

Talking Back

Another strategy that some women have used is 'talking back' to authority as a way of re-asserting their human dignity. This can be empowering, but it can also be difficult, especially if a woman is criticized or punished for speaking up; which is what happened to Gina:

> But every year until I was about seventeen, I went to this clinic ... I had this doctor and he was incredibly impersonal. And these clinics would involve a number of things. First of all, they would take the whole day. Second, you would be a case study and there would be a number of people that would come in and literally record into a tape 'case number 85.6' and this is the progression and everything else ... I always came out of there feeling terrible. And when I got older I would start rebelling. I would still have to go but I would make my mother feel uncomfortable because I would talk back and be insolent to this doctor ... He'd make a comment about my weight and I'd say 'Well, it's not that easy,' or one time I think I made a comment about his weight or something ridiculous. [laughs] When I think about it, it was rude, but I think I was just trying to gain a bit of myself back because I felt so ... like a dehumanizing experience to me.

Using Humour

Many women resist through play, pleasure, and humour. Humour can be a powerful means of resisting ideal standards of body, as Fatima explains:

> We would go to church ... And constantly, women would come up to me and say, 'You poor thing!!!' 'Oh my God!, Pray to God to get better!!!' And we were brought up with you respect your elders [laugh]. So I

would sit there and nod and look away. And they would end up talking to my mother. And they would get personal, ask what happened, what hardships did my mother have to go through because of my illness. What would end up happening is that my sister and I would be over-hearing this such dramatic response and we would be laughing, thinking it was funny [laughs] ... I was considered a burden and a cross, like my mother's cross. And that was soon to become a joke in our family. I'd be leaving for school and I would say, 'OK mom, your cross is going to school now.' I would say it and laugh like it wasn't negative to me.

Rebelling Through the Body

Most women learn to regulate their bodies mainly through messages from families, peers, and systems, all of which monitor their appear-ance, body functioning, and sexual behaviour. Rebellion against social pressures can take the form of smoking, drinking, tattooing, and pierc-ing. It can also involve making radical changes to appearance and defying family, peer, or cultural sexual norms. Jan explains: '[Taking risks] meant like going to my friend's mom's and smoking cigarettes and drinking. That's not such a big risk but coming from my family, it was, where that's just not something that you do and get caught. And boys, too. Boys, I remember.'

Angela, a young Australian and Vietnamese woman, described how she rebelled by defying her culture's gender norms: 'I had to become a bad girl. I was always devious in my own mind, but I smoked, I joined a gang, and we ganged up on people. We stole. I developed the same kind of attitude – kind of "fuck the world I am going to do what I want" attitude.' Instead of defying gender norms, Natasha, an Indo-Canadian woman, rebelled against the cultural markers of biological femaleness:

If my sister or my mom asked me, 'Oh, are you on the rag? Do you have your period now?' I would say 'No' when I really was. Why? Because I don't want it to be talked about. I don't want things that make me so much a woman to be talked about. To be pulled out and distinguished. I think it's resistance. I don't want to be seen as a woman ... I used to wear sports bras for a long time because I didn't want it so defined. Why should I wear underwire when the sports bras are more comfortable? ... I think I always maybe wanted to be a guy. Maybe that's why. Because I think I would always want to play with them at school and I would always resist being a woman. I think they got away with a lot. I used to find it unfair. I still find it unfair.

Kathryn describes making a conscious decision to reject mainstream beauty ideals: 'One day I had hair that was longer than yours and straightened. I went to the hairdressers and she cut it all off to one inch. The hairdresser called my mother and said, "You know what I'm doing? She wants all of her hair cut off." That was when the black movement was very big, and I wanted all my hair cut off.' Like Kathryn, many women interviewed describe feeling liberated after they defied dominant ideals and began experimenting with oppositional ones.

Evading the Body Beautiful

Over the course of their lives many women use less overt strategies to evade body ideals. Getting pregnant and becoming a mother gives some women permission to let go of beauty standards: 'Before, I felt like I had to look a certain way. I don't feel that at all any more. Especially after getting pregnant ... I think I have gotten a lot more self-esteem from being pregnant and looking like shit. So I don't think I have looked very good at all for a good two months. I don't really care about it.' For Salima, a South-Asian Canadian woman of Pakistani heritage, ageing has allowed her to escape the strict dictates of the body beautiful: 'I decided not to colour or dye my hair, and I get comments about that too. There is always people who will say, "You did the streaks. You did the grey streaks." And I kind of laugh and say, "I earned them."'

Questioning Cultural Ideals

The examples I have provided so far have focused on the resistance strategies that are used by the individual to defuse the impact of body ideals or increase their personal agency. Some of the women interviewed have demonstrated their opposition to social values regarding beauty by posing insightful questions concerning the social and cultural roots of their experiences. Feminists have long argued that consciousness raising – reading, speaking, and listening to one another – is the best way women have of understanding the female self in society (de Lauretis, 1986). Through CR, women actively challenge taboos regarding female sexual pleasure and female beauty, and develop their own analyses of how their bodies have been manipulated in the culture. Kasha, a woman with Eastern European roots, remarks:

> Men are allowed to keep their sexuality, whether they're balding or fat. But as soon as a woman breaks out of a mold of what her society considers attractive, that's it ... I guess I am looking for an answer. Why? Why can't we look at women who are larger sexually, why is it comical? ... Is society afraid of sexuality? Is that something people are afraid of? What does it represent that's so horrible and comical? I think people find it comical because they are afraid somehow. This is too big a woman, who's taking up too much space, who's too sexual. So in a way it must represent power and that's why it's being crushed.

Organizing for Change

There is no question that social change movements have contributed to the worldviews of many women and have influenced their attitudes and decisions regarding their bodies. The impact of social movements is evident in women's insights into how culture has shaped their experiences of their bodies: these insights would have been impossible before the feminist, black, and disability rights movements. Women not only identify the roots of problems and ways of improving their own body and self images, but also suggest concrete strategies for social change. Some young women have organized events in their high schools. Others have started groups in their universities and colleges. Shavonne was involved in starting a body image group for women of colour:

> I, myself, and other women of colour, we developed that group for women of colour around body image issues. Because around that time I was very active and would ask questions, like, 'We don't see ourselves anywhere. Like what the fuck is this. We're everywhere, but like in terms of media, magazines, we don't see ourselves.'

Fatima spoke of the need to find ways to speak across differences in order to build understanding and find collective strategies for change:

> I would like to think of a way for many men to support women into a better image and a more realistic image. I don't know if that would ever

happen. I have a lot of doubts about that. The one thing I know is that there is a lot of good that comes out of the women's movement and the disabled movement and other movements. The biggest barrier is for us to do this together. If we could find a way of involving men, it might shift. Or if they could find a way of involving women in stuff that they are dealing with, or not dealing with, it might make it better. There is a lot of separation between everybody, and it's really hurting us.

As women pass through adolescence and move into adulthood, many of them work to resolve their body struggles. They often go through a process of working out problems concerning their feelings about their bodies and their identities. This is a time when they confront confusion about being a woman, being fat, being dark, being disabled, or being biracial; a time when they negotiate their own self-definitions. This negotiation often takes place within a woman's family, friendship circles, networks, and cultural context(s). This does not mean that she internalizes the values of her parents or of the mainstream culture; it is more about her developing a positive sense of her body and self out of many conflicting forces. The solutions a woman finds inevitably evolve and change as she becomes pregnant, gains weight, and ages. She must confront and respond to changing messages concerning her body and being throughout her life.

Conclusion

The varied stories I have offered suggest that there is no simple, neat answer to liberation from body ideals. The women suggest that greater body acceptance is won through the use of shifting strategies, which depend on what avenues for self-assertion are possible in the moment. Solutions to the problem of standards of beauty are always partial. Depending on the social context, women sometimes reinforce one body norm while challenging another. They also employ many different strategies to resist ideals and define themselves, which indicates that freedom exists in the possibility of using many different strategies and practices.

Solutions to the problem of the ideal are as varied as the women who seek them. It is important that we respect and support each woman's responses to this problem, whether or not we agree with those solutions. I offer no final judgments about beauty practices because their implications vary so widely. The only feminist responses I can advocate are these: helping women define and expand options for ways of being in their bodies and their worlds; helping them work through the political, ethical, and health-related dilemmas associated with their practices; and helping them choose their most empowering option, given their historical, cultural, personal, and bodily realities. The varied experiences of the women I have quoted in this chapter suggest that we must continue to create alternative images of beauty and a broader range of options for all of us, so as to provide every woman with expanded definitions of beauty and womanhood.

CHAPTER 6

Men and Feminism:
Relationships and Differences

Amanda Goldrick-Jones

In its broadest sense, patriarchy encompasses a vast network of attitudes, behaviours, and institutional structures that enable men to exercise power and claim privileges. Yet patriarchy has never extended carte blanche privileges to 'all men' at the expense of 'all women.' The offspring of patriarchy – capitalism, racism, heterosexism, and the equation of masculinity with physical power and strength – can turn easily against their own fathers. Patriarchal thought has oppressed and continues to oppress women of all races and classes, but various constituencies of men have also suffered under 'the rule of the fathers': the enslaved, the poor, the disabled, men believing the wrong religion, men of the wrong ethnicity, and men with the wrong sexual orientation.

If the overall goal of feminism is to critique and dismantle patriarchal networks, then it stands to reason that feminism can benefit men – even, in the long run, men who believe they would have to 'give up' power. Indeed, some individual men and men's groups worldwide believe strongly that feminism is advantageous to men, and furthermore that men have a great deal to offer when it comes to doing feminist work. Men have often chosen to adopt feminist values because women they love, admire, or work beside are themselves feminists; for these men, feminism is a means to enhance their personal and professional relationships with women.

Yet as individuals and as members of groups, profeminist men are facing enormous challenges. Many profeminist groups that thrived in the 1970s and 1980s are buckling under the stress of balancing idealistic common goals with the fact that men's experiences of masculinity are profoundly different, and are mediated far more by race, class, physical ability, and sexuality than was first recognized. The internal conflicts within many profeminist organizations – and within many feminist ones – are formidable and are capable of frustrating even the most dedicated. Many profeminist activists have opted out of the organizational scene, and redirected their energies toward improving their relationships with their families and doing community work.

As well, feminist women have sometimes questioned profeminist men's motives or actions. Most feminist women agree that men should critique hegemonic and oppressive notions of 'masculinity' and should do more than pay lip service to feminism (see especially hooks [1992a] and Steinem [1992]); still, men doing feminist work do not automatically earn the trust and support of feminist women. Profeminist men sometimes find themselves wrestling with the question of whether they are 'oppressors' within feminist communities, even while they are being marginalized by the hegemonic masculine culture for their feminist beliefs. Given all these real or potential obstacles, it is hardly surprising that the mass profeminist movement envisioned by idealists in the 1970s and early 1980s has failed to materialize; indeed, there is little indication that such a movement will arise.

Yet men's engagement with feminism since the 1970s has resulted in some accomplishments: a growing critique of hegemonic masculinity, increased public awareness of men's responsibility to end domestic abuse and violence against women, and a greater recognition of how stereotyped images of manhood can damage both men and women. Profeminist men are more likely to see through what Canadian writer and White Ribbon Campaign co-founder Michael Kaufman calls the 'collective hallucination' of masculinity (1992: 17), though this clearer sight doesn't mean that profeminists struggle any less with the contradictions of 'being a man ... [in] a strange world of power and pain' (37).

In this chapter I discuss the accomplishments of profeminist men over the past thirty years, and the challenges facing them, and suggest some possible future directions for profeminist work. I begin by defining what feminism or 'profeminism' means to men engaged in this work. I then outline how the 'men's movement' – mainly in Britain, the United States, and Canada – grew out of feminism in the 1970s. After this I illustrate some ways in which profeminist men in these countries have, through their activist work, both jeopardized and strengthened relations between men and feminism. Then I outline some important conflicts arising among profeminist men themselves, mainly between white, middle-class profeminists and gay, working-class, and Black sympathizers who feel their experiences are being marginalized. In illustrating these conflicts, I am not simply trying to point out 'failures'; I am also trying to show how an awareness of differences has usefully, if traumatically, destabilized the totalizing notion of a unified 'men's movement.' Finally, I summarize the many challenges facing profeminists today, and suggest some future directions for profeminist work in this new millennium.

Why Men Support Feminism

Political Reasons

There is no single totalizing definition or set of strategies for men who believe in feminism, any more than there is for feminist women. However, since about the late eighteenth century a minority of men have consistently and publicly endorsed feminist goals such as higher education for women, votes for women, equal pay and gender equality in workplaces, and the right to birth control and reproductive choice (Kimmel and Mosmiller, 1992; LeGates, 1996). More recently, profeminist men have also taken strong stances against rape and other forms of men's violence toward women. The American-based National Organization of Men Against Sexism – once North America's largest profeminist men's organization – outlined the following goals in its 1990 brochure:

> We work to end crimes and injustices toward women such as domestic and sexual violence, attacks on choice and reproductive rights, sexual harassment, lack of parity, and the global feminization of poverty. We understand pro-feminism to mean challenging ourselves and other men on the ways in which we perpetuate, and benefit from, sexist behaviors. At the same time, we are celebrating the many ways in which men are becoming caring, strong, and non-abusive.

The NOMAS statement combines an endorsement of feminist principles and a commitment to antipatriarchal activism with a male-positive, mutually supportive agenda. Similar ideals are encountered in the documents produced by a range of profeminist groups around the world, including the Canadian White Ribbon Campaign (WRC) against violence toward women, the New Zealand–based Men Opposing Racism and Sexism, and Australia's Men Against Sexual Assault (MASA). As well, these goals are implied in profeminist, promale magazines such as *XY*, published in Australia, and the British men's magazine *Achilles Heel*. Recent large-scale profeminist public activism ranges from the Ending Men's Violence 'Brotherpeace' marches in the United States during the 1980s; to the White Ribbon Campaign's partnerships with Canadian unions, businesses, and the YWCA to distribute White Ribbons nationally and to raise funds for antiviolence projects; to a gender awareness curriculum package for high schools produced several years ago by the Halifax-based Men for Change; to – in a slightly unusual move – MASA's anti–male violence fundraiser in the mid-1990s that sold Australian wine labelled with the organization's logo.

Men who do feminist work generally understand that their goals reach beyond ensuring equal access to established economic, judicial, and political resources. Feminist women are critiquing patriarchal forms of economic and political power and showing how these structures maintain racism, classism, violence, and other forms of oppression; in a similar way, many profeminist men are examining how patriarchal power defines and perpetuates oppressive concepts of masculinity. Some of this work, especially where it explores how men of colour, gay men, and working-class men are victimized by power inequities, intersects with issues of race, sexuality, and class.

Personal Reasons

However, not all profeminist groups or individual men adopt overtly political strategies. In Britain, for example, a number of men who support feminism contend that individual therapeutic 'menswork' should precede political engagement. According to two counsellors at the Everyman Centre (now the Ahimsa Centre) in Devon, a facility that treats violent men and supports their partners, it isn't possible to transform gender relations unless a man has personally reflected on what it means to be a man and has addressed problems or inequities in his relationships with women (Bell, 1998; Wolf-Light, 1998). This task is especially challenging for heterosexual men, many of whom implicitly define masculinity in terms of aggression and/or homophobia.

Personal menswork can also have political effects. By examining masculinities and relations between women and men in subversive ways, the British men's magazine *Achilles Heel* is encouraging radical dialogue between women and men on gender issues (Pratt, 1998). This can be seen as a political act. This link between the personal and the political is appropriate, given that men who support feminism often locate their initial motivation in the personal realm – they were, or are, involved personally or professionally with feminist women. Indeed, the first British men's group was formed, possibly as early as 1971, as 'a response to feminism. Women were developing, and as they fought to change their roles, some men felt pressure to change too ... There was liberation in the air and men wanted a part of that' (What Future for Men? 1990).

In these early days of the profeminist movement, some men were galvanized by feminism's potential to transform gender roles. In the 1980s and 1990s, profeminist men were still inspired by relationships with women 'who defined themselves as feminist' (Pratt, 1998), or they found themselves working alongside feminist women in movements such as environmentalism. A few had been 'brought up in feminist households' (Romalis, 1993). A gay profeminist told me he has always felt much closer to women than to men; he prefers groups comprising women, and feels uncomfortable working only with men. Jack Layton (1993), a co-founder of the White Ribbon Campaign, believes that profeminist men working with feminist women need to 'seek the leadership of the women's movement' by exercising relational skills such as consultation and active listening.

For many profeminist men, feminism is as much about enhancing their personal or professional relationships with the women in their lives as it is about transforming political and social institutions. Given that profeminist men are faced with helping to dismantle patriarchy – a system from which some profeminists materially benefit – it seems only logical that many would gain motivation from strong, positive relationships and open communication with feminist women. In this respect, feminist women can play active roles, not as 'mothers' or naysayers, but as facilitators and enablers for men wishing to educate themselves in feminist thought and do feminist work. As one member of the *Achilles Heel* editorial collective notes, doing feminist work as a man means 'really thinking about [women's] own gender identity and our own gender identity as men. Communication ... cross-communication, really ... the idea that we share a project' (Tuddenham, 1998).

Relationships with Feminist Women

Women and men who support feminism can and do share important goals and engage in complementary projects. But there are some major differences in their motives and, it follows, in their strategies and forms of activism. Many women who come to feminism are motivated by personal experiences of being oppressed because of their sex; they gain energy to fight patriarchy both from their anger and from the solidarity of being with others who have had similar experiences. Yet even this solidarity is problematic; the myth of sisterhood, constructed by white middle-class feminists, has faced necessary challenges from women of colour and from working-class and other marginalized feminists, who would like white, middle-class women to articulate their privilege and the ways in which they themselves are raced as the first step toward dismantling these oppressive structures and attitudes.

Profeminists are also motivated by anger over gender injustice and by the urge to redress that injustice, and their white middle-classness has been similarly challenged. But men encounter a unique conundrum: patriarchy is a male construct, so in order to dismantle it they must admit their own collusion and dismantle their own privileges. Taken to a logical end, this argument demands that profeminists effectively dismantle themselves as men (see especially Stoltenberg, 1989). Thus, one of the greatest challenges profeminists face is how to deal with the guilt of being 'a male oppressor.'

A similar problem of 'men as oppressors' underlies debates about how (if at all) women's studies should work with the still small academic field of men's studies. Men's studies researchers and teachers – a few of whom are women – argue that they are consciously studying men not as 'neutral,' default humans but rather as gendered beings who shape and are shaped by power relations in particular ways *because* they are men. However, some feminist critics believe that 'men's studies' is a redundancy, and more than a few are leery about the potential for men's studies to 'take over' feminism in the academy (Jardine and Smith, 1987; Hanmer, 1990; Canaan and Griffin, 1990). The tensions between women's and men's studies underscore the need for profeminists – within or outside men's studies – to articulate their position as 'oppressors' in patriarchy. The ways they do this, or fail to, are inseparable from their activism and from their success in forming productive relations with feminist groups.

Antisexism in the 1970s: Inspiration, Guilt, Conflict

In Britain, several men's movements developed in the early 1970s, one of which was strongly antisexist and consisted of men whose female partners or friends were active in the women's liberation movement (Cooper, 1990: 6; Sheil, 1990). According to one chronicler of British profeminism, these men were initially 'pushed ... by their feminist colleagues [but] were unsure of their role in the feminist struggle and were thus indecisive about what action they could take' (Cooper, 1990: 6). These groups adopted models of consciousness raising (CR) similar to those in the women's movement, and attempted to integrate therapeutic and CR approaches with antisexist, often socialist discussions and conferences (6). Some of these men, including writer-theorists John Rowan and Victor Seidler, were concerned enough about the relationship between therapy and politics that they created the Red Therapy group, which stayed together from 1974 to 1977. According to Rowan, this group functioned as a 'leaderless therapy group' that also created 'a political critique of ... therapy, personal growth, counselling' (1987: 21).

In Canada during the 1970s, profeminist activism was taking at least two major directions, one of them being a personal analysis of masculinity similar to the one undertaken by British men's groups. The sex role theory being explored at the time by activist-academics like Joseph Pleck (Pleck and Sawyer, 1974; Pleck, 1976) was a significant avenue of thought for Canadian men interested in analysing masculinity. Pleck was a keynote speaker at a men's conference held in 1975 at Ontario's University of Waterloo, at which men-only groups were encouraged to talk about oppressive aspects of the male sex role. Profeminists in Canada also adopted CR methods, and met as much to gain emotional support as to plan forms of activism (see Etkin, 1991: 36).

Action against sexism – especially against men's violence toward women – was a second major direction for Canadian profeminists during this decade. Specific projects are difficult to trace, since Canadian men's groups tended to be small and localized in the 1970s. But Canadian therapist Ron Thorne-Finch notes that a number of profeminist-inspired treatment programs for violent men were being developed, among them a Winnipeg-based group called 'Evolve' (1992: 239). Thorne-Finch comments: 'While many of these counsellors would not have identified their actions as part of a movement of pro-feminist men, their theoretical approach and practical applications placed them firmly within the realm of pro-feminist masculinism – whether or not they were card-carrying members' (238–9).

In the United States as well, the 1970s was a decade for men to take on what was then considered 'the interesting and exciting question of the male response to women's liberation' (Men's Liberation, 1971). To this end they formed groups, published radical newsletters, and organized conferences to support feminist activism and explore the implications of feminism for men. The sense of energy and the generally positive outlook for this work in the early 1970s is captured by a contributor to the newsletter *Brother: A Forum for Men Against Sexism*, who wrote, 'I don't believe I have ever felt so affected by a movement or a social development before in my life' (Men's Liberation, 1971). Besides *Brother*, a number of other radical men's newsletters sprang up in the United States, many with explicit profeminist goals. For example, a newsletter published jointly by the Men's Awareness Network and the Chicago Men's Gathering was 'dedicated to eliminating sexism, supporting the women's movement, and changing men's roles' (Men's Awareness, 1976, p. i). In 1975 the first US Men and Masculinity conference discussed the formation of a national antisexist men's organization, whose principles would be based strongly on feminism. Clearly, the 'men's movement' was inspired by and heavily indebted to feminist theory and activism; some men were even a little envious of the excitement and joy women were experiencing.

In both Britain and North America, a second movement was growing out of CR-inspired groups. This consisted of 'liberationist' men who preferred to focus on understanding masculinities, working toward self-improvement, and forging better relationships with other men. In Britain during the late 1970s, antisexist and liberationist groups initially tried to work together. But the simmering tensions between 'anti-sexist' and 'liberationist' men exploded in 1980 over a proposal to adopt a set of 'Ten Commitments' to feminism. To the antisexists, these Commitments represented an overt endorsement and support of the women's movement as well as a call for men to change themselves. Many of the men at the conference saw the commitments as an admission of male guilt – or, as John Rowan put it, as 'a giant superego sitting on my shoulders shouting in my ear' (Cooper, 1991: 9). The motion to adopt the Commitments was defeated.

According to British profeminist writer Mick Cooper, after this incident the British antisexist/profeminist movement lost enthusiasm and clout, going into 'a steep decline' after 1982 (1991: 9–10) while the liberationist movement gained momentum. Nor were antisexist men's relations with feminist groups going well at this time. Cases in point were two men's projects – Crèches Against Sexism and Cash Against Sexism – which began in 1980 and quickly came into conflict with the women's movement over questions of funding. According to Cooper (1990), the men withdrew funds and volunteer childcare they had been willing to donate to a feminist conference when the women said they preferred to use paid childcare workers. 'This move infuriated many women who felt that the men were using the money to control the women's movement' (9). Stung by this criticism, both Crèches and Cash Against Sexism fell apart. It isn't clear who was blaming whom, but it is reasonable to suspect that a lack of open and respectful communications played a part here. It is also possible that the men were unwilling to recognize and find ways to work through the conundrum of being well-intentioned 'oppressors.'

Men Building Relations with Feminism

The U.K.: Achilles Heel

Since the 1980s, the co-editors of the British 'radical men's magazine' *Achilles Heel* have examined oppressive notions of masculinity and encouraged dialogue to improve relations between men and feminism. The current editorial collective of *Achilles Heel* sees the magazine as 'a forum for discussion of men and masculinity, and a reflection of the diverse and developing ways in which men are experiencing themselves today' (Editorial Collective, 1997, p. 3). The magazine includes articles about women's and feminist issues, especially as these intersect with 'menswork'; it also welcomes 'any contributions and comment from women' and refuses to print 'sexist, racist, or homophobic' material (3). A recent issue of *Achilles Heel* featured an article co-written by a woman and a man discussing practical ways that profeminist men can build trust and work productively with feminist women. Among other things, it recommended that men educate themselves about women's oppression, actively question how men oppress women, listen to women, and engage in coalition work with feminist women (Schacht and Ewing, 1997). Yet *Achilles Heel* is unwilling to locate itself entirely within feminism. It does not take an overtly 'political' position on feminist issues; indeed, it often publishes articles exploring other aspects of men's movements, such as Robert Bly's mythopoetics, that many North American feminists and profeminists would consider problematic. Yet as of 1999, *Achilles Heel* was the only extant profeminist print publication being distributed internationally that not only encouraged dialogue with feminists but also explored a range of perspectives on masculinity.

Canada: The White Ribbon Campaign

Informal histories of Canadian men's movements imply that the heyday for Canadian profeminism was the 1980s and early 1990s (Etkin, 1991; Fisher, 1993; Thorne-Finch, 1992). During that time, profeminist conferences and forums took place regularly in Kingston, Ottawa, Toronto, and Montreal. Profeminist groups active during that time included the Manitoba Men's Network, Men for Women's Choice, Metro Men Against Violence (based in Toronto), Men's Network for Change (based in Kingston), and Halifax's Men for Change. According to Canadian profeminist Ken Fisher (in Thorne-Finch, 1992), in 1989 there were probably 200 men's groups, representing 5,000 men in Canada 'organizing to overhaul hegemonic masculinity' (242).

The White Ribbon Campaign (WRC) is one of the few larger Canadian profeminist organizations to have survived the 1990s, in part because it has emphasized communication and coalition work with feminist groups. Started in 1991 as a male response to the massacre of fourteen young women in December 1989 at Montreal's École Polytechnique, this national campaign against men's violence toward women has been described as a successful attempt to extend profeminist principles 'far beyond what the antisexist men's movement in the United States has been able to imagine possible' (Messner, 1997: 54). Though a number of profeminist groups around the world have worked actively to eliminate violence against women, the WRC is arguably unique in that it has tried to persuade large numbers of men at a national, highly public level to take action on a specific feminist issue – an issue that until the Montreal massacre had been somewhat marginalized in the Canadian public forum.

Feminist Criticisms of the WRC

In its first two or three years of operation, the WRC earned praise and criticism from feminists and profeminists alike. The criticisms focused mainly around the issue of accountability to feminist women's groups. In particular, critics asked whether these men were listening attentively enough to women's concerns, and whether their White Ribbon campaign was diverting attention and resources from women's own antiviolence initiatives. These concerns stemmed partly from the fact that in 1991 and 1992 the WRC timed its 'White Ribbon Week' to culminate on 6 December, the anniversary of the massacre, a day that many feminists had considered women's time to mourn and remember. Thus, there were concerns that men were appropriating women's 'space' and assuming for themselves the power to define 6 December as a day for women (Boulos, 1992; Cole, 1991; Jones, 1992a, 1992b).

As well, some critics wondered whether the WRC's plan to blitz the country with ribbons was a form of empire building. No one knows how many men wore the White Ribbon in 1991 as a symbol of their repudiation of violence against women; estimates vary between '100,000' (Kaufman, 1991) and 'more than a million' (Landsberg, 1992: 16). Critics and even some WRC organizers worried that the ribbon could be interpreted as a popular, token gesture – an easy way out for men who weren't willing to take more concrete action against male violence (Kaufman, 1992; Crowe and Montgomery, 1992; Geigen-Miller, 1992).

Nor were feminist women the only critics of the WRC. In 1992, Kingston's Men's Network for Change 'respectfully' declined to support future White Ribbon campaigns. The network was troubled by the possibility that the media attention resulting from the novelty of men getting involved in a feminist project could 'overpower consideration of the central issues (men's violence against women) in favour of the more newsworthy ... issue of "sensitive new age guys" and their token political gestures' (Jones, 1992b: 6).

Strategic Responses to Feminist Criticisms

The WRC prepared two kinds of responses to these criticisms. Beginning in 1993, the campaign rescheduled White Ribbon Week to late November. From 1992 to 1994, the campaign's 'Frequently Asked Questions' (FAQ) brochures stressed the importance of 'stepping back' from 6 December and treating it a day for men to 'listen' to women rather than speak out. The WRC also produced an 'Organizer's Kit' emphasizing the same point for men wishing to begin a local White Ribbon drive: 'This is a day of intense pain for women and we feel it should be a day for men to step back and listen to the voices of women' ('How ...,' 1992: 12). To this day, the WRC still does not schedule large-scale men's events on 6 December. However, on each anniversary of the Montreal massacre, local WRC organizers do speak with news media about men's antiviolence activities, and men – some wearing the White Ribbons – routinely stand with women at 6 December memorials and vigils.

The second major strategy has been to maintain structures of accountability to feminist women's groups. A formal liaison committee of women and men was set up in 1992, but this proved to be burdensome. The WRC now engages in coalition work and other informal means of contact with feminist and women's groups as circumstances demand (including, says one WRC co-founder, phoning, e-mailing, and chatting in supermarket aisles). According to Michael Kaufman and Jack Layton, co-founders of the WRC, opening lines of communication with feminist women has been a priority for the WRC from the beginning. As Michael Kaufman (1993) has noted, 'We make mistakes, but it's a constant process of learning, trying out things, and looking toward women.' It's noteworthy that Australia's Men Against Sexual Assault has a similar philosophy about the link between accountability and communication, and has invited feminist activist women to attend its meetings and workshops (Pease, 1999; Daphne, 1999). Indeed, for profeminist groups worldwide, an integral part of maintaining good relations with feminism has involved balancing between two extremes: men striking out wholly on their own and possibly making major mistakes, and men relying so heavily on women's leadership that they must effectively ask permission to do anything.

Profeminism and the Politics of Inclusion

Maintaining good relationships with feminist women is one major challenge for profeminist men. An equally serious challenge is working through differences in sexual orientation, race, ethnicity, and class. From the beginnings of men's movements in the 1970s, there was an awareness of and a professed sensitivity toward issues of sexuality and race. Yet the white, middle-class nature of profeminist (as well as other men's) organizations has often been a source of tension among activist men, and has given rise to serious concerns about whether profeminist organizations have fairly represented the spectrum of men and masculinities.

Perspectives of the 'Gay Male'

'Gay liberation' profoundly influenced profeminism and antisexism in the 1970s. These influences have been well documented in the United States and Britain. Two cases from those countries are helpful in illustrating how different perspectives about sexuality can fragment profeminist groups. In Britain, gay men who 'had quite suddenly discovered their energy, their voice, their ability to fight back against the oppression which they felt they had for so long endured' (Sheil, 1990) looked toward Black liberation movements in the United States as their model. Though these men considered themselves antisexist, it is perhaps not surprising that many took a highly radical stance toward masculinity – one that called into question men's relationships with women. A piece in a magazine called *Brothers Against Sexism* took a 1974 national men's conference by storm. Titled 'Coming Out is the Only Way Forward,' the article argued:

> If men are serious about being antisexist, then they must sacrifice the privileges they obtain from women and relate on a sexual level exclusively with men ... Only when men are prepared to risk their masculinity to the extent of becoming homosexual can a men's movement challenge sexism in the way gay liberation has. (in Cooper, 1991: 7)

At the 1974 conference, conflict over this position was intense. According to Cooper, several gay men walked out after accusing their straight counterparts of homophobia (7). Cooper also notes that this event set off a round of self-criticism among antisexist men. As a result, there were no further profeminist conferences and publications until the late 1970s. But in Cooper's analysis, the gay men's criticisms were not far off target and revealed growing weaknesses in profeminism: 'The belief that in changing ourselves through consciousness-raising [men] were liberating women was delegitimized through an intense attack from an oppressed group' (7).

In the United States, gay and straight men's groups showed some initial signs of working together. The first of the many yearly Men and Masculinity (M&M) conferences, held in 1975, included topics such as 'The Black Male Experience' and 'The Gay Male.' The following year's M&M conference ran into trouble for openly supporting gay issues. The conference was to be held at Penn State, but the university administration withdrew its support when it learned that gay-positive topics would be included in the program. In solidarity, the entire conference moved across the street to a Holiday Inn (Men, 1976). By 1978 the M&M Gay Task Force had assumed a high profile, with many gay issues discussed and a number of gay speakers and workshops featured. Among the resolutions passed at the conference was one promising to continue this pro-gay work at future conferences and to fight discrimination against gays. Yet well into the 1980s, critics continued to raise doubts about whether conferences, workshops, and profeminist activism in general were really supportive of gay issues.

Another issue complicating gay men's participation in profeminist conferences and workshops is that these events are often appropriated by straight men as opportunities to work through problems that gays have already dealt with – topics such as 'physicality between men' and 'who does the washing up' (Flood and Dowsett, 1994: 26–7). Given these complications, perhaps it was only a matter of time before a major conflict arose in an American profeminist organization over the free expression of gay experience. One of the first such conflicts was powerful enough to bring NOMAS – which defined itself as both profeminist and gay-positive – to a point of crisis. The catalyst was an article written by one of NOMAS's founders, Jeff Beane, published in the profeminist magazine *Changing Men* in August 1992. The article outlined Beane's experiences as a gay male teen in the late 1950s and early 1960s and described a sexual encounter with a younger boy. In that same issue of *Changing Men* was a discreet ad for the North American Man-Boy Love Association, and another ad for an 'exotic' magazine (Parrish, 1992). The storm of criticism that followed in the wake of this issue called into question NOMAS's commitment to feminist principles. The NOMAS leadership – which had defended the controversial *Changing Men* issue – was accused of 'Old Boy Network tactics' (Parrish, 1992) and even of condoning pedophilia. The following issue of *Changing Men* published criticisms of Beane's article and an apology from the NOMAS executive. But in the eyes of many profeminists and feminists, the organization's credibility had been irreparably damaged.

This conflict occurred in 1992, yet in some ways the tensions within NOMAS over differences in gay and straight perspectives were similar to those that had arisen almost twenty years earlier in Britain. In each case, the failure to resolve the tensions not only created major organizational schisms but also severely compromised the ability of organization members to do solid activist work. There is still an urgent need for gay and straight profeminist men to come up with strategies for working with and through differences arising out of sexual orientation, but this is much easier said than done.

Working through Classism and Racism

Profeminism and Class

No less critical for profeminists is a better understanding of how sexism and masculinity intersect with class to shape economic systems. In Britain, Andrew Tolson (1977) and Victor Seidler (1991) have provided a socialist analysis of class and masculine power that has strongly influenced profeminist thought in that country since the 1970s. When Tolson observed men in the 1970s, he noted that 'working class masculinity is characterized ... by an immediate, aggressive style of behavior' (28) as compared with that of middle-class men. This aggression shapes relationships with other men as well as with women, and can be at odds with feminist goals of gender equity. For Tolson, there is a cause-and-effect relationship between a patriarchal working-class man's demand for absolute power in the home and the fact that the same working-class man is 'individually powerless, a mere calculation of the capitalist economy' (30).

Almost twenty years later, an issue of *Achilles Heel* entitled 'Men and Work' revisited the complex issue of how men's work shapes gender and family relations. In Britain, professional and managerial men are starting to take advantage of job sharing and flexible hours in order, among other things, to 'meet some domestic responsibilities' (Collins and Walton, 1996: 28). But the authors point out that 'manual workers are still under-represented' in job-sharing schemes, 'perhaps because of lower salary levels' (28).

Profeminism and Race

In the United States, profeminist concerns about power differences among men have generally focused more on race than on class. In a March 1976 article in the Men's Awareness Network/Chicago Men's Gathering newsletter, the writer agreed with an earlier article's argument that the 'men's movement is mostly populated by men who "enjoy white skin privilege, class privilege, heterosexual privilege, and male privilege."' Though the writer counterargued that 'a movement has to start somewhere,' he also noted that the American men's movement needed more 'involvement of working class, ethnic/racial minority, and sexual minority men' (Smith, 1976).

Though American men's groups of the 1970s were generally troubled about representation – and this question would continue to haunt national group organizers into the 1980s and 1990s – many profeminists also felt that 'a movement has to start somewhere.' One feminist woman who worked with the group that eventually formed the National Organization of Men in 1982 advised her male colleagues not to 'put [them]selves down' because they were members of a dominant group. In her view, white, middle-class feminists who were struggling with guilt over inclusivity needed to remember that 'being middle-class, white, male and feminist could be a tremendous impetus for deep change in this society ... If white, middle-class, men stand up and say we want change, feminist change, they cannot be interpreted as saying they want *in* to the system – they *are* in the system. It will be clear they're challenging the system' (Ballweg, 1982).

For a time, white, middle-class profeminists in the United States seemed to be succeeding in their attempts at inclusivity. In 1983 the newly fledged National Organization of Men conducted an 'Open Forum' in New York City. Topics at the forum included gay politics and links to antisexist groups, Black men against sexism and racism, and pressures to be a Real Man. In 1984, NOM became the National Organization of Changing Men and mandated seventeen task groups that in theory would allow NOCM to be diverse and representative. These groups included 'Gay Rights,' 'Homophobia,' and 'Racism and Sex Role Issues of Minority Men.' It was anticipated that each task group would have 'considerable power and autonomy,' including the exclusive right to issue statements and initiate actions regarding its particular area (Shapiro, 1982). Commenting on these attempts at inclusivity, profeminist sociologist Michael Messner notes that some aspects of this structure represented a 'rare example' of diverse men working together 'toward common goals' (1997: 101). But at the same time, '[NOCM][1] remained an organization that was made up of predominantly white, professional-class men (and some women.) Although the organization "welcomed and sought Black men's participation ... over the year, few blacks participated"' (quoted in Messner, 1997: 101).

Messner maintains that by the mid-1990s, antiracist work had become 'part of the political discourse of NOMAS' and that more men of colour were taking leadership roles in the organization (1997: 101). However, there are conflicting accounts about how successful NOMAS has been as an inclusive profeminist organization. One crisis point over issues of race was the organization's decision in 1991 to go ahead and hold the annual Men & Masculinity conference in Arizona after the Reverend Jesse Jackson and civil rights groups had called for a tourism boycott of Arizona. That state had rescinded the new national holiday in memory of Martin Luther King. In response to NOMAS's decision, noted radical profeminist John Stoltenberg (author of *Refusing to Be a Man*) resigned his position as chair of the Ending Men's Violence task group (Stoltenberg, 1997). Similarly, another former NOMAS member saw NOMAS's decision as a sign of the organization's 'internal racism' and 'lack of commitment ... to combatting racism' (Parrish, 1992). NOMAS's decision to ignore the Arizona boycott was interpreted by many as confirmation that this mainly white organization wasn't prepared to represent or respect the views of Black men.

In retrospect, it does seem questionable that an antisexist organization created mainly out of the experiences of white, middle-class men could even begin to address the multiple oppressions experienced by Black men. The challenge of eliminating sexism against Black women is complicated not only by what Manning Marable (1997) calls the distortions of racial stereotyping, but also by Black men's experiences of systemic socioeconomic and political discrimination. And there is no agreement among Black theorists about the current state of gender relations. Marable believes that Black women's and men's common struggle against racism 'transcends the barrier of gender, as Black women have tried to tell their men for generations' (447). However, Robert Staples (1997) warns that public schisms between Blacks over sexual relations, notably the 1991 Anita Hill–Clarence Thomas hearings, have the 'potential for increasing tension and conflict between Black men and Black women' (191).

In Canada, profeminist groups have not been as overtly outspoken or as badly fractured over issues of race. From the perspective of an American profeminist writing in 1976, Canada was managing better than the United States to achieve a 'balance' on issues of race and sexism (Smith, 1976). The official focus of many Canadian profeminist groups since the 1970s has been to end men's violence and encourage men to reconceptualize masculinity, and ending racism could be considered part of that agenda. For example, Halifax's Men for Change includes 'antiracist' in its self-definition, and on its website provides many links to antiracist men's organizations. Notably, however, these websites pertain to African-American, not African-Canadian, men's activism. Nor are First Nations issues visible in this landscape. Given the many disadvantages that First Nations men, as well as women, are struggling against (see especially Cassidy et al., 1998), it seems surprising that unlike their American and Australian counterparts, Canadian profeminist men have paid relatively little attention to the matter of how perceptions of race can shape perceptions of masculinity.

Postmillennial Profeminism

Commentators and theorists examining the effects of feminism on men offer guardedly optimistic views, garnished with much caution, about whether men are truly changing. Segal (1990) argues that the past quarter-century or so of feminist thought and activism '*has* made an impact on men as well as women.' Indeed, men 'who occupy spaces where there is already greater equality between women and men,' such as universities and the caring professions, are now commonly showing 'support for feminist principles, as well as some level of practical sharing of housework and childcare' (xxvi–xxvii). Segal also notes the success of the White Ribbon Campaign in creating mass awareness among men about violence against women (xxvii). Even informally, day by day, it's observable that more Western men are sympathetic to feminism than they were a generation ago and that more men are changing in response to women's expectations.

But overall, as Segal implies, 'collective anti-sexist initiatives by men' have had relatively little public impact in Britain and are unlikely to be an effective means of changing the social and political landscape. As Australian profeminist R.W. Connell puts it, 'No huge crowds of men have become feminists' (1995: 226). Clatterbaugh (1997) is pessimistic about the future of a large, politically based profeminist movement in the United States. He points to the troubles of NOMAS, the demise of the profeminist magazine *Changing Men*, and the demise or low circulation figures of smaller antisexist publications (both the Australian magazine *XY* and the British magazine *Achilles Heel* have at least temporarily ceased publication). According to Clatterbaugh, although profeminist activism and theory have contributed substantially to building men's studies as an academic area, 'success in academia is not necessarily a sign of success in the movement' (1997: 198). In fact, he argues, profeminism stands in danger of becoming 'a largely academic discipline, complete with esoteric methodologies, while its political activism fades from sight' (198).

By the early to mid-1990s, NOMAS was in peril. But at the same time, hundreds of thousands of men were packing football stadiums to attend rallies organized by the right-wing Christian 'Promise Keepers,' and millions of Black men were joining the 'Million Man March' to Washington. Profeminism was never an enormously popular movement, even in its heyday, but in the 1970s the prospect of working with women to eliminate gender-based injustice and oppression did engage a number of men. Today, it seems that only small handfuls of men are still actively engaging political, antisexist feminism.

Why are so few men willing to support feminism collectively and publicly? Besides the fact that maintaining non-profit organizations can be exhausting and dispiriting (many former activists have suffered from burn-out), it's extraordinarily difficult to navigate political tensions around not only racism and sexual orientation, but also male privilege and men's relations with feminism. In Clatterbaugh's view, profeminism in the United States has yet to address adequately two major conundrums: how men can face the challenge of helping women achieve equality if this means relinquishing or sharing power with women, and how men can radically change themselves and eradicate violence without learning to hate their own masculinity. The first of these prospects – relinquishing or sharing power – is distasteful or frightening. Movements like the Promise Keepers recognize as much; that group validates patriarchal interpretations of masculinity and does not demand that men fundamentally change their ways of thinking about power and gender relations. The second prospect – essentially, redefining masculinity – can be extremely difficult and painful. Robert Bly's mythopoetic conception of the 'deep masculine,' with its therapeutic emphasis on group work, tries to give men tools to redefine masculinity in positive and empowering ways. But the mythopoetic movement does not fundamentally question the oppressive power relations that helped shape 'mythological' concepts of masculinity in the first place.

These scenarios suggest that men do want to change, but that perhaps rather than the traditional model of men mobilizing around a feminist political issue, profeminist men should consider how feminist principles might be brought be bear on existing men's groups or organizations. Connell (1995) contends that for men, organizations based structurally on feminist principles *'cannot* be the main form of counter-sexist politics among men, because the project of social justice in gender relations is directed *against* the interest they share. Broadly speaking, anti-sexist politics must be a source of disunity among men, not a source of solidarity' (236).

Connell believes that political activists in the area of masculinity, instead of staying within 'pure gender politics,' (237), should form groups based on situations that potentially intersect with gender injustice. He notes how British theorizing on masculinity has benefited from exploring interrelations with class issues such as labour unions, working conditions, and the education of young men (237–8). Connell sees more promise in an 'alliance politics,' in which 'the project of social justice depends on the overlapping of interests between different groups (rather than mobilization of one group around its common interest)' (238).

If profeminist organizations themselves are in peril, there are still many opportunities for men to build productive personal and working relationships with feminist women. Men can (and do) engage in partnership or coalition work with women, listen to and cooperate with experienced feminists, critique (and help other men critique) oppressive masculinities and promote 'male-positive' alternatives, and encourage boys and men to make gender equality part of their lives. Participating in small, local projects with specific goals – coaching boys' and girls' teams, producing films, speaking in schools, taking a women's studies course, promoting forms of gender justice in workplaces, making profeminist or feminist resources available to men on the Web, and (yes) cooking and doing the dishes – can provide some opportunities for men to transform oppressive gender relations.

The mass profeminist movement is no longer as visible as it once was. It may not even be a viable way for most men to incorporate feminism into their lives. Yet as Gloria Steinem (1992) has said: 'Women want a men's movement. We are literally dying for it.' There is reason to believe that men are becoming increasingly aware of the impact of feminism in their lives; that some are questioning the enormous damage wrought by patriarchy; that not all men are resisting feminism; and indeed, that more men are thinking about and enacting feminist principles each day in myriad ways that are perhaps too small to see through a broad sociopolitical lens.

Note

1 NOCM became NOMAS (the National Organization of Men Against Sexism) in 1990; Messner uses this name in his discussion (1997) of the organization's activities before 1990.

CHAPTER 7

Feminism, Reproduction, and Reproductive Technologies

Vanaja Dhruvarajan

Control over reproduction has always been a concern for women everywhere, and there is a commonsense understanding that reproductive technologies (RTs) help women achieve the control they want. In this chapter I consider whether RTs actually do help women control their reproduction. In the first section, I identify old and new RTs (ORT, NRT) and discuss the different ways in which they cater to women's needs.

In the second section I discuss the concerns feminists have regarding the impact of RTs on women. In the third section I discuss feminists' strategies for addressing these concerns. Since feminists do not speak with one voice on this issue, I review some of the more common opinions held by feminists regarding the implications of RTs. Different segments of the feminist movement have different perspectives on RTs; the feelings on this issue are intense and always have been.

Some feminists emphasize individual rights and choices; basically they trust the system as it exists and look for ways to work within it. Other feminists distrust the system and contend that social conditions must be transformed before the solutions they propose can work. Some feminists are pragmatists and are working to achieve the best possible solutions to the problems women face in their social circumstances.

Old and New Reproductive Technologies

Old Reproductive Technologies (ORTs)

ORTs include contraceptive devices that reliably limit the number of pregnancies a women has and spaces them according to her convenience. ORTs also include safe and reliable means for terminating unwanted pregnancies. Most European and North American women, and Third World women, have welcomed these technologies, which have helped them control their reproductive lives.

The women's movement in Canada has always concerned itself with reproductive issues. In 1969, therapeutic abortions were decriminalized. Under the procedure established by federal law that year, abortion committees consisting of physicians had the ultimate say on whether a woman would be permitted to have an abortion (McDaniel, 1985). Feminists argued against so much control being placed in the hands of the medical establishment – which propagates the view that abortion is a technical/medical matter – and mounted a struggle for the right to abortion on demand. They faced strong opposition, since in effect, they were demanding that abortion be treated as an ethical decision rather than a technical/medical one. The media in general labelled their demands extremist and tried to reinforce the authority of the medical establishment. Even though abortion is mainly a woman's issue, the media privileged the ideas and opinions of medical and legal professionals (Lake et al., 1991). However, mainly as a result of relentless campaigning by feminists, the Supreme Court of Canada struck down the 1969 law on the grounds that it was being applied arbitrarily and that it unduly restricted women's access to abortion services. This resulted in a number of court challenges by husbands and boyfriends of women seeking abortions. In 1991 the Mulroney government tried to recriminalize abortion through legislation, but failed; the proposed legislation passed marginally in the House of Commons but was defeated in the Senate. So at the present time abortion is legal in Canada.

There is an ongoing debate about whether abortion services should be subsidized by Medicare. Medicare is under provincial jurisdiction, which means that each province has its own policy, which is affected by the political climate at hand. As a result, access to abortion services is uneven across Canada. In addition to this, abortion services are generally better in large urban centres; it is difficult for women in smaller towns and rural areas to access these services (CARAL, 1995).

Pro-life groups are becoming more and more strident in their objections to abortion on demand. They demonstrate in front of clinics, flash placards showing photographs of aborted fetuses, and harass abortion service providers, sometimes to the point of shooting them or bombing their clinics. All of this is restricting the availability of abortion services in various parts of the country, and reducing the number of doctors willing to perform abortions. Thus, even though abortion is legal in Canada, it does not mean that abortion is always available to women on demand.

Until the 1980s, abortion on demand was central issue in Canadian feminism. Yet for working-class and minority women in Canada, the right to *bear* children is just as important, if not more so. This is because in a racist and classist society such as Canada, poor people and racial minorities are discouraged from reproducing. It became increasingly clear to middle-class feminists that unless the movement broadened its base, it would find it difficult to resist challenges from the pro-life movement. So beginning in the late 1980s, the women's movement in Canada began to redefine its priorities. The struggle now focuses on reproductive freedom, which includes the right to bear children as well as to access abortion services. In the words of the Ontario Coalition for Abortion Clinics:

What we will be demanding is publicly funded clinics in every community, working in every language and providing all the care women need; from safe and effective contraception to abortion; from birthing and midwifery to well-woman and well-baby care; and from sexuality counseling to reproductive technology developed according to women's needs and priorities. We will settle for nothing less. (1992: 452–3)

In Third World countries the 'experts' assume that RTs foster economic development – that population control is in fact a prerequisite for economic development. This 'expert' opinion has filtered into the public consciousness, and now informs public policies. In policy terms, population control has become more important than women's empowerment. RTs have come to be seen as a cornerstone of economic growth (Mies and Shiva, 1993a).

The New Reproductive Technologies (NRTs)

NRTs are used to assist reproduction. Midwives, herbalists, and traditional healers have always tried to help infertile women and impotent men have children. In the present day, science and technology are providing assistance in this area. Technologies such as *in vitro* fertilization (IVF), artificial insemination (AI), and surrogate motherhood, to name a few, are welcomed by many people encountering problems in their reproductive lives. For example, women who have problems conceiving and men who have problems with their sperm count can now have children of their own with the help of NRTs.

Amniocentesis and ultrasound are used to determine fetal health and sex; this helps the parents decide whether to carry the fetus to term. The developing field of genetic engineering is expected to open many more doors to help people control and direct their reproductive lives. For example, it is now possible to manipulate the genetic make-up of children by selectively fertilizing eggs with selected sperm. Also, people can now control the timing of their reproduction by having their embryos frozen and stored. The possibilities seem endless. But the implications of all these changes for human welfare are not clear and can provoke anxiety (Jackson et al., 1993).

The new NRTs inspire awe and wonder. Many people feel overwhelmed by the mysteries of scientific knowledge. They are fascinated by them, and they have come to believe that science leads to human progress. Its rationality, and thus its impartiality, is taken for granted. It is now considered perfectly natural to use knowledge and technology for the benefit of humanity. Some people now actually expect science to correct the imbalances produced by nature. For example, many women who cannot get pregnant in the natural course of their lives now feel it is their right to resort to reproductive technologies to achieve reproduction (Jackson et al., 1993).

Feminist Concerns Regarding Reproductive Technologies

In recent years, developments in RTs have led some to question their utility, and to wonder if the controls over them are sufficient. Those who use RTs are beginning to realize that the biomedical establishment is failing to treat them like active participants in the decision-making process. Many feel that they are patronized and talked down to, and that their feelings and opinions are trivialized. Too often the recipients of RT services are treated as commodities rather than as human beings with agency and control. These experiences are common among IVF patients and users of contraceptives (Williams, 1989; Akhtar, 1986). Furthermore, too often women are not told about the side effects of RTs.

Some people no longer perceive surrogate motherhood as an NRT (Pollit, 1993). It is evolving into a business, in which brokers are creating and exploiting a market for babies. NRTs can now determine whether it is the woman or the man who is infertile. In this context, surrogate motherhood is often pitched as a solution to the problem of infertility. Unfortunately, surrogate motherhood separates biological parenthood from social parenthood. It is left to others to decide whether a sperm donation is needed because the man is infertile, or an egg donation because the woman is infertile. Conceivably, both the egg and the sperm could be collected from donors, fertilized in a petri dish, and implanted in a 'rented' womb. The woman who goes through the pregnancy may not have any right to the child, even though she experiences all the pains and pleasures of pregnancy and childbirth. Thus, having a child can become just a commercial transaction devoid of human emotions. The implications of this are huge. Rothman (1997) reveals how marginalized women can be exploited by affluent people; how those who have money can make the best use of the law; and how the process is profoundly dehumanizing but interpreted as providing a needed service in the capitalist market discourse. She brings the racist, classist, and sexist nature of these practices to the fore.

Misuses of ORTs and NRTs

RTs are being misused. Pharmaceutical companies are interested mainly in getting results, selling products, and maximizing profits. For example, the misuse of DES (the synthetic hormone diethylstilbestrol), a hormone prescribed to prevent miscarriages, has had devastating consequences for many women (Simand, 1989). The welfare of those who are prescribed drugs is often ignored. Often, drugs are prescribed without proper testing and their side effects are not explained carefully enough to those who take them. Contraceptive devices are often marketed recklessly. Unsafe, untested contraceptive devices are given to Third World women and to marginalized women in Western societies.

Abuses are much more widespread in Third World countries. This is because these countries are preoccupied with economic development and there is a widespread conviction that population control is a prerequisite for economic development. Financial agencies such as the World Bank often make population control a precondition for economic assistance. As a result, political and corporate agendas take precedence over the welfare of women (Mies and Shiva, 1993a).

Similar attitudes are encountered among some segments of American medical establishment. For example, *60 Minutes*, an American public affairs program, reported in October 1998 that Quinacrine, a drug that sterilizes women permanently, had been planted in the uteri of more than 100,000 women. The drug was never tested for side effects and was never used on white women in North America. It was distributed in India by two North American doctors, who were convinced that they were doing an important social service to their country. As expressed by one of the doctors, the fear was that the Third World would become overpopulated and that poverty and misery would spread. Third World people in search of opportunities would spill over to North America, the First World. This would increase poverty and misery in North America. The doctors were convinced that population control had to take precedence over the welfare of Third World women.

The drug was distributed without the approval of the U.S. government's regulatory body. When this was brought to public attention by feminists in India, and made headlines, the drug was withdrawn and the U.S. government ordered the drug destroyed. But the doctors in charge were not about to give up. These doctors saw themselves as the saviours of the First World, and further rationalized that they were not making any money out of Quinacrine. They had no sense whatsoever of the inhumanity of their project, nor did they express any concern about the possible side effects of these drugs for poor, illiterate women. These women were not treated as human beings; even worse, they were treated as dangerous wombs in need of control and destruction for the good of the First World way of life.

NRTs have resulted in the abortion of fetuses identified as abnormal. They have also often resulted in the abortion of female fetuses. In Canada, this technology is being marketed in South Asian communities, over strong opposition from feminists in those communities. The doctors promoting this technology contend that they are serving a cultural need of these communities (Dhruvarajan 1994; Thobani 1993). This problem is especially acute in countries such as India (Vanaik, quoted in Mies and Shiva, 1993a: 194; Dhruvarajan, 1994).

Genetic engineering is also being hotly debated. Questions are being raised about the safety, efficacy, and usefulness of RTs. In the absence of ethical and moral guidelines, RTs and genetic engineering techniques may lead to the exploitation of women, especially marginalized women (Corea, 1993). Concerns about the implications of RTs and genetic engineering are now running so deep that an international association against RTs and genetic engineering has been formed:

FINNRAGE (Feminists International Network of Resistance to Reproductive and Genetic Engineering).

Feminist Responses to Concerns about RTs

There is a range of feminist responses to RT issues. Some feminists are concerned with individual rights and choices; others desire to change the system; still others are more pragmatic, and consider the issues one at a time. Liberal feminists tend to focus on rights and choices, more radical feminists on changing the system. Pragmatists are found in both camps.

Individual Rights and Choices

Liberal feminists tend to argue that RTs help women achieve equality with men. The argument goes that women have unequal status because they are responsible for reproducing the species. Technology can help women transcend this natural constraint (Firestone, 1972). This need felt by many liberal feminists to transcend nature has arisen in a historical context in which nature is constructed as inferior to culture. Men are defined as closer to culture, women as closer to nature. The differences between men and women in the area of reproduction are used to legitimize gender hierarchy. Thus, many feminists perceive RTs as a means for women to gain control over their reproductive lives – that is, to transcend nature (Mies and Shiva, 1993a).

This argument assumes that scientists are rational and value-neutral. Nevertheless, the misuses of RTs by scientists and by the entrepreneurs who market scientific discoveries are a rapidly growing concern. Liberal feminists are thoroughly convinced that scientists contribute to human progress through their research, and that the biomedical establishment can be trusted; they also believe in free markets. But they also accept that safeguards are necessary to protect people from the failings of individual scientists, technologists, and entrepreneurs, and that the altruism of scientists and doctors is not beyond scrutiny. In sum, these feminists attribute any problems with RTs to individual indiscretions, not to the workings of the biomedical and capitalist system.

These feminists contend that in a democracy with a free market economy, the best solution to problems with RTs is building safeguards. Doing so provides all citizens with equality of choice. As

Andrews writes (1986, 1987), in 'My Body, My Property,' if all people are legally the owners of their own bodies, then the biomedical establishment and the entrepreneurs in the capitalistic economy cannot use reproductive body parts and fluids for their benefit without the consent of individuals. Body parts and fluids, whether they are needed for research or for sale, cannot be appropriated without the consent of individuals, who legitimately own their own bodies. Thus, the role of the state is to enact laws giving individuals control over their own bodies. The misuse and exploitation of individuals will end once these institutional safeguards are in place. These feminists have faith in the biomedical system and in the free market economies. They also have faith in the state to mediate between individual citizens and the biomedical and capitalist establishments. They also assume that once individual property rights are enshrined in law, all people will have the opportunity to exercise these rights.

These feminists argue that it is up to individuals to decide what to do with their bodies and body parts. They do not see anything wrong with the idea of women engaging in commercial transactions. If we are ready to sell the products of our minds, what is wrong with selling the products of our physical bodies? In the opinion of these feminists, the products of the mind belong to a higher order than the products of the physical body. They subscribe to a mind–body dualism and privilege the mind. The critical question they ask is, 'Can a given individual give informed consent, make an informed choice?' If the answer is *yes*, the given individual is exercising options and making informed decisions. This argument holds in the context of selling one's eggs, becoming a surrogate mother, going through an IVF treatment, using a contraceptive device, or having an abortion, and so on.

The belief that nature has been unfair to women and that technology can help right these wrongs has a certain plausibility. The intent is to enable women to compete with men in a free market economy. With the help of technology, women become similar to men and thereby become capable of achieving gender equality. RTs enable women to avoid pregnancy, space children according to their convenience, solve problems of infertility, make children in alternative ways, and so on. It is in this context that RTs are perceived as beneficial. The only impediment is that those who control this knowledge – namely, scientists and technicians, as well as the entrepreneurs who market scientific products – may misuse that knowledge to exploit people.

This discourse focuses on providing women with opportunities for freedom and self-determination; but it pays little attention to the condition of women's lives. Only women who control their own lives can exercise options. Class, race, and gender inequality place women in vulnerable positions in terms of wealth, power, and status, and this reduces their opportunities to exercise free choice. It is not enough to have the information to make an informed choice if one's life circumstances make it impossible to act on that choice. Mies and Shiva (1993a) point out that freedom and self-determination are just as important to Third World women as they are to women in North America. But when conditions are oppressive, Third World women cannot act in their self-interest. To provide for their families, to have the basic necessities of life, women may agree to sell parts of their bodies, become surrogate mothers, get tubectomies done, and so on. Similar predicaments surface for poor and marginalized women in Western countries.

We should also be concerned about how laws are enacted, interpreted and enforced. Money is power, and legal battles are expensive and time-consuming. Most women who are poor do not have the time or money to mount a legal challenge when their rights are intruded on. Clearly marginalized groups are in a vulnerable position, whatever the law's actual intent. Also, multinational and transnational corporations have tremendous power – power that often overrides the powers of states. So the question of choice is spurious for many Third World women, most of whom suffer from poverty and illiteracy. They find themselves caught in power plays between international agencies and state governments, who are more interested in population control than in women's empowerment (Mies and Shiva, 1993a).

It is in this context that the commercialization of reproductive processes and the commodification of reproductive parts and fluids are considered dangerous (Saulnier, 1997). Once these enter the free market arena, they are treated just like any other kind of property. Scientists, technologists, and entrepreneurs are governed by the profit motive. Women's welfare and empowerment are no longer overriding concerns. Motherhood ceases to be a relationship and becomes a saleable commodity. Once it is reduced to that level, there can be a significant loss of control over abuses. This is especially true in the context of surrogate motherhood.

Transforming the System

Radical feminists tend to argue that building institutional safeguards to ensure reproductive choice is not enough because the problem is systemic – that is, it is integral to how reproduction is 'done.' Science and technology are projected as rational and value neutral; in fact they are gendered, raced, and classed.

Historically, women have been excluded from scientific enterprise. In the enlightenment paradigm, which is the prevailing philosophical framework, women are constructed as 'other' – as beings to be dominated and controlled. Because of their procreative capacities, women are conceptualized as closer to nature and therefore as inferior. This perspective is possible because nature is defined as inferior to (man's) culture (Jordanova, 1993). The biomedical model of reproduction approaches the human body as a mechanism. The scientific and technological innovations developed from this model have promoted the subordinate position of women, and conceptualized women as constellations of body parts and fluids to be mechanically manipulated. The procreative functions of women's bodies are perceived as natural resources to be exploited and used according to the needs and will of those in control. Women's bodies are medicalized and controlled by the biomedical establishment (Mies and Shiva, 1993a).

Radical feminists contend that the discourse on motherhood is developing in such a way that the technodocs – that is, the doctors using NRTs – are being praised for their ability to transcend nature. Claims are being made that children born as a result of RTs are of superior quality to those born through natural processes (Mies and Shiva, 1993a). These new methods of reproduction use the genetic materials and body fluids of women and men, and use women as receptacles. The symbiotic relationship between mother and child is thereby ruptured, and the experience of motherhood, which ought to develop naturally between the fetus and the mother, is thereby denied. The use of technology to reveal the movements of the baby is promoted as strengthening the development of bonding between mother and child. It is assumed that for the fetus to develop normally, the mother's behaviour must be controlled. In sum, the interests of the fetus and the interests of the mother are treated as antagonistic. It has become common to treat the interests of the fetus as more important than those of the . mother. In this way the natural processes of pregnancy and motherhood are made unnatural and artificial. In these circumstances, the experience of motherhood becomes alienating and dehumanizing (Mies and Shiva, 1993a).

The constructing of non-Europeans as 'different' and therefore inferior is part of the colonial heritage. Europeans perceived their culture as naturally superior, so they considered themselves justified in exploiting non-Europeans and their lands. Within this cultural ethos, the science of eugenics developed, and promoted the notion that some 'races' were superior to others (Valverde, 1992). Morgan elaborates on the psychological impact of these technologies on women:

> Internalizing the language, beliefs and values of the patriarchal reproductive technologists contributes to a profound experience of psychological oppression for women ... Living under psychological oppression, women come to feel fragmented, devalued, infantilized, dehumanized, degraded and rendered invisible ... One dangerous effect ... is other political and economic forms of oppression come to be seen as normal, justified, or our 'problem' and fail to be identified as oppression. (1989: 61–2)

Radical feminists see a link between the eugenics movement and RTs. The practice of judging some people to be unfit for reproduction on the basis of race, class, gender, or ability is a legacy of the eugenics movement of earlier centuries. The practice of denying NRTs such as *in vitro* fertilization to Black, poor, single, lesbian, and disabled women is based on the same logic as the eugenics movement.

Population control is considered vital to economic development. Malthusian principles of population growth are accepted uncritically, and government policies are informed by those principles. Third World women are treated not as human beings capable of rational decision making, but as statistics. They are often used as guinea pigs for new products. In fact, certain products have been developed specifically for Third World consumption. These products are supposed to be more suitable for mass consumption. They are provider-controlled, in the sense that women do not play an active role in taking them. NorPlant and Quinacrine are two such drugs. Many of them have side effects. Third World women, especially the poorest, are forced to accept these technologies without regard to their health and well-being (Akthar, 1986).

Many financial bodies, including the World Bank, provide development loans to Third World countries on the condition that they control their populations. In turn, these countries accept Western knowledge of population control without questioning it. The practice of applying RTs to selectively abort fetuses on the basis of sex or fetal abnormalities has become commonplace in the Third World. For example, scientific methods such as gametrics have been developed to prevent the conception of female fetuses. If these practices become widespread, 'it will render women more than ever an "endangered species," in countries with a strong patriarchal preference for boys' (Vibhuti Patel, an Indian feminist, in Mies and Sahiva, 1993: 194). Science has been declared value neutral; scientists are believed to be working for human progress. These assumptions are no longer even questioned.

In the relentless quest to accumulate profit, progress is defined as the accumulation of material and goods, and the concept of sustained growth does not acknowledge that resources are limited. In such a framework, new frontiers for capitalist exploitation must constantly be identified. Environmental degradation and mass poverty on a world scale are direct results of capitalist patriarchy, and science and technology operate within this framework. Throughout all this, commodification of the female body is happening at an accelerated pace. Scientists are concentrating on technological fixes for fertility problems; meanwhile, not enough attention is being paid to the impact of environmental degradation on human fertility. Once female bodies are declared to be property, market forces can exploit them in different ways. Human beings become atomistic body parts and fluids to be used for profit. And at all times, marketing campaigns are creating demand for the new products that result (Mies and Shiva, 1993a).

Radical feminists contend that the scientific knowledge developed in a racist, sexist, heterosexist, and ableist sociocultural milieu will be used to perpetuate hierarchical relationships. Such an environment influences the types of scientific discoveries that are made. At present there are no ethical guidelines regarding the types of scientific research undertaken (Mies and Shiva, 1993a). Guidelines have been developed only to set limits for the uses of discoveries already made. Radical feminists argue that scientific/technological research should be put on hold until the sociocultural milieu becomes egalitarian. Promoting biomedical research before that goal is achieved will only buttress capitalist patriarchy, at which point it will be too late to talk about an egalitarian society.

RTs are being promoted, these feminists argue, not to improve the human condition, and not to contribute to human welfare, but rather to aid the relentless pursuit of profit through sustained progress. The capitalist world view does not recognize that resources are limited. Instead, as one area dries up and stops yielding profit, the search renews for new areas. Right now, the biomedical field is considered to be among the most very profitable. While this holds true, women's bodies will continue to be commodified and fragmented as new technologies develop new products for the market. The logic of the marketplace is all-powerful, and its discourse has been carefully developed to project the notion that technology is satisfying actual needs.

Corea (1993) vividly describes the kind of fears envisioned by many radical feminists, if NRTs and genetic engineering are allowed to continue developing as they are now. She speculates on what could happen if techniques currently used to breed animals are applied to human reproduction. Concerns like these are motivating radical feminists to argue that the further development of RTs and genetic engineering should be put on hold until gender, race, and class inequalities are addressed and an egalitarian society established.

Pragmatic Approach

Pragmatic feminists argue that rejecting technological innovations is like throwing out the baby with the bathwater. They agree that people must be vigilant, but they also warn against paranoia. They reject the idea expressed by radical feminists that these technologies could lead to widespread femicide, pointing out that the available technology is not a cost-effective way to reproduce the species. Besides, women serve men and societies in ways other than reproducing the species (Delphy, 1993).

Pragmatic feminists do not agree that RTs go against nature and make pregnancy and childbirth artificial and contrived (Delphy, 1993). They consider that argument essentialist. Historically, women have suffered because of essentialist arguments – that is, arguments that women are closer to nature. They agree that RTs are used in alienating and dehumanizing ways, but don't agree that women should reject all technology. In their view, women should emphasize human agency instead of privileging nature. Pragmatic feminists also argue that each technology should be evaluated on its merits, and that they shouldn't all be painted with the same brush and declared unacceptable.

Furthermore, rejecting all technology is not viable, because of the prestige that science and technology carry in today's society. More importantly, many women consider RTs empowering and enabling and don't want to give them up (Sawicki, 1993). It is not fair to deprive people of the opportunity to benefit from these innovations. The focus should be on making sure that these technologies are woman-friendly.

Pragmatic feminists suggest a strategy of active engagement by women at the levels of research, policy, and practices. Women must make their voices heard in research to ensure that any new knowledge gained will not be applied to perpetuate sexism in society. Feminists have developed guidelines to ensure that it won't (Eichler, 1988). Women must participate in constructing alternative discourses so that the cultural framework that mediates social practices includes women's perspectives (Sawicki, 1993). For example, the pronatalist discourses that are being constructed by the biomedical establishment in the context of IVF and AI should be countered with alternative discourses. In the same, way antinatalist discourses are being constructed to sterilize Third World women in the name of economic development; these should be countered to give women in those countries control over their reproductive lives. Institutional safeguards must be established to prevent misuse of this knowledge to the detriment of women. These initiatives must be followed through to ensure that conditions exist for all women to exercise their freedom of choice. Clearly, reproductive rights cannot be conceptualized in isolation: they are an integral part of economic, legal, and political rights.

Pragmatic feminists also argue that ethical guidelines should be developed so that RTs promote human welfare instead of simply feeding the patriarchal capitalist establishment (Sherwin, 1989). Colodny (1989), discussing the politics of birth control in a reproductive rights context, contends that the feminist goal is to ensure that all women take control of their bodies, their fertility, and their sexuality. This goal, she is convinced, can be achieved only through organized efforts among women. She provides some details regarding this objective:

> Until we live in a society of the future, where women are truly autonomous, women will not have free choice. The sexism, the racism and the classism of the society in which we live will limit our choices. But we can push our society to the limit. We can organize to make a non-capitalist, non-patriarchal, non-racist world a reality. None of us as individuals can finish our own personal work of resocializing ourselves until the society as a whole is reorganized. The objective reality of sexism simply creates too many barriers. And society, as a whole, can't be reorganized unless we undo the oppressive aspects of our female socialization and claim our

power to criticize, to stand up for our rights, and to organize with others
to achieve the recognition of those rights from governments. (1989: 44)

Wagner and Lee (1989: 239) provide a model of feminist health care
in which it is necessary to mobilize a social movement. They offer the
following glimpse at the central principles of this model:

It would be care that covers the whole spectrum of women's reproductive lives, is universally accessible, integrates services and counseling,
respects and validates all sexual and reproductive choices, and is accountable to the women of its community. Most fundamentally, this means
health care that empowers women – that provides what women need,
comes from women's lived experiences and enhances their control over
their lives.

The thrust of the pragmatic feminists' argument is that the feminist
community must engage actively in the politics of reproduction. Organized feminist efforts have had some impact in this area. In Canada
the federal government established a Royal Commission on RTs after
extensive feminist lobbying. The report, published in 1993, offers recommendations that address many of the feminists' concerns. For example, it recommends against legalizing the sale of reproductive body
parts and fluids, and against legalizing contractual surrogacy. In 1996
a bill was introduced in Parliament to make contractual surrogacy
illegal. In 1994, after decades of struggle, midwifery was recognized as
a profession in Ontario, over very stiff opposition from the medical
establishment, which continues to campaign against it.

The dumping of untested contraceptives in Third World countries is
being actively resisted by feminists in various countries, including
India. It has also led to legal challenges and has sometimes resulted in
certain contraceptives, such a Quinacrene, being withdrawn.

After protests against family and heterosexist biases, IVF and AI
are now available to single women and lesbians. But the prohibitive
cost of these procedures still deprives working-class women of these
services.

Conclusion

The goal of achieving gender equality by transcending our reproductive nature in an effort to become similar to men has to be carefully

evaluated. Is this the kind of equality we should aspire for? Do we not lose our sense of who we are if we separate ourselves from our bodies? Should we not be arguing that difference should not mean inequality? Instead of adopting a dualistic paradigm, should we not be thinking holistically?

Radical feminists do insist on such an orientation, and critique the liberal feminist position. The problems we encounter with the biomedical model and capitalist patriarchy are systemic. Building institutional safeguards by guaranteeing individual rights to choose goes only so far. This is because those who occupy lower rungs of the social ladder in a hierarchical society are not able to exercise their options. The feminist goal of achieving an egalitarian society necessarily involves systemic transformation. We need to build a society based on principles of cooperation, nurturance, and harmony. We must accept and respect differences. Radical feminist contributions provide insights into how we can develop such a society, but transforming society in this image cannot be done quickly.

Certain issues need immediate attention. For example, contractual surrogacy and the sale of body parts and fluids should be made illegal. The advantages of IVF should be carefully assessed before that technology is endorsed and approved. The economic and human costs of this procedure, in addition to promoting pro-natalism are causes for concern. Since the implications of genetic engineering are virtually unknown, it would be wise to put this technology on hold until proper ethical guidelines for researching and applying it are developed. Theories of economic development developed in the West, inspired by capitalist greed and a racist mindset that makes population control a prerequisite for financial aid, must be deconstructed and reevaluated to end the misery of millions of Third World women. Technology that means death to female fetuses should be stopped.

Feminists who take a pragmatic approach suggest that we ask, 'What is possible and what is feasible?' before adopting a particular stand. The suggestion that feminists should be engaged at all levels of decision making – including research, policy, and practices – to ensure that they are woman-friendly makes eminent sense. But in a social context where power is distributed unevenly, this participation remains an ideal rather than a reality. Women in general, including racial and other minorities, do not have equal access to decision making. The boardrooms, the legislatures, and the scientific and technological establishments are certainly not inclusive at the present time.

In these circumstances the concerns expressed by radical feminists cannot be ignored. This is especially so in a context where the general public is not aware of the implications of all the changes that are taking place.

One of the major tasks requiring immediate attention is to raise public awareness about the amoral and unethical practices among the elites in the biomedical and patriarchal-capitalist establishments. Feminists can be catalysts in this. Organized efforts are necessary at this juncture. Resistance to changes that negatively affect social life must come from the grassroots, and must be broad-based and widespread. The struggle to usher in an egalitarian society is as urgent as ever, and must be guided by a vision for a better future.

CHAPTER 8

Thinking about Violence

Jill Vickers

A great achievement of women's movements worldwide has been their success in 'breaking the silence' about male violence against women in intimate relationships. As a result of women's collective efforts, we now realize that such violence is a risk for all girls and women and takes many forms, including rape, battering, psychological abuse, sexual abuse, incest, and femicide. Women's movements have created shelters, safe houses, and crisis centres to aid women, who are often literally fleeing for their lives. All are vulnerable before birth, in childhood and as adults; from young women struggling to resist date rape and sexual harassment to their grandmothers experiencing 'granny bashing.' In Western countries some groups of women face higher risks of violence than others; and far beyond the domestic sphere, violence pervades the lives of women living under repressive regimes and in war zones.

All feminists – indeed, most women – agree that violence is wrong and must stop. No women's movement argues that 'violence against women is acceptable' or that fighting against it is not important. Why, then, have we included violence as an issue about which we must 'think through difference'? Surely, if there is an issue on which all women agree, isn't this it? In all of the forty-three countries reported on in *Women and Politics Worldwide* (1994), a desire for security and freedom from violence was the top priority of women's movements. However, women had somewhat different 'takes' on a number of violence-related questions. Most mainstream Western women see violence through a gender lens focused on their personal security; to them, violence is more or less synonymous with wife beating, rape, and sexual harassment. But marginalized women in the West, especially refugees, as well as women outside the West, have often experienced a broader range of violent acts, including war, genocide, mass rape as a strategy of war, forced removals, torture and being 'disappeared' by state security forces. From the Second World War to the collapse of the Soviet Union, all except one of the world's 120 wars were waged in the Third World. Most were anticolonial conflicts (Sivard, 1991). And in many countries, women have had to mobilize against state violence. Moreover, although states promise security to their women citizens, many do not deliver, especially when the violence occurs in the private sphere. Amnesty International's 1993 Annual Report revealed that repressive governments existed in 161 of the UN's 181 member countries (Moussa, 1998–9). Among those most vulnerable to repressive governments or to the lack of effective governments are women and children. In 1994 alone, 4 million women and children were turned into refugees by armed conflicts and human rights violations (Moussa, 1998–9). Mainstream Western women focus on *violence against women* as the key issue; other women also face violence affecting their children, male partners, and family members. Some suggest that the mainstream Western feminism's focus on violence against women is deflecting attention from public, societal violence, and from the role of women in perpetuating violence as mothers with their children, as teachers or caregivers, and as citizens implicated in racism or colonialism. When we look through a gender lens, the focus is mainly on male violence against women and children in intimate relationships. But when we apply concepts such as gendered racism, the facts of public violence and of violence experienced by men come into focus. Moreover, we must keep in mind how the changes described as 'globalization' interact with issues of women's security from violence. We know that the proportion of women in abject poverty has risen sharply as the trends of globalization are manifested. Are those same trends reducing women's security from violence? If so, which women are most vulnerable? Are there countervailing trends? Will belonging to the global economy 'club' mean that countries and corporations will have to protect vulnerable citizens better? But can they protect them? And if so, who will make them expend the resources needed for more effective security measures?

In this chapter, we explore two aspects of the broad problem of women's experiences of violence. First, we outline mainstream women's experiences of violence in Western countries which until recently enjoyed relatively higher levels of public security, at least for white populations. This book was written before the awful acts of terrorism in the United States, which shattered the security of ordinary citizens in Western countries in ways it is yet too soon to absorb. We then consider how marginalized women and their men folk experience violence in Western countries and in Third World and postcommunist countries, where levels of public violence are usually much higher. Tragically, one consequence of globalization may be the diminishing of difference in insecurity such that more women will fear the threat of violence. Then we explore how women think about violence in terms of their different experiences of it. What is violence? What causes it? What role do women play in perpetuating it? And how should those who commit violent acts be dealt with by the state and the community? We conclude this chapter by outlining the efforts of international feminist networks to situate women's security from violence within human rights discourse and within the understanding of development in the UN system.

Mainstream Experiences of Violence

Arguably the most distinctive feature of second-wave, mainstream feminism in Western countries was the opening up to scrutiny of the violence girls and women experience in their most intimate relationships. First-wave feminists in the West – active between 1890 and 1950 – were also concerned with violence, but it was mainly the violence of warfare that preoccupied them. In the second wave, radical feminists broke the silence about violence in intimate relationships. As Ann Duffy argues, 'the issue of violence against women is at the heart of much feminist analysis and action' and 'unites feminists across other political lines' (1998: 132). Second-wave, mainstream feminists developed a gender lens to conceptualize violence as violence against women. Bunch and Carrillo, for example, assert that 'sexism kills' (1998: 231) before birth, in childhood, and in adulthood. Moreover, 'this is not random violence ... The risk factor is being female' (Hensing, in Bunch and Carrillo: 234). This idea that women experience violence *because of* their gender is a core feature of accounts. Historically, violence in intimate relationships was condoned or permitted in Western societies, so second-wave feminists faced an uphill battle to get 'domestic' violence taken seriously by the state, by the institutions of civil society, or by academic researchers and professionals, especially doctors, lawyers, and judges. For example, since the 1970s white feminists in English Canada and Quebec have been seeking to define violence against women, to determine its frequency, and to get governments, the police, and the media to take it seriously and act to protect its victims and prevent its occurrence. A complex war of statistics has emerged. For example, the percentage of women who report experiencing violence in intimate relationships varies depending on how violence is defined. Part of the uphill battle is persuading the mainly male 'powers that be' that violence in intimate relationships must be treated seriously and that it is not a trivial or private matter to be resolved within the family or relationship.

In the struggle to establish that domestic and relationship violence exists – that it is a serious problem and must be treated earnestly – second-wave feminists, in conjunction with action researchers and sympathetic professionals, have mapped the contours of intimate violence in most Western societies. Although there are still many differences of opinion over scope and definition, consensus has been reached in some areas. In Western countries, in intimate relationships women and girls experience incest, child abuse, battering, marital rape, date rape, and murder, as well as psychological abuse; all of these result in fear, health problems, and control of women's actions. Many second-wave feminists define violence rather broadly, as an abuse of power in which one person uses violence or threats of violence to control the actions of another person (Catin and Clément, 1998: 73). By this definition, violence includes one-on-one acts and threats of violence such as sexual harassment in the classroom or the workplace, as well as abuse from caregivers and professionals. Strong efforts have been made to reveal these acts of violence, and feminists have lobbied energetically to get laws changed and to make public services more responsive. In many jurisdictions, feminists have also created shelters for women who are fleeing intimate violence or experiencing rape, and networks of self-help groups to support women who have experienced various forms of abuse. In this section I briefly explore three aspects of this large and complex project.

Iris Marion Young (1990b) identified violence as one of five dimensions of oppression. Violence and threats of violence are the chief means of maintaining the subordination of women; that being said, to some degree *all* systems of dominance are maintained through violence and threats of it. The oppression of women, however, also relies on women's sense of inadequacy, weakness, and vulnerability; too many women accept male control in exchange for protection from strangers, only to experience violence from their 'protectors.' Women do not have to experience violence and threats directly to be affected by these things; knowledge of other women's experiences, as spread through media reports and popular culture, can generate a sense of fear that can in turn control their minds and actions. Notwithstanding all this, the murder of women by partners is an excellent measure of the broader problem of violence against women in intimate relationships. Ontario researchers found recently that between 1974 and 1994, between 63 per cent and 76 per cent of all women homicide victims in the province were killed by an intimate partner (Gartner et al., 1998).[1] In Canada and Ontario, men outnumber women as homicide victims by 2 to 1, and as offenders by 7 to 1. Thus, 98 per cent of all women killed in Ontario in the study period were killed by men, but only 17 per cent of adult male victims were killed by women (Gartner et al., 1998: 164–5). Here again, a gender lens reveals an important gender gap.

Women tend to be more afraid of violence from strangers, yet for most white mainstream women, intimate partners and family members are far more dangerous. The *Violence Against Women Survey* (Statistics Canada, 1993), action research, and research from academics all document that 'statistically the greatest risk to women's safety comes from men who are known to them' (Haskell and Randall, 1998: 115). Women often use avoidance strategies to avert violence; this limits their freedom of movement and ability to participate in society. For example, poor, elderly, and disabled women are more likely to stay at home, because they cannot afford costlier, self-protective strategies such as taking taxis and having alarm systems installed (118–19). Young university and college women organize to demand better lighting and emergency telephones. They also join with men in student union 'walk home' programs.

Myth #1 – 'It isn't rape if he buys you dinner.'
Myth #2 – 'It isn't battering if he says he loves you.'

Statistics about women's health reveal a great deal about the incidence of violence against women and where it occurs. Statistics Canada's 1995 report *Women in Canada: A Statistical Report* (3rd ed.) noted that the life-time prevalence of wife assault was 29,000 per 100,000

– that is, 29 per cent of all women who had ever been married or had ever lived in a common law relationship had been assaulted or sexually assaulted by their intimate partners (104). Consequently, the health damage from such violence potentially exceeds that from cancer, heart disease, strokes, and arthritis. Not all cases of intimate assault and sexual assault result in death, but many result in serious injuries that damage women's health and make them more fearful and less able to act independently. Shelters for women victims of violence and their children are always full – a clear indication of the severity of the problem.

Difference and Experiences of Violence

Women marginalized in Western societies because of race, sexuality, disability, poverty, age, or internal colonialism (i.e., indigenous women) experience significantly higher levels of violence than white, mainstream women. Also, they experience different *kinds* of violence, with structural violence and random acts of public violence featuring prominently. Until recently, women in Western countries were mostly secure from random acts of terrorism. But all women are vulnerable to violence as long as systematic male dominance and the ideologies that support it persist. But women marginalized because of such differences are much more vulnerable. For example, Statistics Canada data show that the rates for intimate femicide are five to ten times higher for aboriginal women than for non-aboriginal women (in Gartner et al., 1998: 159). A 1989 report by the Ontario Native Women's Association revealed that indigenous women experience violence in intimate settings at eight times the rate of other women (in Duffy, 1998: 145). Women with disabilities also reveal significantly higher rates of violence. Despite controversy about its composition (i.e., the accusation that marginalized women were underrepresented), the 1993 Canadian Parliamentary Panel on Violence Against Women reported that lesbians, teenagers, and seniors are also especially vulnerable. In fact, this body found that just over half (51 per cent) of all sexual assaults were on women between the ages of sixteen and twenty-seven.

What do these much higher levels of vulnerability mean in terms of relationships among women in women's movements, shelters, and crisis centres, which are usually dominated by white, mainstream women? Three first-hand experiences reveal the reality behind the often confusing and sometimes controversial statistics. First, the experiences of indigenous women are so different from those of white, mainstream women that we must use the framework of continuing colonialism to explain it. According to this structural approach, 'the conditions of colonialism' create the circumstances in which violence by indigenous men and women occurs, as well as violence *against* indigenous people by white men and women (Frank, 1993; Bachmann, 1993). Patricia Monture-Okanee's text 'The Violence We Women Do: A First Nation's View' (1992) explores this perspective. It is also useful to consider the mechanics of the conflicts between white and indigenous women up close. Bonita Lawrence, a working-class, lesbian/ bisexual woman of Metis origin, reports her story, which began when she was in an abusive relationship with a white man:

> It was at this juncture that I first encountered shelter workers. Their casual words too often seemed to divide 'battered women' into 'deserving' and 'troubled' categories. The 'troubled' women were women like me – angry and self-destructive, with poor self-control, who tended to remain with their abusers even if they had no children. The 'deserving' women were the ones that the shelter workers seemed interested in helping; they were unequivocally blameless in their victimization; ordinary (white) women struggling against all odds to protect themselves and their children from abusive men – without any of the complications which I manifested ... I walked away from such encounters feeling entirely worthless. According to these women, who were, after all, 'experts,' the battered woman's movement was not about me, it was about 'real' battered women: the innocent victims of all-powerful men. (1996: 7)

Lawrence's sense of being an 'undeserving' battered woman actually increased her vulnerability, and she entered a second abusive relationship with a man, also of indigenous heritage:

> My experiences have led me to certain conclusions about the shelter movement, and its relationship to the survivors it speaks for, particularly those women marginalized by race and class. Generally speaking, I have found that my own ways of conceptualizing experiences of abuse have not been reflected in most feminist presentations I have heard about wife abuse, nor in the practices of shelter workers. Without detracting from the valuable intervention by feminist activists in saving women's lives, *I have been* personally *unable*, for a good many years, *to 'see myself' in the decontextualized models of 'the battered woman'* which have been presented

within feminist discourse, models which expressly repudiated connections between violence and a woman's marginality, addictions, or low
self-esteem – precisely the problems which have scarred my own life and
those of the women in my family. (1996: 15, my emphasis)

Similar experiences have been reported by lesbians who experienced
violence from female partners. Adrienne Blenman (1991) broke the
silence on this taboo subject, which doesn't 'fit' mainstream assumptions that violence against women is done by men. A Black lesbian,
she observed about her experience:

The question I remember being uppermost in my mind was why was I
being beaten by a woman? I didn't connect my abuse to the abuses
suffered by women at the hands of their male partners. I believed that as
a lesbian, I was safe from violence in my relationships because women
didn't hit each other. I think it was this belief that kept me involved [in
the abusive relationship] for so long. (1991: 61)

bell hooks (1988) has argued that violence in adult intimate relationships re-exposes wounds and vulnerable areas resulting from childhood abuse; as a result, the wounded person feels betrayal as well as
pain. The loss of trust is felt by the victim, but the perpetrator is also
often wounded. Blenman observed about her abusive female partner:
'One of the main factors contributing to the abuse was my partner's
homophobia, even though she was involved with a woman. Homosexuality went against every new religious belief she held. In a way,
every time she hit me, she was beating up on the lesbian part of
herself' (1991: 61).

Women with disabilities are also especially vulnerable. Rochelle, in
'Busting the Myth,' asserts: 'If other women feel like a target for assault, then I feel like the bull's-eye. I use a wheelchair, and I figure if
someone's out there looking for an easy hit, it's me' (1993: 113). Her
analysis highlights the extreme vulnerability of many women with
disabilities and their frequent exclusion from mainstream women's
movements and from the shelters and centres they have created. Girls
and women with disabilities are assaulted much more often than able-
bodied women, and the more disabled they are, the higher the rate:

You wouldn't think anybody would pull a woman out of her wheelchair
to rape her, or hit a little kid with her crutches, but it happens. Boy-

friends do it, spouses do it. Strangers, friends, families ... teachers, doctors, even the counsellors and caretakers supposedly there to help, do it. It happens in homes, hospitals, schools, in accessible buses and taxis. If a woman with a disability seeks help from services for victims of violence, she'll find most are not built to accommodate her physical needs. (113)

Rochelle and others in her group chose to get training in Wen-Do, a self-defence project for women with restricted mobility. In introducing these rarely heard voices of women who are especially vulnerable to violence because they are marginalized by their 'difference,' I am not trying to imply that all shelters are *deliberately* inhospitable to Blacks, lesbians, indigenous women, or women with disabilities. My point, rather, is that the framework of analysis commonly accepted in shelter work constructs an undifferentiated women as the victim of undifferentiated male violence. How are we then to understand the relationship between shelter workers' knowledge and the diverse understandings that highly vulnerable, marginalized women have developed of the violence they experience?

Jacquelyn Campbell in her 1998 article 'Interdisciplinarity in Research on Wife Abuse: Can Academics and Activists Work Together?' explores the conflict between academics and activists in this field of research. Campbell tells us that the two sides even employ different terminology: many (but not all) sociologists talk about 'domestic violence,' whereas most activists talk about 'wife abuse' or 'violence against women' (308). In North America, activists began antirape and antibattering movements in the 1970s, and developed analyses that saw male violence against women as a key mechanism in the patriarchal oppression of women. But men were not the only source of violence; nor were women the only victims – far from it. The conflict between the research tradition, which viewed 'family violence' as part of family dysfunction, and shelter-based and movement understandings has escalated. Academic and legal specialists are now taking up the issue, and politicians are moving funding levels up and down according to the level of media hype.

Campbell concludes, that after three decades of media hype, of backlash, of professionals getting on the bandwagon and young feminists accusing them of perpetuating 'victim feminism,' shelter activists have saved women's lives for little pay while doing incredibly difficult work. Often, shelter activists have been blamed for concepts that come not from their discourse but from some strand of academic or professional research. For example, research that attempts to answer the question 'Why does she stay?' has applied the behavioural framework of 'learned helplessness' to women who refuse to leave an abusive partner (Campbell, 1998: 312). This thread of research has been especially harmful to Black and indigenous women – who tend not to look like pathetic victims – especially when it is used in courts to defend women who have killed their abusive partners. These women don't seem to be 'good victims'; nor do they accept the analyses offered about violence by either professionals or shelter activists. Partnership research that draws on the insights of the combatants in the minefield of violence against women *and* that includes the insights of marginalized and highly vulnerable women would be an important first step toward resolving this complex conflict.

Women outside Western countries also face far different experiences with violence. As I noted earlier, Amnesty International has assessed 161 countries as repressive to some degree, so clearly state violence, war, terrorism, and civil strife are crucial contexts within which women and girls experience violence. Refugee women and children, of whom there are many millions, are especially vulnerable to violence in camps (Moussa, 1998). Note, however, that public violence and intimate violence are usually linked. Bunch and Carrillo (1998) report that often – in Mexico, for example – violence is present in at least 70 per cent of families, and that two-thirds of wives in Papua New Guinea and over two-thirds of wives in South Korea have been beaten. They also report high levels of femicide, abortion of female fetuses, and female infanticide. Where both sexes receive similar care and nutrition, there are 105 females for every 100 males; yet in South and West Asia, North Africa, and China there are roughly 90 million 'missing women' – in those regions men outnumber women by the approximate ratio of 100 to 94. Clearly, this gender gap reflects violence against women to at least some degree.

Some Western feminists believe that the higher levels of violence experienced by marginalized women in the West and by women in Third World and postcommunist countries can be attributed to 'barbaric' cultural practices. These interpretations have now been revealed as 'orientalist,' and third-wave feminists are insisting we delve more deeply to understand why these patterns exist. One explanation is poverty, which is the aftermath of colonialism and neocolonialism. How do factors like poverty and colonialism set up patterns which make women – indeed all people – vulnerable to violence? Colonialism involved the invasion and takeover, usually by military force to some degree, of already occupied land. Until the 1950s most countries outside of Europe either were or had been colonies. Colonialism did not end peacefully: wars were usually required to end the colonial relationships that had made Europeans and white settler descendants so affluent. White settlers and their descendants tried to justify the exploitation they perpetrated by conceptualizing those whose lands they had taken as inferior – as 'primitive' or 'savage' or asserting that the lands were empty. This mindset was also used to legitimize the brutality with which survivors were treated. So, for example, indigenous peoples became Canada's poorest inhabitants. Force was used to keep them on reserves and away from their lands; to place their children in residential schools; and to practise the casual rapes and assaults commonly inflicted on 'dirty Indians' by 'superior' whites.

Europeans found it easy to justify systematic, state, and casual violence against those they had colonized. Similarly, the mindset that blames victims for their own mistreatment is used to legitimize and/ or tolerate violence against the poor wherever they are found, be it in rich nations or in countries made poor by colonialism and by neocolonial exploitation.

Differences in How Women Think about Violence

Beyond the agreement that violence against women is unacceptable and must stop, differently situated women may disagree about (1) what constitutes violence, (2) what causes violence, (3) women's roles in perpetrating violence, (4) how those who commit violent acts should be dealt with. These differences are important not just in terms of academic theory, but also in terms of the activities and structures of women's movements. In some Canadian shelters for battered women they have led to conflicts. For example, some mainstream shelter workers believe that violence is part of 'man's nature,' whereas many indigenous women and women of colour believe that poverty, racism, and colonialism affect men's behaviour. Some of the (still too few) Black, Asian and indigenous women working in shelters believe that white women refuse to admit their complicity in the structural violence of racism, and point out that young, poor, non-white men are the most frequent victims of violence, often at the hands of the (still mainly white) police. Moreover, lesbians are now seeking services that recognize their realities. The ability of women's movements to create and sustain coalitions to achieve shared goals will be less than it could be as long as mainstream women think their experiences are universal, and their analyses universally valid. In fact, women's experiences with violence vary considerably, and so do their understandings of violence.

Comparatively speaking, white mainstream women in the West have long enjoyed high standards of personal security. They face little threat of overt violence. They were taught by their mothers to 'get help from a policeman when you are in trouble,' and they do; this reflects the fact that they don't need to fear being 'disappeared' by the policeman, or beaten, ignored, or unjustly incarcerated. Influenced by first-wave feminists, many second-wave, mainstream feminists deplore violence in all forms. Many women worldwide, however, live under repressive regimes that use violence against them, and some believe their communities must use force to ensure their future security. As Yuval Davis notes:

> Feminists from the Third-world justifiably argue against ... an automatic condemnation of all acts of violence ... without taking into account who carries out the violent campaigns and why. They would also argue that they could not afford the luxury of being anti-militarist because the national liberation of oppressed people can only be carried out with the help of an armed struggle. (1997: 113)

Women who have fled to Western countries to escape violence often find it hard to convey their experiences. And mainstream Western women find it hard to understand women who themselves have taken up arms. Yet we must come to understand those experiences if we are to learn to work together to ensure that women and their families are secure. Sadly, one effect of globalization has been the introduction of previously secure women to mass terrorism, which makes solidarity in the fight for justice and peace a high priority.

Violence? What's That?

In 1983, *Canadian Women's Studies/les cahiers de la femme* devoted an issue to the subject of violence (Vol. 4, no 4). Its dramatic cover showed a young white woman with a black eye and a bruised cheek. The articles reveal what violence *meant* at the time for the English-Canadian women's movement: men battering their wives and partners, male-inflicted incest, pornography focused on male, violence-triggered sexuality, male-on-female rape, sexual harassment, and the homophobic violence suffered by lesbians. Articles about how to run shelters and change laws were also featured. The security concerns of racial-minority, aboriginal, and poor women were addressed in only one brief article, which described the abuse experienced by 'Indian' women at the hands of indigenous men, why they 'took it,' and how indigenous children were taken by away Children's Aid because their parents drank. In all but one of the articles, women were the victims of violence and men the perpetrators. The hot debate was whether pornography caused men's violence and if it should be censored. All of this was seen through a violence-against-women gender lens. This violence-against-women agenda reflected the experiences of white, mainstream women, who controlled the politics of second-wave women's movements in the early 1980s. Some important voices and experiences of violence were absent: older women about 'granny-bashing'; immigrant women about war, torture, and terrorism and about relatives being 'disappeared'; indigenous women about violent dispossession, incarceration, abuse in residential schools, and violence turned inward to manifest itself in alcoholism, glue-sniffing, and suicide.

In the eighteen years since, many things have changed. In Canada, 6 December has become the day we commemorate the fourteen women killed in Montreal in 1989 because they were studying engineering and – so their murderer believed – as feminists were taking study places away from men. A firestorm of controversy ensued: some women wished to grieve in an all-women setting; others compared the crime to the crimes of 'ordinary' men who batter and rape. In the wake of the massacre, women's movements became more open to new voices. A movement against violence against women led by men began (the White Ribbon campaign). The concept developed that violence existed on a continuum, and this made it possible to show links between personal and institutional violence. This idea provided the framework for a 1991 issue of *Canadian Women's Studies* in which women and men discussed men's violence as a shared problem. 'Difference' was incorporated into several articles, which explored the experiences with violence of race-minority women and women with disabilities. Perhaps the most significant breakthrough was an article that examined women's violence against other women. In the same issue was a poem written by Rita Kohli, 'Musings of a South Asian

Woman in the Wake of the Montreal Massacre,' which challenged white women to add racism to their definition of violence, since race-minority and indigenous men are also often victims of racism and violence.

At a 1992 conference, Patricia Monture-Okanee, a Mohawk, challenged mainstream feminists' premise that violence is best seen through a gender lens. Insisting that her race and her gender 'are all in one package' (1992: 193) she argued that her entire community, including men and boys, were suffering from the violence of racism and internal colonialism. The title of her presentation – 'The Violence We Women Do' — focused on the fact that women do violence to one another and to men through their involvement in oppressive systems such as racism, even if they don't directly inflict a blow or pull a trigger. She challenged feminists to support her people in their quest for justice: 'I do wish you would come stand beside me ... Only then will we stop doing violence to each other' (194). She assumed that white, mainstream women are not just passive victims but can exert power for good or ill.

The early 1990s also marked the end of the Cold War and a concomitant expansion of women's experiences of violence. For women, 'liberation' from communism meant an end to the security that communist states had provided, although many women supported the changes. As part of ethnic cleansing, violent 'new nationalisms' tolerated and even fostered atrocities such as mass rape. In Latin America, dictatorships were toppled, with women playing active roles in challenging repressive regimes, establishing democracy, and restoring security. Some who suffered violence, including torture, in these struggles immigrated to Western countries, bringing with them experiences of a much broader range of violence. As a result of all this, violence has come to be seen as a continuum. The notion that there is a continuum of violence reflects the fact that violence is 'done' everywhere, from the most intimate settings to the most public. (Note that 'continuum' does not imply grades of severity. Although 'continuum' is the commonly used term, 'spectrum' is perhaps a better one.) Moreover, it assumes that public violence is as important for women worldwide as violence in intimate settings. Violence, approached this way, includes both intentional acts and structural violence. Figure 8.1 lists some major forms of violence as they affect women around the world. Note that we could also construct a comparable list of forms of violence that affect men.

Figure 8.1. Different forms of violence as they affect women's security

War	Rape, ethnic cleansing, mass rape as a policy of war
Massacres	Mass murders of women because they are women
Gang rape	Gang rape to regulate women's behaviour
Cultural violence	Porn, movies, TV, magazines, pop music, 'high' culture
Structural violence	Threats and fears that limit what women feel they can safely do. But also complex systems involving violence such as racism.
Marital, partner, and date rape	
Stranger rape	
Sexual harassment	At work, school
Battering	By spouse, children, grandkids, caregivers
Child abuse	Battering and sexual abuse
Gender-based murder	E.g., dowry deaths
Medical violence	E.g., abortion of female fetuses
Massacres and terrorism	Terrorist acts that target women

What Causes Violence?

When women have different experiences of violence, they may develop different explanations of its causes and different proposals concerning what should be done about it. For example, ideology and religious beliefs influence how women explain violence against them and in their societies. Moreover, until the 1960s and 1970s few even acknowledged the existence of violence in intimate relations. In the violence-against-women framework, a single cause was asserted: men and the patriarchal system they had created were seen as the cause of violence against women. This was set in opposition to the belief of researchers in sociology and psychology, and of professionals, that 'family dysfunction,' not male dominance, caused 'family violence.' This did not accord with the 'common sense' of white, mainstream women in Western countries, who mostly experienced violence from individual men. Some offered a *biological explanation* of men's violent nature – that is, they argued that men were 'naturally' more aggressive than women. Many first-wave feminists in Western countries also saw men as 'naturally' violent war mongers – again a commonsense view, since few women in Western countries fought wars as soldiers. (Had they known the history of women warriors in Africa and elsewhere, their views might have been different.) They also saw women as natural peacemakers, believing that their experiences as mothers made them desire peace and hate war. Others advanced a *social constructionist explanation*, arguing that how men were socialized made them more violent than women. Biological and socialization explanations of male violence provided a gender lens but failed to explain lesbian violence, terrorism in which women participate, or the effects of racism, colonialism, and prejudice based on poverty or disability.

Second-wave, radical feminist ideology located violence as central to patriarchy (systematic male dominance). This launched antiviolence movements through which women demanded protection from rape, battering, incest, and pornography. These movements also created safe houses and shelters for victims of male violence. Theories that saw violence as a natural and inevitable part of maleness mirrored arguments that men were using to exclude women from citizenship, work outside the home, political power, and even education. The idea was that women could not be citizens because of their unaggressive nature, since citizens had to be able to defend their country as soldiers. Within a violence-against-women framework, biological and social constructionist views can be highly persuasive, since both represent classic, radical-feminist explanations that violence is part of 'man's nature.' Socialization theories reflect liberal feminist beliefs in the efficacy of education.

When we look at the continuum of violence, including situations in which women exercise power over others or collaborate in structural forms of violence such as colonialism and racism, these explanations are less persuasive. Men everywhere are still far more likely than women to hold power, so it is still easy to conclude that women are always helpless victims at the mercy of men. Indeed, everywhere men are more likely than women to be perpetrators of violence. But when we consider all aspects of violence, we see that some women benefit at others' expense from organized, institutionalized power, and that in some relationships women may be abusers of power. Moreover, men are more often victims of violence than women when these other forms of violence are considered. Furthermore, not all power relationships are harmful to the less powerful; power can also involve energy, knowledge, and skill in leadership roles. For example, parents have power over their children, and most exercise it without abuse to teach, guide, restrain, and inspire them on their journey toward adulthood. Power imbalances, however, provide the structural context in which abuses of power occur – abuses that take the form of violence or altered or constrained behaviour because of threats of violence. These abuses of power most often take place within countries between adults and children or frail seniors, between men and women, between dominant and marginalized groups, and between the able-bodied and those who are sick or disabled. This is a common thread among forms of violence. In trying to deal with abuse resulting from power imbalances, women often try to create a more level playing field. Economic or physical dependency is often part of unequal relationships, and can often result in abuse. Note that between or among countries, inequalities resulting from colonialism, military superiority, or economic imbalances form the context within which violence may occur. However, this does not exhaust modern forms of violence, including transnational violence not disciplined by states, such as terrorism.

Violence as an Abuse of Power

Thus, we can understand that in many cases, violence is an extreme form of the abuse of power in relationships of unequal power. It manifests itself in different ways, with different degrees of intensity, and it cuts across boundaries such as class, race, and ethnicity. Though violence manifests itself in interpersonal relationships, it is also structured into human institutions. War and slavery, for example, are ancient human institutions involving organized violence. On the other hand, mass terrorism depends on modern forms of communication and transportation. State institutions such as the military, prisons, and the police have a monopoly over the legitimate use of force and may abuse it, especially against marginalized peoples. In theory, these coercive institutions exist to protect citizens from potential violence from 'outsiders' and deviant insiders. In practice, many women must organize to protect themselves and their families against the very state institutions that are supposed to protect them. Even in democracies, in which state violence against citizens is less common, vulnerable minorities are exposed to violence without state institutions acting to protect them, and may experience violence from the state agents themselves, such as the police. The same is true of women in most societies, because their relative powerlessness vis-à-vis their partners in intimate relationships makes them vulnerable to violent abuses of power. The ideology that the private sphere and the public sphere should be separate has led those in power (mostly men) in modern state institutions, and in the institutions of civil society such as churches and the media, to justify violence ('she asked for it') or to minimize it ('it doesn't happen often'). Abuses of power experienced by those marginalized because of race, sexual orientation, age, disability, class, caste, or ethnicity are also often 'justified' or minimized. As we've seen, people in these categories are most vulnerable to violent abuses of power (Levinson, 1989).

How do we explain the existence of these unequal power relationships that tend toward violence? One theory is that unequal access to and control of resources creates conditions in which violent abuses of power can occur. For example, in patriarchal societies men are considered superior by definition and so worthy of better entitlements. Similarly, white supremacist ideology assumes non-whites to be inferior and so unworthy of equal entitlements. Colonial ideology considered those conquered to be 'pagan,' 'savage,' or 'primitive'; this justified violence against them, and not acting against violence among them. In intimate relationships, women, children, and frail seniors rarely have control over resources and as a consequence are more vulnerable to violent abuses of power. At the societal level, women's lack of political power as a group is evident when we consider male dominance of parliaments, bureaucracies, armies, police forces, and courts around the world. Their lack of collective economic power is evident in the worldwide discrepancy between men's and women's pay levels and property. Everywhere women work more hours than men do and have less property; yet everywhere they are far poorer. This collective lack of political and economic clout contributes to the violence women experience. So struggles against women's inequality are also struggles against violence. Marginalized minorities also lack political representation: few are judges or bureaucrats, and their control of economic resources may also be limited. These groups are more likely to experience violent abuses of power such as dispossession, imprisonment, death in custody, and racist harassment, including from the institutions of the state. They are also more likely to experience intimate violence and violence from those paid to educate them or care for them in other institutions.

Another explanation of violence in relationships of unequal power points to the prevalence of ideologies that legitimize the use of violence when conflict arises. In competitive and militaristic societies, aggressive behaviour is considered part of daily life and dominant conceptions of masculinity valorize tough, aggressive behaviour. Cooperative behaviour is seen as 'wimpy,' and those who advocate co-operation and peaceful coexistence are seen as weak. Women's traditional association with peacemaking makes them seem inappropriate as leaders; macho men are favoured. These ideologies are reflected in popular and high culture. National myths portray the conquest of continents and the triumph over nature and 'savage' enemies. Moreover, these ideologies portray women as passive, as in 'western films,' with their gallant white soldiers and settlers rescuing white women and children.

There are two additional approaches to explaining violence, especially against women. The first points to the importance of *imitation*: those with power are more likely to abuse it violently when they see this happening elsewhere (directly and through the media), especially if the perpetrators are admired and successful and get away with it. There is evidence that wife and child abuse are learned behaviours: abusers were often themselves abused as children or witnessed the abuse of their parents – most often their mothers (see Gauthier et al., 1998). European colonialism and, more recently, the near global distribution of movies and television from Western countries (typically the United States) has popularized the ideologies that underwrite violent abuses of power.

A complex relationship between violence against women and 'development' or modernity has been identified. In 'Why Male Violence against Women Is a Development Issue' (1994), written for the United Nations Development Fund for Women, Christine Bradley concluded that violence against women, including rape, wife-beating, and sexual harassment, was exacerbated by modern conditions and rapid development. She noted that in one study, conducted in Papua New Guinea, 55 per cent of urban men surveyed reported 'bashing' their wives. Her study revealed that force and threats of force are often used to prevent women from attending meetings and from participating in development programs – especially those providing women with income – and to negate the effects of development programs such as family planning programs. Bradley concluded: 'Where men are expected to be dominant ... [they] may respond to any perceived threat to their superior position by using force and violence' (1994: 18). Other studies corroborate this. Indeed, in conditions of 'modernity' which is the goal of development projects worldwide – women and children and others with limited power experience higher levels of violence both in intimate relationships and in the public realm.

Figure 8.2. Four kinds of explanations

---

1. Unequal resources create exploitable power imbalances.
2. People are violent because of ideologies that valorize violence.
3. People are violent in imitation of others who use violence, especially those admired who 'get away with it.'
4. Men are violent when development creates dislocation and stress, or when modernization programs have results that challenge male dominance.

In contrast to the older explanations, these tentative explanations of connections between abuse of power and violence help us move away from a narrower, violence-against-women approach toward a more broad-based framework. This lets us focus on the fact that when women experience violence, it is usually at the hands of men, especially in intimate relationships. But this is not to deny that women may also perpetrate violence or that children, indigenous and racial-minority people, the frail elderly, and those who are sick or have disabilities are also especially vulnerable to violent abuses of power. Nor do these explanations account for forms of violence by those without power.

What Should Be Done about Violence?

Women's responses to violence are diverse. Figure 8.3 lists some of the different responses to violence by women's movements around the world.

In this section we focus on conflicts over how to deal with violence – especially conflicts between white, mainstream women in Western societies, who look to their states to prosecute violent men, and aboriginal and racial-minority women; and between Western and 'Third World' women who have developed other approaches, often because they cannot trust 'their' state to act on their behalf. For example, some marginalized women know that their partners, fathers, sons, and brothers are already more likely than mainstream men or women to be victims of police violence, that they are imprisoned more often, and that they are more likely to die in police custody than white men. So they support community healing approaches or collective direct action against perpetrators rather than legal action. Disagreements about how violent men should be dealt with have emerged especially within the contexts of racism and colonial oppression. For example, 'Take Back the Night' demonstrations, in which mainly white, mainstream feminists march through neighbourhoods that are usually 'no go' ar-

Figure 8.3. Common women's movements' responses to violence

War	Antiwar activism
Ethnic cleansing/apartheid	Silent testimony ('Women in Black')
World trade in sex slaves	Campaigns to get sex oppression in definitions of refugee status
	Rescue campaigns
Massacres of women	Gun control campaigns
Gang rape, stranger rape	Safe houses, shelters
Partner rape and date rape	Campaigns to make rape in marriage illegal
	Campaigns against legal harassment (rape shield laws)
	'No Means No' campaigns; education
Partner battering	Shelters; campaigns for prosecution; provision of second-stage housing
Child assault/incest	Support groups; legal action
Cultural violence	Antipornography campaigns, campaigns against war toys and TV violence
Structural violence	'Take Back the Night' marches; self-defence campaigns
Sexual harassment	Campaigns for legal remedies
	UN survey
Abortion of female fetuses	Campaigns against sex-specific abortions.

eas for 'nice' women, may have lynch-mob overtones for the Blacks and other dark-skinned people who actually have to live in those neighbourhoods. Since white women have long been 'protected' (i.e., controlled) by white men through images of the rapist as a 'dark stranger,' collective actions of this sort are complicated by a race dynamic. Oppressive systems that privilege some women because of their class, race, sexuality, or able body, while victimizing other women and their menfolk, preclude real security for either. To end personal violence, we must fight structural violence. But marginalized women face an especially difficult dilemma: on the one hand, they want and need relief from the violence they suffer from partners, brothers, sons, and fathers; on the other, they are well aware that by approaching the police and the courts, they are exposing their partners to the violence of racism or homophobia that is embedded in those institutions. It is important to realize that the responses of marginalized women vary significantly. Some though not all indigenous women favour community healing approaches, especially because so many men and women are involved (Davies, 1994). And Black women, lesbians, ethnic minority women, women with disabilities, and some indigenous women are demanding shelters and other services adapted to their needs.

Women's movements everywhere have adopted many common strategies such as safe houses, shelters, hot lines, and education campaigns. But collective security practices also exist in the women's cultures of many 'Third World' countries. For example, in some parts of Africa, women engage in the practice of *sitting on a man*, in which they descend as a group on the residence of an offender to demonstrate their anger about his breach of their rights, or about his actions against a woman or women. In Brazil, all-woman police stations have been established; these also draw on ideas of mutual aid. Women's movements in countries with developed welfare states are demanding that their governments make a woman's right to security an actual right of citizenship. Mainstream movements are struggling to have battering and rape recognized as crimes that police forces and courts must take seriously. Most Western governments have responded to these demands, but often by passing legislation that deals with each kind of violence separately; they have not responded to the systemic pattern of violence that is sustained by male dominance. Marginalized and vulnerable women are often expected to pursue remedies to violence through the courts, where they may be subjected to further abuse; for example, the still mainly male actors (police, lawyers, judges) in that system may blame them for their own victimization (e.g., 'You asked for it,' 'You must have provoked it'). Canada's rape shield legislation, which women's groups lobbied for to protect women from such secondary abuse, has been controversial because it seems to restrict the accused's ability to defend himself as vigorously as his lawyer can.

Most Western governments, with the support of mainstream women's movements, have criminalized various forms of violence against women and insist on homogenous application of the laws. But as I noted earlier, far more men marginalized by poverty, race, and internal colonialism are incarcerated than white mainstream men. A clear conflict of interest is evident here between mainstream women, who are most likely to be listened to by governments and courts, and women marginalized because of race, sexuality, colonialism, or poverty. For example, the Australian state of New South Wales maintains eighty-three refuges for battered women. Its feminist Status of Women Minister in 1997 told me during an interview that wife bashing 'is always against the law and must always be punished.' She rejected programs that worked with perpetrators of violence to change their behaviour instead of incarcerating them on the grounds that 'you can't do that and not have a diminishment of the fact that it is a crime ... Why should the limited resources for women go to fund programs for men? ... I have an unforgiving view. They've clearly broken the law and should be punished.'[2] Most groups seeking alternative approaches in NSW were immigrants or aboriginals. Only two of the eighty-three shelters in NSW were aboriginal-specific, although aboriginal women experience the highest levels of violence in the state. In 'Third World' countries, where welfare state services are less common, shelters and other self-help projects usually function outside the state. In Western countries, state-funded shelters and crisis centres are increasingly professionalized and controlled by state policies. But mainstream feminists believe state responsibility for women's security is central to their rights as citizens.

Women's agitation against violence in all its forms – and especially against violence against women – has entered the international arena. Transnational networks of women have developed the idea that violence against women should be understood as a human rights issue, and also that it is a result of 'development,' in ways current approaches fail to comprehend. In the 1990s the idea that women's rights, including the right to security and the right to freedom from violence, should be considered human rights was introduced at the 1993 World Congress on Human Rights. Feminists from many countries rejected the idea that a distinction should be drawn between private and public abuse and that 'privacy' excuses governments from acting to protect girls and women from violence wherever it occurs. In the 1990s the human rights community began to respond to all this, as did some governments. For example, Canada has made gendered violence grounds for gaining refugee status. Human Rights NGOs are beginning to explore gender-specific forms of violence as human rights abuses.

The *UN Declaration on the Elimination of Violence Against Women*, adopted by the General Assembly, was a landmark document in three ways: First, it *'situated violence against women within the discourse on human rights'* and affirmed that security of the person is a human right. Second, *'it enlarged the concept of violence against women'* to include physical, sexual, and psychological violence and threats of violence wherever they occur, including in the private, family realm. Third, *'it pointed to the gender-based root of violence'* (Bunch and Carrillo, 1998: 237). In the debate within the UN system, it was asserted that both gender and economics were factors in violence, especially as they affected women and children made refugees by war and poverty. To a significant degree, the 'women's rights are human rights' approach to violence reflects mainstream, Western feminist analyses. Indeed, some non-Western governments and activists seeking women's advancement assert that the UN's human rights declarations reflect Western rather than universal values so this approach must be viewed with caution by feminists seeking a global understanding of this crucial issue.

The dynamic character of women's debates worldwide is reflected in the ongoing conflict in the international arena about how to interpret practices such as female circumcision. Many Western critics argue within a 'women's rights are human rights' framework for zero tolerance of such practices; some 'Third World' researchers and activists for women's rights counter that such practices may be ritualized and rendered harmless to girls and women, as male circumcision is within Jewish religious practice. They stress that when zero tolerance human rights campaigns are conducted in ignorance of the cultural values to which millions of men and women are committed, those campaigns are less likely to succeed than campaigns that are sensitive to these cultural values. Far better, many believe, to raise the status of women within the context of specific cultures, and to avoid applying Western-derived norms, which are in any event viewed with suspicion by those who are resisting globalization, secularism, and modernity. Those who advocate Western-derived norms for women regardless may unwittingly contribute to forces that increase violence against them. Here especially, respect for local women's perspectives is crucial to their security.

Conclusion

Within Western countries and in a global context, the issues concerning violence against women are both simple and complex. Women are resisting violence everywhere, and have mobilized to ensure security from violence for themselves and their families. That being said, differently located women have quite different views about the causes of violence against them, and about how the roots of that violence can be addressed. Mainstream, Western women consider state protection from violence to be a right of citizenship. Marginalized women and women in some countries outside the West consider it unwise to trust the state in this way, and prefer community-level approaches and collective security practices for building women's solidarity. If scholars on women are to develop a 'one world' approach, they must explore these differences, and listen to and respect differently located women's views.

Notes

1 1,206 women were killed. This study could not break the data down by race because the research agreement with the Ministry of the Solicitor General prevented them from compiling 'statistics based on social, cultural, regional, linguistic, racial or ethnic group' from the coroners' records. They were able to document 'intimate femicides' of indigenous women from other sources.
2 Interview with Jill Vickers, Sydney, November 1997.

CHAPTER 9

Feminists and Nationalism

Jill Vickers

Western feminism has had a rocky relationship with other 'big' identity movements, including nationalisms. One reason is that male leaders often see women's movements as competitors for women's loyalties, and fear that if women pursue their gender interests through women's movements, their support for other causes will be weakened. Ann McClintock observes: 'All too frequently, male nationalists have condemned feminism as divisive, bidding women hold their tongues until after the revolution' (1993: 7). Especially outside the West and in former colonies, nationalists often view feminism with suspicion as 'an American contagion' (Margolis, 1993: 383). But many feminists seem equally suspicious of nationalism. 'The (implicit) self-representation of Western women as educated, as modern, as having control over their bodies and sexualities and the freedom to make their own decisions' (Mohanty, 1991: 36) is widespread; yet most mainstream feminist accounts of nationalism see women as controlled and manipulated by movements dominated by men. Why is there this hostility between nationalisms and feminisms, especially when we consider that in many countries, women gained rights *because* they participated in nation building and national liberation movements? Mainstream feminists often believe that women involved in nationalist movements are not 'real feminists,' or are 'dupes' of male political leaders who control them (Mohanty, 1991: 57) Given these paradoxical views, why do most women's studies texts ignore the involvement of many millions of women worldwide in nationalist movements? And why do many mainstream, Western feminists consider it impossible for women to be both feminists and nationalists?

Western theorists of nationalism have virtually nothing to say about women, and until recently, few Western feminists paid any attention to nationalism either. White, mainstream feminists in the United States, who had the greatest influence on stand-alone feminism and identity politics, have failed to understand 'Americanism' as nationalism, mainly because they are located in the most powerful country on earth. Their ideas of 'universal sisterhood' have denied the importance of national identity to 'women.' Other white, Western feminists are more conflicted. Given Europe's history of violent nationalist conflicts, feminists are more aware of nationalist movements, albeit equally disapproving. Scottish and Catalan feminists, however, have linked their movements to the nationalist movements of their communities. Most francophone feminists in Quebec have constructed their identities as feminists within the framework of Quebec nationalism, as in the 1970s slogan: 'No liberation of Quebec without liberation for women; No liberation for women without liberation for Quebec' (Lamoureux, 1987). In their analysis of the parallels between the oppression of women and that of Quebec, they were influenced by the anticolonial theories then fuelling national liberation movements in the Third World – theories that tied the two movements strongly together. Similar linkages have been made by women involved in anticolonial nationalisms around the world. Moreover, in settler states many indigenous peoples are expressing their anticolonialism and desire for autonomy within a nationalist framework, and many indigenous women have rejected feminism as a white women's ideology that also implicates non-white immigrants in ongoing, internal colonialism.

In this chapter I explore relationships between feminists and nationalism in four contexts. However, I reject the possibility of generalizing on a global basis. I argue that feminisms and nationalisms take different forms in different contexts; this means that relationships between them also vary. Both 'isms,' after all, are historically and geographically situated and shaped by a nation's location in global systems of colonialism and neocolonialism. Both also vary over time and have different meanings for and effects on women who are differently located in the same country with respect to race, language, ethnicity, and sexual orientation. Nonetheless, we can discern patterns in these relationships by comparing women's experiences with nationalism movements, and by comparing nationalists' experiences with feminism.

Given the complexity of the relationships, and given the tensions between feminisms and nationalist movements, and given the issue's absence from most women's studies agendas, we must first ask, 'Why bother with nationalisms?' There are four main reasons. First, cross-cultural analysis (Basu, 1995; Jayawardena, 1986; Nelson and Chowdhury, 1994) shows that relationships to nationalist movements are an issue for many women's movements, although the kinds of nationalist movements that women encounter have changed over time. Moreover, globalization has strengthened nationalisms, which in itself suggests that this is an important topic for scholarship on women. Second, the results of women's associations with nationalisms vary from positive and productive to negative and destructive, so it is important for feminist scholars to identify which kinds of nationalist movements produce positive results for women. Given the hideous consequences of some contemporary nationalist movements for women – consider the former Yugoslavia – it is important to explore how women can achieve positive goals of gender justice in alliances with nationalist movements. Third, feminist nationalisms and (less clearly) modernizing nationalism are systemically linked to women's achievements of legal and political rights, so it is important to explore this relationship further. Neglect in this area of research makes it unclear if this is so generally and if so why, but the dangers to women of violent nationalisms are such that continued neglect must obstruct the progress of feminism. Finally, there is some evidence that nationalities in which woman participate as autonomous actors are more likely to proceed peacefully and democratically in seeking their goals.

This chapter has five parts. First I overview the small body of Western, feminist literature on nationalisms. Then I examine three recent feminist frameworks that theorize relationships between gender and nation: Yuval-Davis (1997), who develops the concepts of nationed gender and gendered nations; Pettman, who distinguishes between dominant nationalisms and anticolonial nationalisms as they effect women; and Lois West, who initiates a theory of feminist nationalism. Then I explore women's involvements in nationalism in settler societies, including Canada, by examining the ideas of Micheline de Sève (1997), who contends that feminists give much to and gain much from women-friendly democratic nationalisms, and Haunani-Kay Trask (1979), who has analysed the relationship between women and Native Hawai'ian nationalism. Then I explore analyses of relationships between feminism and nationalism in postcolonial countries. Here I focus on the differences in the consequences for women between anti-colonial and national liberation movements, and between modernizing and antimodern nationalisms. I note that women's emancipation was part of imperialism's justification for colonial occupation, and thereby created an ambiguous context for postcolonial feminists. Finally I focus on women's experiences of nationalism in the former Yugoslavia, and observe that xenophobic nationalisms target women as reproducers of population, language, faith, and culture in an especially dangerous way. Bosnian Muslim feminist Indijana Hidovic Harper (1993) illuminates women's experiences with some aspects of these nationalisms. My approach is to explore relationships between feminism and nationalism in different contexts (see Figure 9.1).

Feminists and Nationalism

Historically, feminisms and nationalisms have been competitors: each represents an ideology that sets out to capture the loyalty of individuals by creating a shared identity, and to mobilize them to demand collective liberation. But the fates of these two 'isms' have also been intertwined. The predominant view of Western feminists is that nationalisms are bad for women – that they deny women agency, use them as reproducers, and manipulate them as boundary markers between nations controlled by men. This view was universalized by Robin Morgan in *Sisterhood is Global*: 'Women seem cross-culturally to be deeply opposed to nationalism' (1984: 23). Ann McClintock asserted: 'All nationalisms are gendered, all are invented, and all are dangerous' (1993: 61). Philomeda Essed maintained: 'Nationalism nourishes and is nourished by the subordination of women' (1995: 54). These views are based mainly on observations from Europe and from places where virulent, nationalist conflicts have devastated women's and men's lives. But as we will show, elsewhere and in other circumstances women have pursued both feminist and nationalist goals in peaceful, democratic movements.

Western European history offers us several reasons why feminisms and nationalisms have long been perceived as antithetical to each other. First, in Western Europe nationalisms were tools of 'modernization' – that is, they were means for consolidating nation-states by suppressing internal minorities whose ethnic, linguistic, and religious ways impeded centralization and standardization. They served this function

Figure 9.1. Categories of relationships between feminism and nationalism

Type of nationalism	Where	When	Type of relationship between nationalism and feminism
Modern nation-state formation	Europe	18–20C	Primarily negative
Modernizing anti-colonial nationalisms	Asia Middle East	Late 19C Early 20C	Primarily positive Mostly rights for elites
Antimodern, anticolonial, and anti-Western	Middle East	Mid 20C to 21C	Primarily negative
Revolutionary settler society	U.S., Latin	18C to 21C	Primarily negative
Non-revolutionary settler society	New Zealand, Canada, Australia	19C & 20C	Primarily positive
• Internal nationalisms	Quebec Scotland Catalonia	20/21C	Initially negative but positive after restructuring Mostly positive Mostly positive
Indigenous nationalisms	Fouth world encapsulated w/i settler and postcolonial societies	Pre-invasion 20/21C	Mixed
Postcommunist	e.g., ex-Yuogslavia, Russia	Late 20C, early 21C	Mostly negative

even before industrialization created the conditions for autonomous women's movements to emerge.[1] Glenda Sluga argues, in fact, that 'the central event of modern European nationalism, the French Revolution, involved a differentiation of masculine from feminine forms of national citizenship' (1998: 87). Participatory citizenship in the civic realm was now to be gendered, and the gender of the citizen was male. In most European nations, public space and the ideology of masculine bourgeois citizenship excluded women except as faithful wives and mothers of male citizens. Second, the Western European nation-states that froze women out were also the main colonial powers, and their nationalisms became implicated in imperialist ideology ('the white man's burden'). Although European women were not directly involved in creating nationalist ideologies or colonial power systems, they played unacknowledged roles in their administration and taught imperialist ideas as wives, teachers, missionaries, nurses, and so on (Chaudhuri and Strobel, 1992). Finally, nationalisms in Europe were implicated in many bloody wars in which women suffered greatly. Clearly, most European feminists have good reasons to believe that nationalism is bad for women.

American feminists are antinationalist mainly because their country is a neo-imperial superpower, so 'Americanism' doesn't strike them as nationalism.[2] Yet American feminists see *other* people's separatist or national liberation movements as nationalisms – and usually disapprove. French feminist Ginette Castro's 1984 study of American feminism showed just how much American mainstream feminism has been shaped by 'Americanism.' Castro further contends that American feminists are largely unaware of their own nationalism, and that this has led them to ignore the engagement of millions of women world-wide with their own nationalisms. Many of the 'feminist nationalist' movements identified by West – Hawai'ian, Puerto Rican, Black, Chicana, Filipino, South Korean – are in fact internal to the United States or within its sphere of influence. Many English-Canadian feminists uncritically share these Americans' views with respect to Quebec and First Nations women's engagements with nationalisms. This is ironic, since English-Canadian women have benefited significantly from their association with English-Canadian nationalisms (Vickers, 2000). For example, between 1890 and the end of the First World War they were rewarded for participating in nationalist 'Canadianization' efforts with the vote, which most non-white women were denied.

In some Western countries, feminists believe they can achieve feminist goals by allying themselves with nationalism. Quebec political scientist Micheline de Sève contends that engagement with *all* political movements, including nationalism, must be part of women's responsibility as equal citizens, so should be a goal of feminism. In her view, mainstream, Western feminists have lost sight of this goal: 'Somewhere on the road, we let fall centre ground political issues as if they were not gendered or ... were less women's business ... As women, we still act as if national issues were not rightly ours ... [yet] we must take responsibility as ... citizen[s]' (1997: 113). Lois West's study of alliances between feminists and nationalists reveals a number of positive inter-actions in what she calls feminist nationalism. She believes that 'women in feminist nationalist movements are struggling to define and reconceptualise their relationships to states, nations and social move-ments as activists central to the debate, not as passive recipients' (1997).

What are we to make of these different perspectives? First, note that it is mainstream feminists in Western countries – that is, those who are part of the dominant culture, who are most likely to view nationalism negatively. Cynthia Enloe (1989) believes this is because in the past two centuries nationalisms have been patriarchal in character, have marginalized women, and have often justified their oppression while inflating male pride and political authority: 'Nationalism has typically sprung from masculinized memory, masculinized humiliation and masculinized hope' (1989: 44). Pettman (1996) argues that only women of dominant groups that control the state, or of groups that aspire to be dominant in their own states, can benefit from nationalisms. Most Western feminists, however, doubt that *any* type of nationalism can benefit *any* woman in the long run. In Europe, feminist movements emerged *after* the first waves of nationalism receded; as a result, women's movements became critiques of the inequalities concealed in visions of shared nationhood (Parker et al., 1992). Most Euro-American feminists also believe that 'in anti-colonial struggles, ... feminist pro-grams have been sacrificed to the cause of national liberation and, ... after ... independence, women have been consigned to their former "domestic roles"' (Parker et al., 1992). Many postcolonial feminists and feminist nationalists disagree, but the conclusion confirms many women's actual experiences.

Yuval-Davis notes that this debate was largely ideological and that a deadlock developed between 'the nationalists' and 'the feminists' (1997: 118). The empirical basis for the debate was incomplete, since far too few women's experiences were being considered. For example, Scandinavian women's experiences were ignored, as were the largely positive experiences of women's movements in Canada, New Zealand, and Australia, which emerged at the same time as their colonial na-tionalisms, not *after* nationalist fervour had receded. Nationalists faced with integrating large numbers of immigrants saw white settler women as allies, at least for a time. Moreover, the belief of Western feminists that Third World women gained little from their interaction with anti-colonial nationalist movements is not substantiated by the evidence. Nelson and Chowdury (1994) conclude that modernizing nationalisms produced gains for women in terms of their political and legal rights. Scholarship undertaken by Third World feminists shows that modernizing, anticolonial nationalisms can have positive results for women. Jayawardena (1986), for example, discusses the feminist elements associated with anti-imperialist, nationalist movements in twelve Asian and Middle Eastern countries in the late nineteenth and early twentieth centuries. She demonstrates that feminism, far from being invented in the West, was active in these countries, and that nationalist struggles were not always inhospitable to women. Her research demonstrates that women worked both for the independence of their nations *and* for improvements in how women were treated in those new nations. She also insists that feminist and Third World nationalist movements must both be understood against a backdrop of imperialism and capitalism. Scholte sees 'identity politics' as '*alternative forms* of collective identity [that] often bypass ... the nationality principle' (1996: 566, my emphasis); in contrast, Jayawardena shows that nationalists and feminists worked together to gain independence from colonial domination, and that such struggles often had positive results for women in terms of citizenship rights, education, access to employment, and ability to advance women's goals. Women's studies scholarship needs to start introducing questions about which women are 'affected' and 'when.'

Moreover, feminisms and nationalisms change over time, as do the relationships between them. Before the 1960s, French-Canadian nationalism was largely inhospitable to feminism and often cast women in selfless reproductive and spiritual roles. The reimagined democratic nationalism that has emerged since 'the Quiet Revolution'[3] has provided a new context within which a new, feminist nationalism has been able to emerge. Sylvia Walby (1992) suggests that when nation-states are undergoing fundamental changes (restructuring), women can often pursue feminist goals in movements that are normally male-dominated or hostile to feminism. Quebec is one case in which the participation of feminists within the restructuring of nationalism made it less prone to violence and more democratic. In Quebec, a reimagining of modernizing nationalism based in the Quebec state provided an opportunity for women to articulate their own interests and to organize around them; this changed the nature of Quebec nationalism.

Once we understand that neither nationalism nor feminism takes only one form, or only one correct form, we can start to make sense of competing views, because it becomes clear that interactions between them historically differ from place to place, across time, and for differently located women. Mainstream women in many Euro-American states often are not aware of the links between their state's nationalism and its history as a colonial or neocolonial power. In contrast, minority women and Third World and indigenous women are often compelled to be aware of these macro forces, and so are more likely to combine feminism quite deliberately with other collective identities.

Three Recent Feminist Frameworks on Gender and Nation

In this section I examine three attempts to make sense of the different relationships between gender and nation and/or between feminisms and nationalisms. The work of Yuval-Davis rejects 'westocentric' (1997: 25) theories of nationalism, for two reasons: they ignore women's role in nationalist movements and ideologies, and they ignore the experiences of non-Western peoples or see them only as reactive to Western forms. Her account of the complex relationship between gender and nation shows how the structures, ideas, and processes of nationalisms are gendered. As Vickers has argued (1984; 1987; 1994a), women's power to reproduce groups physically by bearing children, and to transmit collective identities across time by rearing them, has made nationalisms gendered, in that sex/gender is key to both the material and symbolic dimensions of nationalisms. Yuval-Davis adopts gender as her basic category, and focuses mainly on discourse.

In *Woman–Nation–State*, Anthias and Yuval-Davis identified five major ways that women have participated in national processes (1989: 7):

1 As biological reproducers of ethnic collectivities.
2 As reproducers of the boundaries of ethnic groups and nations.
3 As reproducers of collective's ideologies and transmitters of their cultures.
4 As signifiers of ethnic and national differences – that is, how women dress or act are symbols in making, reproducing, and changing ethnic and national categories.
5 As participants in national military, economic, and political struggles.

Yuval-Davis (1997) also theorizes that relationships between nation and gender vary with the bases of commonality used by particular nationalist movements.[4] She hypothesizes three dimensions of nationalist projects relating to gender relations:

- The *genealogical dimension* of nationalist projects. She sees this as 'constructed around the specific origin of the people (or their race)' (21), and as associated with the European concept of *Volknation*, which has been used to construct 'the most exclusionary/homogeneous visions of "the nation"' (21). The nation is perceived as based on shared blood or common origins.
- The *cultural dimension* of nationalist projects, in which 'the symbolic heritage provided by language and/or religion and/or other customs and traditions is constructed as the "essence" of "the nation"' (21). This is associated with the European concept of *Kulturnation*, which permits assimilation but has little tolerance of unassimilable differences.
- The *civic dimension* of nationalist projects, which 'focuses on citizenship ... as determining the boundaries of the nation and thus relates it directly to notions of state sovereignty and specific territoriality' (21). She associates this with *Staatnation* or civic nationalism, in which any citizen can be part of the nation.

Which of these three bases of commonality a specific nation uses will affect its openness to women.

Yuval-Davis also introduces the concepts 'nationed gender' and 'gendered nations' to break assumptions of universalism in both feminist accounts and general theories of nationalism. In her view, all of our experiences of gender occur within a national culture, and all manifestations of nations are gendered. So the forms that gender relations take cannot be generalized in 'patriarchy,' as stand-alone feminists theorize. Gender relations are heterogeneous; they are also set in historical contexts that frame their specific content. Yuval-Davis illustrates how nationalist projects use concepts of gender and how women both resist and cooperate with nationalisms. She also shows how the role of women in biological and cultural reproduction makes them central to nationalist projects and often subject to male control. From all of this, we can pull two questions:

- Which basis for commonality or solidarity used by a nationalism is the least/most open to feminist goals?
- Which is least/most likely to attract cooperation as opposed to resistance from women – especially those also committed to feminist projects?[5]

Clearly, answering these questions is a task of historical and empirical research that is long overdue. Nationalisms cannot be theorized simply as 'bad' or 'good' for women.

Australian Jan Jindy Pettman (1996) sees all nationalisms as gendered, with women being used as markers of nations' boundaries and as 'territory across which the boundaries of nationhood are marked' (1996: 45). She shares Western feminists' negative conceptualization of nationalisms, but has also developed a framework that provides important insights about the relationship between gender and nation for women's studies. She sees nationalisms as taking two basic forms:

- *Dominant nationalisms* are used by those in control of a state or an imperialist project to mobilize 'public and institutional power to dominate, exclude, even destroy others' (1996: 52)
- *Counternationalisms or anticolonial nationalisms* are mobilized against dominant settler groups, European empires, and Western domination (1996: 53–4).

Pettman argues that both kinds of nationalism are gendered, and that women's sexuality and reproductive powers are always targets of male control.

Pettman recognizes that feminist nationalisms are a possibility, but concludes:

Nationalist movements and communal identities pose particular problems for feminists. The powerful appeal of nationalism and communal values extend to women too ... There is often a difficult relationship between nationalism, women's rights and feminist struggles, although these are negotiated in different ways over time and place. Nationalist movements mobilise women's support and labour, while simultaneously seeking to reinforce women's female roles and femininity. (1996: 61)

Pettman also notes that although nationalist men may support women's rights within nationalist movements, 'more often, women are asked to set aside "sectional interests" until the national cause is secured' (1996: 61).

The third analysis is by American scholar Lois West. She begins with 'the dilemma of women who had not yet achieved full citizenship rights yet were asked to support the nationalist cause in time of war.' It was this context that led first-wave feminists to reject nationalism, as in Virginia Woolf's famous declaration that 'as a woman, I have no country' (1997: xi–xii). Case studies of movements in Europe, Africa, the Middle East, Asia, the Pacific Islands, and the Americas lead West to conclude: 'Various types of feminist and nationalist movement activists on both a grassroots and elite level work today for the identification with their national group ... while simultaneously fighting for what they define as the rights of women within their cultural context' (xiii). These she calls feminist nationalist movements. She believes that feminist nationalists must juggle the competing demands of women's rights, civil rights, and nationalist struggles. In the process, they 'are reconstructing meanings of both nationalism and feminism within culturally specific contexts' (xv). For West, this means going beyond an understanding of feminism as a universal phenomenon detached from culture; and going beyond understanding gender as a mere variable in studies of nationalism. She believes that nationalisms are inherently and differently gendered and that restricting our understandings of nationalism to their ethnicity is problematic. Her project is 'to incorporate gender, viewed here as the struggle for women's rights, into a definition of nationalism that places women at the centre and acknowledges feminist nationalism as a process of interaction developed between women and men, and not solely by men' (xxx).

West identifies three models of feminist nationalist movements: national liberation social movements, which arose in colonial contexts when nationalist movements were seeking independence from external, imperial control; movements against neocolonialism, which arise where colonialism has ended formally but neocolonialism continues, as in the Philippines; and 'identity-rights movements that wage struggles internal to their societies' (xxx) against internal neocolonialism or for (collective) identity rights. In this category, West includes feminist nationalists in Quebec and African-Americans and Chichanas in the United States. She sees the Hawai'ian and Quebec movements as both struggles for identity rights and decolonization movements. She argues that women in these contexts are active in reconstructing nationalism and feminism 'by redefining the private and public realms as not mutually exclusive and binary but as complementary and unitary' (xxxi).

West's framework has several drawbacks. First, her categories are incomplete. As Pettman notes, women can also gain space within dominant nationalisms that can permit the emergence of feminist national-isms, as when English-Canadian women gained legal and political rights in Canada because of their active role in nation-building. Sec-ond, West's framework conflates neocolonialism, whereby foreign pow-ers persist in their influence long after being expelled, with continuing colonialism, whereby white settler states encapsulate indigenous peoples. This is an important distinction, because although women in many states facing neocolonialism adopt forms of feminism, many indigenous women facing continuing colonialism do not, perceiving 'First World feminism' as complicit in their oppression. West also con-fuses women's activism in nationalist movements with feminist activ-ism. Because many indigenous women explicitly reject feminism as representing values unacceptable to their cultures, it is not appropri-ate to class them as instances of feminist nationalism.

Gender and Nation in 'Settler Societies'

In this section I apply insights from the frameworks explored above to the new nation-states (including Canada) that were created by white settlers in territories previously occupied by indigenous peoples.[6] In settler societies, different relationships emerged between gender and nation, with two distinctive patterns. The earliest appearance of na-tionalism was among white creoles in Latin America and the United States, who found themselves patronized as inferiors by those born in Europe (Anderson, 1991). These countries were formed through revo-lutions against the European powers that had settled them – revolu-tions that took place before conditions had emerged for autonomous women's movements. In contrast, the countries of the late British Em-pire, including Australia, Canada, and New Zealand, never rebelled, instead winning independence by slow stages. In these countries a form of colonial nationalism developed (Eddy and Schreuder, 1988) in which white women of British origin played a significant role. Indeed, the early enfranchisement of white women was the end result of a symbiotic emergence of colonial nationalism and maternal feminism, as men recruited women to help in nation-building projects. There weren't enough men to perform the many nation-building activities, and this enabled women of British origin to claim full citizenship for themselves through their work in the public realm. By the mid-nine-teenth century they were working as teachers, government employ-ees, medical workers, home missionaries, social and settlement workers, journalists, library builders, and community leaders – sometimes even as police and magistrates. The role of Canadian women of British origin was especially important; the large francophone population never fully accepted British rule, and a rebellious Metis population resisted it. Women participated actively in this dominant, internally imperialist nationalism, and gained rights for which they had been advocating within a framework of maternal feminism.[7]

Non-Dominant Nationalisms

The settler states displaced indigenous occupants. In South Africa and Canada they also conquered European peoples of Dutch and French origins. French-Canadian nationalism has taken various forms over the past two centuries, and its openness to changes in women's roles has varied accordingly. Since 'the Quiet Revolution' of the late 1960s, however, it has become a democratic movement operating within Quebec, where francophones are a majority. Francophone feminists have forged a close relationship with this new nationalism,[8] which though still a minority force in Canada, is dominant in Quebec. As LeClerc and West have demonstrated, franco-Quebec feminists are nationalists and believe that their project of an equal society is most likely to be achieved in an autonomous (but not necessarily sovereign) Quebec. Some of them are fully integrated into nationalist movements, while others occupy an independent position through the Fédèration des Femmes, from which they regularly assess the fit between their goals and those advanced by nationalist politicians. De Sève argues: 'Feminism begins with the claim to [the] autonomy of every woman, but it doesn't stop there ... What brings us together as well as what distinguishes us, our identity as feminists and Quebecoises is indivisible' (1992: 110).

Feminists in Quebec have had a complex relationship with nationalism. Their nation defines itself as a minority within Canada and within English-speaking North America. Its language and culture are threatened by the corrosive dominance of English as a world language. A decentralized federation would provide Quebec with significant powers, and French Canada's relatively large population (over 25 per cent of Canada's) would allow a nation centred in Quebec to act as a majority in many ways provided other nations accommodated it.[9] Franco-Quebec feminists have moved away from private, familial, and religious defences of language and identity toward a secular, state-based approach, and this has done much to make them allies in democratic nationalist movements; they no longer feel like tools or symbols of male-dominated movements. When de Sève argues, 'As a feminist, I want the world to be mine through and through,' she is asserting her right to be a full citizen of a democratic nation. She contends that women must accept responsibilities as well as demanding rights – if we demand a share in power, we must also accept responsibility.

For women who are members of smaller, less secure minorities – especially non-white minorities – such assertions of citizenship may not be possible. The clearest case of this is women's relationships to indigenous nationalisms, to which we now turn.

Indigenous Nationalisms

In many settler societies we find encapsulated, indigenous nations seeking self-determination. Many indigenous women see their futures within these nations. Donna Awatere, for example, after long involvement in the New Zealand women's movement, concluded:

> The first loyalty of white women is to the White Culture and the White Way. This is true as much for those who define themselves as feminists ... This loyalty is seen in their rejection of the sovereignty of Maori people and in their acceptance of the imposition of the British culture on the Maori ... The oppressor avoids confronting the role they play in oppressing others ... White feminists do this by defining 'feminism' for this country and by using their white power, status and privilege to ensure that their definition of 'feminism' supersedes that of Maori women. (1984: 4)

Haunani-Kay Trask describes Hawai'i as a nation struggling against American occupation. She rejects 'First World feminism,' associating it with the whites who occupy her islands, suppress her language, religion, and culture, and oppress her people. Her commitment to native Hawai'ian nationalism focuses on land rights, language revival, and self-determination. Trask is committed to 'traditional women's issues' – reproductive rights, equal opportunity, and ending domestic violence. To her, feminism in the continental United States 'seems more and more removed from the all-consuming struggles against our physical and cultural extinction as indigenous peoples' (1997: 191). 'First World' feminism is 'just too white, too American,' because white women have structured its agenda so that only those issues they define as feminist are included (190). She concludes: 'What concerns white women of the ruling culture is rarely what concerns Native women in colonised cultures' (194). So although women in both contexts objectively have some interests in common, Hawai'ian women's solidarity with their menfolk is more important to Trask than any goals they might share with white women. Moreover, she supports gender interests across and within the sovereignty movement, not a feminist movement that would pit white and native Hawai'ian women against white and native Hawai'ian men.

Trask's critique of 'First World feminism' shows the problems inherent in an approach that 'recognizes' difference without understanding its causes. Like indigenous women everywhere, Trask asks, 'Why is land, our mother, not a women's issue?' Native Hawai'ian nationalism shows how 'women's issues' are linked to land rights and continuing colonialism. For example, native Hawai'ian women's health has suffered significantly because without land on which to grow traditional crops, they must eat a Western diet that they cannot tolerate and that (as elsewhere) results in very high levels of diabetes and other illnesses. Trask insists: 'Any exclusive focus on women neglect[s] the historic oppression of all Hawai'ians and the large force-field of imperialism' (190). For example, feminists are concerned about 'women' being poor, but rarely link the diseases of poverty – that is, diseases resulting from poor housing, low education, and high incarceration levels – to colonialism and neocolonialism. Trask concludes: 'We are the colonised; they are the beneficiaries of colonialism. That some feminists are oblivious to this historical reality does not lessen their power in the colonial equation' (192).

Indigenous women in Canada also have complex relationships with nationalism. Many express their collective identity in the concept of First Nations. Although often portrayed in mainstream feminist texts only as forgotten and oppressed, many First Nations women occupy positions of leadership in their nations and see their destinies as women tied to the destiny of their nations. Mohawk women, for example, are playing important roles in the resistance against continuing Canadian and Quebec colonialism and in the struggle for self-government. But at the same time, other Indian and Metis women – many of them urban dwellers, and some of them denied status as 'Indians' – may not believe that First Nations movements have space for their concerns. These differences have focused in recent years on whether the Canadian Charter of Rights and Freedoms should apply within self-governing First Nations. The Native Women's Association of Canada

(NWAC) has demanded that it be applied, arguing that women will be victimized by (mainly male-dominated) Indian governments if no protections exist. The NWAC interprets the abuse that indigenous women experience mainly through a gender lens, and has concluded that the Charter would provide protection. In contrast, traditional Indian women see the gendered harms that indigenous women experience as mainly a consequence of continuing colonialism, remembering that many indigenous cultures were egalitarian until the colonial state imposed male dominance through the Indian Act (Monture-Angus, 1995). First Nations scholarship traces the existence of Indian nations (without states) and confederacies of nations prior to white contact (Alfred 1995: 182). In its present mode, indigenous nationalism is a form of politics that involves some Indian and Metis women who are concerned with gendered harms but who see those harms as caused mainly by continuing colonialism.

Feminism and Anticolonial Nationalisms

In this section we explore the relationships between feminism and nationalism in 'Third World' countries in two different contexts. First, we focus on women's relationships with national liberation movements that adopted *modernizing nationalisms*, drawing on the analysis of Sri Lankan Kumari Jayawardena (1986), who explores positive associations in Asia and the Middle East in the early part of the century. We then consider *antimodern nationalisms*, which emerged – mainly in the Middle East – in the second half of the twentieth century. We explore Valentine Moghadam's analysis (1994) of women's relationships with anti-Western movements, and conclude that there is more political space for autonomous feminist activism within modernizing anticolonial movements, although those movements sometimes constrain women's emancipation and control their politics. Yet even within some antimodern nationalisms, women may find political space to pursue the goals of women's advancement, although in many cases hostility to women's equality may be central to the movement's opposition to Western values.

Relationships with Anticolonial, Modernizing Nationalisms

Jayawardena notes that the status of women was an intrinsic part of the logic of modernizing, anticolonial nationalisms in the Third World.[10] 'Many reformers of Asia ... argued that "Oriental backwardness" was partly due to women's low status' (1986: 11–12). The general assumption was that to resist colonialism and expel the Europeans, colonized peoples had to embrace 'modern' (i.e., Western) social organizations, and strengthen their economies and secular institutions. Many imperialists once asserted the status of women was the barometer of 'civilization.' In this context, male reformers had two objectives: 'to establish ... a system of stable, monogamous, nuclear families with educated and employable women such as was associated with capitalist development and bourgeois ideology; and yet to ensure that women would retain a position of traditional subordination within the family' (15). Third World feminists struggled for women's rights and made their struggles an integral part of nationalist resistance movements. The relationships they established varied between regions, and so did their achievements. In this section I focus on India as an illuminating example of how the process works.

Partha Chatterjee (1986) shows that in India, anticolonial nationalism was a response to the complex problem of how to mobilize large numbers of people against British imperialist ideology, which asserted that its rule was justified because Indians were so 'backward' they could not be left to rule themselves. This ideology held that the colonizers ruled because they were modern and superior and so occupied the 'moral high ground.' According to Chatterjee (1993), the struggles over nationalism were inherently gendered. Women were assigned the role of protectors of Hindu culture and spirituality; although it might be necessary to imitate the West in the public realm with regard to the material aspects of life, the spiritual aspects that made Indian civilization superior and unique had to be protected within the private realm, where women were. Gandhi's teachings, in contrast, were antimodern, rejecting both colonial rule and Western modernity, including industrialism. In his view, only India's spiritual heritage and potential could demonstrate Indians' superiority to the British and thereby persuade the colonizers to leave. According to Gandhi, both women and men had to be the guardians of India's spirituality in a symbiosis of interdependent roles.

Nationalist debates were gendered in a second way: having 'new' modern women was part of being a modern nation ready for independence, given that imperialist ideology justified colonialism in part because of the 'backward' treatment of women. Women were active participants in the struggle for Indian Independence, which gained them legal and political rights; and they established a tradition of women's political participation. Women in the movement were feminist in the sense that they conceptualized women as oppressed because of their sex as well as by the British and struggled against both oppressions. Educated Indian women informed the world of India's modernity through their vision of women's public roles. But Indian nationalism also assigned women responsibility for cultural and spiritual things protected in the home.[11] As in the West, women's citizenship coexisted with male dominance. Chatterjee links the material/spiritual distinctions found in most Indian nationalism to an outer/inner distinction: women's relationship to the home, where the spiritual was to be preserved, came to represent the essence of Indian nationalism. The demands on women were contradictory: they were to be modern, educated, and active in the public sphere, but they were also to accept the primacy of their private mission as mothers and as transmitters of cultural and spiritual values within enduring families led by men.

In Chatterjee's analysis, 'Indian nationalism' was basically Hindu nationalism. Hansen's analysis (1995) of the involvement of women in the contemporary Hindu nationalism movement suggests that the fundamental ambivalence about modernity that marked earlier nationalist movements persists to this day. Hindu nationalism is now dominant in India, and is seeking to turn India from a secular into a Hindu state. Many educated, middle-class Hindu women have become active in women's nationalist groups, some of which are radical and autonomous. Hansen uses the concept of *controlled emancipation* to explain the strategy of Hindu nationalist leaders, who allow women sufficient 'emancipation' that they can participate in radical political action, but at the same time restrict their independence in other ways. This helps explain some aspects of the relationship between feminist and nationalist movements, and not just in India. Modernizing, Third World nationalisms are ambivalent about modern Western values; this is evident in the material/spiritual distinction. Some educated and upper class/caste women have rejected some aspects of modernity (e.g., public roles) in favour of family roles. Those who do participate in public life nonetheless are expected to preserve values in private that conflict with Western modernity.

Relationships with Antimodern Nationalisms

Nelson and Chowdhury (1995) identify 'the changing nature of nationalism' as one of four main international forces affecting women's status in the past three decades. They have established a dichotomy between modern nationalisms, which are based on universalism and secularism in the public sphere, and antimodern nationalisms, which they associate with the rise of religious fundamentalisms (1995: 6–7). They believe that the former expanded women's rights, while the latter works to constrain them. In essence, they see modern, secular nation-states and their civic nationalisms as safe for women and as promoting their rights and opportunities; and they fear ethnic and religious nationalisms, which they regard as dangerous for women. This picture may be somewhat biased. The existence of antimodern nationalisms and of antimodern elements within modernizing nationalisms is nothing new: Gandhi, though he was opposed to Western modernity, argued for the emancipation of both women and untouchables. Nor are modern nation-states as secular, universalist, and 'civic' as they seem on the surface; they certainly don't seem so to minorities. In states that seem characterized by civic nationalism, an ethnic nationalism often exists, and a dominant form of religion controls the state and its institutions. Nonetheless, anticolonial or anti-Western nationalisms that are also antimodern are different in character and some have involved gender apartheid and intense oppression for women.

Valentine Moghadam, in *Gender and National Identity* (1994), explores the gender dynamics of nationalism in antimodern movements for Islamization. Anti-modern nationalisms vary. Those involving the conflict between Islam and the West (many centuries old) involve cases (Afghanistan, Algeria, Bangladesh, Palestine) that raise issues for women in their starkest form. Moghadam agrees with Jayawardena that in the past in Asia and the Middle East 'feminism and nationalism were complementary, compatible and solidaristic' (3). But she concludes: 'This has changed. Today, feminists and nationalists view each other with suspicion if not hostility, and nationalism is no longer assumed to be a progressive force' (3). This is because both nationalism, under the influence of religious fundamentalism, and feminism have changed in such a way that the two projects have become less rather than more compatible. She explains the changes in nationalisms as involving the substitution of religion for secular doctrine in the nationalist text: 'If the nation is defined as a religious entity, then the appropriate models of womanhood are to be found in scripture' (4). She concludes: 'Nationhood has been recast in these terms in the latter part of the twentieth century, and this has distinct implications for definitions of gender, for the position of women and for feminism as an emancipatory project' (4).

Moghadam believes that disillusionment with nationalism is wide-spread, especially where leftist ideology has subsumed 'the woman question' under the national question. In many parts of the Third World, the failure of secular, modernizing regimes (Sudan, Iran) and the collapse of state socialist regimes has resulted in a backlash to the values of Western modernization. But Islamization raises especially important questions about modernization, and about the Eurocentrism of values long assumed – falsely – to be universal. In Afghanistan a tribal-Islamist opposition fought a secular, Marxist-inspired government and rejected its reform program, which included the emancipation of women. Veiling and unveiling exemplify the underlying issues. For many women who share Islamist, anti-Western values, the veil is a political symbol they embrace willingly. For urban women faced with sexual harassment everywhere, covering up may mean relief and greater mobility. In modernist Turkey, however, a politician is forbidden by law to wear the veil and prevented from taking her seat in the legislature for doing so; in Iran the veil is compulsory; and in Afghanistan, with its regime of gender apartheid, not wearing the veil was a capital crime. In Algeria or Egypt, some women wear the veil voluntarily as a sign of cultural integrity or antimodern views, but others wear it to evade intimidation by male vigilantes, who seek to reassert control over women in a world in which they cannot control their own lives. In this backlash against Western, modern values, how women dress and behave has become part of a conflict of increasing violence.

Islamist women in Egypt believe that existing states oppress women, along with men, because they are based on the Western or state-social-ist models of a secular state and not on true Islamic laws. They reject the *label* of feminism, which they consider a Western ideology that creates enmity between men and women; but at the same time they argue for the advancement of women, especially in terms of interpreting Islamic law. Some women also work from secular Marxist and Muslim feminist positions (Karam, 1998), so alignments between feminists and nationalists in secular states such as Egypt are complex. In officially Islamic states like Iran, there are two main groups within the women's movement: secular feminists, who adopt liberal or socialist ideas, and Muslim women, who seek the advancement of women from within an Islamist perspective. Like the Islamists in Egypt, the latter seek a true Islamic state; they contend that the current regime is male chauvinist and are seeking women's involvement in the judiciary, in accord with the Koran (Tabari, 1987). Women working within an Islamist nationalist framework reject some of the content of Western feminism, but they are still seeking political, economic, and social justice for women. They do not align themselves with the West or with secularism; most would join with nationalists seeking a true Islamic state. Yet Western feminists have demonized Islamist movements, and consider it impossible that Muslim women aligned with such nationalisms could consider themselves feminists or work for the advancement of women.

In these nationalist struggles, gender politics are central. As in modernist anticolonial nationalisms, how women act and how they dress become important as nationalist symbols. Islamist women welcome the changes; non-Islamist women see them as a form of social control incompatible with feminism. But the impact of Islamist nationalisms is not uniform: in Afghanistan, women virtually disappeared from the public realm; whereas in Iran they are active and visible. Bangladesh is an especially provocative case: in that country two women – representatives of their respective dynasties – dominate politics, and a feminist movement is contesting woman-hostile elements of Islamist nationalist doctrine.

Gender and Nationalism in the Postcommunist World

Sholte reminds us that 'nationality has been a question of privilege within the world system. "Insiders" have enjoyed certain entitlements that have simultaneously been denied to "outsiders," for example ... residence, passport, suffrage, welfare provisions' (1996: 570). In this process, nationalisms construct who is 'in' and who is 'out.' Economic globalization has loosened the ties between dominant and minority groups within nation-states. As large populations are dislocated by global economic and political changes, the security of being a national becomes especially important. The collapse of many of the artificial states imposed by colonial powers in Africa and Asia resulted in nationalist conflicts that had devastating consequences for millions of women. The collapse of the Soviet Union and the countries created by communist imperialism in Eastern Europe had similar consequences. In this section I explore the relationships between feminisms and nationalisms in the aftermath of the collapse of the former Yugoslavia.

The Yugoslav socialist state was established in 1945 with six socialist republics (Bosnia, Herzegovina, Croatia, Macedonia, Montenegro, Serbia, and Slovenia) and two autonomous socialist republics (Kosovo and Vojvodina). Yugoslavia was intended to be a multinational state and it contained nations with very different histories. Some had once been part of the (Christian) Austro-Hungarian Empire, others part of the (Muslim) Ottoman Empire. Language, religion, culture, and history created conflicts among them.[12] Yugoslavian state socialism, like Western modernism, was universalist and opposed nationalisms internal to the state: 'In 1971 ... Tito defined nationalism as a terrible disease, which, like cancer, treacherously erodes not only the individual organism, but soon also the whole state body' (Godina, 1998: 421). Nationalism was repressed. But at the same time, Yugoslav leaders, like their Soviet counterparts, manipulated nationalist enmities and pitted national groups against one another in order to maintain their control. As a result nationalism was not eliminated – it was perverted.

In the break-up of Yugoslavia and the resulting wars, nationalisms repressed for three decades by the Yugoslav state-socialist leadership resurfaced, and women's roles and behaviour became a battleground for many conflicts. In large part through the efforts of the Women in Black group, it became known in the West that mass rape was being used as an act of war in the former republics of Yugoslavia. Indijana Hidovic Harper describes the conflict between Bosnian Muslims and Bosnian Serbs (1993). A Western, European feminist, and part of the Muslim middle class, she was raised in Bosnia 'to be a woman of ... my own making' (1993: 102). The ease with which this descendant of generations of women doctors, lawyers, and teachers combined her feminism with her identity as a Muslim and a Bosnian Yugoslav was shattered by the collapse of the Soviet Union and Yugoslavia, by the rise of radical Islamist movements, and by the wars that followed. The values that characterized the Bosnian Muslim community were a product of complex political forces: first the Ottoman Empire, then the Austro-Hungarian Empire, and finally secular, state-socialist Yugoslavia shaped their identity and their relationships with their Orthodox Serb and Catholic Croat neighbours. It was largely an ethnic identity: the Muslim community was mostly secularized. Bosnian nationalism was women-friendly, and the liberation of Muslim women in Bosnia was seen as a mark of its progressiveness – a quality it held in common with many modernizing nationalisms.

Serbian nationalism, which fuels many post-Yugoslav conflicts, is not women-friendly. Socialist Yugoslavia had an official policy of gender equity that was 'derived from ... Marxist ideology, a belief in modernization, and a recognition of women's contribution to the Second World War.' In state-socialist Yugoslavia, women legally had equal political rights and were active in the paid workforce and in the political system at about the same rate as women in Western Europe and North America. Serbian nationalism rejects state-socialist values, including gender equity, in favour of a return to traditional pro-Serbian patriarchal values.

Before the Kosovo War, the dominant, state nationalism in Serbia – where the proportion of women in Parliament dropped in 1990 from 29 to 1.6 per cent – delivered a mixed message to Serbian women. On the one hand, under Milosevic they were seen as 'enemies of the Serbian people' if they demonstrated against anti-abortion policies (Hidovic Harper, 1993); on the other, they were portrayed as emancipated relative to Albanian women in Kosovo, who were described as baby machines. This and the wars provoked a nationalist-inspired demographic 'crisis.' Serbian women were urged to bear more soldiers to defend the nation. The Albanians, the Gypsies, and the Muslims were declared to have 'irrational' birthrates, and Serbian women were pressured to accelerate their reproduction and to give up their roles in the public sector (Korac, 1996). In sum, Serb nationalism was coercively pronatal.

Women in all of the region's communities have suffered as a result of the links that have been forged between embattled nationalisms and reproductive capacity. Serious contractions in women's choices have resulted from macropolitical change, such as nationalist-inspired wars. Hidovic Harper concludes: 'My individual choices, once so limitless, have been brought down to a precious few. I am identified as part of my community and will be viewed in whichever way it is viewed, treated in whichever way it is treated' (1993: 107). Too often, once security and affluence are stripped away, women receive protection only from those with whom they share a primary identity.

Conclusion

In this chapter I have explored the relationships between gender and nation, and between feminists and nationalisms, over time and in various parts of the world. I found a number of different perspectives on nationalism, ranging from suspicion and rejection to more positive evaluations of women combining democratic nationalism with feminism, as in Quebec. Many indigenous women still fighting internal colonialism are committing themselves to indigenous nationalisms and rejecting 'white' feminisms. Clearly, there is no single, universal relationship between gender and nation, although all nations are gendered. The extent to which feminists can work within nationalist movements varies considerably across time and place. Democratic nationalist movements offer opportunities for women to participate in seeking feminist goals. Others do not.

Many predicted that globalization would mean the end of nationalism; they were wrong. As globalization weakens nation-states and forces more and more transnational links, nationalisms are likely to reassert themselves even more strongly, and affect the world's women even more profoundly. For this reason, nationalism is an important field of research for women's studies. A one-world approach to scholarship on women requires us to do more than simply recognize diversity. We must also understand why women's experiences vary, and why the relationship between feminisms and nationalisms ranges from repressive to productive. By exploring women's experiences in different contexts and times, we can begin to understand this most complex relationship.

Notes

1 See Held, 1996, 'The Development of the Modern State,' in Hall et al., *Modernity*: 55–89. It is common to assume that feminism and women's movements are themselves a product of modernity and therefore of the modern nation-state. This account works for Europe but not for colonized states, the Fourth World or the settler states established in 'the new world.'

2 American thought has always assumed its exceptionalism. American thinkers see themselves as 'the first new nation' and as the manifestation of a universal form destined to prevail over the American continent (at least), as the idea of manifest destiny implies. So American nationalism since the American Revolution, which combines classical liberalism and manifest destiny, seems to 'Americans' not to be nationalism at all but rather a universal creed: 'Americanism.'

3 Until the 1960s, French-Canadian nationalism was antimodern and stressed preserving language and culture via large, religious families and a rural lifestyle. Since the 1960s francophones in Quebec have relied on their majority status within the province, which has used its state powers

to preserve and promote language and culture. This 'Quiet Revolution' was a project of liberal modernization that sought autonomy, and women took up different roles than they had in 'the battle of the cradles' that marked earlier English/French nationalist contests. More recently, a left-inspired, national liberationist form of nationalism has been growing in strength, and many feminists of more classes are participating. The fact that this new nationalism focuses on Quebec's state has had the result of Acadian nationalism diverging from it.

4 Note that aspects of more than one of them may be used in a particular project, and the basis may change over time.

5 Note that nationalist movements often use a mixture. Nor are the categories self-evident. For example, de Sève contends that 'civic nationalism' is often an ethnic nationalism (geneological or cultural) that had gained control of the state.

6 There are also cases in which the invading society was neither white nor European. For example, the indigenous peoples of Japan were displaced by peoples from the mainland of Asia.

7 This combination made their activism compatible with their roles as mothers since, their nationalism was also pronatalist.

8 Quebec nationalism has two distinct strains: one embodied in the Quebec Liberal Party, which is autonomist, and the other in the Parti Québécois, which is sovereigntist.

9 Acadians and francophones in other provinces have thus been rendered vulnerable minorities, looking mainly to the protection of the Charter of Rights and Freedoms. Their members have different views.

10 Not all of the countries she studied were actually occupied by Western powers. For example, Japan and Iran were not. There, movements were modernizing in an imperialist context – usually to forestall occupation.

11 Note that 'Indian' nationalism was officially a civic nationalism and led to the creation of a secular state, although with different personal status codes for the different religious groups. (So Hindu women and Muslim women have aspects of their personal status governed by different codes.)

12 I am relying on Vesna Godina, 'The Outbreak of Nationalism on Former Yugoslav territory,' *Nations and Nationalism* 4(3), 1998: 409–22.

CHAPTER 10

Religion, Spirituality, and Feminism

Vanaja Dhruvarajan

Religion often invokes the deepest of human emotions and commitments. Spiritual expression may well be a basic human need, and religion provides by far the most important avenue for it. Religion in one form or another is present in all known societies. As sociologists have consistently pointed out, religion serves many important functions in social life.

Religion provides meaning for life and specifies the purpose of life. It provides answers to bewildering questions and uncertainties such as these: Where did we come from? What happens after we die? Why is there so much suffering in life? Why does it seem that good people suffer while bad people escape unpunished? By providing answers to these questions, religion motivates people to live, achieve, and strive.

Among communities of believers, religion provides a sense of belonging. It underscores people's moral and emotional ties to other people. Rituals and ceremonies help followers of a given religion develop common bonds, and motivate them to rededicate themselves to a common purpose.

Religion also legitimizes the places people occupy within their social hierarchy. It naturalizes social relationships.

Belief systems and ritual practices influence a people's way of life. They set the tone and tenor of life. They provide a framework for organizing both social and personal life. Religion varies in its impact on individuals, but no one escapes religion entirely – not even those who are not overtly religious. That is because belief systems are embedded in institutional structures.

Both women and men need answers to the perplexing questions of life, and to make sense out of their lives. They also need to belong to a community with a shared history. They need camaraderie so that they can celebrate life and obtain comfort and solace in times of trouble. Although this eternal quest is universal, the kinds of answers women get from most of the dominant world religions are often different from the one's men get because these religions are patriarchal.

All of the major world religions are patriarchal and accord women a subordinate status in the gender hierarchy. Women are believed to be biologically and spiritually inferior to men. They have a body that is periodically unclean due to menstruation and childbirth; they are impulsive and morally deficient; and they have uncontrollable sexual urges. It is argued that these qualities legitimize the subordinate position accorded to them within patriarchal families and the religious communities. As they are socialized into their families and communities, women learn to accept their lower status. The resulting inequalities are routinely reproduced, with each generation transmitting its values to the next. The rituals and symbols of patriarchal religions foster the development of an emotional conviction that gender hierarchy is natural and normal.

The consequences of all this are far-reaching for women. They are not allowed to occupy leadership positions; they can function only as helpers and supporters of male leaders; and they cannot participate in many rituals and ceremonies. As well, rituals focus on the *male* life cycle and on male life experiences; those of women are excluded. They regulate and control women's sexuality. They assign women to mundane activities while their men engage in scholarly and spiritual enterprises.

In all three monotheistic religions – namely Christianity, Judaism, and Islam – the divinity is conceptualized as male. In Hinduism, which is polytheistic, goddesses are present, but they have a lower status and are considered secondary to the primary godheads. Buddhism is non-theistic and focuses on ethical and moral behaviour; however, it privileges male leadership in spreading the teachings of religion. Confucianism is neither monotheistic nor polytheistic. Its teachings are derived from proclamations of Confucius, which have a clear patriarchal bias. In the context of all these religions, women are integrated into the religious fold under terms and conditions beneficial to men, and this bolsters men's authority and privilege.

Even though the world's major religions are obviously gender biased, it is important to remember that there are significant variations in religious practices and in people's degree of adherence to religious tenets. The followers of any given religion are never a homogeneous group; for example, they vary on the basis of history, geographical location, caste, class, race, ethnic background, and sexual orientation. Even though they have some things in common, they also vary significantly. They often vary in their interpretations of the same religious scriptures, and this can legitimize particular religious practices.

Generally speaking, in the patriarchal religions discussed in this chapter, gendered teachings are adhered to most stringently by the most orthodox branches. Such teachings affect the behaviour of men and women, the rituals they follow, and their relative position in authority structures. They also regulate the sexuality of men and women.

Religious traditions are not homogeneous. Evangelical Christianity is different from the Christianity practised by the Quakers. Roman Catholicism is more conservative than many forms of Protestantism. Within Judaism there is a great deal of variation between the Orthodox, Conservative, and Reform branches, with the first being the most rigid and the latter the least rigid.

Islam as practised in Iran is much more conservative than Islam as practised in Malaysia. Hinduism does not have a centralized authority structure, which means it is practised differently in different regions in India. For example, Hinduism as practised in Rajastan in north India is very conservative; in Kerala, a southern Indian state, it is much less so.

Feminists have different opinions about the usefulness of religion for women. Many accept that women may need religion as much as men do, to satisfy their need for spiritual expression; but they also realize that it is a double-edged sword for them. Women are faced with similar spiritual questions, yet adhering to the kinds of religions that prevail today often means accepting a subordinate position. This tension between the need to nurture spiritual aspects of one's life and the need to validate the intrinsic worth of women as persons is evident in feminist dialogues. There is no unanimity among feminists in their response to the world's patriarchal religions (Cooey et al., 1991; Downing, 1993; Gross, 1996). Though they generally agree that patriarchy must ultimately be dismantled and that gender equality must be achieved, they differ over strategies to achieve these goals. Some feminists have called for the transformation of religion, others for its rejection. In this chapter I discuss both strategies in some detail and critically evaluate them.

Transformation

Many feminists aspire to sacralize ordinary life, and promote an integrated, holistic way of life that avoids dualistic conceptions. They point out the dangerous consequences of dualistic thought for everyone – both men and women – as well as for the environment and all living beings on earth. Dualistic thinking has led to hierarchical conceptions that privilege some over others. Man/woman, culture/nature, sacred/profane, heaven/earth, soul/body, spirit/matter – the former in each pair is valorized. This sort of mindset leads us to focus on aspects of life considered superior, and to neglect those aspects which are considered inferior (Gross, 1996; Goldenberg, 1990; Downing, 1993; Cooey et al., 1991).

As a consequence of dualism, men are identified with those aspects of life that are considered to be of greater intrinsic worth, and women with those aspects that are considered to be of less worth. Everything that is susceptible to change, decay, and death is perceived as belonging to a lower order and therefore despised. Life on earth is to be lived by aspiring to transcend it, to reach a better place. This sojourner attitude has led to the neglect of the environment and the destruction of plants and animals; the devaluation of relationships and community, resulting in widespread alienation and discontent; and the despising of the body and its functions, resulting in militarism and the normalization of violence (Gross, 1996; Goldenberg, 1990).

Feminists have consistently aspired to transcend dualisms and live life to the fullest here and now. They aspire to sacralize the profane and to treat the earth as our home. They emphasize the unity of body and soul, spirit and matter, and argue that experience should provide the basis for spirituality. They also promote the importance of leading an embodied life and of accepting ageing and death as part of life. Such an outlook leads to a revaluation of everyday life, to the nurturing of the environment, and to the realization that resources are limited. Life is to be lived in harmony with nature and in cooperation with communities of other people. The regenerative capacities of the human body and of nature itself are to be celebrated. Such a way of life will be filled with contentment, peace, and friendship and suffused with a sense of well-being (Goldenberg, 1990; Cooey, 1991; Gross, 1996).

The explicit purpose of these feminist efforts is to transform patriarchal religions. As Gross points out:

> Often feminists talk about their visions by using metaphors from women's traditional occupations of cooking. It is frequently said that religious feminism is not about getting our piece of the pie, or our *fair* share of the pie. It is about developing a whole new recipe and a whole new method of baking, which is more basic, threatening and inspiring or even more accurate, religious feminism is about the coexistence, flourishing and interaction of quite a few recipes. (1996: 199)

These feminists insist that postpatriarchal religion must speak to women's experiences. It must recognize and celebrate the full humanity of women and men, not just that of men. Women must participate in naming the reality that has been denied to them historically under patriarchy. The end result of transformation will be a paradigm shift from an androcentric model of humanity to one that is gender inclusive – or as some feminists refer to it, androgynous (Gross, 1996).

Feminists involved in this project agree on the ultimate goal but not on how to reach it. In this, there are two dominant strategies. The first involves working within patriarchal religions to bring about transformation. Due to shortage of space, I will not be able to discuss in full detail the various efforts at transformation. Instead I will highlight some of the significant feminist efforts in each of the major religious traditions. These feminists are of the opinion that all major religions contain the seeds of their own transformation. Because they are redeemable, it is worthwhile trying to redeem them. Within each tradition we find many feminists who are struggling to transform their religion in such a way that women can identify themselves with it and feel validated, inspired, and empowered (Gross, 1996; Richardson, 1981; Renzetti and Curran, 1999; Dhruvarajan, 1996; Cooey, 1991; Downing, 1993; Stuckey, 1998).

Then there are feminists who find patriarchal religions as they are practised now dehumanizing for women, but who are certain that women do need religion, just as men do. Their solutions involve establishing new religious traditions by discovering and recovering women's experiences and giving importance to women's full humanity. Some of these feminists advocate a return to nature and the sanctifying of that relationship (Gaard, 1993; Mies and Shiva, 1993). Other feminists are trying to recover the lost traditions of prebiblical times and to construct new traditions that speak to women's needs (Gross, 1996; Stone, 1976; Gimbutas, 1974). This strategy involves working outside established religious traditions (Goldenberg, 1990; Stuckey, 1998; Downing, 1993; Gross, 1996).

Transformation by Working within Religious Traditions

Religious followers in all traditions who argue for transformation believe that patriarchal religions are redeemable and worth redeeming. They are firmly convinced that these religions are not inherently patriarchal, but are that way because of how sacred texts have been interpreted. Careful rereading of scriptures reveals that these religions can become gender inclusive. Employing this conviction, people in these traditions are striving to interpret the scriptures from an androgynous perspective, to develop inclusive language in liturgy, and to ensure that rituals and ceremonies celebrate and recognize male *and* female life experiences and life cycles. This movement has been inspired in large part by feminist ideals of gender equality. I will discuss Judaism and Christianity together, because the initiatives in these traditions are quite similar. I will discuss Islam and Hinduism separately. Because of shortage of space, I will restrict my discussion to these four religions.

Judeo-Christian Tradition

Inclusive language. Many feminists under Christianity have focused on developing gender-inclusive lectionaries. This effort has been led by the National Council of the Church of Christ, a Protestant denomination. There is a clear link between language and consciousness, so it is important to develop gender-inclusive language for the deity and humanity if a paradigm shift is to be brought about. The deity is perceived as transcending gender as well as race and colour. As much as possible, 'sovereign' is used instead of 'Lord.' 'God, the Father' becomes 'God, the Father and Mother,' and so on (Gross, 1996: 202). The practice of using only masculine pronouns in addressing the congregation, or in prayer, is avoided by either using the plural form or by using both the masculine and feminine pronouns. Similar efforts are being made in Reformist Judaism; for example, both forefathers and foremothers of religion are recognized, rather than just forefathers (Plaskow, 1991; Stuckey, 1998; Gross, 1996).

Ritual practices. In a significant sense, rituals transform conscious-ness. The religious community rededicates itself by affirming the basic tenets of religious teachings through the performance of rituals. Ritu-als recognize and celebrate important milestones in people's lives. In patriarchal religions it is the milestones of men's lives that are usually recognized and celebrated. But as a result of feminist interventions, milestones in women's lives, such as menstruation, pregnancy, and childbirth, are beginning to be celebrated. This is true under Reform Judaism (Gross, 1996).

Leadership in the religious hierarchy. Who conducts the rituals? Who officiates at the ceremonies? Who are in positions of authority? An-swers to all these questions are important because they affirm and validate the intrinsic worth of men and women. Historically, women have been denied these opportunities. In most of the Protestant de-nominations, feminists are actively involved in the struggles to ordain women. They have consistently argued that it is important for women to be in positions of authority. Only when they are will they be able to participate in church policy decisions and in reinterpreting scriptures in such a way that they are women-friendly. These feminists also main-tain that women should have the same rights as men to respond to a religious calling and lead congregations (Hole and Levine, 1971). The ordination of women, feminists point out, will symbolically transform the image of the church as feminine; women will then be seen as people rather than as mystical and mythical constructs of the male imagination. Women ministers will also establish a direct link to God; this will elevate the status of women and explode the myth that only men can have a direct connection to God. Gender relations in churches will cease to be hierarchical, since they will question the commonsense assumption that men are leaders and women are followers (Hole and Levine, 1971).

Under Reform and Conservative Judaism, feminists are struggling for the right of women to be ordained as rabbis. They are also playing a significant role in introducing various rituals that respond to women's needs and concerns. In Reform Judaism, personal ethics are empha-sized over the rabbinical laws inspired by the Talmud. Gender equal-ity is also emphasized. Women are permitted to sing during rituals and are counted in the *minyan* (the minimum number required to hold a prayer meeting). Women are being ordained as rabbis; sexist prayers are being eliminated. Women and men are working together in temple activities. Initiation ceremonies are being performed for both boys (*bar mitzvah*) and girls (*bat* or *bas mitzvah*). As a result of feminists' efforts, women-focused rituals such as Rosh Chodesh (celebration of new moon) have been introduced. Gay and lesbian weddings are being performed. It is believed that the problem is not with Judaism's religious texts, but rather with how they are interpreted, by whom, and in what ideological context. It is accepted that religious teachings need not be gendered and can be used to free both women and men. Clearly, consistent efforts are being made to make Reform Judaism gender inclusive. Under Orthodox Judaism, all of these rights and privileges are denied to women (Gross, 1996; Stuckey, 1998).

The reform movement in Christianity has succeeded in almost all Protestant denominations. The ordination of women is now permitted. Inclusive language is being used in prayers. Rituals and symbols are becoming more and more inclusive. The number of women enrolled in divinity colleges is increasing (Gross, 1996; Stuckey, 1998).

Many feminists are firmly convinced that changes in one aspect of religion will bring about changes in others; before almost anyone realizes, a new order will be in place. As Gross metaphorically writes: 'It's like the hemstitch on a skirt. If you pull it, before you know what has happened, the whole thing comes undone.' She quotes a conversation between a mother and daughter. The daughter had just returned from Sunday school at a church where the minister is a woman. The mother asked, 'Do you think it is possible that God is a woman?' The daughter replied, 'Well, if Kathy can be a minister, I guess God could be a woman' (Gross, 1996: 201).

Woman-Church Movement. This movement originated in Roman Catholicism, within which women's aspirations to redefine religion to make it gender inclusive have consistently been stifled. Feminists involved in the movement have described this movement as a church in exodus. Those involved in it are mostly white, middle-class women who refuse to renounce Christianity yet also refuse to compromise their feminist principles. They consider the movement a temporary measure until Roman Catholicism transforms itself to become gender-inclusive. When that happens, there will be no need for separate women-churches because the religion will be androgynous. At present, women-churches speak to the spiritual needs of women and provide an environment for them to realize their full humanity. The movement is essentially a community of worshippers that focuses on women-centred rituals. Besides rituals commemorating milestones in a woman's life cycle, it also has healing rituals for victims of various forms of abuse or divorce, rituals celebrating personal sexuality, such as coming out as a lesbian (Gross, 1996).

Within Judaism there are similar women's communities in the context of Orthodox Judaism, within which women are forbidden to participate in public demonstrations of their faith. These communities have women-centred rituals such as Rosh Chodesh, where women engage in 'myth making and ritual making.' An anthology edited by Debra Orenstein, *Life Cycles: Jewish Women on Life Passages and Personal Milestones* (1994), includes many such new rituals. Persistent efforts by feminists have made it possible to undertake innovations like these.

Hinduism, the dominant religion in India, does not have a centralized authority structure. Even though the basic tenets are generally accepted, such as belief in the authenticity of Vedas as sacred scriptures, and belief in the transmigration of souls and the principle of Dharma, there are variations across the country in terms of the degree of adherence to behavioural prescriptions in the area of gender relations. In lower castes, Hinduism is practised as an oral tradition; in upper castes, Hindu scriptures have primacy. As one result, upper-caste Hindus tend to be more conservative and rigid in their gender-role prescriptions. There are marked differences in Hinduism between north and south, urban and rural, and so on (Dhruvarajan, 1989; Young, 1993).

There is a goddess tradition in Hinduism, and it has played a significant role in women's lives. For example, exceptional women and women in positions of authority are more easily accepted and respected in the Hindu tradition. Women's ability to achieve is rarely questioned. But in general, goddesses are integrated into the patriarchal framework as the docile consorts of male gods. These goddesses run a poor second to male gods who are held up to women for emulation. Thus, the existence of goddesses does not raise women's stature, but rather bolsters male hegemony (Dhruvarajan, 1989; Bucchetta, 1993).

Nevertheless, there are some goddesses who are wise, strong, caring, and compassionate. For example, the patron goddesses of villages are popular among the lower castes, who see them as mother goddesses who care for the welfare of the villagers by whatever means necessary (Dhruvarajan, 1989). These wise, strong, and autonomous goddesses have been devalued and stigmatized by people of upper castes, who adhere to scriptural traditions. Recently, feminists have been retrieving these goddesses in all their glory, beneficence, autonomy, and wisdom (Gupta, 1991).

Women in the Hindu tradition also have their own rituals and ceremonies, which recognize significant events in a woman's life cycle such as menstruation, pregnancy, and childbirth. But these do not have scriptural sanction, so they have a low status. Nevertheless, women, especially in villages, observe these rituals very diligently. Re-evaluating these rituals is in the interest of women, and some efforts are being made to do so (Dhruvarajan, 1989; 1996).

Female gurus are becoming more and more common. In the past there were female saints who defied Hindu traditions of marriage and motherhood, but these saints were not gurus, who can have followings of their own and act as spiritual guides to their devotees. The saints of yesteryear do not provide examples for today's women to emulate. In recent years, however, female gurus are commanding their own followings, not only among women but also among men (Young, 1993).

In Hinduism, divinity is both imminent and transcendent, and can manifest itself as male or female (Dhruvarajan, 1989, 1996; Young, 1993; Bucchetta, 1993). Hinduism's polytheistic nature gives feminists hope that they can redeem the religion for the benefit of women. Unfortunately, in some parts of India patriarchal interpretations of Hinduism predominate, and as a result its androgynous aspects have been neglected. That being said, Hinduism is practised in different ways depending on which aspect of the tradition is valourized. It is not unusual to find different communities in India emphasizing different aspects of Hinduism. This gives feminists hope that Hinduism can provide a validating and empowering environment for women. But feminists will have to work increasingly to highlight Hinduism's women-friendly aspects and make them acceptable to the general population.

Islam

The dominant feminist response to Islam is to reinterpret its traditions in androgynous and gender-neutral terms. One such effort is portrayed in the video *Women and Religion,* in which Dr Leila Ahmed, the author of *Women and Gender in Islam,* argues that the Qu'ran was first interpreted in a particular historical period, by a particular group of people, most of whom were misogynistic men. From all this it can be concluded that other interpretations are possible, and that it is possible for feminists in an egalitarian societal context to interpret the Qu'ran in terms favourable to women. Many Islamic women are certain that their religion can be reformed and made woman-friendly. So are many Islamic scholars, such as Hassan (1991) and Berktay (1998).

Ahmed points out that Islam is practised differently in different places and cultural contexts. Anti-Western and anti-feminist attitudes explain some of these variations. Also, modernization and industrialization have led to significant demographic transitions – for example, rural–urban migration. Quite possibly, these upheavals have led to rigidification of social practices. Local histories and traditions have also been factors in this. In sum, there are many forms of Islam, and one can deduce from this that a woman-friendly version of it is possible.

Ahmed notes that in the past, Muslim women were allowed to inherit property and control the disposal of that property. Also, that purdah is not inherently a Muslim custom. In fact, it was prevalent among elite women around the Mediterranean – even Christian women practised it. As well, purdah itself takes many forms. It is worn differently by rural and urban women. Some do not wear it at all, while others do. The veil itself can be of different shapes and sizes. In other words, this is a *negotiated* custom, not an inherent part of Islam. All that Islam stipulates is that both men and women dress modestly. Yet conceptions of modesty vary across time and place. Berktay (1998: 188) quotes a Muslim Arab woman protesting against the custom in 1928:

What is this unjust law [of veiling] which is permeated with the spirit of Tyranny and oppression? It is in violation of the book of God and his prophet, may God bless his soul. This law is the law of the victor, the man who subdued the woman with physical force. Man tampered with God's book to make this law. He prided himself on his tyranny and oppression, even as those hurt him, too. He made the law independently, not permitting the woman to share in a single letter. So it came out in accordance with his desires and contrary to the will of God.

Viewed historically, women have participated in various activities generally thought of as forbidden. They have played roles that are generally considered masculine. For example, A'ishah, one of Muhammad's wives, led an army into battle and won. The question is, what is the essence of religion? If there are variations in interpretation, is it conceivable that a new, gender-neutral interpretation is possible? Ahmed seems convinced that it is. She argues that Muslim women strongly believe that Islam is just.

Hassan (1991) arrives at similar conclusions. She shows how Islamic traditions are not unitary and monolithic. She identifies many inconsistencies in Islamic teachings and points out internal contradictions. For example, she writes:

> In spite of the Qur'anic affirmation of man-woman equality, Muslim societies in general have never regarded men and women as equal, particularly in the context of marriage ... The alleged superiority of men to women that permeates the Islamic tradition is grounded not only in Hadith literature [sayings attributed to Prophet Muhammad], but also in popular interpretations of some Qur'anic passages. (1991: 54)

Hassan (1991) contends that much of the problem arises from the fact that in general, men have been the interpreters of religious teachings and women have been kept fairly ignorant of the primary sources of religious teachings. In her opinion, women should take the lead in understanding and interpreting the primary sources of Islamic teachings.

Transformation by Working outside Religious Traditions

Feminists who are convinced that patriarchal religions are beyond redemption prefer to work outside established religious traditions to transform religious ways of life. They contend that because of male godheads, male-centred rituals and ceremonies, and sexist language in liturgy, patriarchal religions privilege men in no uncertain terms. Patriarchal myths and symbols have infiltrated the psyche of believers to such an extent that they animate their thinking and imagination. Women can never feel at home in religions like these, nor can they become an integral part of them. These religions do women harm. Carol P. Christ claims:

> Worship of a male deity keeps women in a state of psychological dependence on men and male authority, while at the same time creating the impression that female power is not legitimate. That women and men

may not be aware of these messages does not lessen their impact. (in Gross, 1996: 225)

According to these feminists, reformists' efforts to define the deity as genderless, to develop inclusive language and rituals, and to re-interpret scriptures in a woman-friendly manner are inadequate to make patriarchal religion acceptable to women.

They also contend that imagining God as the great patriarch in heaven sanctifies both sexism and hierarchy. When God is cast in a domination/subordination relationship, unequal relations between castes, classes, races, and people with different sexual orientations are legitimized. Hierarchical relations are normalized, and treated as self-evident realities of everyday life. Thus, these feminists argue, patriar-chal religions sanctify not only gender bias, but also biases of race, caste, class, ethnicity, and sexual orientation (Richardson, 1981).

Some feminists argue that the concept of 'God' represents the necro-philia of patriarchy, whereas 'Goddess' affirms life. They are reluctant to include men in their movement because men are identified with the necrophilia of patriarchy:

There is no way to remove male/masculine imagery from God. Thus when writing/speaking 'anthropomorphically' of ultimate reality, of the divine spark of being, I now choose to write/speak gynemorphically. I do this because God represents the necrophilia of patriarchy, where-as Goddess affirms the life-loving, be-ing of women and nature. (Daly, 1978: xi)

Goldenberg (1990: 197) writes: 'Both the facts and the fantasies of the Goddess movement function to crack the edifice of patriarchy by encouraging the emergence of suppressed patterns of language, vi-sions, dreams and theories.' Jane Leverick, a practising witch, docu-ments various practices of goddess worshippers, drawing on her own involvement with a group of women in Winnipeg, who meet and worship the goddess on a regular basis. These women consider their practices a very meaningful alternative to patriarchal religious tradi-tions (personal communication).

Other feminists argue that it is important to work with men who are also concerned about transcending the dualistic mindset of patriarchy to bring about a transformation of religion. In particular, eco-feminists have been able to transcend racial and cultural differences to make alliances for a common cause. Although these feminists reject patriarchal religions, they agree that spirituality is important in human life. So they look for other ways of fulfilling this need. Giving the deity a female name is considered crucial. Some of them consider nature as divinity, and personify it as Goddess (Mies and Shiva, 1993).

These feminists argue that the purpose of life is to live in harmony with nature. The earth is our home, and we should protect and preserve all of its resources and life forms. Its resources are limited, so we must endeavour to live in such a way that we do not deprive those who come after us by destroying and squandering those resources in our own lifetimes.

Other feminists delve into prebiblical times to reclaim the Goddess (Stone, 1978; Gimbutas, 1974). In the Wicca movement, the Goddess is conceptualized as both transcendent and imminent – she is out there, and she is within all of us:

> The simplest and most basic meaning of the symbol of Goddess is the acknowledgment of female power as beneficent and independent ... A second important implication of the Goddess symbol for women is the affirmation of the female body and life cycle, especially the sacredness of uniquely female body processes. The third implication of goddess symbolism is the positive valuation of female will, especially in ritual practice of feminist witchcraft. Finally, ... goddess symbolism is important in coming to value women's relationships with each other. (Christ, in Gross, 1996: 226)

Feminist theologians describe Goddess as connected to the entire universe. Starhawk writes:

> Each individual self is linked by ties of blood and affection to the coven, which in turn is a part of the larger human community, the culture and society in which it is found and that culture is part of the biological/ geological community of Planet Earth and the Cosmos beyond, the dance of being which we call Goddess. (in Goldenberg 1990: 202)

The rituals and symbolism of Goddess worship emphasize embodied life (Goldenberg, 1990). Regenerative work performed on a daily basis is considered important, because it maintains and replenishes life. Regenerative functions of the body are celebrated. For this reason, life cycle ceremonies signifying the milestones of women's lives are celebrated. Life is to be lived joyfully (Gross, 1996).

Relations and community are considered important because life is to be lived in cooperation with other people. For these feminists, 'to be' means 'to be in a relationship.' They are critical of the patriarchal privileging of individualism and autonomy. Goldenberg (1990: 211) argues that the patriarchal definition of transcendence is 'a wish for something beyond body, beyond time and beyond specific relationships to life.' She calls for a reconceptualization of the notion of transcendence:

> A transcendence that is life-oriented would involve feelings of connection instead of separation. It might be possible for transcendence to refer to a state of knowing oneself to be part of other human lives – to knowing that one's life is linked with other lives ... Our visions of happiness, of peace, of contentment must be as embodied as life itself.

Working to eliminate oppression and inequality is considered a feminist spiritual goal. Since life is embodied, differences among people are to be recognized, accepted, and celebrated:

> Just as rebellion against finitude is blamed for environmental degradation and disregard for the earth, so insufficient attention to the primacy of relationships is seen as a cause for the alienated quality of modern life, and the acceptance of violence, aggression and warfare as normal by large segments of modern society. (Gross, 1996: 241)

Rejection

Marxist/socialist feminists advocate rejecting religion and focusing on elevating the economic and political status of women. They do not see any point in trying to make religions women-friendly. Their firm conviction is that religion is bad, not only for women but also for societies in general. They argue that religions have fostered conflict between groups by strengthening ethnocentric attitudes. These attitudes have led to intolerance, of and to people being constructed as insiders and outsiders (Sarkar and Butalia, 1996). Historically, religious proselytization has led to devaluation of people and destruction of cultures. By promoting narrow loyalties, religions have legitimized the domination of one given religious group over others. In Canada, the treatment of aboriginal peoples testifies to these arguments. Similar examples abound around the world.

The emergence of a community among followers of a given religion is often accomplished at a personal cost to people at the lower rungs of the social ladder. The dominant sectors of religious communities have long used religion to legitimize hierarchy in social relations and their own privileged positions (McGuire, 1992). History is full of such examples. In nineteenth-century England the puritan ethic was used to justify the wealth and power of capitalists, who perceived their privileges as ordained by God or merited on the basis of holy grace. Poor people, on the other hand, were exhorted to endure their suffering in this world so that they could enjoy salvation in the next. In a similar vein, some aspects of Hinduism legitimize the caste system, which differentiates people on the basis of parentage and accords higher status and greater privileges to upper castes.

Karl Marx (Bottomore, 1964, translation; Engels 1972) argued forcefully that religion perpetuates inequalities among people, including gender, class, and race inequalities. Religion neutralizes dissent among marginalized groups by diverting their attention to otherworldly affairs and attributing low status to the vagaries of personal fate. In this way, religion legitimizes hierarchical social structures. Also, by invoking a sense of community among believers, religion prevents people from questioning the system. Dominant groups use arguments in the spiritual domain, which cannot be verified in any way, to convince subordinate groups that they deserve the positions they are occupying (Roberts, 1995). Religion's mystique clouds the judgment of women and of other marginalized people, and renders them unable to see who is benefiting from the status quo, and who is losing because of it. All of this false consciousness leads people, including women, to misdirect their energies and efforts, and to contribute to maintaining the status quo in all types of unequal relations instead of trying to change the system.

Marxist and socialist feminists point out that religions promote ethnocentric attitudes and legitimize hierarchical relationships, and thus make solidarity more difficult to achieve. Values emerge from the material conditions of life, so if the egalitarian values that would nurture spirituality are to be brought out, the material conditions of women must change. Feminists' time and effort are best spent developing strategies to change women's material conditions. Communities are necessary to foster resistance and promote change. But communities should be based on common interests rather than otherworldly concerns. Once women develop solidarity on the basis of common concerns and common goals, they will be able to generate a viable social movement that will bring about change in gender relations. Making alliances with men who subscribe to these concerns and goals will only strengthen the movement by broadening its base.

Marxist and socialist feminists also believe that organized religion is not really necessary to satisfy the spiritual needs of women – or men, for that matter. If spirituality means the ability to transcend oneself and identify with something that unites all people and responds to their concerns, any cause can achieve that goal. For example, a commitment to dismantle capitalism and patriarchy – which are dehumanizing all societies – can invoke a sense of dedication and commitment (Omvedt, 1993). Organized religion is not necessary to promote an ethical and moral life. Concern for the welfare of all people can help people forge alliances across gender, class, race, and ethnic barriers. Commitment to such a goal can have strong spiritual significance and bring about personal fulfilment. It is best for feminists to focus on bringing about tangible improvements in human relationships.

Prospects for the Future

My study of religion emphasizes the importance of addressing issues pertaining to gender equality. The argument made by Marxist and socialist feminists – that it is better for us to focus our time and effort on economic and political aspects – is not convincing because it is based on the assumption that there is a one-way relationship between material aspects of life and value systems – that material conditions determine the nature of value systems. In fact, there is a reciprocal relationship between these two aspects of life. It is true that patriarchal, class-biased religions arise under social conditions in which people are marginalized on the basis of gender and class/caste. But it is also true that economic and political decisions are made within a value framework and that religion has always provided such a framework.

Conceptions about women's body, mind, and sexuality have often resulted in a denial of freedom of movement for women – for example, under Islam and Hinduism (Accad, 1997; Dhruvarajan, 1989). The kind of work deemed appropriate for women and the location of that work are influenced by these conceptions. For example, in many societies midnight shifts are not considered appropriate for women, whereas piece work done at home and part-time work are considered appropriate. In other societies women can work only among women, because mixing the sexes is taboo. Clearly, economic activities are influenced by gender conceptions.

The ideals of traditional womanhood have the effect of assigning particular jobs to women. This has the effect of promoting the ideal of women sacrificing themselves to others' service, whatever their suffering. For example, in the Hindu religious context, women are exhorted to spend their lives exclusively as mothers and wives (Dhruvarajan 1989). Even when women are permitted to work for pay, only certain types of jobs are considered appropriate for them. Their entry into 'non-traditional' arenas such as engineering is perceived as an intrusion into men's fields. Marc Lepine, who shot fourteen female students at the École Polytechnique in Montreal in 1989, was unable to gain admission to that engineering college and believed that feminists had deprived him of his rightful place in society.

Under patriarchal religions, many women accept religious tenets as a given, develop a negative body image and self-image, and do not participate actively in the political and economic arenas to argue on their own behalf. More importantly, they become willing participants in the reproduction of gender inequality. In patriarchal societies, commonsense sexism is all-pervasive and gender inequality is routinely reproduced in daily life. In other words, sexism is systemic in such societies. Patriarchal religions have been largely responsible for this state of affairs. So it is vital that women raise their critical consciousness regarding the impact of patriarchal religions on their lives. As Downing (1993: 78) states: 'Such personally empowered women might be able to engineer significant social and political changes as well.' Gross elaborates on this point:

This polarization of psychological empowerment on the one hand, and economic, political, or legal empowerment on the other hand, is unwise. Goddess religion surely could be useful for feminists working for social change, for the psychological empowerment that comes with saying 'goddess' is one source for regenerating the energy needed to continue working for economic, political, or social justice issues. And without ongoing psychological and spiritual renewal, social activists usually burn out or become embittered and ineffective. (1996: 226)

In developing countries such as India, development policies are gender biased. When men are perceived as heads of households and women as merely supportive, the resulting policies serve to reinforce dominant/subordinate relations between men and women (Dhruvarajan, 1996). Where patriarchal religious tenets have become law, women are faring even worse: 'In a Sharia state, attempt to resist the established order is an existential question, a matter of life and death. This being the case, it should not be so surprising that the great majority of women opt to act obediently' (Berktay, 1998: 189). In the context of evangelical religions, many women accept male hegemony in the certainty that it provides security and stability in family relationships (Stacy and Gerard, 1997).

Obviously, women's activism must not restrict itself to the economic arena, or the political arena, or the religious arenas. Struggles to transform patriarchy need to be all-encompassing. Spretnak points out the significance of such an orientation:

> Like feminist goals in education, law, health care, etc. feminist goals in spirituality are ultimately humanist, new ways of knowing and being. We must develop a cohesive cosmology; we must design models of affirmation and integration.
>
> Women's spirituality exposes revisionist history and sustains us in our struggle; and more than being just a tool to aid us while we fight for a better life, it *is* a key to the better life. We are forming a new sensibility of that which cannot be quantified – of that which gives birth to possibilities, which is difficult to control, which does not serve hierarchical ordering – and, therefore, has been fiercely denied. We refuse to acquiesce any longer to being the 'other', the 'non-being'. Ours is a working activist philosophy of existence – on our terms.
>
> At the centre of our expanding spiral is a creative self-love and self-knowledge. We have barely tapped the power that is ours. We are more than we know. (Spretnak, 1978: 396)

We also need to recognize the rise of religious fundamentalism around the world. In some countries where Islam is the dominant religion, religious fundamentalists are renewing the orthodox version of Islam in the name of the struggle against Western cultural hegemony. They perceive the forces of modernization as corrupting people's moral sensibilities. They readily accept the technological aspects of modernization, but vehemently reject those which contribute toward gender equality. In their view, national and cultural identity can only be maintained by imposing restrictions on women's lives, as ordained by the conservative, misogynist interpretation of Islam.

In India, under the Bharatiya Janata Party (BJP) government, the traditional model of Hindu womanhood is being revived. That regime is constructing India as a mother Goddess and casting her sons as protectors. On TV screens and through the radio, motherhood is constantly being portrayed as sacred. At present, the BJP is receiving strong support from Hindu fundamentalist groups. Motherhood is being romanticized as the personification of selflessness, sacrifice, and suffering. This reinstatement of traditional ideals of femininity is considered necessary to establish an Indian national identity.

In North America there is some evidence of a backlash against feminist gains of the past few decades, especially the gains made in reproductive rights and rights for homosexuals. These new rights, and the laws that codify them, are reviled by fundamentalist groups, whose biggest fear is the erosion of the traditional, patriarchal family. Religious fundamentalists are strongly against laws that legitimize homosexual lifestyles and that give women control over their bodies (i.e., the right to abortion on demand). Campaigns against these laws have generated violence against homosexuals and abortion service providers.

Religious fundamentalists have different concerns in different regions of the world. For example, Islamic fundamentalism is fundamentally anti-imperialist and anti-Western. Hindu fundamentalism focuses on developing an Indian national identity. In North America, the main target of fundamentalists is the liberal agenda, be it social or economic. But everywhere, fundamentalists propagate heterosexual norms, traditional families, and male hegemony. Considering this, it cannot be denied that religion is doing much to determine the destiny of women in all present-day societies.

Religion has often contributed toward group conflict by promoting ethnocentrism; but it has also played an important role in resistance movements against different kinds of oppression. For example, in Latin American countries the Church has provided a forum for political struggles, just as it did for Black people in the United States during the civil rights era. By fostering a sense of community among followers, religion can help people mobilize against injustice and oppression. Religion can also provide people with the spiritual strength to persevere in their struggles, even when prospects for success seem bleak.

The problem of burnout is very real in all resistance movements, and religion can provide moral strength and stamina. Our goal as women has to be to construct religion in such a way that we are able to retain its positive aspects while rejecting its negative ones.

The goal of feminists in the transformation of religion is to establish a gender-inclusive paradigm in place of patriarchy. Feminists reject the dualistic conception of life and are striving to replace it with a holistic and integrated perspective of life. Their main purpose is to ensure that religion is grounded in the human experiences of both women and men, and that the full humanity of women and men is recognized. To achieve this goal, some feminists work within given religious traditions, others outside these traditions.

Some feminists advocate developing alliances across religions. I agree with Cooey et al. (1991) when they argue that an interfaith dialogue is important to promote truly postpatriarchal religions. We can learn from the experiences of those feminists who are struggling within or outside their religious traditions to arrive at strategies to dismantle patriarchy and usher in postpatriarchal religious ways of life. Perhaps different strategies are appropriate in different contexts. A continuous dialogue among all those who are working for a common goal should help us devise workable strategies for raising critical consciousness among all those who have internalized patriarchal strictures. Gross expresses a similar sentiment:

> Borrowing various symbols from different traditions to construct a brand new religion is a worthwhile project, if the goal is transformation of patriarchal world religions. Whatever symbol is useful must be used to construct that new movement. Whatever is useful to build a new movement to achieve this goal must be encouraged. (Gross, 1996: 246)

Culpepper (1991) shows how working from the margins can actually help people develop bold new visions for the future. Borderlands are a fertile ground for resisting established authority structures (Anzaldua, 1997). bell hooks contends that margins are places where oppositional politics can be nurtured (1984). This is because, as Mary Douglas writes (in Berktay 1998:13), 'all margins are dangerous ... Margins are where any thought system is weakest.' It is important that we support feminists' various efforts in different contexts to resist patriarchal religions and envision new religious ways of life. These visions need to be popularized if we are to usher in postpatriarchal religious ways of life. To achieve this end, feminists would do well to build coalitions. This will make it easier to stem the tide of religious fundamentalism across the globe by raising critical consciousness among all people regarding the negative impact of patriarchal religions.

Conclusion

Women are not a homogeneous group. Our lives are affected by social, cultural, historical, political, and geographic factors. Diverse experiences can lead to divergent needs and expectations; it follows that our struggles against patriarchal religions are necessarily varied. It is difficult to argue that one type of struggle, or one type of solution, is better than another. People have to negotiate their own lives and decide which strategies are possible and/or feasible for them. Women are often deterred from defying traditions by loyalty to their families and their religious and ethnic communities, even when they aspire to a better life. Also, immediate needs and concerns determine the strategies that they adopt. But feminists must continue to raise critical consciousness among all people.

The various strategies for confronting religion discussed in this chapter are in no way exhaustive, but they suggest the complexities of the issues involved. Thinking through these issues helps us become aware of the available options. Every individual woman has to decide which is the best possible strategy in her own context to achieve a post-patriarchal religious way of life.

CHAPTER 11

Feminism and Social Transformation

Vanaja Dhruvarajan

Inequalities persist worldwide. They are built into structures and reinforced through social practices. Pervasive ideologies of sexism, racism, and classism, among others, legitimate these inequalities. Cross-cultural insight shows that the historical legacy of colonialism and the globalization of free markets have done much to establish systems of oppression (Mies and Shiva, 1993a). These systems are interrelated yet distinct – none is reducible to another. Rather, as Huey-Li suggested in 1993, the patriarchal, dualistic, hierarchical, mechanist world view provides the conceptual roots for *all* kinds of exploitation and domination (1993). Dominant groups impose their beliefs and values on subordinate groups in their attempts to control them. These beliefs and values come to be built into institutional structures, and our lived experience occurs within those structures. As these practices are routinized, people come to accept them as normal and natural.

In an article about the disaster in Bhopal, India, in 1984, Jaising and Satyamala (1994) discuss the awesome power of transnationals and the inability of nation-states to protect their own citizens. The Union Carbide Corporation is a transnational company (TNC) that manufactures deadly chemicals. At one of its factories in the densely populated city of Bhopal, an accident attributed to human error killed thousands of people. Millions more were poisoned, and deadly fumes were released into the environment. Even though this disaster resulted from the company's own reckless behaviour, it has not been possible to hold it accountable. On a global level, legal and political support is accorded to corporations, not to the people who suffer as a result of their neglect. Countries that at one time were under colonial rule have become victims of economic domination by developed countries. Even though they are politically independent, these nation-states do not have enough economic clout to stand up to TNCs. Until the legal framework is changed so that the welfare of people and the protection of environment take precedence over the economic interests of TNCs, the situation will not improve. In the current political climate there is more interest in promoting the interests of capital around the globe than in protecting people and the environment. This is one example of how the hegemonic status of rich capitalist countries enables them to impose laws that serve the interests of TNCs at the expense of vulnerable and helpless people.

Disasters such as the one in Bhopal are part of a pattern. In their quest to maximize profits, big corporations pollute the air and water in all countries – including the affluent North – with impunity. Only in recent years has awareness of this problem been growing. But nothing significant has been done to curb the power of TNCs so that they will stop exploiting people to satisfy their capitalistic greed.

Colonization and imperialism have led to the development of stereotypes about Third World people. They are perceived as biologically inferior and morally deficient. Historically, the superior and morally 'upright' Nordic races have been considered their legitimate rulers, with the right to control and educate them. Belief systems like this have sanctioned colonization and imperialism (Said, 1979).

Third World women are routinely conceptualized as weak and docile victims of patriarchy. Elisabeth Bumiller, an editor for the Style page of the *Washington Post*, wrote a book in 1990, *May You Be the Mother of a Hundred Sons*, which became a bestseller. She wrote this book after making a handful of trips to some Indian villages. She spoke to her respondents through an interpreter because she did not know the local language. Her conclusion was that village women in India are either prisoners or slaves – ignorant, traditional, dependent, passive, and pathological. She concluded this without taking into account either their social context or their history. She also failed to comprehend the diversity of their experiences. At the same time, she conceived herself as a secular, autonomous Western woman in control of her destiny. Even though she presented this analysis with the best of intentions, her conclusions have done significant harm to Indian women by perpetuating the negative stereotypes about them that have prevailed since colonial times.

Popular accounts such as Bumiller's are replicated by feminists working in academia. *Frogs in the Well*, edited by Juliet Minces (Zed Press: 1980), is another example. In their attempts to show how Third World women are different from themselves, these scholars tend to construct a homogenous category of Third World women. Then they assume almost by definition that these women are under the domination of a monolithic patriarchy. At the same time, they implicitly construct themselves as autonomous agents in full control of their own destinies and as models for us to emulate. Both these constructions raise problems. Women in the Third World experience patriarchy differently because of their caste/class, regional differences, ethnicity, and so on. Note also that if all Western women were autonomous agents, we would not need a women's movement in the West. This type of portrayal is detrimental to women in the Third World: 'Feminist theories which examine our cultural practices as "feudal residues" or label us "traditional," also portray us as politically immature women who need to be versed and schooled in the ethos of Western feminism. They need to be continually challenged' (Amos and Parmar, in Mohanty et al., 1991: 57).

The West has imposed a Western model of development on Third World people – a model based on the assumption that what is good for the West is good for everyone else. Too many Westerners are convinced that Third World people need to be educated, directed, and controlled by the First World. Many Third World countries have a long history of exemplary achievements, but these achievements have been downgraded in this world in which Western cultures and nations enjoy hegemonic status (Tinker and Bramsen, 1992).

Politicians and scientists in various disciplines have taken it on themselves to curb population growth in the Third World by whatever means necessary and without considering the welfare of the people involved. They attribute problems such as poverty and environmental degradation to unfettered population growth in the Third World (Population Conference, Cairo, 1994). In doing so, they forget that similar growth occurred in Europe during the Industrial Revolution. The Europeans solved that 'problem' by colonizing the Americas, Africa, and Australia. They also forget that First World people are the ones consuming most of the earth's resources. The consumer ethic and capitalist greed are the main causes of poverty and environmental degradation. The problem is not lack of wealth, but rather how existing wealth is distributed.

The West's policies and practices must be understood in the context of Western imperialism, cultural hegemony, and the dominant military-industrial complex:

> Contemporary imperialism, is in a real sense, a hegemonic imperialism exercising to a maximum degree a rationalized violence taken to a higher level than ever before – through fire and sword, but also through the attempt to control hearts and minds. For its content is defined by the combined action of the military-industrial complex and the hegemonic cultural centers of the West, all of them founded on the advanced levels of development attained by monopoly and finance capital, and supported by the benefits of both the scientific and technological revolution and the second industrial revolution itself. (Abdel-Malek, in Mohanty et al., 1991: 54)

Unequal relationships among people of different races and ethnic groups get built into institutional structures (Dhruvarajan, 1994). These institutions systematically maintain and reproduce dominant and subordinate relationships among various groups of people. For example, universities produce and disseminate Eurocentric and androcentric knowledge as universally applicable scientific truth. Any deviation from that 'truth' is attacked as wrong-headed, deviant, deficient, and generally lacking.

Those who make decisions about curricula and program administration usually belong to dominant interest groups. As a result, the experiences of marginalized groups are left out of the curricula, or they are recast from Eurocentric and androcentric perspectives. Most people are not conscious of dominant and subordinate relationships in society; they take as a given the privileged position enjoyed by dominant groups. Most people contend that Canada is a democratic society that provides equal opportunity to all people. They do not take into account the enduring legacy of past racism, ethnocentrism, and sexism. As Henry and colleagues write: 'Canada suffers from historical amnesia. Its citizens and institutions function in a state of collective denial' (1995: 1). To correct this orientation, we must begin teaching history from the perspective of a Cherokee Indian grandmother or a black mother in slavery, as Joseph puts it (in Hale, 1992: 418). Only then will everyone understand that imperialism, racism, and sexism are embedded in the dominant culture. An inclusive curriculum taught by inclusive professoriate is needed if systemic imperialism, racism, ethnocentrism, classism, and sexism are to be eliminated.

Similar arguments can be made about other institutions, such as the economy and the political system. When certain institutional structures are in place, marginalized people are routinely denied equal opportunity. Only after we understand how institutions work will we have sufficient insight to transform them. In the 1980s this understanding led to feminist activism to make the academy gender inclusive. In the wake of this activism, women's studies departments and programs were established. Many feminists are now struggling to make the academy more inclusive of marginalized groups and their perspectives (Bannerji et al., 1991).

As people go about their lives within institutional structures, unequal relationships between groups become routinized and normalized. People come to accept these relationships as natural. Both dominant groups and subordinate groups come to accept and abide by the values and beliefs of dominant groups. As a common result, subordinate groups internalize oppression and dominant groups internalize dominance. But some members of subordinate groups resist internalizing oppression and develop oppositional values and belief systems. This is how dominant belief systems come to be resisted by counter-hegemonic movements. Women's liberation, gay liberation, and national liberation, are only three examples of counter-hegemonic movements. In every case the objective is to dismantle the hegemonic status of dominant groups: to question their privilege and their naturalized right to impose their will on all others.

Families and communities can bring out social change by altering their daily practices. Examples: introducing initiation ceremonies for daughters *and* sons; casting an Asian woman as the main character in a Shakespearian play; permitting women and minorities to join men-only clubs; letting the mother sit in the big chair at the dinner table that had always been reserved for the father. All of these acts subvert old behaviour patterns. Changes like these will have the cumulative effect of redefining power relations among different groups. Kandiyoti (1997) argues that many women in patriarchal settings actively strategize, negotiate, and bargain to empower themselves. So, probably, do other marginalized groups. These strategies may well bear fruit in the long run; even so, collective social activism is probably more effective as a means of changing society.

For any social movement to develop, the most important first step is for subordinated peoples to develop critical consciousness of their status (Friere, 1999). Once people recognize their subordinate status, they can begin to envision a better life for themselves. These visions inspire and motivate subordinate groups to engage in collective activism to transform existing relationships. Organized efforts are necessary to restructure institutions: new blueprints for a better life, with new values and belief systems, must be developed. By developing critical consciousness, people are able to purge themselves of internalized oppression; having done so, they are able to protest as individuals against existing patterns of oppressive relationships. Such behaviour can disrupt social life and annoy dominant groups, but patterns of dominant and subordinate relationships can be difficult to transform. Also, these protests can easily be quelled by those in dominant positions. Usually, sporadic outbursts of discontent among marginalized groups are easily contained by established authorities. Meaningful transformation can occur only where there is carefully organized resistance.

History is full of examples demonstrating that those with power and privilege are reluctant to relinquish either. The only way to convince them that they ought to share power with the powerless is to make them realize that the current state of the world is as dehumanizing to them as it is to those they are dominating. They also need to be shown that they also have something to gain by giving up their current dominant status and adopting a new way of life. As Kate Young has argued (1988), it is in everyone's strategic interest to stem the tide of environmental destruction, global poverty, consumerism, and deterioration of the quality of life. Dominant groups must be made aware of how they achieved their privilege, and how they maintain their privilege. They must be made fully aware of the consequences of their actions for the lives of others. Even then, there is no guarantee that they will be ready to relinquish their privilege. Efforts to raise the consciousness of dominant groups must continue, but it is even more important to focus on those who are oppressed. Coalitions among all groups experiencing oppression offer broad-based support to resistance movements, and can make dominant groups realize that the maintenance of their hegemonic position is not viable.

Feminism provides an alternative world view – one that extends to women the prominence they deserve. Because as women we do not have political power, we have to unite and speak with a strong voice to advance feminist agendas. However, women are a heterogeneous category. Building solidarity among women requires that we address concerns of all women. This means that gender, race, class, ethnicity, sexual orientation, and ability must all become feminist issues.

The chances of success in bringing about social transformation are greater when there is broad-based support for resistance. This is where coalitions are necessary. Coalitions become easier to form when we can establish a sense of community across differences based on and inspired by a shared vision of a better future for all.

During the second wave of feminism, the feminist dictum 'the personal is political' was used to mobilize women. Because this movement was led by white, middle-class women, the focus was on analysing patriarchy to raise critical consciousness of gender subordination. When women from marginalized groups argued that in addition to gender, race/ethnicity, class, sexual orientation, and ability were important in determining the life experiences of all people, the women's movement adopted the approaches of diversity and cultural pluralism.

Multiculturalism, or cultural pluralism, was adopted as an approach to explain differences among groups. But the descriptive treatment of differences gives the illusion all cultures are on par with one another. The reality is that the cultures of dominant groups have hegemonic status. As a result, marginalized cultures are evaluated in comparison with dominant cultures. Similar arguments can be made about approaches that focus on diversity of experiences among people of different classes and races. Cataloguing differences is informative, but it does not shed light on the power differentials between dominant and subordinate groups. When we focus on differences without analysing relations of power, we can end up blaming the victims. For example, poverty and alcoholism among aboriginal people is often perceived as an 'inside' problem, and assumed to be caused by some deficiency in native people's culture or personality. The history of the exploitation these people have suffered at the hands of dominant groups is completely left out in this analysis.

To analyse the impact of several systems of inequality, the approach 'matrix of domination,' suggested by Collins (1986), is useful. The objective here is to show how gender, race, ethnicity, class are all simultaneous interacting systems of action and meaning; these systems intersect with one another and are interlocked to produce particular types of experiences for all people. These experiences become crystallized in institutional structures. As a consequence, unequal relationships among people are routinely reproduced in daily life.

In various chapters of this book, we have discussed a given issue and shown that women differ in the positions they take in accordance with their social location. Because of space limitations we have had to limit the number of issues we discuss. This book has not covered all important women's issues but we hope that the analytical scheme we have offered can be extended to analyse other issues. We have tried to include diverse voices of experience in each chapter, to give an idea as to what it means to be in a particular position of marginality. We have not been able to include the experiences of every marginalized group in every chapter, but we have tried to achieve a fairly good representation. Because the experiences of all groups are located across dimensions of race, class, sexuality, and so on, our analytical scheme here can be applied to analyse the experiences of any group of the reader's own choosing.

We have not used exactly the same analytical strategies in all chapters; however, we have followed the assumption that the differences among women across dimensions of race, class, sexuality, ability among others must be taken into account to understand and explain the diversity of experiences. We have also accepted that these differences manifest themselves in power disparities. Only when these disparities are clearly understood can light be shed on viable oppositional and liberatory strategies.

By identifying the specificity of women-of-colour experiences, Dhruvarajan shows in chapter 3 how white privileges are maintained at the expense of non-whites. For example, she shows how mainstream art is defined as real art and the art of non-whites as ethnic art, which privileges the former while devaluing the latter. In a similar vein, Goldrick-Jones in chapter 6 argues that for pro-feminist men true masculinity involves occupying a dominant position and enjoying privileges that are denied to women and marginalized men. These men find relinquishing that power and privilege or sharing it with others distasteful, painful, and frightening. Vickers in chapter 8 shows how violence is one of the devices used in societies to maintain systems of race, class, and gender hierarchy. The interlocking nature of belief systems of hegemonic masculinity, heterosexism, and racism need to be deconstructed before any changes can be brought about. Ghorayshi in chapter 4 argues that the character and composition of the Canadian labour force have changed but hierarchies of gender and race have remained. At the top of the occupational ladder, white men are overrepresented; at the bottom, aboriginal and women of colour are overrepresented. Injuries of sexism in both the paid and unpaid work, and injuries of racism pervasive in society at large, maintain and reproduce these hierarchies. Dhruvarajan, in chapter 7, shows how the devaluation and economic domination of Third World people have resulted in the imposition of birth control measures that are detrimental to the health of poor Third World women. This illustrates the interlocking nature of racist belief systems and patriarchal capitalist systems.

Rice, in chapter 5, shows how the intersections of gender, race, and ability, and so on produce different kinds of experiences of body image for differently located women. White women suffer from eating disorders while trying to live up to the white model of beauty; nonwhite women suffer because racism precludes them from being considered beautiful. Women with disabilities suffer because they are considered deficient. Vickers in chapter 9 shows how engagement with mainstream feminism and/or nationalism varies with the history of intergroup encounters. Women from colonized/dominated groups consider involvement with national movements imperative for the survival of their groups. Some of them may see feminism as practised currently as irrelevant for addressing their concerns – a view held by many aboriginal women in Canada and elsewhere. On the other hand, feminists in Quebec do not consider it a problem to involve themselves in the separatist movement while holding feminist aspirations. Dhruvarajan, in chapter 10, shows how organized religions maintain and perpetuate social inequalities on the basis of gender, race, class, and culture. Even feminists interested in transforming world religions seem to prefer working within their traditions instead of working across religions to produce a liberatory spirituality.

Besides making detailed analyses of the significance of various dimensions of social status in order to understand and explain the experiences of different groups of women, the authors of all chapters show that a clear understanding of how disparities manifest themselves among women sheds light on viable oppositional and liberatory strategies. Insights into particular strategies addressing specific issues of concern for women are provided in various chapters. In the following sections, I discuss the need to raise critical consciousness at different levels. I also describe feminist visions for a better life, identify challenges to feminist efforts, and assess prospects for coalition building to transform the existing social order. In this context, I will draw on the insights provided in some of the chapters.

Critical Consciousness

Critical consciousness among people needs to be raised at various levels if we are to provide conditions conducive to bringing about social transformation. In this section I identify several of these levels and discuss them in some detail. The following discussion is in no way exhaustive but it gives somes idea of the complexities of this process.

For social transformation to happen, individuals have to be motivated to use their human agency. They must purge themselves of negative self-concepts. Only people who are convinced that they deserve a better life can be motivated to apply themselves to this task. In his discussion on alienation, Howard McGary states:

> Fragility and insecurity of this self [is] caused by the way people who are victims view and define themselves. According to this view, even if the external constraints were removed, the self would still be estranged because it has been constructed out of images hostile to it. (1994: 134)

Being in the margins, and being told repeatedly that they are unworthy and less deserving, and that they do not have equal entitlements, leads people to lower their expectations and consider themselves less capable. Removing such negative images is a difficult task. bell hooks (Video: 'Conversations') states that when she compares her Black students with white students, the difference between the two is that white students act as though they belong in the university and that they are entitled to all the attention they get. They expect to achieve and to be in control of their lives. Black students are more hesitant, even though they are just as bright and just as capable. They hesitate to expect too much for the future. This reveals clearly how a hostile environment sends messages to children and affects their aspirations. Children need parents and teachers who believe in them and who encourage them on a daily basis. They need a supportive environment in families, in schools, and in communities in general. They need to learn about the accomplishments of Black people over time. They also need to understand the processes of domination that led to the devaluation and subordination of Black people. They need to have inspiring role models such as bell hooks and Martin Luther King Jr. In such an environment and with conscious effort, Black students can achieve and thrive.

Similar arguments can be made about other marginalized groups such as women and people with disabilities. Persistent efforts on individual, institutional, and ideological levels are necessary to raise consciousness so that internalized oppression can be ended. Rice in chapter 5 argues that the models of beauty promoted by dominant cultures need to be divested of their hegemonic status for all women to accept and feel comfortable with their bodies. Vickers in chapter 8 shows how the empowerment of women is necessary to dismantle oppressive structures. The need to raise consciousness regarding systemic racism and sexism is discussed by Dhruvarajan in chapters 3 and 10 respectively. In chapter 3 she shows how racism has become part of commonsense knowledge. In chapter 10 she demonstrates how sexism is institutionalized in the world's major religions. Ghorayshi in chapter 4 contends that to end gender and race inequalities in the labour force, systemic sexism within families must be addressed, as well as systemic racism and sexism in the economy.

Just as it is necessary to get rid of internalized oppression, so is it necessary to get rid of internalized domination. Barb Thomas (1994) walks us through her life to show how she became conscious of her privileged position and the underprivileged positions of marginalized people. The realization that both dominance and subordination are socially constructed helps people embark on processes deconstruction and social transformation. Thomas discusses how she learned to accept white privilege as natural while growing up in an English Loyalist family. She shows how she lived like a fish in a fishbowl, and only became aware of the bowl after she became an adult and was exposed to the real lives of 'Others.' She discusses how her critical consciousness was raised and how she learned to understand her own position in Canadian society. Her article illustrates how race, class, and gender are interlocking systems that produce particular experiences and structure particular social institutions, which in turn reproduce experiences of privilege over generations.

She wrote her article as a letter to her daughters, who are confronting the resistance of minorities who refuse to accept their subordinate position. She advises her daughters never to blame themselves for the racism that pervades Canadian society because they had no part in causing it. But adds that they must take responsibility for admitting they enjoy privileges because of that legacy, and do what they have to do to correct the ills of the past. Inaction amounts to complicity. She also discusses the difficulties involved in challenging the system. But the costs are much higher for marginalized groups, who become targets of anger and hostility in the hands of those with power and privilege. White people who involve themselves in antiracist activities are commended for doing so and often rewarded. Peggy McIntosh (1995) in her article 'White Privilege and Male Privilege' discusses how she became aware of white privilege after persistent effort on her part. Similar arguments can be made regarding raising awareness about other kinds of privilege such as class, ability, and heterosexuality.

Changing the system to become just and caring is difficult indeed. More often than not, people take their privileges for granted and dwell on their disadvantages. Razack and Mary Louise Fellows call this behaviour 'the race to innocence' (Razack 1998: 14). An important prerequisite for coalition building is making a critical analysis of our own positions. This helps us understand how knowingly or not we can oppress others as well as be oppressed ourselves. Awareness of this will help us exert ourselves so that we will not be a part of the problem but rather part of the solution.

Once we understand the processes through which privileges are accrued, maintained, and reproduced we can transform those processes to stem the tide of oppression and domination. Instead of conceptualizing the challenges faced by oppressed groups as 'woman problem,' 'race problem,' 'aboriginal problem,' 'gay/lesbian problem,' 'problems of homeless people,' we can learn to analyse how all of these 'problems' are caused by how our social life is organized. Once we organize social life to respond to the needs and concerns of all people, and to treat all people as equally deserving of a good life, we will not have these 'problems.' We will all be involved in finding solutions by examining how we live and how our lives affect other people.

June Jordon (1998) relates her experiences as a Black lesbian in Black communities. She criticizes many Black women for privileging racism over heterosexism. She rejects the argument that sexuality in some way belongs to the private domain whereas race relations belongs in the public domain and that struggles against racism should therefore take precedence. She argues effectively that there should be no hierarchies of oppression and that it is dangerous to make such constructions. She shows how all patriarchal societies are constantly preoccupied with controlling women's sexuality. The ideology of compulsory heterosexuality adhered to by most societies devalues and stigmatizes all other forms of sexual orientations, including homosexuality and bisexuality.

Accad (1997), in her article about the lives of women in one Islamic country, shows how freedom and individuality are denied to women in the name of controlling their sexuality and channelling it in socially appropriate ways. She comments on how such restrictions prevent women from realizing their full humanity. Audre Lorde reinforces this view: 'My fullest concentration of energy is available to me only when I integrate all the parts of who I am, openly, allowing power from particular sources of my living to flow back and forth freely through all my different selves, without the restriction of externally imposed definition' (in Collins 1990: 230).

There can be no coalition building among people of different races and sexual orientations until it is understood that there are no hierarchies of oppression. Awareness of this should motivate us to support all struggles for emancipation.

Women with disabilities identify similar problems with regard to coalition formation. 'Perceiving disabled women as childlike, helpless, and victimized, non-disabled feminists have severed them from sisterhood,' write Stuart and Ellerington (1990: 16). This is the biggest impediment to coalition formation. The women's movement has not been sensitive to the needs of women with disabilities. Women with various disabilities have been treated badly by other women. Serious attempts have not been made to reach out and include these women in decision-making processes. If a strong women's movement is to be created, women with disabilities must be included and their needs must be addressed. Women with disabilities will participate in the movement only when they are accepted as true partners.

Can men be allies? Can they participate alongside women in liberation struggles? For many feminists, these are important questions. Marable (1997) argues that not all men can be considered oppressors. Like women, men occupy ambivalent positions in the sense that they can be oppressors and the oppressed at the same time. Black men are oppressed on the basis of their race (and often class), just like black women. They are compared with white, middle-class men, who personify hegemonic masculinity, and of course, when judged in this manner, Black men come up short. Their access to opportunity structures is limited because their masculinity is maligned and they are stigmatized on the basis of their race. It is true that many Black women suffer from sexism at the hands of Black men. But if Black men's consciousness is raised and they give up their role as oppressors of women, they can become allies in the project of resisting racism and imperialism.

Similar arguments can be made about other marginalized groups of men, such as men with disabilities, gay men, and men from lower classes. All of these groups suffer from unequal access to opportunity structures. Also, all people, including all men, suffer as a result of environmental degradation and the excesses of capitalism. So, it is possible for men to become allies, provided that they relinquish their role as oppressors of women.

Goldrick-Jones, in chapter 6, argues that even though profeminist men have been unable to mobilize a viable movement across race, class, and sexuality, they can be counted on as allies on specific issues. In addition, these men can involve themselves in myriad small ways – cooking and doing dishes, taking women's studies courses, and so on – and this can bring about gradual change in gender relations.

Visions for a Better Future

Critical analysis of the current state of affairs has led to envisioning a better future. Many feminists have articulated such visions, which have a remarkable convergence of broad principles. They all embrace harmony with nature, cooperation and mutual respect among people, and a pervasive concern for justice and care of all people. These visions promote a holistic, interdependent world view, as well as social relations that emphasize cooperation (Mies and Shiva, 1993a).

A holistic approach to life encompasses several interrelated, interconnected and irreducible goals. Within this perspective, reproduction of life and the maintenance of health and well-being of all people are placed at the front and centre of societal and individual objectives. This involves measuring success in life not by the amount of money one has, or by the number of goods collected, or by the degree of control over other lives. It means becoming aware of the impact of our own lifestyles on others, and learning to live in ways that promote not just our own health and well-being but everyone else's. It means learning to resolve conflicts through peaceful means and to resist wasting resources on armed conflict. Resources can then be spent on reproducing life and coexisting peacefully. We come to understand that difference does not mean inequality, and that one style of life is not necessarily better, and that life should be lived in a non-exploitative manner. Feminists involved in transforming religions are providing models of spirituality that are life-affirming, community oriented, and environmentally friendly. These models, which embody the principles discussed above, are described in detail in chapter 10.

A holistic approach also means perceiving nature and the environment not as something 'out there,' but rather as something intimately connected to our lives. If we ruin the environment, we ruin our own health and well-being (Mies and Shiva, 1993). We must avoid the tendency to think in dualistic terms. For example, we must learn not to dichotomize our lives as private and public, and not to apply different principles to organize our lives in different domains. This means that the work we do to earn a living should be consistent with the principles we live by in our private lives. Thus, we cannot justify working in a nuclear plant that produces hazardous materials and pollutes the environment, and then retreating to our suburban homes where we breathe fresh air and provide a pollution-free environment for our children. Those who cannot move to the suburbs will be condemned to live in a polluted environment. Also, when we subscribe to the ethic of consumerism we are encouraging multinational corporations to exploit vulnerable people to produce goods at a cheap price. We need to see the connections between our habits and the exploitation of vulnerable people. In chapter 7 Dhruvarajan shows how the rights discourse results in further entrenchment of capitalist market economy around the globe to the detriment, of all women, especially those who are marginalized on the basis of class, race, and sexuality. The profit-driven research agenda in the biomedical field means further alienation for women (people) from their reproductive functions. We need to rethink the role of science and technology in human life. We need to become critically aware of the indiscriminate use of reproductive technologies – technologies based on research that does not consider its own impact on human welfare. In democratic societies an enlightened electorate can strengthen the state so that it provides viable opposition to the power of multinationals. The state in such circumstances can be, as Vickers argues in chapter 9, an ally for feminist aspirations.

The implications of such a vision of life are that every aspect of our lives as we live them now has to be transformed. At the present time in most societies, women are in charge of life-sustaining activities but are themselves marginalized and powerless, since life-sustaining activities generally have low priority for most national governments. Women tend to bear the brunt of this neglect. The feminization of poverty is a worldwide phenomenon: 'It must be recognized that there are deep contradictions in economic policies of restructuring and globalization. Current structural adjustment policies do not reduce poverty or create meaningful work for people and the detrimental impact on women is an inherent, not an accidental, feature of these programmes' (Vienna NGO Forum, 1994: 3).

It is important that we reject the mythical norms propagated by dominant groups. Coalition building to transform society is possible only if we reject the dominant paradigm in its entirety. Rejecting some aspects of that paradigm while retaining others will not result in a non-exploitative society (Lorde, 1995). Raising critical consciousness regarding how relations of power are reproduced can leave us intellectually debilitated, morally disempowered and personally depressed, as Cornel West (1998) writes. This is especially true for those who are marginalized and do not see a way out. The present paradigm has failed to fulfil promises of happiness, freedom, dignity, and peace, even for those who have profited from it. As Mies and Shiva (1993a) note, rich people from affluent countries fly to unspoiled lands to get away from the stressful routines of their lives and to get in touch with themselves. Articulating visions for a better world can be empowering. bell hooks contends that coalition building across differences is possible when we have a shared vision for a better future (1994).

Coalition building is not easy. It requires patience and perseverance. The difficulties that arise are mainly due to differences in power among groups – differences resulting from the historical legacy of exploitation and domination. As Kate Young has argued (1988), if everyone – that is, both those in dominant positions and those in subordinate positions – agrees that it is in everyone's strategic interest to stem the tide of environmental destruction, global poverty, and consumerism, it will be possible to develop solidarity across differences.

Prospects for the Future

No movement can succeed without broad support from the grassroots. Feminist gains have been impressive in the past few decades precisely because the movement has been able to elicit such support from different segments of the population. The various chapters in this book have recounted these gains. Nevertheless, the movement is also faced with challenges that threaten to erode the gains it has made (Steuter, 1995).

The feminist movement is often spoken of as comprising collective behaviour and voluntary activity. This gives the impression that resistance among feminists is sporadic and disconnected – a sort of leisure activity. There is no awareness that feminism is a conscious, organized movement to transform the existing social order. One reason for such labelling is the way it is organized.

Women are a heterogeneous group, and their concerns and preoccupations vary with class, race, sexual orientation, nationality, and ability, so coalitions are often formed on the basis of particular issues at a particular time. For example, for women with disabilities, accessibility is an important issue; for poor women everywhere, including those in Third World countries, reproductive technologies pose problems; for women of colour, systemic racism is a daily concern. Women often mount resistance to address these issues by enlisting support from as many groups as possible. Even though at first glance it seems all these issues are disconnected and are unique to particular groups of people, careful analysis reveals that they are in fact interconnected. Such an analysis reveals that all these problems confronted by different groups of people are a result of how social life is organized around the goal of maximizing profit by any means possible. If the centrepiece of societies were the promotion of human welfare, all activities would be organized to achieve that goal.

Also, it is difficult to organize women worldwide on the basis of a single issue. In that sense the feminist movement is different from other movements, such as national liberation movements and civil rights movements. Women's struggles necessarily have to take place on different levels. The goal of feminist movements is to transform the social order in its entirety; this means changing every aspect of life in society. These movements need to address internalized dominance and subordination, relations of power at the interpersonal and institutional levels, and hegemonic values and belief systems.

It is important to make connections between particular issues of concern in a given locality on the one hand, and the broad principles of the feminist project on the other. Such analyses can help mobilize support from the grassroots. But it must be realized that not all women can participate in all struggles. For example, in patriarchal families some women's lives are constrained in such a way that they cannot participate in activities outside the home. Yet these women can influence the daily practices that *are* under their control. In my study of the lives of women in an Indian village, I showed how a few women whose consciousness had been raised were trying very hard to give their daughters a life better than their own by providing opportunities for education and by encouraging them to achieve. They were doing this at some personal risk to themselves. These women were trying to change the life chances of their daughters; by succeeding they could eventually transform the patriarchal family, at least for some women. Women who live under less restrictive conditions can participate more easily in projects of social change.

The media play an important role in disseminating information about feminist movements. Feminists have tried to use the media to promote their goals; regrettably, most of the coverage they have received has been negative. We need to explore ways of reaching the public to counter the media's influence and to raise critical consciousness among the broader population.

Until recently, feminist policies and practices in Canada focused on the interests of white, middle-class women (Agnew, 1993). Historically, mainstream feminist struggles for gender equality have not included women of colour. When the suffragists campaigned for women's voting rights, they meant right for *white* women (Kline, 1989). Women of colour were not included even in the white feminist utopia (Mukherjee, 1993a). Valverde (1992) notes that a leading first-wave Canadian feminist, Emily Murphy, believed that the 'Nordic' races were inherently superior and that feminism was for white women only. The largest grassroots feminist organization, the Women's Christian Temperance Union (WCTU), employed both scientific theories (which were strongly racist at the time) and evangelical discourses on race to establish white privilege. During second-wave feminism, women of colour were excluded and marginalized as white feminist analysis and social practices focused exclusively on the issue of sexism. Spellman (in Agnew, 1993: 224) captures this spirit:

> Although it [feminism] acknowledges that some women are black, some are white, some are rich, some are poor, if we insist that nevertheless they are all the same, as women, that differences among women reside in some non-woman part of them, then these differences will never have to make a difference for feminism. For it is the women part of any woman

that counts, and if differences among women can't lodge these then differences among women finally don't really matter.

Coalition formation between women of colour and mainstream women is very unlikely in these circumstances. Such a venture becomes even more difficult when non-white women see white women as beneficiaries of their own hardship. For example, aboriginal women gave up the notion of a sisterhood relationship with white women when the law of the land favoured white women. For example, when a native woman married a non-native man she lost her treaty status, yet a white woman gained that status when she married an Indian man (Maracle, 1993).

By and large, white women are the beneficiaries of Black women's hardships. An excellent example is the situation of domestic workers from the Caribbean. The perception of most women of colour is that white women, along with white men, have been the beneficiaries of colonialism, imperialism, and racism. In recent years the feminist movement, led by white, middle-class women, has focused on combating sexism, and the beneficiaries generally have been those same white, middle-class women. A movement that focuses exclusively on sexism cannot solve the problems faced by women of colour. The identity of women of colour is a fusion of racial, ethnic, gender, and class identities (Lorde, 1984). This has done much to increase the social distance between mainstream women and women of colour. Women of colour tend to see white women as part of the problem rather than part of the solution (Mies, 1986).

Construction of people of colour as 'the other' has driven a wedge between mainstream feminists and feminists of colour and prevented coalition formation. These constructed images reflect past social relations and determine present ones. If social change is to come, these images must be discarded in favour of positive ones that recognize and respect differences.

The process of constructing new images is complex. All of us must critically examine our own assumptions regarding relationships among people of different classes, races, and ethnic groups. As June Jordan argues, we should avoid constructing hierarchies of oppression and take into account class differences between and within groups. Racial privileges and class privileges both lead to the exploitation of poor women. Prejudices can prevail among women of colour toward each other, and these must be addressed (Sheth and Handa, 1993). We must examine these issues systematically and analyse how we arrived at our assumptions. This will make us aware of how our social locations limit our consciousness and determine our concerns and preoccupations (Bannerji, 1995). This exercise will help us understand the concerns of those who are in different social locations (Razack, 1993). As we expose ourselves to analyses of different experiences in different social locations, we learn to empathize with the predicaments of others. Social practices must be informed by these understandings. Even while investing our energies in causes in which we strongly believe, we must support other feminists as they continue their own struggles. Even more important, we must make sure we are not part of the problem.

Developing a sense of community among feminists opens doors for us to know each other's cultures, histories, and motivations. This is an important beginning for understanding and respecting one another. I agree with Gaard (1993) that we cannot borrow from other cultures to solve our problems, but must instead look inward and draw strength from our own cultural heritage. We must learn to respect one another for doing the best we can within the limits imposed by our social and cultural locations, and to support other people's struggles to transcend their locations.

In recent years, mainstream feminists have begun to recognize that they must acknowledge the significance of race, ethnicity, and class in feminist theorizing. Sometimes, only lip-service has been paid to these issues (Kline, 1989). As Dionne Brand observed in her keynote address to the 1992 Annual Conference of Canadian Research Institute for the Advancement of Women (CRIAW), some feminists seem to chant gender, race, and class like a mantra, without carefully reflecting on the implications. Nevertheless, some serious attempts are being made to integrate these issues into feminist theory and practice. Our own work is collaborative across differences; we think this is a useful approach because it brings multiple perspectives to the fore.

The differences we consider include personal attributes and histories. Our experience suggests that collaboration among those with similar ideological orientations is much easier. Otherwise even if we agree on the ultimate goals, there can be difficulties identifying appropriate strategies for achieving those goals.

There have been many collaborative efforts among mainstream feminists and women-of-colour feminists to revise feminist theories – for example, Mies and Shiva (1993a), Mohanty et al. (1991), Anderson and

Collins (1995), and Bannerji et al. (1991). In recent years in Canada, some feminist practices have been informed by such theorizing. For example, recent political activities of the National Action Committee (NAC) include the appointment of women of colour to the executive and taking positions on issues of concern for women of colour. In 1993 the Women's Legal Education and Action Fund published a special issue of its newsletter: *Litigating Equality: Race and Gender*. In 1992 the Canadian Research Institute for the Advancement of Women (CRIAW) produced an information tool on, by, and for racial minority and immigrant women in Canada (*Learning from Diversity*). Many white feminists have supported the struggles of domestic workers in Canada, to the detriment of their own personal interests. Several mainstream feminists have spoken out against the media's targeting of Asian Indian women for fetal sex determination services (*The Globe and Mail*, 10 December 1990). These are all very important beginnings that can create a positive environment for coalition-building.

These beginnings are mainly due to constant struggles by women of colour in North America and around the world. The first two UN Conferences on women – Mexico City (1975) and Copenhagen (1980) – were beset with problems as the world's women attempted to forge alliances, develop solidarity, and speak for the interests of women. These conferences revealed deep differences among women, mainly between First World and Third World women. First World women preferred to focus exclusively on sexism, whereas Third World women insisted on including issues relating to racism and poverty. In the third UN Conference on women, in Nairobi, the document 'Forward Looking Strategies' was adopted almost unanimously by the women attending, who represented the world. A similar document was generated at the latest UN conference on women, in Beijing. This document delineates women's concerns around the world and emphasizes the need for women to influence world events (UN Chronicle, 1995).

The World March of Women 2000, which took place in October of that year, brought together women from 157 countries. This global campaign was initiated by the Federation des Femmes du Quebec (FFQ) and united over 5,000 organizations around the world. Bringing together so many women of so many backgrounds involved a remarkable effort. The march focused on ending poverty and violence. These causes struck a chord among the multitude of women. This project raises hope for the future of collaborative efforts to challenge hegemonic power structures.

In Canada, the struggles of many women of colour have brought the issue of race into feminist discourse. Women of colour have been organizing autonomously and lobbying the public and the government on their own behalf (Black, 1988). My own experience working in both mainstream and women-of-colour organizations leads me to believe that women of colour are better off directing their energies into their own organizations. We can express our concerns much more effectively working with like-minded other women of colour. The same approach also makes it easier to build coalitions with mainstream organizations. When individual women of colour are asked to participate in mainstream organizations, it works much better if they go as representatives of women-of-colour organizations. The chances of our ideas and opinions being taken seriously are better in these circumstances. Also, it is better for women of colour to attend these meetings in pairs so as to avoid feeling isolated. When there is at least one other person who supports a given position, that position becomes easier to articulate.

As Maracle (1993) writes, our mutual survival requires that we cut the strings that tie us to patriarchy and find a new thread to bind us together. hooks (1994) echoes the same conviction when she argues that all women, including women of colour, should plan for their future even though it is difficult to forget the painful memories of the past. The main goal should be social transformation for all people. All feminists should try to foster conducive conditions for coalition building.

The challenges to feminist efforts to change the existing system are formidable indeed. But history is full of examples of people changing their life circumstances against seemingly impossible odds. Participants in these movements have often drawn on their spiritual strength and their unshaken faith in the validity of their causes. They have applied themselves to these struggles to the very end, inspired by the vision of a better future. How can one forget the efforts of people like Mahatma Gandhi, Martin Luther King Jr, and Nelson Mandela and their millions of cohorts! The challenges that feminists face are no less daunting. The vision of a caring and compassionate world where equality and justice prevail for all people should inspire all of us to work toward that goal.

BIBLIOGRAPHY

Abdo, Nahla. 1993. 'Race, Gender and Politics: The Struggle of Arab Women in Canada.' In *And Still We Rise: Feminist Political Mobilizing in Contemporary Canada*, edited by Linda Carty. Toronto: Women's Press.

Accad, Evelyne. 1997. 'Sexuality and Sexual Politics: Conflicts and Contradictions for Contemporary Women in the Middle East.' In *Through the Prism of Difference*, edited by M.B. Zinn et al. Toronto: Allyn & Bacon.

Acker, Joan. 1995. 'The Future of Women and Work: Ending the Twentieth Century.' In *Gender in the 1990s: Images, Realities, and Issues*, edited by E.D. Nelson and B.W. Robinson. Scarborough: Nelson Canada.

Afshar, Haleh. 1993. *Women in the Middle East: Perceptions, Realities, and the Struggle for Liberation*. New York: St Martin's Press.

– ed. 1996. *Women and Politics in the Third World*. London and New York: Routledge.

Afshar, Haleh, and C. Denis. 1998. *Women and Adjustment in the Third-world*. Basingstoke: Macmillan.

Aggarwal, Pramila. 1987. 'Business as Usual in the Factory.' *Resources for Feminist Research* 16(1): 42–4.

Agnew, John. 1987. *Place and Politics*. Boston: Allen & Unwin.

Agnew, Vijay. 1990. 'Women's Work with Women.' *Polyphony* 12(2–3): 64–72.

– 1993. 'Canadian Feminism and Women of Colour.' *Women's Studies International Forum* 16(3).

– 1996. *Resisting Discrimination*. Toronto: University of Toronto Press.

Ahmad, Akbars, and Hastings Donnan, eds. 1994. *Islam, Globalization and Postmodernity*. London: Routledge.

Ahmad, Fawzia. 1994. 'How Do You Identify?' *Canadian Women's Studies*, April 1994.

Ahmad, S., G. Waller, and C. Verduyn. 1994. 'Eating Attitudes and Body Satisfaction among Asian and Caucasian Adolescents.' *Journal of Adolescence* 17: 461–70.

Aitkin, Susan. 1998. *Making Worlds: Gender, Metaphor and Maternity*. Tuscon: University of Arizona Press.

Akhtar, Farida. 1986. *Depopulating Bangladesh: A Brief History of the External Intervention into Reproductive Behaviour of a Society*. Dacca: UBINIG.

Alfred, Gerald L. 1995. *Heeding the Voices of Our Ancestors: Kahnawake Mohawk Politics and the Rise of Native Nationalism*. Toronto, New York, Oxford: Oxford University Press.

Alpha, Catherine. 1997. 'Catching Rainbows.' *Status of Women Journal*. March.

Amott, Teresa, and Julie Matthaei. 1991. *Race, Gender, and Work: A Multicultural Economic History of Women in the United States*. Montreal/New York: Black Rose Books.

Anderson, Benedict. 1991. *Imagined Communities: Reflections on the Origins and Spread of Nationalism*. London: Verso.

Anderson, Margaret L., and Patricia H. Collins, eds. 1995. *Race, Class and Gender: An Anthology*. Belmont, CA: Wadsworth.

Andrews, Lori B. 1986. 'My Body, My Property.' In *Hastings Centre Report*. 28–37.

– 1987. 'Feminist Perspectives on NRTs.' In *Briefing Handbook: Reproductive Laws for the 1990s*. Newark, NJ: Women's Rights Litigation Clinic and Institute for Research on Women. Rutgers Law School.

Ang, Len. 1995. 'I am a feminist but ... "Other" women and postnational feminism.' In *Transitions: New Australian Feminisms*, edited by B. Caine and R. Pringle. Sydney: Allen & Unwin.

Anonymous. 1974. Portland Feminist Coordinating Council Forum on the Role of Men in the Women's Movement. 19 March.

Anthias, Floya, and Nira Yuval-Davis. 1989. *Woman-Nation-State*. London: Macmillan.

Anzaldua, Gloria. 1997. 'La Conciencia de la Mestiza: Towards a New Consciousness.' In *Through the Prism of Difference: Readings on Sex and Gender*, edited by B. Zinn et al. Toronto: Allyn & Bacon.

Apostle, R., Don Clairmont, and Lars Osberg. 1985. 'Segmentation and Wage Determination.' *Canadian Review of Sociology and Anthropology* 22: 30–56.

Appadurai, Arjun. 1996. *Modernity at Large*. Minneapolis: University of Minnesota Press.

– 1998. 'Dead Certainty: Ethnic Violence in the Era of Globalization.' *Development and Change* 29(4): 905–25.

Armstrong, Pat, and Hugh Armstrong. 1990. *Theorizing Women's Work*. Toronto: Garamond Press.

Asch, A., and M. Fine. 1988. 'Shared Dreams: A Left Perspective on Disability Rights and Reproductive Rights.' In *Women with Disabilities: Essays in Psychology, Culture and Politics*, edited by M. Fine and A. Asch. Philadelphia: Temple University Press.

Ashford, Lori S. 1995. 'New Perspectives on Population: Lessons from Cairo.' *Population Bulletin* (1).

Awatere, Donna. 1984. *Maori Sovereignty*, Aukland, NZ: Broadsheet.

Bachmann, Ronet. 1993. *Death and Violence on the Reservation*. New York: Auburn House.

Bakker, Isabella, ed. 1994. *The Strategic Silence: Gender and Economic Policy*. London: Zed Books.

– 1996. *Rethinking Restructuring: Gender and Change in Canada*. Toronto: University of Toronto Press.

Balibar, Etienne, and Immanual Wallerstein. 1988. *Race, Nation, Class: Ambiguous Identities*. New York: Verso.

Ballweg, M.L. 1982. Letter to national council members. 24 July.

Bandarage, A. 1997. *Women, Population and Global Crisis*. London: Zed Books.

Bannerji, Himani. 1987. 'Introducing Racism: Notes Towards an Anti-Racist Feminism.' *Resources for Feminist Research* 16: 10–12.

Bannerji, Himani, et al. 1991. *Unsettling Relations: The University as a Site of Feminist Struggle*. Toronto: The Women's Press.

– 1993. 'Popular Images of South Asian Women.' In *Returning the Gaze: Essays on Racism, Feminism and Politics*, edited by H. Bannerji. Toronto: Sister Vision Press.

– 1995. *Thinking Through*. Toronto: Women's Press.

Bannerji, Kaushalya. 1993. 'No Apologies.' In *A Lotus of Another Colour: An Unfolding of South Asian Gay and Lesbian Experience*, edited by R. Ratti. Boston: Alyson Publications.

Barndt, Deborah, ed. 1999. *Women Working the NAFTA Chain*. Toronto: Second Story Press.

Bartky, S. 1990. *Femininity and Domination: Studies in the Phenomenology of Oppression*. New York: Routledge.

Basu, Amrita, ed. 1995. *The Challenge of Local Feminisms: Women's Movements in Global Perspective*. Boulder, San Francisco and Oxford: Westview Press.

Becherman, Gordon, and Graham Lowe. 1997. *The Future of Work in Canada: A Synthesis Report*. 146. Ottawa: Canadian Policy Research Network.

Bell, C. 1998. Personal interview. 29 January.

Benaria, Lourdes, and Shelley Feldman, eds. 1992. *Unequal Burden: Economic Crisis, Persistent Poverty and Women's Work*. Boulder: Westview Press.

Benokraitis, N., and J. Feagain. 1995. *Modern Sexism: Blatant, Subtle, and Overt Discrimination*. 2nd Edition. Englewood Cliffs, NJ: Prentice Hall.

Berkeley Brother. 1973. 'About Us.' *Brother: A Forum for Men Against Sexism.* Berkeley, CA: n.p.

Berktay, Fatmagul. 1998. *Women and Religion.* Montreal: Black Rose Books.

Bissoondath, N. 1991. *Selling Illusions: The Cult of Multiculturalism in Canada.* Toronto: Penguin Books.

Black, Naomi. 1988. 'The Canadian Women's Movement.' In *Changing Patterns: Women in Canada,* edited by S. Burt. Toronto: McClelland & Stewart.

Blenman, Adrienne. 1991. 'The Hand that Hits Is Not Always Male,' *Canadian Women Studies,* 11(4): 60–2.

Blishen, B.W., et al. 1987. 'The 1981 Socio-economic Index for Occupations in Canada.' *Canadian Review of Sociology and Anthropology* 24: 465–88.

Blondin, G. 1997. *Yamoria: The Lawmaker, Stories of the Dene.* Edmonton: Newest Press.

Bolaria, B. Singh, and Peter S. Li. 1988. *Racial Oppression in Canada.* Toronto: Garamond Press.

Bordo, S. 1993. *Unbearable Weight: Feminism, Western Culture and the Body.* Los Angeles: University of California Press.

Bottomore, T.B., trans. 1964. *Karl Marx: Selected Writings in Sociology and Social Philosophy.* New York: McGraw-Hill.

Boulos, P.J. 1992. White Ribbon Campaign. 8 December. Online posting. WMST-umdd.umd.edu. 5 April. 993.

Boyce, R., ed. 1999. *The Communication Revolution at Work: The Social, Economic and Political Impacts of Technological Change.* Montreal: McGill-Queen's University Press.

Boyd, M. 1975. 'The Status of Immigrant Women in Canada.' *Canadian Review of Sociology and Anthropology* 12: 406–23.

Bradbury, B. 1984. 'Women and Wage Labour in a Period of Transition: Montreal, 1861–1881.' *Histoire Sociale/Social History* 17: 115–31.

– 1995. 'The Home as Workplace.' In *Labouring Lives: Work and Workers in Nineteenth-Century Ontario,* edited by P. Craven. Toronto: University of Toronto Press.

Bradley, Christine. 1994. 'Why Male Violence Is a Development Issue.' In Miranda Davies, comp., *Women and Violence.* London and New Jersey: Zed Books.

Brah, Avtor. 1992. 'Difference, Diversity, Differentiation.' In *Race, Culture and Identity,* edited by Donald and A. Rattansi, London: Sage.

Brant Catellano, Marlene. 1991. 'Women in Huron and Ojibwa Societies.' *Transition.* December.

Bridgman, Rae, et al. 1999 *Feminist Fields: Ethnographic Insights.* Peterborough, Ontario: Broadview Press.

Briskin, L., and L. Yanz, eds. 1983. *Union Sisters: Women in the Labour Movement*. Toronto: The Women's Press.

Brodie, Janine. 1994. 'Shifting the Boundaries: Gender and the Politics of Restructuring.' In *The Strategic Silence: Gender and Economic Policy*, edited by Isabella Bakker. London: Zed Books.

Brown, L. 1987. 'Lesbians, Weight and Eating: New Analyses and Perspectives.' In *Lesbian Psychologies*, edited by the Boston Lesbian Psychologies Collective. Chicago: University of Illinois Press.

Brown, Rosemary. 1989. *Being Brown*. Toronto: Random House.

Buchanan, K. 1993. 'Creating Beauty in Blackness.' In *Consuming Passions*, edited by C. Brown and K. Jasper. Toronto: Second Story Press.

Bucchetta, P. 1993. 'All Our Goddesses Are Armed: Religion, Resistance and Revenge in the Life of a Militant Hindu Nationalist Woman.' *Bulletin of Concerned Asian Scholars* 25(4): 38–52.

Buchignani, N. 1983. 'Some Comments Made on the Elimination of Racism in Canada.' *Canadian Ethnic Studies* 15(2): 119.

Bulbeck, Chilla. 1998. *Re-Orienting Western Feminisms*. Cambridge: Cambridge University Press.

Bumiller, Elisabeth. 1990. *May You Be the Mother of a Hundred Sons*. New York: Fawcett Columbine.

Bunch, Charlotte, and Royanna Carrillo. 1998. 'Global Violence Against Women: The Challenge to Human Rights and Development.' In *World Security: Challenges for a New Century*, 3rd ed., edited by M.T. Klare and Y. Chandrani. New York: St Martin's Press.

Burt, Sandra. 1995. 'The Several World's of Policy Analysis: Traditional Approaches and Feminist Critiques.' In *World Security: Challenges for a New Century*, edited by M.T. Klare and Y. Chandrani. New York: St Martin's Press.

Burt, Sandra, and Lorraine Code. 1995. *Changing Methods: Feminists Transforming Practice*. Peterborough: Broadview Press.

Butler, J. 1990. *Gender Trouble: Feminism and the Subversion of Identity*. New York: Routledge.

Buvinic, Maya, Margaret A. Lycette, and William Paul McGreevey, eds. 1983. *Women and Poverty in the Third-world*. Baltimore: Johns Hopkins University Press.

Calliste, Agnes. 1989. 'Canada's Immigration Policy and Domestics in the Caribbean: The Second Domestic Scheme.' In *Race, Class, Gender: Bonds and Barriers*, special issue of *Socialist Studies* 5: 113–65.

– 1992. 'Women of Exceptional Merit: Immigration of Caribbean Nurses to Canada.' *Canadian Journal of Women and the Law* 6: 85–102.

Campbell, Jacquelyn. 1998. 'Interdisciplinarity in Research on Wife Abuse.' In *Women's Studies in Transition: The Pursuit of Interdisciplinarity*, edited by

K. Conway-Turner et al. Newark: University of Delaware Press/London: Associated University Press.

Camper, C., ed. 1994. *Miscegenation Blues: Voices of Mixed Race Women.* Toronto: Sister Vision Press.

Canaan, J.E., and C. Griffin, 1990. 'The New Men's Studies: Part of the Problem or Part of the Solution?' In *Men, Masculinities and Social Theory,* edited by J. Hearn and D. Morgan. London: Unwin Hyman.

Canadian Gallup Poll. 1994. *Report on the Behaviour and Attitudes of Canadians with Respect to Weight Consciousness and Weight Control.* Toronto: Canadian Gallup Poll Limited.

Canadian Panel on Violence Against Women. 1993. *Changing the Landscape: Ending Violence-Achieving Equality,* Ottawa: Minister of Supply and Services Canada.

Canadian Teacher's Federation. 1990. *A Cappella: A Report on the Realities, Concerns, Expectations and Barriers Experienced by Adolescent Women in Canada.* Ottawa: Canadian Teacher's Federation.

CARAL – Canadian Abortion Rights Action League. *The ProChoice News* (quarterly newsletter).

Carty, Linda, ed. 1993. *And Still We Rise: Feminist Political Mobilizing in Contemporary Canada.* Toronto: Women's Press.

Carty, Linda, and Dionne Brand. 1989 '"Visible Minority" Women: A Creation of the Canadian State.' In *Resources for Feminist Research* 17: 39–40.

Cassidy, B., R. Lord, and N. Mandell. 1998. 'Silenced and Forgotten Women: Race, Poverty, and Disability.' In *Feminist Issues: Race, Class, and Sexuality,* 2nd ed., edited by N. Mandell. Scarborough: Prentice Hall Allyn and Bacon Canada.

Castro, Ginette. 1990. *American Feminism: A Contemporary History,* translated by Elizabeth Loverde-Bagwell. New York and London: New York University Press. Publ. in French 1984.

Catin, Solange, and Michèle Clément. 1998. 'Les origines et les orientations du Centre de recherche interdisciplinaire sur la violence familiale et la violence faite aux femmes (CRI-VIFF),' *Resources for Feminist Research* 26(3/4): 71–7.

Cavendish, R. 1982. *Women on the Line.* London: Routledge and Kegan Paul.

Chapkis, W. 1986. *Beauty Secrets: Women and the Politics of Appearance.* Boston: South End Press.

Charmaz, K. 1995. 'The Body, Identity, and Self: Adapting to Impairment.' *The Sociological Quarterly* 36(4): 657–80.

Chatterjee, Partha. 1986. *Nationalist Thought in the Colonial World: A Derivative Discourse.* London: Zed Books.

Chaudhuri, Nupur, and Margaret Strobel, eds. 1992. *Western Women and Imperialism: Complicity and Resistance*. Bloomington: Indiana University Press.

Chen, Martha Alter. 1995. 'The Feminization of Poverty.' In *A Commitment to the World's Women*, edited by Noleen Heyzer. New York: UNIFEM.

Chossudovsky, Michel. 1998. *The Globalisation of Poverty*. London: Zed Books.

Clatterbaugh, K. 1997. *Contemporary Perspectives on Masculinity: Men, Women, and Politics in Modern Society*. 2nd ed. Boulder: Westview.

Code, Lorraine. 1995. 'How Do We Know? Questions of Method in Feminist Practice.' In *Changing Methods: Feminists Transforming Practice*, edited by Sandra Burt and Lorraine Code. Peterborough: Broadview Press.

Cohen, C., R. Wilk, and B. Stoeltje, eds. 1996. *Beauty Queens on the Global Stage: Gender, Contests and Power*. New York: Routledge.

Cohen, M. 1982. 'The Problem of Studying "Economic Man."' In *Feminism in Canada*, edited by A. Miles and G. Finn. Montreal: Black Rose.

Cohen, Yoland, ed. 1989. *Women and Counter-Power*, Montreal: Black Rose Books.

Cole, S.G. 1991. 'Remembering Montreal.' *NOW* (December 5–11): 14, 17.

Cole, Sally, et al., eds. *Feminist Fields, Ethnographic Insights*. Peterborough, ON; Broadview Press.

Collins, L., and P. Walton. 1996. 'Changing Work Patterns for Men.' *Achilles Heel: The Radical Mens' Magazine*. 20 (Spring/Summer): 28–30.

Collins, Patricia Hill. 1986. 'Learning from the Outsider Within: The Sociological Significance of Black Feminist Thought.' *Social Problems* 33: 514–32.

– 1990. *Black Feminist Thought: Knowledge, Consciousness and the Politics of Empowerment*. Boston: Unwin Hyman.

Collins, T., M. Schneider, and S. Kroeger. 1995. '(Dis)Abling Images.' *Radical Teacher* 47: 11–14.

Colodny, Nicki. 1989. 'The Politics of Birth Control in a Reproductive Rights Context.' In *The Future of Human Reproduction*, edited by Christine Overall. Toronto: The Women's Press.

Conboy, K., N. Medina, and S. Stanbury, eds. 1997. *Writing on the Body: Female Embodiment and Feminist Theory*. New York: Columbia University Press.

Connell, R. W. 1995. *Masculinities*. Berkeley: University of California Press.

Connelly, Patricia. 1978. *Last Hired, First Fired: Women and the Canadian Work Force*. Toronto: Women's Press.

Cooey, Paula M. 1991. 'Post-Patriarchal Reconstruction of Inherited Christian Doctrine.' In *After Patriarchy*, edited by Paula M. Cooey et al. New York : Orbis Books.

Cooper, M. 1990. 'A History of the Men's Movement.' In *Searching for the Antisexist Man*. London: Achilles Heel Publications. 1–14.

Corea, Gene. 1993. 'The Reproductive Brothel.' In *Women's Studies: Essential Readings*, edited by Stevi Jackson. New York: New York University Press.

Creese, G., N. Guppy, and M. Meissner. 1991. *Ups and Downs on the Ladder of Success*. Ottawa: Statistics Canada.

Creese, Gillian, and Daiva Stasiulis. 1996. 'Introduction: Intersections of Gender, Race, Class and Sexuality.' *Studies in Political Economy* 51: 15–64.

Crowe, C., and C. Montgomery. 1992. 'Putting on a Ribbon Isn't Nearly Enough.' *The Globe and Mail*. 27 November: 25.

Crowley, T. 1995. 'Rural Labour.' In *Labouring Lives: Work and Workers in Nineteenth-Century Ontario*, edited by P. Craven. Toronto: University of Toronto Press.

Culpepper, Emily. 1991. 'Political Journey of A Feminist Freethinker.' In *After Patriarchy*, edited by Paula Cooey et al. New York: Orbis Books.

Daly, Mary. 1978. *Gyn-Ecology: The MetaEthics of Radical Feminism*. Boston: Beacon Press.

Daphne, M. 1999. Personal interview. 9 May.

Darwin, C. 1981/1871. *The Descent of Man and Selection in Relation to Sex*. Princeton, NJ: Princeton University Press.

Das Gupta. 1987. 'Involving Immigrant Women: A Case of Participatory Research.' *Canadian Woman Studies* 8: 14–15.

Davies, Miranda. 1994. *Women and Violence: Realities and Responses Worldwide*, London: Zed Books.

Davis, K. 1995. *Reshaping the Female Body: The Dilemma of Cosmetic Surgery*. New York: Routledge.

Davis, L. 1995. *Enforcing Normalcy: Disability, Deafness and the Body*. New York: Verso Press.

Day, D. 1990. *Young Women in Nova Scotia: A Study of Attitudes, Behaviour and Aspirations*. Halifax: Nova Scotia Advisory Council on the Status of Women.

de Lauretis, T., ed. 1986. *Feminist Studies, Critical Studies*. Bloomington: Indiana University Press.

de Sève, Micheline. 1992. 'The Perspectives of Quebec Feminists.' In *Challenging Times*, edited by Constance Backhouse and David Flaherty. Montreal and Kingston: McGill-Queen's University Press.

– 1996. 'Women's National and Gendered Identity,' unpublished, available from the author, Montreal.

– 1997. 'Gendered Feelings About Our National Issues.' *Atlantis* 21(2).

Dei, George J. Sefa. 1996. *Theory and Practice: Anti-racism Education*. Halifax: Fernwood Publishing.

Delphy, Christina. 1993. 'New Reproductive Technologies.' In *Feminist Frameworks: Alternative Theoretical Accounts of the Relations Between Women and Men*, edited by A.M. Jagger and P.S. Rothenberg. Toronto: McGraw-Hill Ryerson.

Derricotte, T. 1997. *The Black Notebooks: An Interior Journey*. New York: W.W. Norton.

Desai, Nira, and Maitreyi Krishnara. 1987. *Women and Society in India*. New Delhi: Ajanta.

Dhruvarajan, Vanaja. 1989. *Hindu Women and the Power of Ideology*. Granby, MA: Bergin and Garvey.

– 1990. 'Women of Colour in Canada: Diversity of Experiences.' In *Women Changing Academe*, edited by S. Kirby et al. Winnipeg: Sororal Publishing.

– 1992. 'Conjugal Power Among First Generation Hindu Asian Immigrants in Canada.' *The International Journal of Sociology of the Family* 22.

– 1994. 'Hindu Asian Indian Women, Multiculturalism and Reproductive Technologies.' In *Racial Minorities, Medicine and Health*, edited by B.S. Bolaria and R. Bolaria. Halifax: Fernwood Publishing.

– 1995. 'Addressing Systemic Discrimination with a Focus on Racism and Ethnocentrism.' In *The Bulletin: Simon Fraser University*, 8(2).

– 1996. 'Hinduism, Empowerment of Women and Development in India.' In *Labour, Capital and Society* 29(1&2): 16–40.

Dickenson, Peter. 1998. 'In Another Place Not Here: Dionne Brank's Politics of (Dis)Location.' In *Painting the Maple*, edited by V. Strong-Boag et al. Vancouver: UBC Press.

Downing, Marymay. 1993. 'For Her, or Against Her? The Power of Religious Metaphor.' *Limited Edition: Voices of Women, Voices of Feminism*, edited by Geraldine Finn. Halifax: Fernwood.

Driedger, D., and A. D'aubin. 1992. 'Women with Disabilities Challenge the Body Beautiful.' *Healthsharing Magazine* 12(4): 35–41.

Driedger, Leo, and R.A. Mezoff. 1981. 'Ethnic Prejudice and Discrimination in Winnipeg High Schools.' *Canadian Journal of Sociology* 6(1) Winter: 1–19.

duCille, A. 1996. *Skin Trade*. Cambridge, MA: Harvard University Press.

Duffy, Ann. 1998. 'The Feminist Challenge: Knowing and Ending the Violence.' In *Feminist Issues: Race, Class and Sexuality*, edited by N. Mandell. Scarborough: Prentice Hall Allyn & Bacon Canada.

Eddy, John, and Deryck Schreuder, eds. 1988. *The Rise of Colonial Nationalism: Australia, New Zealand, Canada and South Africa First Assert Their Nationalities, 1880–1914*. Sydney: Allen & Unwin.

Editorial Collective. 1997. *Achilles Heel: The Radical Mens' Magazine* 22 (Summer/Autumn): 3.

Egeagwali, G., ed. 1995. *Women Pay the Price: Structural Adjustment and the Caribbean*. New Jersey: Africa World Press.

Eichler, Margrit. 1987. 'The Relationship Between Sexist, Non-sexist, Women-centred and Feminist Research in the Social Sciences.' In *Women and Men*, edited by G. Hofmann Nemiroff. Montreal: Fitzhenry and Whiteside.

– 1988. *Nonsexist Research Methods: A Practical Guide*. Winchester, Mass.: Allen and Unwin.

– 1993. 'Some Minimal Principles Concerning New Reproductive Technologies.' In *Women's Studies: Essential Readings*, edited by S. Jackson. New York: New York University Press.

Elson, Diane. 1987. *The Impact of Structural Adjustment and Women: Concepts and Issues*. Development Studies: University of Manchester.

Elson, Diane, and R. Pearson. Reprinted 1997. 'The Subordination of Women and the Internationalization of Factory Production.' In *The Women, Gender and Development Reader*, edited by Nalini Visvanathan et al., London: Zed Books.

Engels, Frederick. 1902. *The Origin of the Family, Private Property, and the State*. Chicago: Charles H. Kerr.

Enloe, Cynthia. 1989. *Bananas, Beaches and Bases: Making Feminist Sense of International Politics*. London: Pandora.

Erlandson, David, et al., eds. 1993. 'Foreword.' In *Doing Naturalistic Inquiry: A Guide to Methods*, by D. Erlandson et al. Newbury Park, London, and New Delhi: Sage.

Essed, Philomeda. 1991. *Understanding Everyday Racism: An Interdisciplinary Theory*. London: Sage.

Etkin, M. 1991. 'The Men's Movement.' *Canadian Dimension* (January–February): 35–7.

Fanon, Frantz. 1963. *The Wretched of the Earth*. New York: Grove Press.

– 1967/1952. *Black Skin, White Masks*, translated by C. Lam Markmann. New York: Grove Weidenfeld.

Featherston, E. 1994. *Skin Deep: Women Writing on Color, Culture and Identity*. Freedom, CA: The Crossing Press.

Feldman, W., E. Feldman, and J.T. Goodman. 1988. 'Culture Versus Biology: Children's Attitudes toward Thinness and Fatness.' *Pediatrics* 81(2): 190–4.

Fine, M., and A. Asch, eds. 1988. *Women with Disabilities: Essays in Psychology, Culture and Politics*. Philadelphia: Temple University Press.

Firestone, Shulasmith. 1972. *The Dialectic of Sex*. New York: Bantam Books.

Fisher, B., and R. Galler. 1988. 'Friendship and Fairness: How Disability Affects Friendship between Women.' In *Women with Disabilities: Essays in Psychology, Culture and Politics*, edited by M. Fine and A. Asch. Philadelphia: Temple University Press.

Fisher, K. 1993. 'Men's Groups: Accountable to Whom? for What?' *Canadian Dimension* (March–April): 41–4.

Flannery, R. 1995. *Ellen Smallboy: Glimpses of a Cree Woman's Life*. Montreal: McGill-Queen's University Press.

Fleras, A., and J.L. Elliot. 1995. *Unequal Relations*. Scarborough, ON: Prentice Hall Canada.

Flood, M., and G. Dowsett. 1994. 'Movement in a Straight Line.' *XY: Men, Sex, Politics* (Spring): 26–7.

Fox, B. 1980. *Hidden in the Household*. Toronto: The Women's Press.

Frank, G. 1988. 'On Embodiment: A Case Study of Congenital Limb Deficiency in American Culture.' In *Women with Disabilities: Essays in Psychology, Culture and Politics*, edited by M. Fine and A. Asch. Philadelphia: Temple University Press.

Frank, Sharlene. 1993. *Family Violence in Aboriginal Communities: A First Nations Report*. Victoria, BC: Report to the B.C. Government.

Fraser, Nancy. 1997. *Justice Interruptus*. New York and London: Routledge.

Freedman, R. 1984. 'Reflections on Beauty as It Relates to Health in Adolescent Females.' In *Health and the Female Adolescent*, edited by S. Golub. York: Harrington Park Press.

Freire, Paulo. 1999. *Pedagogy of the Oppressed*. New York: Continuum.

Gaard, Greta. 1993. 'Ecofeminism and Native American Cultures: Pushing the Limits of Cultural Imperialism.' In *Ecofeminism: Women, Animals, and Nature*, edited by G. Gaard. Toronto: Garamond Press.

Gabriel, Chris, and Katherine Scott. 1993. 'Women's Press at Twenty: The Politics of Feminist Publishing.' In *And Still We Rise: Feminist Political Mobilizing in Contemporary Canada*, edited by Linda Carty. Toronto: Women's Press.

Ganage, C. 1986. *Double Day, Double Bind*. Toronto: The Women's Press.

Gard, M., and C. Freeman. 1996. 'The Dismantling of a Myth: A Review of Eating Disorders and Socioeconomic Status.' *International Journal of Eating Disorders* 20(1): 1–12.

Garland, R. 1995. *The Eye of the Beholder: Deformity and Disability in the Graeco-Roman World*. Ithaca, NY: Cornell University Press.

Gartner, Rosemary, Myrna Dawson, and Maria Crawford. 1998. 'Women Killing: Intimate Femicide in Ontario, 1974–1994.' *Resources for Feminist Research*, 26(3/4): 151–73.

Gaskell, Jane. 1993. 'What Counts as Skill: Reflections on Pay Equity.' In *Work in Canada: Readings in the Sociology of Work and Industry*, edited by G. Lowe and H. Krahn. Scarborough: Nelson Canada.

Gauthier, Lorraine, et. al. 1998. 'La formation en matière de violence faite aux femmes et aux enfants en Ontario français.' *Resources for Feminist Research* 26(3/4): 13–33.

Geigen-Miller, P. 1992. 'White Ribbon Easy Way Out for Many Men, Activist Says.' *London Free Press* (5 December): C9.

Geschiere, Peter, and Birgit Meyer. 1998. 'Globalization and Identity: Dialectics of Flow and Closure.' *Development and Change* 29(4): 601–14.

Ghorayshi, Parvin. 1990. 'Manitoba's Clothing Industry in the 1980s: Change and Continuity.' In *The Political Economy of Manitoba*, edited by J. Silver and J. Hull. Canadian Plains Research Centre: University of Regina.

– 1990a. *The Sociology of Work: A Critical Annotated Bibliography*. New York: Garland Publishing.

Gimbutas, Marija. 1974. *The Goddesses and Gods of Old Europe, 6500–3500 B.C.* Berkeley: University of California Press.

Godina, Vesna. 1998. 'The Outbreak of Nationalism on Former Yugoslav Territory: A Historical Perspective on the Problem of Supernational Identity.' *Nations and Nationalism* 4(3): 409–22.

Goetz, Anne Marie. 1988. 'Feminism and the Limits of the Claim to Know: Contradictions in the Feminist Approach to Women in Development.' *Millenium: Journal of International Studies* 17(3): 477–96.

Goldenberg, Naomi R. 1990. *Returning Words to Flesh*. Boston: Beacon Press.

Goldrick-Jones, A. 1998. 'Politics and Profeminisms Across the Pond: Personal Reflections.' *Achilles Heel: The Radical Men's Magazine* 23 (Summer): 32–4.

Gordon, M-D. 1993. 'Why Is This Men's Movement So White? An Open Letter.' *Changing Men: Issues in Gender, Sex, and Politics* 26 (Summer/Fall): 15–17.

Gortmaker, S., A. Must, J. Perrin, A. Sobol, and W. Dietz. 1993. 'Social and Economic Consequences of Overweight in Adolescence and Young Adulthood.' *The New England Journal of Medicine* 329(14): 1008–12.

Gottlieb, Amy. 1993. 'What about Us? Organizing Inclusively in the National Action Committee on the Status of Women.' In *And Still We Rise: Feminist Political Mobilizing in Contemporary Canada*, edited by Linda Carty. Toronto: Women's Press.

Government of Canada, House of Commons. 1984. *Equality Now! Report of the Special Committee on Visible Minorities in Canadian Society*.

Greaves, Lorraine, Alison Wylie, et al. 1995. 'Women and Violence: Feminist Practice and Quantitative Method.' In *Changing Methods: Feminists Transforming Practice*, edited by Sandra Burt and Lorraine Code. Peterborough: Broadview Press.

Greenhill, Pauline. Forthcoming. 'Folk and Academic Racism: Concepts from Morris and Folklore.' *Journal of American Folklore*.

Grewal, Inderpal, and Caren Kaplan, eds. 1994. *Scattered Hegemonics*. Minneapolis and London: University of Minnesota Press.

Gross, Rita N. 1996. *Feminism and Religion*. Boston: Beacon Press.

Guba, Egon. 1993. 'Foreword.' In *Doing Naturalistic Inquiry: A Guide to Methods*, by D. Erlandson et al. Newbury Park, London and New Delhi: Sage.

Gupta, Lina. 1991. 'Kali the Savior.' In *After Patriarchy*, edited by J.M. Cooey et al. New York: Orbis Books.

Gupta, Tanya Das. 1986. *Learning from Our History*. Toronto: Cross-Cultural Communications Centre.

– 1996. *Racism and Paid Work*. Toronto: Garamond Press.

Hahn, H. 1992. 'Can Disability Be Beautiful?' *Social Policy* 18(3): 26–31.

Hahnel, Robin. 1999. *Panic Rules*. Cambridge, MA: South End Press.

Hajnal, V. 1995. 'Can I Do A Good Job of Both Family and Work? Decisions Regarding Offspring.' In *Young Women and Leadership*, edited by C. Reynolds and B. Young. Calgary: Detslig Enterprises.

Hale, Sylvia M. 1992. *Controversies in Sociology*. Toronto: Copp Clark Pitman.

Hall, C. 1995. 'Asian Eyes: Body Image and Eating Disorders of Asian and Asian American Women.' *Eating Disorders: A Journal of Treatment and Prevention* 3(1): 8–19.

Hall, Stuart. 1990. 'Cultural Identity and Diaspora.' In *Identity, Community, Culture, Difference*. London: Lawrence and Wishart.

Hanmer, J. 1990. 'Men, Power and the Exploitation of Women.' In *Men, Masculinities and Social Theory*, edited by J. Hearns and D. Morgan. London: Unwin Hyman.

Hansen, Thomas Blom. 1995. 'Controlled Emancipation: Women and Hindu Nationalism.' In *Ethnicity, Gender and the Subversion of Nationalism*, edited by F. Wilson and B. Folke Fredericksen. London: Frank Cass.

Haraway, Donna. 1991. 'Situated Knowledges: The Science Question in Feminism and the Privilege of Partial Perspective.' In *Simians, Cyborgs, and Women: The Reinvention of Native*, edited by Donna Haraway. New York: Routledge.

Harding, Sandra. 1991. *Whose Science? Whose Knowledge? Thinking from Women's Lives*. Ithaca, NY: Cornell University Press.

Harper, Indijana Hidovic. 1993. 'Personal Reactions of a Bosnian Woman to the War in Bosnia.' *Feminist Review* 45 (Autumn): 102–7.

Harris, A., and D. Wideman. 1988. 'Construction of Gender and Disability in Early Attachment.' In *Women with Disabilities: Essays in Psychology, Culture and Politics*, edited by M. Fine and A. Asch. Philadelphia: Temple University Press.

Hartmann, Heidi. 1981. 'Unhappy Marriage of Marxism and Feminism: Towards a More Progressive Union.' In *Women and Revolution*, edited by L. Sargent. Boston: South End Press.

Haskell, Lori, and Melanie Randall. 1998. 'The Politics of Women's Safety: Sexual Violence, Women's Fear and the Public/Private Split.' *Resources for Feminist Research* 26(3/4): 113–49.

Hassan, Riffat. 1991. 'Muslim Women and Post-Patriarchal Islam.' In *After Patriarchy*, edited by P.M. Cooey et al. New York: Orbis Books.

Henry, Francis, et al. 1995. *The Colour of Democracy: Racism in Canadian Society*. Toronto: Harcourt Brace & Company.

Henry, Francis, and Effie Ginsberg. 1992. 'Racial Discrimination in Employment.' In *Everyday Life*, edited by L. Tepperman and J. Curtis. Toronto: McGraw-Hill Ryerson.

Hevey, D. 1992. *The Creatures Time Forgot*. London: Routledge.

Heyzer, Noleen, ed. 1995. *A Commitment to the World's Women: Perspectives on Development for Beijing and Beyond*. New York: UNIFEM.

Higginbotham, E. 1992. 'We Were Never on a Pedestal: Women of Colour Continue to Struggle with Poverty, Racism and Sexism.' In *Race, Class and Gender*, edited by M.L. Anderson and P. Hill Collins. Belmont, CA: Wadsworth.

Higgins, P. 1992. *Making Disability: Exploring the Social Transformation of Human Variation*. Springfield, IL: Charles C. Thomas.

Hill, A., and R. Bhatti. 1995. 'Body Shape, Perception and Dieting in Preadolescent British Asian Girls: Links with Eating Disorders.' *International Journal of Eating Disorders* 17(2): 175–83.

Hole, Judith, and E. Levine. 1971. *The Rebirth of Feminism*. New York: Quadrangle Books.

hooks, b. 1984. *Feminist Theory: From Margin to Center*. Boston: South End Press.

– 1988. *Talking Back: Thinking Feminist, Thinking Black*. Toronto: Between the Lines.

– 1992a. 'Men in Feminist Struggle: The Necessary Movement.' In *Women Respond to the Men's Movement*, edited by K.L. Hagan. San Francisco: Pandora.

– 1992b. *Black Looks: Race and Representation*. Toronto: Between the Lines Press.

– 1993. *Sisters of the Yam: Black Women and Self-Recovery*. Toronto: Between the Lines Press.

– 1994. *Outlaw Culture: Resisting Representations*. London: Routledge.

How to Organize the WRC in Your Community, School, Group, or Workplace. 1992. Toronto: White Ribbon Campaign.

Huffman, M., S. Velasco, and W. Bielby. 1996. 'Where Sex Composition Matters Most: Comparing the Effects of Job Versus Occupational Sex Composition of Earnings.' *Sociological Focus* 29(3): 189–207.

Hughes, M., and Hertel, B. 1990. 'The Significance of Colour Remains: A Study of Life Chances, Mate Selection, and Ethnic Consciousness Among Black Americans.' *Social Forces* 68(4): 1–16.

Hutchinson, M. 1985. *Transforming Body Image*. New York: The Crossing Press.

Interrante, J. 1983. 'Dancing along the Precipice: The Men's Movement in the 80's.' *M: Gentle Men for Gender Justice* (Spring): 3–6.

Issennman, B. Kobayashi. 1997. *Sinews of Survival: The Living Legacy of Inuit Clothing*. Vancouver: UBC Press.

Jackson, S., et al. 1993. 'Science, Medicine & Reproductive Technology: Introduction.' In Stevi, Jackson, ed., *Women's Studies: Essential Readings*. New York: New York University Press.

Jaising, Indira, and C. Sathyamala. 1994. 'Legal Rights ... and Wrongs: Internationalizing Bhopal.' In *Close to Home: Women Reconnect Ecology, Health and Development Worldwide*, edited by V. Shiva. Philadelphia: New Society.

James, Carl E., and Adrienne Shadd. 1994. *Talking About Difference*. Toronto: Between the Lines.

Jardine, A., and P. Smith, eds. 1987. *Men in Feminism*. New York: Routledge.

Jayawardena, Kumari. 1986. *Feminism and Nationalism in the Third-world*. London: Zed Books.

Jhappan, Radha. 1996. 'Post-Modern Race and Gender Essentialism or a Post-Mortem of Scholarship.' *Studies in Political Economy* 51: 15–64.

Johnson, Laura, and Robert Johnson. 1982. *The Seam Allowance: Industrial Home Sewing in Canada*. Toronto: The Women's Press.

Johnson, Rhonda, Winona Stevenson, and Donna Greschner. 1993. 'Peekiskwetan.' *Canadian Journal of Women & the Law* 6: 153–73.

Jones, C. 1992a. 'Kingston Report: White Ribbon Reflections.' *Men's Network News* 3(1): (Winter): 7.

– 1992b. 'Kingston Respectfully Dissents.' *Men's Network News* 3(2) (Summer): 6, 14.

Jordanova, Ludmilla. 1993. 'Natural Facts: An Historical Perspective on Science and Sexuality.' In *Women's Studies: Essential Readings*, edited by S. Jackson. New York: New York University Press.

Jordon, June. 1998. 'A New Politics of Sexuality.' In *Race, Class and Gender*, 2nd edition, edited by M.L. Andersen and P.H. Collings. Toronto: Wadsworth Publishing Company.

Kallen, Evelyn. 1989. *Label Me Human: Minority Rights of Stimatized Canadians*. Toronto: University of Toronto Press.

Kandiyoti, Deniz. 1997. 'Bargaining with Patriarchy.' In *Through the Prism of Difference*, edited by M. Zinn et al. Toronto: Allyn & Bacon.

Kaplan, Caren. 1998. 'On Location.' In *Making Worlds*, edited by S.H. Aiken. Tucson: The University of Arizona Press.

– 1999. *Between Women and Nation: Nationalizing Transnational Feminisms and the State*. Durham, NC: Duke University Press.

Kaplan, Caren, and Inderpal Grewal. 1999. 'Transnational Feminist Cultural Studies: Beyond the Marxism/Poststructuralism/Feminism Divides.' In *Between Woman and Nation: Nationalism, Transnational Feminisms, and the State*. London: Duke University Press.

Karam, M. Azza. 1989. *Women, Islamisms & the State: Contemporary Feminism in Egypt*. New York: St Martin's Press.

Kaschak, E. 1992. *Engendered Lives: A New Psychology of Women's Experience*. New York: Basic Books.

Kaufman, M. 1991. 'The Future of the White Ribbon Campaign.' Unpublished report, 25 January.

– 1992a. *Cracking the Armour: Power, Pain and the Lives of Men*. Toronto: Penguin.

– 1992b. 'Facing the Issues of Violence Together.' *The Globe and Mail* (1 December): A23.

– 1993. Personal interview. 3 December.

Kendall, Diana, et al. 1996. *Sociology in our Times*. Toronto: Nelson.

Khosla, P. 1993. *Review of the Situation of Women*. Toronto: National Action Committee on the Status of Women.

Kimmel, M.S., and T.E. Mosmiller, eds. 1992. *Against the Tide: Pro-Feminist Men in the United States, 1776–1990: A Documentary History*. Boston: Beacon Press.

Kline, Marlee. 1989. 'Women's Oppression and Racism: A Critique of the "Feminist Standpoint."' In *Race, Class, Gender: Bonds and Barriers*, edited by J. Vorst et al. Toronto: Between the Lines.

Kohli, Rita. 1993. 'Power or Empowerment: Questions of Agency in the Shelter Movement.' In *And Still We Rise: Feminist Political Mobilizing in Contemporary Canada*, edited by Linda Carty. Toronto: Women's Press.

Korac, Maja. 1996. 'Understanding Ethnic-National Identity and Its Meaning: Questions from Women's Experience.' In *Women's Studies International Forum* 19(1/2): 65–74.

Krahn, Harvey, and Graham Lowe. 1988 and 1998. *Work, Industry and Canadian Society*. Toronto: Nelson Canada.

Kumar, Radha. 1995. 'From Chipko to Sati: The Contemporary Indian Women's Movement.' In *The Challenge of Local Feminisms: Women's Movements in Global Perspective*, edited by Amarita Basu. San Francisco: Westview Press.

Kumar, Satish. 1996. 'Gandhi's Swadeshi: The Economics of Permanence.' In *The Case Against the Global Economy and For a Turn Toward the Local*, edited by J. Mander and E. Goldsmith. San Francisco: Sierra Club Books.

Lacovetti, F. 1987. 'Trying to Make Ends Meet: An Historical Look at Italian Immigrant Women, The State and Family Survival Strategies in Post-War Toronto.' *Canadian Woman Studies/Les cahiers de la femme: Mediterranean Women* 8(2): 6–11.

Lake, Robert, Judith Scrimger, and Marie Riley. 1991. 'Pursuing Order: Ten Years of Editorial Coverage of the Abortion Issue in *the Globe and Mail*.' *Atlantis* 17(1).

Lamoureux, Diane. 1987. 'Nationalism and Feminism in Quebec: An Impossible Attraction.' In *Feminism and Political Economy*, edited by H.J. Maroney and M. Luxton. Toronto: Methuen.

Landsberg, M. 1992. 'Canada: Will Ribbons Keep Men's Violence under Wraps?' *Ms* (November–December): 16–17.

Larkin, J., C. Rice, and V. Russell. 1996. 'Slipping Through the Cracks: Sexual Harassment, Eating Problems and Problems with Embodiment.' *Eating Disorders: A Journal of Prevention and Treatment* 4(1): 5–26

Lawrence, Bonita. 1996. 'The Exclusion of Survivor's Voices in Feminist Discourse on Violence against Women.' *Voix Feministes/Feminist Voices* 2 (November). Ottawa: Canadian Research Institute for the Advancement of Women.

Layton, J. 1993. Personal interview. 31 August.

Lazreg, Marnia. 1994. 'Women's Experience and Feminist Epistemology: A Critical Neo-rationalist Approach.' In *Knowing the Difference: Feminist Perspectives in Epistemology*, edited by K. Lennon and M. Whitford. London: Routledge.

LeClerc, Patrice, and Lois A. West. 1997. 'Feminist Nationalist Movements in

Quebec: Resolving Contradictions.' In *Feminist Nationalism*, edited by Lois West. New York: Routledge.

Lee, J. 1993. 'Women in Academia: A Growing Minority.' In *Perspectives on Labour and Income*. Ottawa: Statistics Canada. Cat. 75-001E.

Lee, J., and J. Sasser-Coen. 1996. *Blood Stories: Menarche and the Politics of the Female Body in Contemporary U.S. Society*. New York: Routledge.

LeGates, M. 1996. *Making Waves: A History of Feminism in Western Society*. Toronto: Copp Clark.

Lennon, Kathleen, and Margaret Whitford. 1994. *Knowing the Difference: Feminist Perspectives in Epistemology*. London: Routledge.

Levine, M., L. Smolak, A. Moodey, M. Shuman, and L. Hessen. 1994. 'Normative Developmental Challenges and Dieting and Eating Disturbances in Middle School Girls.' *International Journal of Eating Disorders* 15(1): 11–20.

Levinson, David. 1989. *Violence in Cross-Cultural Perspective*. Newbury Park, CA: Sage.

Li, Huey-Li. 1993. 'A Cross Cultural Critique of Ecofeminism.' In *Ecofeminism: Women, Animals, Nature*, edited by G. Gaard. Philadelphia: Temple University Press.

Li, Peter. 1994. 'A World Apart: The Multicultural World of Visible Minorities and the Art World of Canada.' *Canadian Review of Sociology and Anthropology* 31(4).

Lian, J., and D. Matthews. 1998. 'Does the Vertical Mosaic Still Exist? Ethnicity and Income in Canada, 1991.' *Canadian Review of Sociology and Anthropology* 35(4): 461–77.

Lim, Linda Y.C. 1997. 'Capitalism, Imperialism and Patriarchy: The Dilemma of Third-World Women Workers in Multinational Factories.' Reprinted 1997 in *The Women and Development Reader*, edited by Nalini Visvanathan et al. London: Zed Books.

Linton, S., S. Mello, and J. O'Neill. 1995. 'Disability Studies: Expanding the Parameters of Disability.' *Radical Teacher* 47: 4–10.

Little, M. 1998. *No Car, No Radio, No Liquor Permit*. Toronto: Oxford University Press.

Lobel, Kerry. *Naming the Violence: Speaking Out About Lesbian Battering*, The Seal Press.

Lorde, Audre. 1984. *Sister Outsider*. Freedom CA: The Freedom Press.

– 1993. 'AUDRE LORDE: Reflections.' *Feminist Review* 45 (Autumn): 4–9.

– 1995. 'Age, Race, Class and Sex: Women Redefining Difference.' In *Race, Class and Gender*, edited by Margaret L. Anderson and Patricia Hill Collins. New York: Wadsworth.

– 1998. 'Age, Race, Class and Sex: Women Redefining Difference.' In *Race, Class and Gender*, 2nd ed. Toronto: Wadsworth.

Luxton, Meg. 1986. 'Two Hands for the Clock: Changing Patterns in the Gendered Division of Labour in the Home.' In *Through the Kitchen Window: The Politics of Home and Family*, edited by M. Luxton and H. Rosenberg. Toronto: Garamond Press.

Lynn, M., and M. Todoroff. 1995. 'Women's Work and Family Lives.' In *Feminist Issues: Race, Class, and Sexuality*, edited by N. Mandell. Scarborough: Prentice Hall Canada.

Macionis, John, and Linda Gerber. 1997. *Sociology*, 3rd Canadian ed. Scarborough: Prentice Hall.

Mama, A. 1995. *Beyond the Masks: Race, Gender and Subjectivity*. New York: Routledge.

Mangena, Oshadi. 1994. 'Against Fragmentation: The Need for Holism.' In *Knowing the Difference: Feminist Perspectives in Epistemology*, edited by K. Lennon and M. Whitford. London: Routledge.

Marable, Manning. 1997. The Black Male: Searching Beyond Stereotypes. In *Through the Prism of Difference: Readings on Sex and Gender*, edited by M.B. Zinn et. al. Toronto: Allyn & Bacon.

Maracle, Lee. 1993. 'Racism, Sexism and Patriarchy.' In *Returning the Gaze: Essays on Racism, Feminism and Politics*, edited by H. Bannerji. Toronto: Sister Vision Press.

Margolis, Diane Rothbard. 1993. 'Women's Movements Around the World: Cross-Cultural Comparisons.' In *Gender and Society* 7(3): 379–99.

Maroney, Heather Jon, and Meg Luxton, eds. 1987. *Feminism and Political Economy: Women's Work, Women's Struggle*. Toronto: Methuen.

Maynard, Mary. 1994. '"Race," Gender and the Concept of "Difference" in Feminist Thought.' In *The Dynamics of 'Race' and Gender*, edited by H. Afshar and M. Maynard. London: Taylor & Francis.

McClintock, Ann. 1993. 'Family Feuds: Gender, Nationalism and the Family' in *Feminist Review* 44 (Summer).

McDaniel, S.A. 1985. 'Implementation of Abortion Policy in Canada as a Woman's Issue.' *Atlantis* 10(2): 74–91.

McGary, Howard. 1994. 'Alienation and the African-American Experience.' In *Alienation and Social Criticism*, edited by R. Schmitt and T.E. Moody. New Jersey: Humanities Press.

McGuire, Meredith B. 1992. *Religion: The Social Context*. Belmont, CA: Wadsworth.

McIntosh, Peggy. 1995. 'White Privilege and Male Privilege: A Personal

Account of Coming to See Correspondences Through Working in Women's Studies.' In *Race, Class and Gender*, edited by M.L. Anderson and P.H. Collins. Boston: Wadsworth.

McLuhan, M., and B.R. Powers. 1989. *The Global Village*. Oxford: Oxford University Press.

Men Supporting Men. 1976. 2nd Men & Masculinity Conference Program. State College, PA.

Men's Awareness Network/Chicago Men's Gathering Newsletter. 1976. No. 3/6.

Men's Liberation: Responding to the Women's Movement. 1971. *Brother: A Forum for Men Against Sexism*. Berkeley. n.p.

Menzies, H. 1996. *Whose Brave New World: The Information Highway and the New Economy*. Toronto: Between the Lines.

Messner, M.A. 1997. *Politics of Masculinities: Men in Movements: The Gender Lens Series in Sociology*. Thousand Oaks, CA: Sage.

Mies, Maria. 1982. *Lace Makers of Marsapur*. London: Zed Press.

– 1983. 'Towards a Methodology for Feminist Research.' In *Theories of Women's Studies*, edited by G. Bowles and R. Klein. London: Routledge and Kegan Paul.

– 1986. *Patriarchy and Accumulation of Capital on a World Scale: Women in the International Division of Labour*. London: Zed Books.

– 1996. 'Liberating Women, Liberating Knowledge: Reflections on Two Decades of Feminist Action Research.' *Atlantis* 21(1): 10–24.

Mies, Maria, and Vandana Shiva. 1993a. *Ecofeminism*. London: Zed Books.

– 1993b. *Ecofeminism Renders Women an Endangered Species*. Halifax: Fernwood.

– 1994. 'The Myth of Catchup Development.' In *Ecofeminism*, edited by Maria Mies and Vandana Shiva. London: Zed Books.

Minces, Juliette. 1980. *The House of Obedience: Women in Arab Society*. London: Zed Press.

Minh-ha, Trinh. 1987. 'Not You/Like You: Post-Colonial Women and the Interlocking Questions of Identity and Difference.' Lecture given at the Feminism and the Critique of Colonial Discourse Conference. UC – Santa Cruz. April. Printed in *Inscriptions* 3(4).

Moe, B. 1991. *Coping with Eating Disorders*. New York: Rosen Publishing Group.

Moghadam, Valentine, ed. 1994. *Gender and National Identity: Women and Politics in Muslim Societies*. London: Zed Books.

Mohanty, Chandra T., et al. 1991a. *Third World Women and the Politics of Feminism*. Bloomington: Indiana University Press.

– 1991b. 'Under Western Eyes: Feminist Scholarship and Colonial Discourses.' In *Third-World Women and the Politics of Feminism*. Bloomington: Indiana University Press.

- 1992. 'Feminist Encounters: Locating the Politics of Experience.' In *Destablizing Theory: Contemporary Feminist Debates*, edited by M. Barrett and A. Phillips. Stanford, CA: Stanford University Press.

Montero, Gloria. 1979. *We Stood Together: First-hand Accounts of Dramatic Events in Canada's Labour Past.* Toronto: James Lorimer.

Monture-Angus, Patricia. 1995. *Thunder in My Soul: A Mohawk Woman Speaks.* Halifax, NS: Fernwood Publications.

Monture-Okanee, Patricia. 1992. 'The Violence Women Do: A First Nations View.' In *Challenging Times*, edited by Constance Backhouse and David Flaherty. Montreal: McGill-Queen's University Press.

Moodley, Kogila. 1984. 'The Predicament of Racial Affirmative Action: A Critical Review of Equality Now.' *Queen's Quarterly* 91(4): 795–806.

Moraga, C., and G. Anzaldua, eds. 1983. *This Bridge Called My Back: Writings by Radical Women of Colour.* New York: Kitchen Table Women of Colour Press.

Morgan, Kathryn P. 1989. 'Of Women Born? How Old Fashioned. New Reproductive Technologies and Women's Oppression.' In *The Future of Reproduction*, edited by C. Overall. Toronto: The Women's Press.

Morgan, Robin. 1994. *Sisterhood is Global.* Garden City, NJ: Anchor Books.

Mosmiller, T. 1992. 'Pro-feminist, Gay/Bi Affirmative, Enhancing Men's Lives & Proud! The Men's Movement in the United States.' Draft manuscript. 25 pp.

Moussa, Helen. 1998–9. 'Violence Against Refugee Women: Gender Oppression, Canadian Policy, and the International Struggle For Human Rights.' *Resources for Feminist Research* 26(3/4): 78–111.

Mukherjee, Arun P. 1993a. 'Right out of Herstory: Racism in Charlotte Perkins Gilman's "Herland" and Feminist Literary Theory.' In *Returning the Gaze: Essays on Racism, Feminism and Politics*, edited by H. Bannerji. Toronto: Sister Vision Press.

Mukherjee, Arun P., ed. 1993b. *Sharing Our Experience.* Ottawa: Canadian Advisory on the Council of Women.

Nain, Gemma Tang. 1991. 'Black Women, Sexism and Racism: Black or Antiracist Feminism.' *Feminist Review* 37 (Spring): 1–32.

Nash, J. 1983. 'The Impact of the Changing International Division of Labor on Different Sectors of the Labour Force.' In *Women, Men, and the International Division of Labor*, edited by J. Nash and M.P. Fernandez Kelly. Albany: State University of New York Press.

National Council of Welfare. 1985. *Poverty Profile 1985.* Ottawa: Supply and Services Canada.

National Eating Disorder Information Centre. 1989. *An Introduction to Food and Weight Problems.* Toronto: National Eating Disorder Information Centre.

Nelson, Barabara, and Najama Chowdhury, eds. 1994. *Women in Politics World-wide.* New Haven and London: Yale University Press.

Ng, Roxanna. 1986. 'Immigrant Women in Canada: A Socially Constructed Category.' *Resources for Feminist Research* 15 (March): 13–14.

Nourbese Philip, Marlene. 1992. *Frontiers: Essays and Writings on Racism and Culture.* Stratford: The Mercury Press.

Obasi, E. 1996. 'Structural Adjustment and Gender Access to Education in Nigeria.' *Gender and Education* 9 (2).

Omvedt, Gail. 1993. *Reinventing Revolution: New Social Movements and the Socialist Tradition in India.* Armonk; M.E. Sharpe, Inc.

Ontario Coalition for Abortion Clinics. 1992. 'The Campaign for Free-Standing Abortion Clinics.' In *Debates in Canadian Society,* edited by Ronald Hinch. Scarborough, Ontario: Nelson Canada.

Orenstein, Debra. 1994. *Life Cycles: Jewish Women on Life Passages and Personal Milestones.* Woodstock, VT: Jewish Lights Publishing.

Parker, A., et al., eds. 1992. *Nationalisms and Sexualities.* New York: Routledge.

Parrish, G. 1992. 'Male Supremacy and the Men's Pro-feminist Movement: The Dubious Legacy of the National Organization for Men Against Sexism.' *Oh! brother.* 26 January 1998. www.igc.apc.org/nemesis/ACLU/oh!Brother/

Paxton, S. 1996. 'Friendships, Body Image and Dieting in Teenage Girls: A Research Report.' *National Eating Disorder Information Centre Bulletin* 11(2): 1–4.

Paxton, S., E. Wertheim, K. Gibbons, G. Szmukler, L. Hillier, and J. Petrovich. 1991. 'Body Image Satisfaction, Dieting Beliefs and Weight Loss Behaviours in Adolescent Girls and Boys.' *Journal of Youth and Adolescence* 20(2): 361–79.

Pease, B. 1999. Personal interview. 5 May.

Pettman, Jan Jindy. 1992. *Living in the Margins: Racism, Sexism and Feminism in Australia.* Sydney: Allen & Unwin.

– 1996. *Worlding Women: A Feminist International Politics.* London and New York: Routledge.

Phillips, P., and E. Phillips. 1983. *Women and Work: Inequality in the Labour Market.* Toronto: James Lorimer.

Phizacklea, A. 1983. *One Way Ticket: Migration and Female Labour.* London: Routledge and Kegan Paul.

Pierce, J.W., and J. Wardle. 1993. 'Self-esteem, Parental Appraisal and Body Size in Children.' *Journal of Child Psychology and Psychiatry* 34(7): 1125–36.

Plaskow, Judith. 1991. 'Transforming the Nature of Community.' In *After Patriarchy,* edited by Paula M. Cooey et al. New York: Orbis Books.

Pleck, J.H. 1976. 'The Male Sex Role: Definitions, Problems, and Sources of Change.' *Journal of Social Issues* 32: 155–64.

Pleck, J.H., and J. Sawyer, eds. 1974. *Men and Masculinity*. Englewood Cliffs, NJ: Prentice-Hall.

Polanyi, Karl. 1957. *The Great Transformation*. Boston: Beacon Press.

Pollit, Katha. 1993. 'The Strange Case of Baby M.' In *Feminist Frameworks: Alternative Theoretical Accounts of the Relations Between Women and Men*, edited by A.M. Jagger and P.S. Rothenberg. Toronto: McGraw-Hill Ryerson.

Pratt, S. 1998. Personal interview, 25 January.

Prentice, A., and S. Mann Trofimenkoff, eds. 1985. *The Neglected Majority: Essays in Canadian Women's History*. Vol. 2. Toronto: McClelland & Stewart.

Pumariega, A., C. Gustavson, J. Gustavson, P.S. Motes, and S. Ayers. 1994. 'Eating Attitudes in African-American Women: The Essence Eating Disorders Survey.' *Eating Disorders: A Journal of Prevention and Treatment* 2(1): 6–16

Radforth, I. 1995. 'The Shantymen.' In *Labouring Lives: Work and Workers in Nineteenth-Century Ontario*, edited by P. Craven. Toronto: University of Toronto Press.

Rahnema, Majid, and Victoria Bawtree, eds. 1997. *The Post-Development Reader*. London: Zed Books.

Ralston, Helen. 1988. 'Ethnicity, Class and Gender Among South Asian Women in Metro Halifax: An Exploratory Study.' *Canadian Ethnic Studies* 20(3).

Razack, Sherene. 1993. 'Storytelling for Social Change.' In *Returning the Gaze: Essays on Racism, Feminism and Politics*, edited by H. Bannerji. Toronto: Sister Vision Press.

– 1998. *Looking White People in the Eye: Gender, Race, and Culture in Courtrooms and Classrooms*. Toronto: University of Toronto Press.

Renzetti, Claire M., and Daniel J. Curran. 1999. *Women, Men & Society*. Toronto: Allyn & Bacon.

Reuther, Rosemary. 1992. *Gyia and God*. San Francisco: Harper and Row.

Reynolds, Cecilia, and Beth Young. 1995. *Women and Leadership: In Canadian Education*. Calgary: Detselig Enterprises.

Rice, C. 1995. *Promoting Healthy Body Image: A Guide for Program Planners*. Toronto: Ontario Prevention Clearinghouse.

– 1996. 'Trauma and Eating Problems: Expanding the Debate.' *Eating Disorders: A Journal of Prevention and Treatment* 4(3): 197–237.

Rice, C., and L. Langdon. 1991. 'Women's Struggles with Food and Weight as Survival Strategies.' *Canadian Women's Studies* 12(1).

Rice, C., and V. Russell. 1995a. 'EmBodying Equity: Putting Body and Soul into Equity Education, Part I: How Oppression is Embodied.' *Our Schools, Ourselves* 7(1): 14–36.

– 1995b. 'EmBodying Equity: Putting Body and Soul into Equity Education, Part II: Strategies for Change. *Our Schools, Ourselves* 7(2): 42–54.

– *Embodying Equity: Working With Young Women at the Intersections of Body, Self and Society*. Unpublished manuscript.

Richardson, Laurel W. 1981. *The Dynamics of Sex and Gender*. Boston: Houghton Mifflin.

Ridington, J. 1989. *Who Do We Think We Are? Self-Image and Women with Disabilities*. Toronto: DisAbled Women's Network (DAWN) Canada.

Roberts, Helen, ed. *Doing Feminist Research*. London: Routledge and Kegan Paul.

Roberts, Keith A. 1995. *Religion in Sociological Perspective*. Belmont, CA: Wadsworth.

Rochelle, R. 1993. 'Busting the Myth.' *Canadian Women Studies* 13(4).

Rodriquez-Tomé, H., F. Bariaud, M.F. Cohen Zardi, C. Delmas, B. Jeanvoine, and P. Szylagyi. 1993. 'The Effects of Pubertal Changes on Body Image and Relations with Peers of the Opposite Sex in Adolescence.' *Journal of Adolescence* 16: 421–38.

Romalis, L. 1993. Personal interview. 31 August.

Rooks, N. 1996. *Hair Raising: Beauty, Culture, and African American Women*. New Brunswick, NJ: Rutgers University Press.

Root, M., ed. 1996. *The Multicultural Experience: Racial Borders as the New Frontier*. London: Sage.

Rothman, Barbara K. 1997. 'On Surrogacy.' In *Through the Prism of Difference: Readings on Sex and Gender*, edited by M.B. Zinn et al. Toronto: Allyn & Bacon.

Rousso, H. 1988. 'Daughters with Disabilities: Defective Women or Minority Women?' In *Women with Disabilities: Essays in Psychology, Culture and Politics*, edited by M. Fine and A. Asch. Philadelphia: Temple University Press.

Rowan, J. 1987. *The Horned God: Feminism and Men as Wounding and Healing*. London: Routledge and Kegan Paul.

Russell, K., M. Wilson, and R. Hall. 1992. *The Color Complex: The Politics of Skin Color among African Americans*. Toronto: Anchor Books.

Said, Edward, 1979. *Orientalism*. New York: Vintage.

Sainsbury, Diane, ed. 1994. *Gendering Welfare States*. London: Sage.

Samuels, T.J. 1992. *Visible Minorities in Canada: A Projection*. Toronto: Race Relations Advisory Council on Advertising. Canadian Advertising Foundation.

Sarkar, Tanika, and Butalia Urvashi. 1996. *Women and the Hindu Right*. New Delhi: Kali for Women.

Saulnier, Christine. 1997. 'Mapping Conflictual Rights Discourse: Women Centered Strategies and NRGTS.' In *Equality and Justice*, edited by D. Hearne and M.L. Lefebure. Montreal: John Abbott College Press.

Sawicki, Jana. 1993. 'Disciplining Mothers: Feminism and the New Reproductive Technologies.' In *Feminist Frameworks: Alternative Theoretical Accounts of the Relations Between Women and Men*, edited by A.M. Jagger and P.S. Rothenberg. Toronto: McGraw-Hill Ryerson.

Schacht, S.P., and D.W. Ewing. 1997. 'Sharing Power: Entering Women's Space.' *Achilles Heel: The Radical Men's Magazine* 22 (Summer/Autumn): 34–6.

Schiebinger, L. 1993. *Nature's Body: Gender in the Making of Modern Science*. Boston: Beacon Press.

Scholte, Jan Aart. 1996. 'The Geography of Collective Identities in a Globalizing World.' *Review of International Political Economy* 3(4) (Winter): 565–607.

Segal, L. 1990. *Slow Motion: Changing Masculinities, Changing Men*. London: Virago.

Seidler, V.J. 1991. *Men, Sexual Politics, and Socialism. The Achilles Heel Reader*, edited by V.J. Seidler. London: Routledge.

Sen, Gita, and Caren Grown. 1987. *Development, Crises and Alternative Visions*. New York: Monthly Review Press.

Shapiro, B. 1982. 'Join the National Task Groups! Draft proposal for National Organization of Men.' n.p.

Sheil, D. 1990. 'The Men's Movement in Britain.' Unpublished manuscript. 4 pp.

Sherwin, Susan. 1989. 'Feminist Ethics and New Reproductive Technologies.' In *The Future of Reproduction*, edited by Christine Overall. Toronto: Women's Press.

Sheth, Anita, and Anita Handa. 1993. 'A Jewel in the Frown: Striking Accord between Indian Feminists.' In *Returning the Gaze: Essays on Racism, Feminism and Politics*, edited by H. Bannerji. Toronto: Sister Vision Press.

Shiva, Vandana. 1997. *Biopiracy: The Plunder of Nature and Knowledge*. Toronto: Between the Lines.

Shukla, Sandyha. 1997. 'Feminisms of the Diaspora Both Local and Global: The Politics of South Asian Women Against Domestic Violence.' In *Women Transforming Politics*, edited by Cathy J. Cohen, Kathleen B. Jones, and Joan C. Tronto. New York: New York University Press.

Silvera, Makeda. 1983. *Silenced*. Toronto: Williams-Wallace.

Simand, Harriet. 1989. '1938–1988: Fifty Years of D.E.S. – Fifty Years Too Many.' In *The Future of Reproduction*, edited by C. Overall. Toronto: The Women's Press.

Sinclair, Deborah. 1985. *Understanding Wife Assault: A Training Model for Counsellors and Advocates.* Publications Ontario.

Sivard, Ruth. 1991. *World Military and Social Expenditure, 1987 and 1991.* Washington, D.C.: World Priorities.

Sluga, Glenda. 1998. 'Identity, Gender and the History of European Nations and Nationalisms.' In *Nations and Nationalism* 4(1) (January): 87–111.

Smith, R. 1976. 'The Men's Movement: One Perspective.' In *Men's Awareness Network/Chicago Men's Gathering Newsletter* 3(6). n.p.

Spitzack, C. 1990. *Confessing Excess: Women and the Politics of Body Reduction.* Albany: State University of New York Press.

Spivak, Gayatri, C. 1990. *The Post-Colonial Critic: Interviews, Strategies, Dialogues,* edited by S. Harasym. New York: Routledge.

Spretnak, Charlene. 1978. 'The Politics of Women's Spirituality.' In *Chrysalis: A Magazine of Women's Culture* 6.

Stacy, Judith, and Susan E. Gerand. 1997. 'We Are Not Doormats: The Influence of Feminism on Contemporary Evangelicals in the United States.' In *Through the Prism of Difference: Readings on Sex and Gender,* edited by B. Zinn et al. Toronto: Allyn & Bacon.

Staffieri, J.R. 1967. 'A Study of Social Stereotype of Body Image in Children.' *Journal of Personality and Social Psychology* 7: 101–4.

Standing, G. 1989. 'Global Feminization Through Flexible Labor.' *World Development* 17: 1077–95.

Stanley, Liz, and Sue Wise. 1983. *Breaking Out: Feminist Consciousness and Feminist Research.* London: Routledge and Kegan Paul.

Staples, R. 1997. 'Anita Hill, Sexual Harassment, and Gender Politics in the Black Community.' In *Through the Prism of Difference: Readings on Sex and Gender,* edited by M.B. Zinn et al. Toronto: Allyn & Bacon.

Stasiulis, Daiva. 1990. 'Theorizing Connections: Gender, Race, Ethnicity and Class.' In *Race and Ethnic Relations in Canada,* edited by Peter Li. Toronto: Oxford University Press.

Statistics Canada. 1992. *Canada's 125th Anniversary Yearbook.* Ottawa: Statistics Canada.

– 1995. *Women in Canada: A Statistical Report. Third Edition. Target Groups Project.* Ottawa: Statistics Canada.

Steinem, G. 1992. 'Foreword.' In *Women Respond to the Men's Movement,* edited by K.L. Hagan. San Francisco: Pandora.

Steuter, Erin. 1995. 'Women Against Feminism: An Examination of Feminist Social Movements and Anti-Feminist Countermovements.' In *Gender in the 1990s,* edited by E.D. Nelson and B.B. Robinson. Scarborough: Nelson Canada.

Stoltenberg, J. 1989. *Refusing to Be a Man: Essays on Sex and Justice*. Portland, OR: Breitenbush.

– 1997. 'Re: [profem] male supremacy and the men's pro-feminist movement.' *Oh! brother*. 26 January 1998. www.igc.apc.org/nemesis/ACLU/oh!Brother.

Stone, Merlin. 1976. *When God Was a Woman*. New York: Dial Press.

Story, M., F. Hauck, B. Broussard, L. White, M. Resnick, and R. Blum. 1994. 'Weight Perceptions and Weight Control Practices in American Indian and Alaska Native Adolescents.' *Archives of Pediatric Adolescent Medicine* 148: 567–71.

Strickland, Susan. 1994. 'Feminism, Postmodernism and Difference.' In *Knowing the Difference: Feminist Perspectives in Epistemology*, edited by K. Lennon and M. Whitford. London: Routledge.

Striegel-Moore, R., and A. Kearney-Cooke. 1994. 'Exploring Parents' Attitudes and Behaviours about Their Children's Physical Appearance.' *International Journal of Eating Disorders* 15(4): 377–85.

Stuart, Meryn, and Glynis Ellerington. 1990. 'Unequal Access: Disabled Women's Exclusion from the Mainstream Women's Movement.' In *Women and Environments*. Spring.

Stuckey, Johanna H. 1998. *Feminist Spirituality*. Toronto: Center for Feminist Research.

Székely, E. 1988. *Never Too Thin*. Toronto: The Women's Press.

Tabari, Azar. 1987. *In the Shadow of Islam: The Women's Movement in Iran*. London: Zed Books.

Tan, M., ed. 1998. *The Virtual Workplace*. Hershey, PA: Idea Group.

Taylor, W. 1991. 'The Logic of Global Business: An Interview with ABB's Percy Barnevik.' *Harvard Business Review* 69: 103–13.

Thobani, Sunera. 1993. 'Fighting Sex Selection Technology.' In *Sharing Our Experience*, edited by A. Mukherjee. Ottawa: Advisory Council on the Status of Women.

Thomas, Barb. 1994. 'Learning from Discomfort: A Letter to my Daughters.' In *A Hunger So Wide and So Deep: American Women Speak out on Eating Problems*, edited by B. Carl Thompson. Minneapolis: University of Minnesota Press.

Thompson, B. Carl. 1994. *A Hunger So Wide and So Deep: American Women Speak Out on Eating Problems*. Minneapolis: University of Minnesota Press.

– 1996. 'Multiracial Feminist Theorizing About Eating Disorders: Refusing to Rank Oppressions.' *Eating Disorders: A Journal of Treatment and Prevention* 4(2): 104–13.

Thorne-Finch, R. 1992. *Ending the Silence: The Origins and Treatment of Male Violence against Women*. Toronto: University of Toronto Press.

Tiggemann, M., and E. Rothblum. 1988. 'Gender Differences in Social Consequences of Perceived Overweight in the United States and Australia.' *Sex Roles* 18(1/2): 75–86.

Tinker, Irene, ed. 1990. *Persistent Inequalities – Women and World Development.* Oxford: Oxford University Press.

Tinker, Irene, and Michelle B. Bramsen. 1992. *Women and World Development.* Washington D.C.: Overseas Development Council.

Tolson, A. 1977. *The Limits of Masculinity: Male Identity and Women's Liberation.* New York: Harper and Row.

Trask, Hounani-Kay. 1997. 'Feminism and Indigenous Hawai'ian Nationalism.' In *Feminist Nationalism*, edited by Lois West. New York: Routledge.

Tseëlon, E. 1995. *The Masque of Femininity: The Presentation of Women in Everyday Life.* Nottingham: Nottingham Trent University.

Tuddenham, R. 1998. Personal interview. 25 January.

Tyagi, S. 1996. 'Writing in Search of a Home: Geography, Culture and Language.' In *Names We Call Home: Autobiography on Racial Identity*, edited by B. Thompson and S. Tyagi. New York: Routledge.

Valverde, Mariana. 1992. 'When the Mother of the Race is Free: Race Reproduction, and Sexuality in First-Wave Feminism.' In *Gender Conflicts: New Essays in Women's History*, edited by F. Iacovetta and M. Valverde. Toronto: University of Toronto Press.

Van Kirk, S. 1980. *Many Tender Ties: Women in Fur Trade Society, 1670–1870.* Winnipeg: Watson and Dwyer.

Vickers, Jill. 1983. 'Memoirs of an Ontological Exile: The Methodological Rebellions of Feminist Research.' In *Feminism in Canada*, edited by A. Miles and G. Finn. Montreal: Black Rose.

– 1987. 'At His Mother's Knee: Sex/Gender and the Construction of National Identities.' In *Women and Men*, edited by G.H. Nemiroff. Montreal: Fitzhenry & Whiteside.

– 1994a. 'Notes Toward a Political Theory of Sex and Power.' In *Power/Gender*, edited by H.L. Radtke and S. Henderickus Stam. London, California, New Delhi: Sage.

– 1994b. 'Difficult Choices: Knowledge Strategies for Feminist Social Science and the Knowledge Needs of Women's Movements.' In *Quilting a New Canon*, edited by U. Parameswaran. Toronto: The Women's Press.

– 1997. *Reinventing Political Science: A Feminist Approach*, Halifax: Fernwood.

Vickers, J., L.P. Rankin, and C. Appelle. 1993. *Politics as if Women Mattered.* Toronto: University of Toronto Press.

– 2000. 'Feminisms and Nationalisms in English Canada.' *Journal of Canadian Studies* 35(2): 128–48.

Vienna NGO Forum. 1994. *Call to Action*. United Nations.

Visvanathan, Nalini, et al., eds. 1997. *The Women, Gender and Development Reader*. London: Zed Books.

Wagner, Vicki Van, and Bob Lee. 1989. 'Principles into Practice: An Activist Vision of Feminist Reproductive Health Care.' In *The Future of Human Reproduction*, edited by Christine Overall. Toronto: Women's Press.

Walby, Sylvia. 1992. 'Women and Nation.' In *International Journal of Comparative Sociology* 33(1/2): 81–100.

– 1997. *Gender Transformations*. London: Routledge.

Waring, Marilyn. 1988. *If Women Counted: A New Feminist Economics*. New York: Harper Collins.

Warren, C. 1986. *Vignettes of Life: Experiences and Self Perceptions of New Canadian Women*. Calgary: Detselig Enterprises Limited.

Wendell, S. 1996. *The Rejected Body: Feminist Philosophical Reflections on Disability*. New York: Routledge.

West, Cornel. 1995. 'Race Matters.' In *Race, Class and Gender*, 2nd edition. Toronto: Wadsworth.

West, Lois, ed. 1997. *Feminist Nationalism*. New York: Routledge.

Westley, R. 1997. 'White Normativity and the Racial Rhetoric for Equal Protection.' In *Existence in Black: An Anthropology of Black Existential Philosophy*, edited by L. Gordon. Routledge: New York.

What Future for Men? 1990. *Achilles Heel: The Radical Men's Magazine*. (Autumn). 15 January 1998. www.stejonda.demon.co.uk/achilles/leaderlo.html

Who Gets In? NFB 1989. 52 min. VHS Emigration, Immigration and Government Policy.

Williams, Linda S. 1989. 'No Relief Until the End: The Physical and Emotional Costs of InVitro Fertilization.' In *The Future of Reproduction*, edited by C. Overall. Toronto: The Women's Press.

Wilson, M., and K. Russell. 1996. *Divided Sisters: Bridging the Gap Between Black Women and White Women*. Toronto: Anchor Books.

Wolf-Light, P. 1998. Personal interview. 30 January.

Wood, S., ed. 1989. *The Transformation of Work?* London: Unwin Hyman.

XY philosophy. 1997. *XY: men, sex, politics* 7(2) (Spring): 2.

Yeatman, Anna. 1994. 'Postmodern Epistemological Politics and Social Science.' In *Knowing the Difference: Feminist Perspectives in Epistemology*, edited by K. Lennon and M. Whitford. London: Routledge.

Yee, May. 1993. 'Finding the Way Home Through Issues of Gender, Race and Class.' In *Returning the Gaze*, edited by H. Bannerji. Toronto: Sister Vision Press.

Young, I. 1990. *Throwing Like a Girl and Other Essays in Feminist Philosophy and Social Theory*. Indianapolis: Indiana University Press.

Young, Iris Marion. 1990. *Justice and the Politics of Difference*. Princeton, N.J. Princeton University Press.

– 2000. *Inclusion and Democracy*. New York: Oxford University Press.

Young, Kate. 1988. *Women and Economic Development*. Oxford: Berg Publishers.

Young, Katherine. 1993. 'Hinduism.' In *Today's Woman in World Religions*, edited by A. Sharma. Albany: State University of New York Press.

Yuval-Davis, Nira. 1997. *Gender and Nation*. London, Thousand Oaks, and New Delhi: Sage.

Zack, N., ed. 1997. *Race/Sex: Their Sameness, Difference, and Interplay*. New York: Routledge.

Zinn, Baca M., et al. 2000. *Gender Through the Prism of Difference*. Toronto: Allyn & Bacon.

– 1997. *Through the Prism of Difference: Readings on Sex and Gender*. London: Allyn & Bacon.

Zuhur, Sherifa. 1992. *Revealing, Reveiling: Islamist Gender Ideology in Contemporary Egypt*. Albany: State University of New York Press.

Vanaja Dhruvarajan is a senior scholar and professor of sociology at the University of Winnipeg. She completed her undergraduate education in India in 1959 and got her Masters and PhD from the University of Chicago in 1964 and 1981 respectively. Her teaching and research interests are globalization, family and socialization, gender and antiracism, women and development, and women and media. She has done research in India and Canada and has published two books and several articles. She served as president of the Canadian Sociology and Anthropology Association from 1998 to 2000, as president of the Canadian Women's Studies Association in 1986–7, and as Ruth Wynn Woodward–endowed chair in Women's Studies at Simon Fraser University in 1994–5. She has also served on the boards of several professional, government, and community organizations.

Parvin Ghorayshi is a sociology professor at the University of Winnipeg. Her research interests include feminist theories and gender relations. She is the author of *Women and Work in Developing Countries* (1996). Her most recent articles have appeared in the *Canadian Journal of Development Studies, Women and Politics,* and *Antropologie et Société.* She is presently engaged in a research project on rural women.

Amanda Goldrick-Jones was born and raised in Vancouver. As a language and rhetoric student at the University of British Columbia, she completed her BA in 1981 and her MA in 1983, then taught writing for six years. In 1990 she began exploring relationships between feminism and communication in greater depth during her studies at Rensselaer

Polytechnic Institute in Troy, NY, where she received her PhD in communication and rhetoric. She has taught at the University of Winnipeg's Centre for Academic Writing and in women's studies since 1994. Her publications have focused on men's relations with feminism, gender politics, and feminism and computer-mediated communication.

Carla Rice is a clinical program specialist at the Regional Women's Health Centre in Toronto, where she runs the Body Image Project, a program providing clinical support, training opportunities, and research focused on body image and identity formation across the life span. Recently she worked with disability organizations to develop the Disability and Physical Differences project and has been involved in a joint project with the Toronto District School Board, exploring connections between equity and health. She is working to complete her PhD in women's studies at York University and has taught feminist research methods and women and health courses at the undergraduate level.

Jill Vickers, a professor of political science, has taught women's studies, Canadian studies, and feminist political science at Carleton University for more than thirty years. At Carleton she has also played a number of administrative roles. She has been active in the women's movement, including as president of the Canadian Research Institute for the Advancement of Women, parliamentarian of the National Action Committee on the Status of Women, and secretary-treasurer of the Canadian Women's Studies Association. Some recent publications include *Politics as if Women Mattered: A Political Analysis of the National Action Committee on the Status of Women* with Pauline Rankin and Christine Appelle; *Reinventing Political Science: A Feminist Approach*; a special millennium issue of the *Journal of Canadian Studies – Women and Nationalisms: Canadian Experiences*, coedited with Micheline de Sève; and *Women's Movements and State Feminism: Integrating Diversity into Public Policy*, with Pauline Rankin.

INDEX